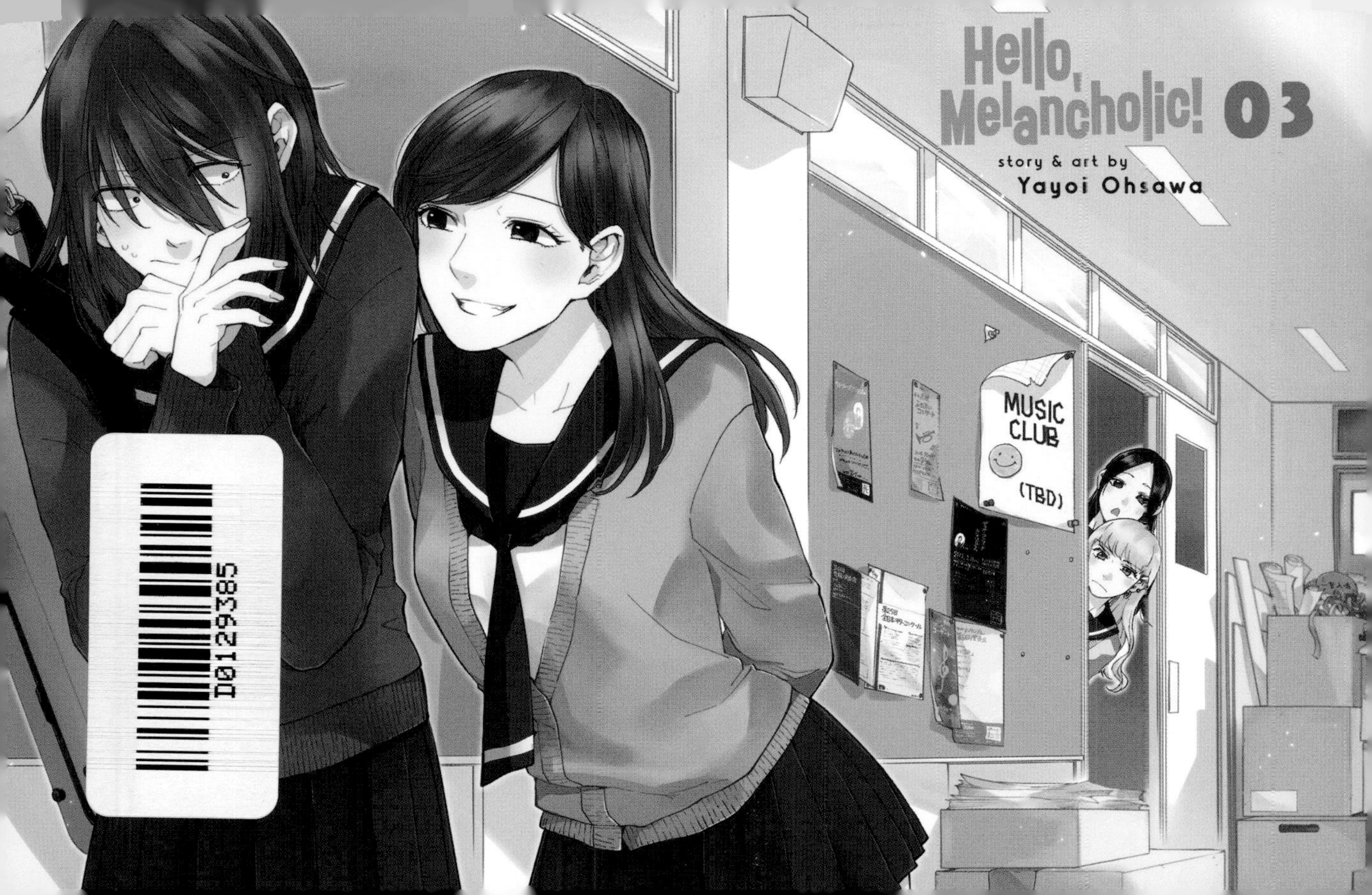
Hello, Melancholic! 03
story & art by
Yayoi Ohsawa
MUSIC CLUB
(TBD)

Hello, Melancholic!

story & art by
Yayoi Ohsawa

CONTENTS

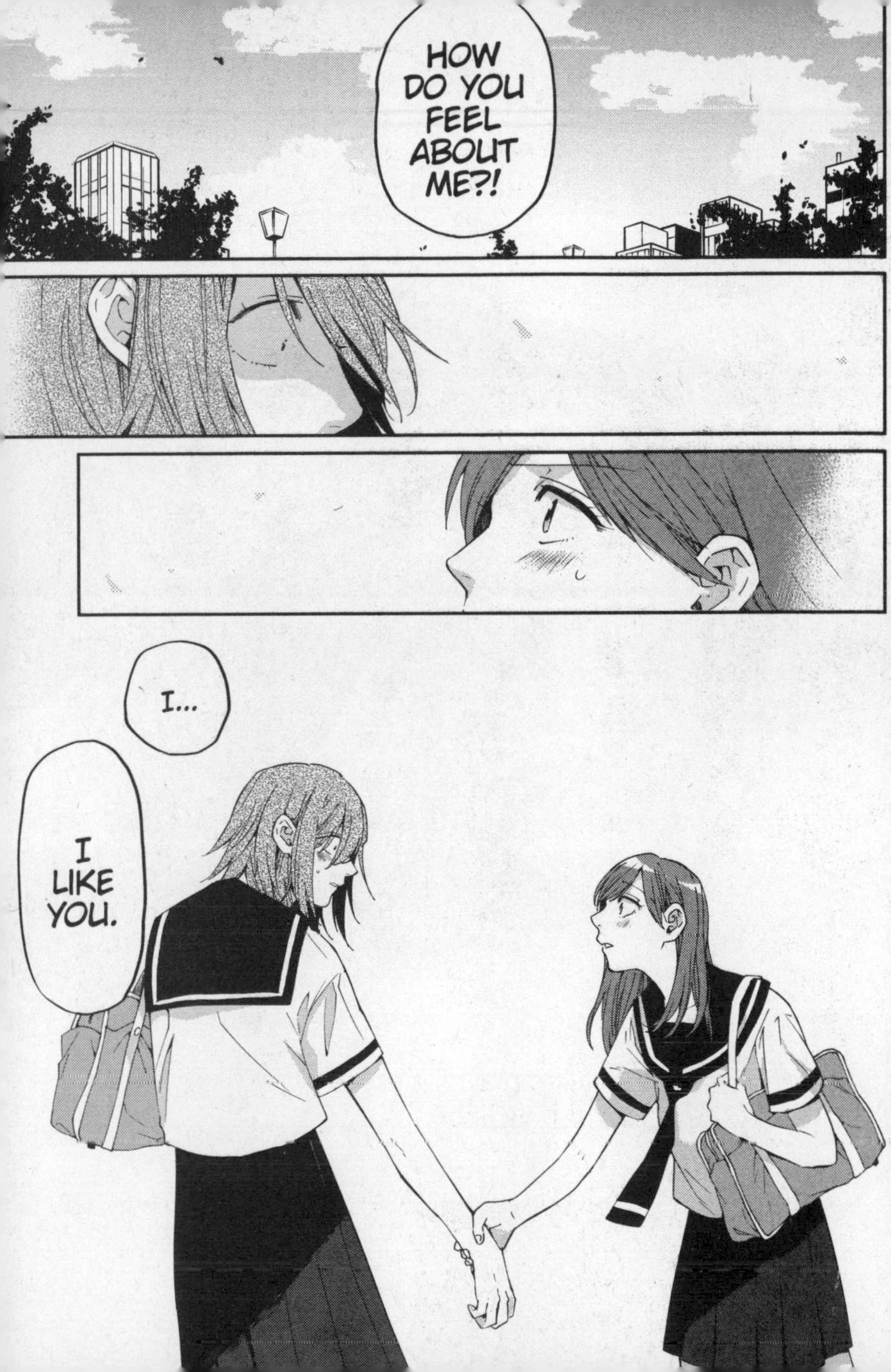
HOW DO YOU FEEL ABOUT ME?!
I...
I LIKE YOU.

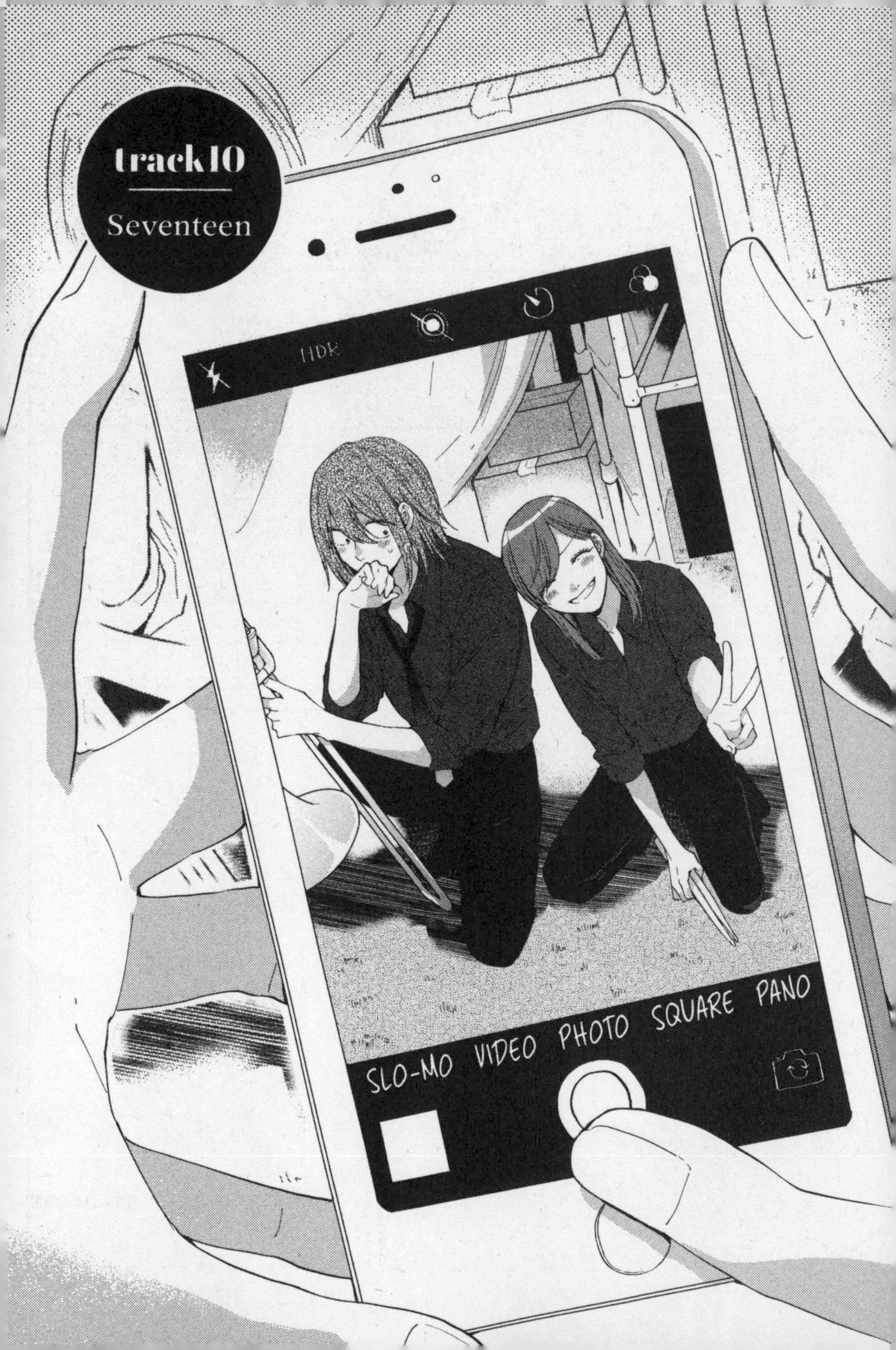
track10
Seventeen
HDR
SLO-MO VIDEO PHOTO SQUARE PANO

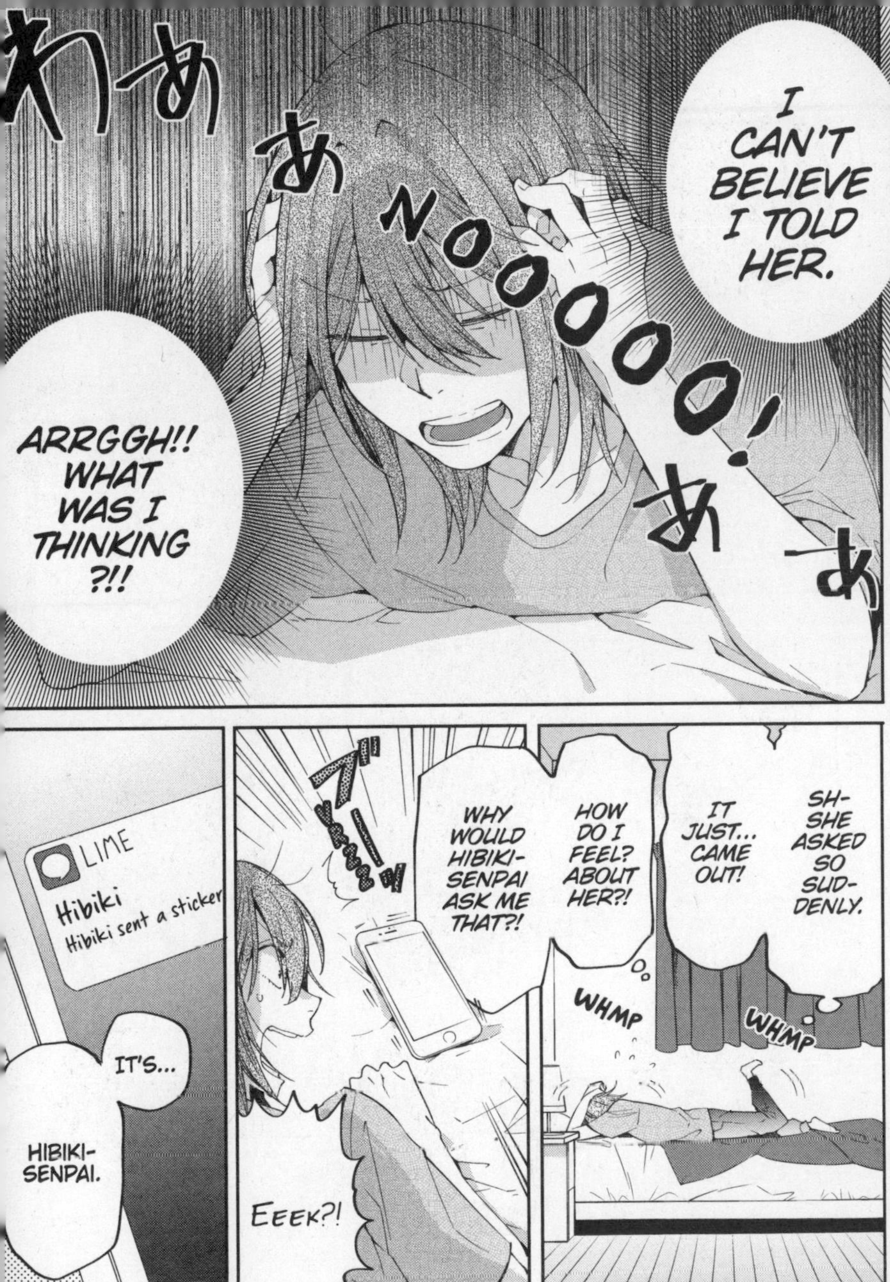
I CAN'T BELIEVE I TOLD HER.
わあ
あ
NOOOOOO!
あ
あ
ARRGGH!! WHAT WAS I THINKING?!!
SH-SHE ASKED SO SUD-DENLY.
IT JUST... CAME OUT!
HOW DO I FEEL? ABOUT HER?!
WHY WOULD HIBIKI-SENPAI ASK ME THAT?!
WHMP
WHMP
EEEK?!
LIME
Hibiki
Hibiki sent a sticker
IT'S...
HIBIKI-SENPAI.

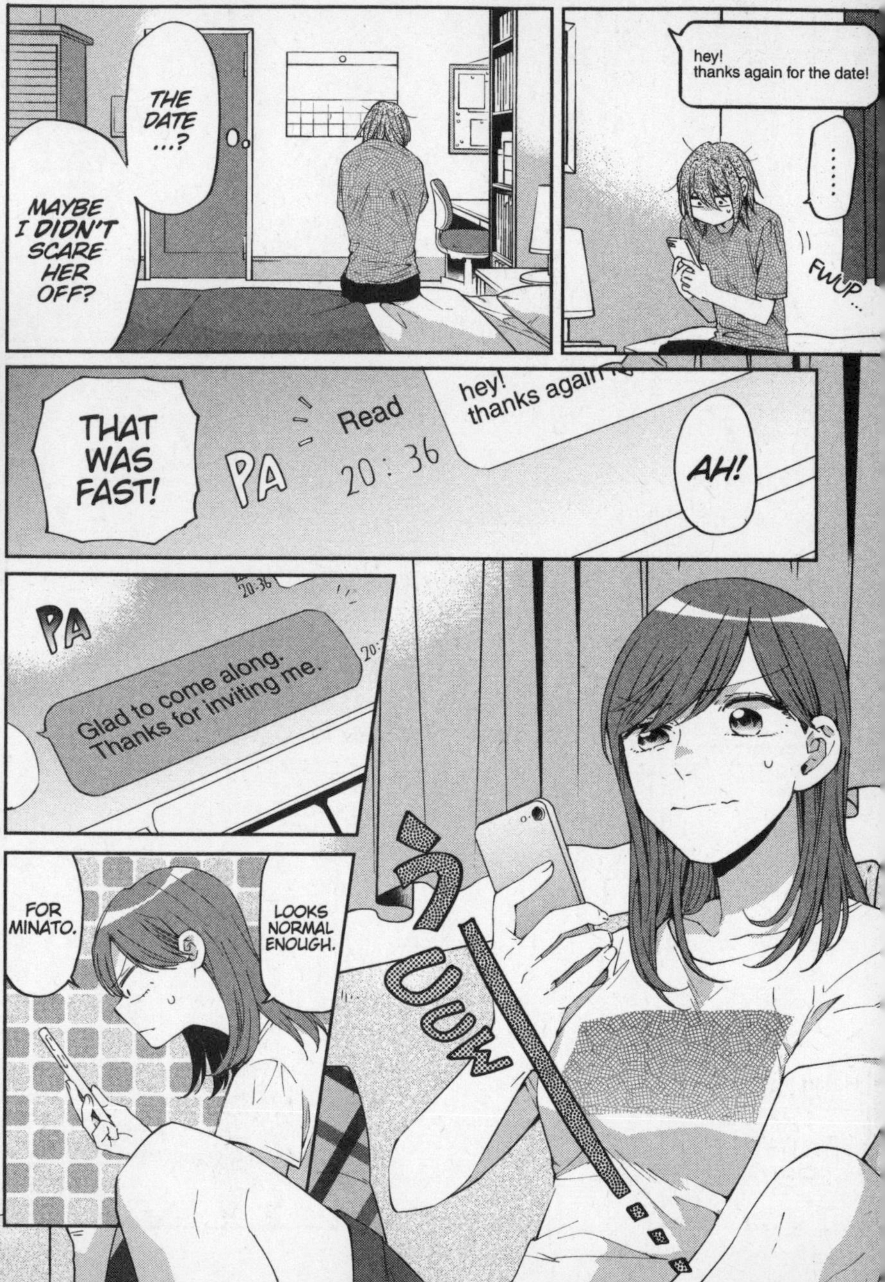
hey!
thanks again for the date!
......
FWUP...
THE DATE...?
MAYBE I DIDN'T SCARE HER OFF?
AH!
hey!
thanks again
Read
20:36
PA
THAT WAS FAST!
PA
20:36
Glad to come along.
Thanks for inviting me.
LOOKS NORMAL ENOUGH.
FOR MINATO.

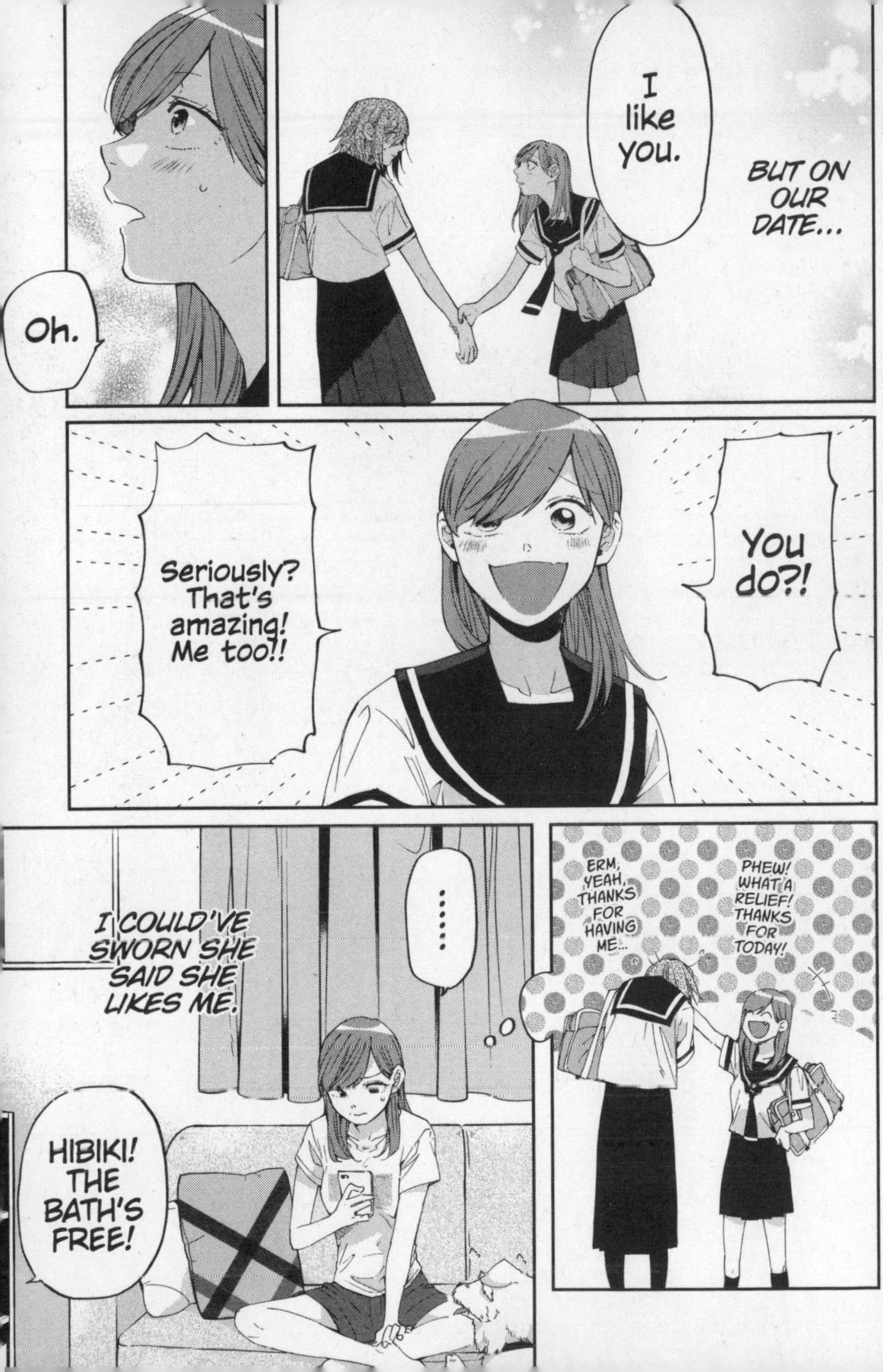
BUT ON OUR DATE...
I like you.
Oh.
You do?!
Seriously? That's amazing! Me too!!
PHEW! WHAT A RELIEF! THANKS FOR TODAY!
ERM, YEAH, THANKS FOR HAVING ME...
......
I COULD'VE SWORN SHE SAID SHE LIKES ME.
HIBIKI! THE BATH'S FREE!

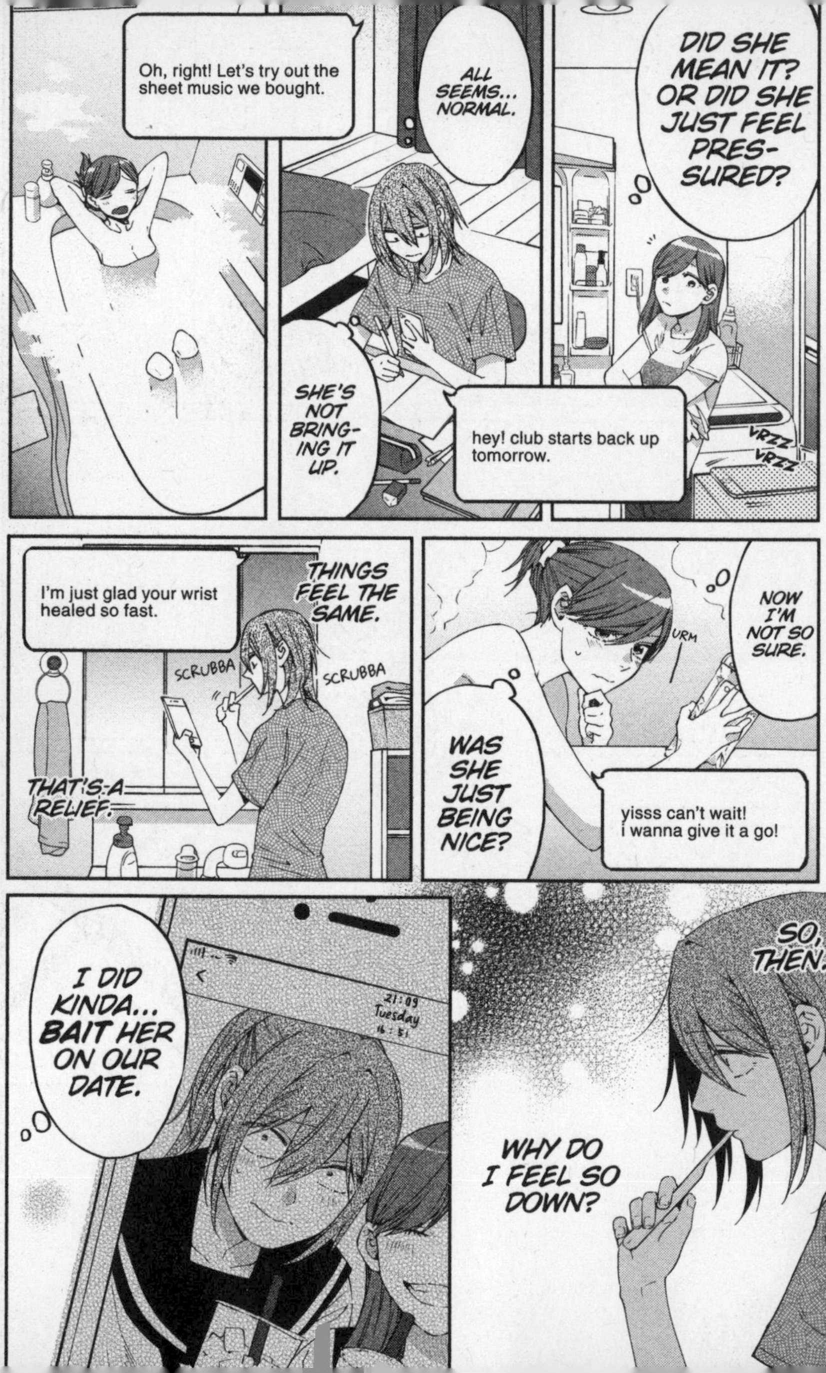
DID SHE MEAN IT? OR DID SHE JUST FEEL PRES-SURED?
VRZZ VRZZ
hey! club starts back up tomorrow.
ALL SEEMS... NORMAL.
SHE'S NOT BRING-ING IT UP.
Oh, right! Let's try out the sheet music we bought.
NOW I'M NOT SO SURE.
URM
WAS SHE JUST BEING NICE?
yisss can't wait! i wanna give it a go!
THINGS FEEL THE SAME.
I'm just glad your wrist healed so fast.
SCRUBBA
SCRUBBA
THAT'S A RELIEF.
SO, THEN...
WHY DO I FEEL SO DOWN?
I DID KINDA... BAIT HER ON OUR DATE.
21:09
Tuesday
16:51

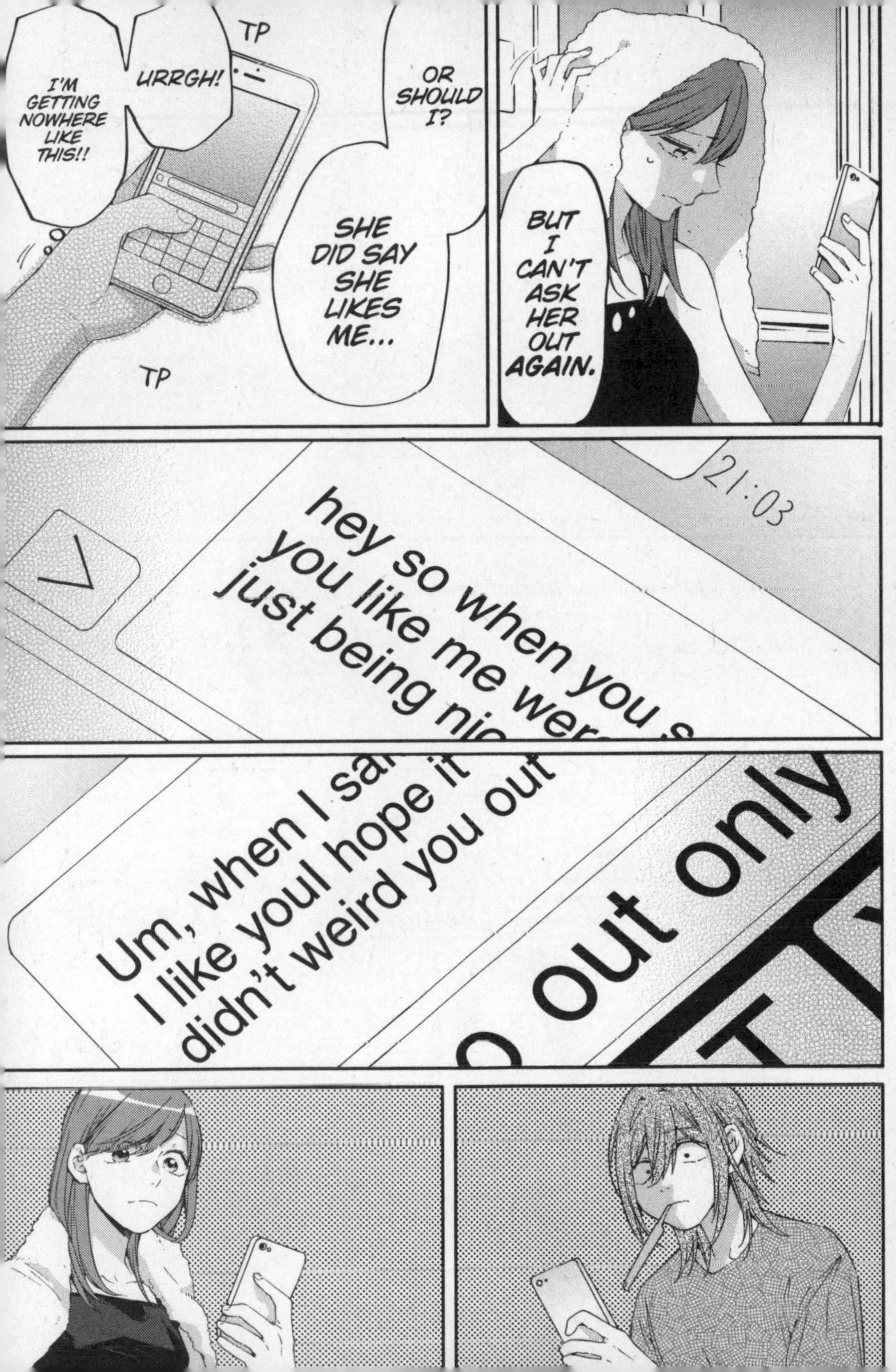
BUT I CAN'T ASK HER OUT AGAIN.
OR SHOULD I?
SHE DID SAY SHE LIKES ME...
TP
URRGH!
I'M GETTING NOWHERE LIKE THIS!!
TP
21:03
hey so when you
you like me were
just being ni
Um, when I sa
I like youI hope it
didn't weird you out
out only

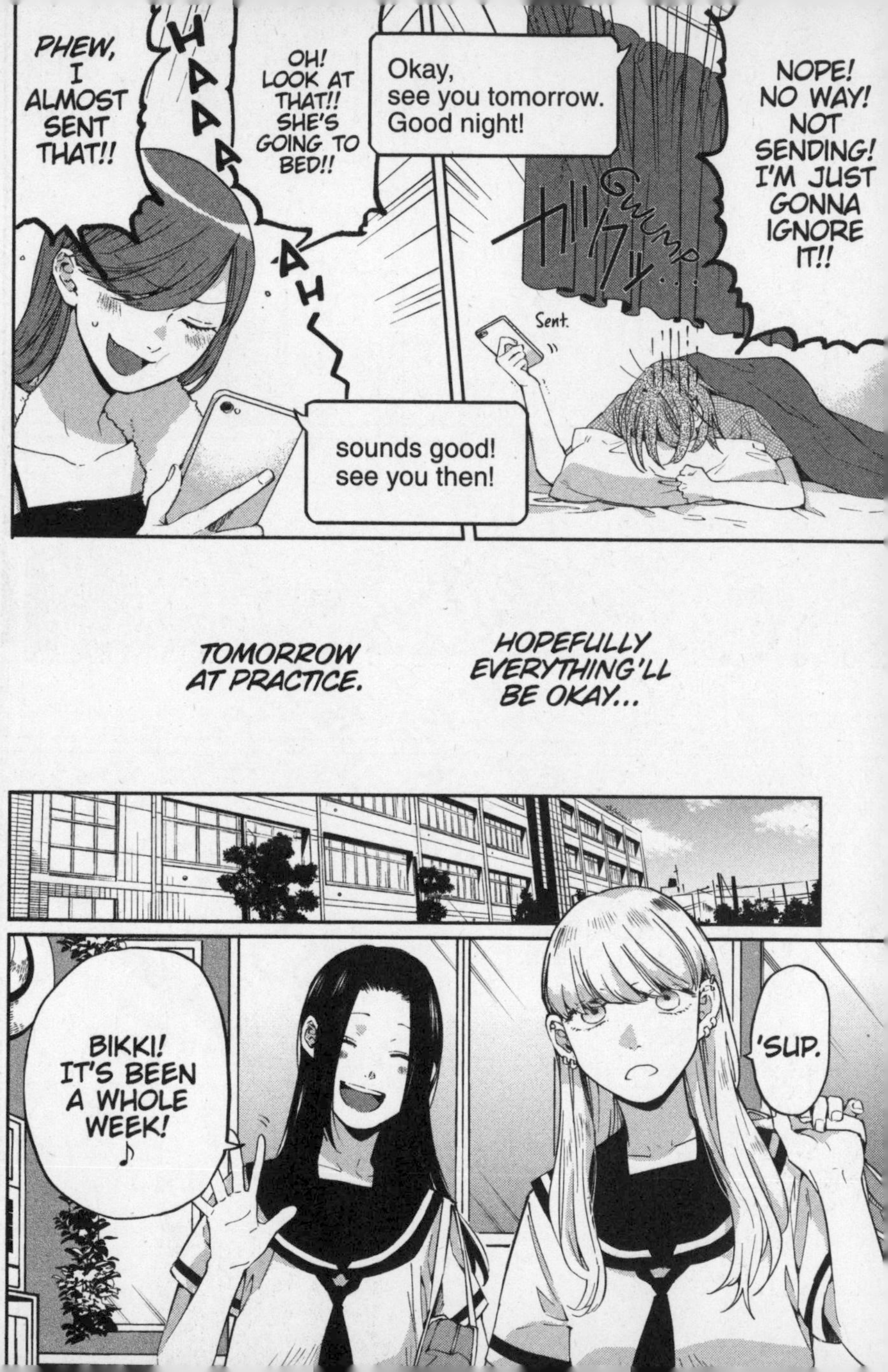
NOPE! NO WAY! NOT SENDING! I'M JUST GONNA IGNORE IT!!
Okay, see you tomorrow. Good night!
GWUMP...
Sent.
OH! LOOK AT THAT!! SHE'S GOING TO BED!!
HAAAAH
PHEW, I ALMOST SENT THAT!!
sounds good! see you then!
HOPEFULLY EVERYTHING'LL BE OKAY...
TOMORROW AT PRACTICE.
'SUP.
BIKKI! IT'S BEEN A WHOLE WEEK! ♪

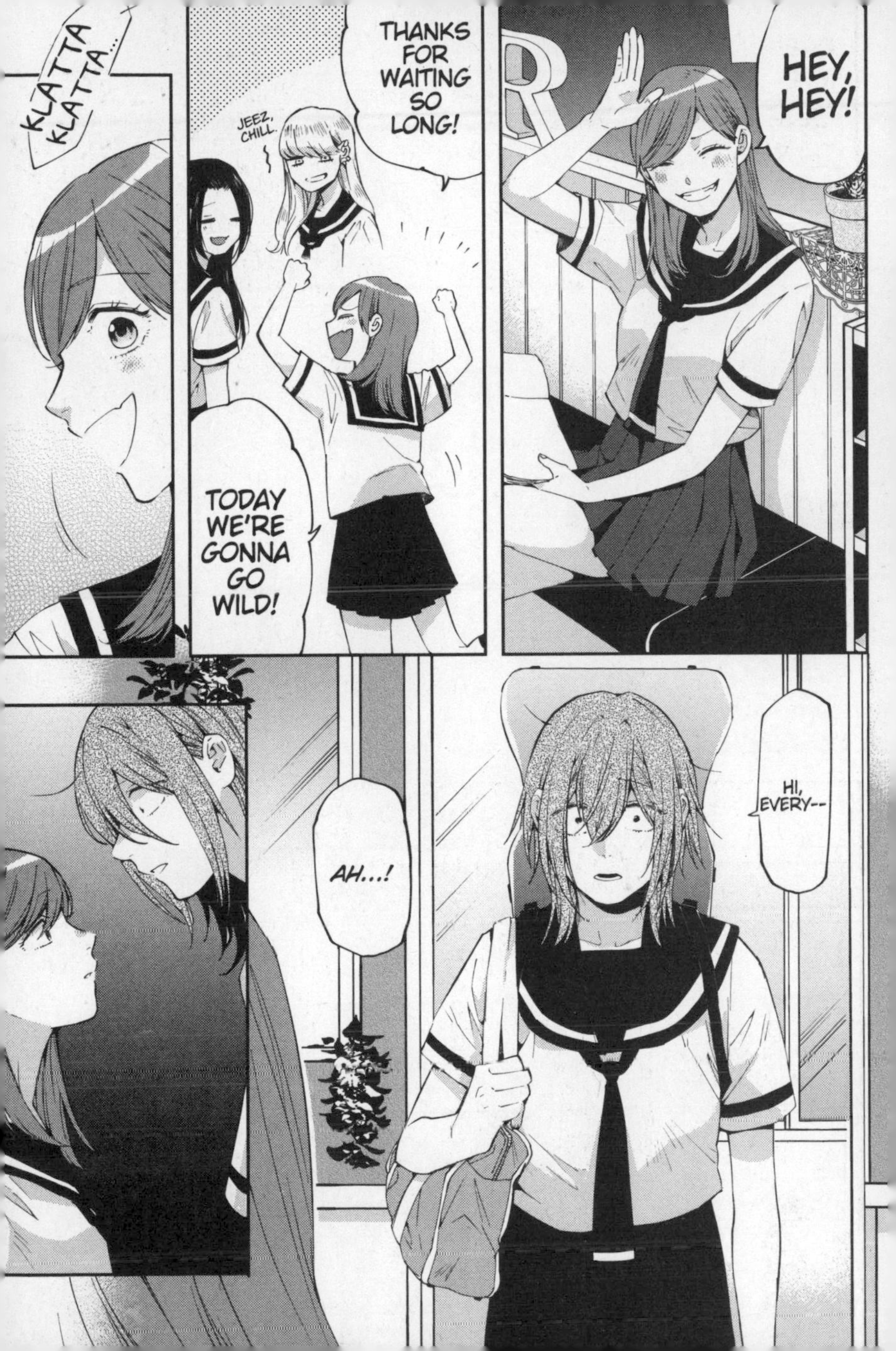
HEY, HEY!
THANKS FOR WAITING SO LONG!
JEEZ, CHILL.
TODAY WE'RE GONNA GO WILD!
KLATTA KLATTA...
HI, EVERY--
AH...!

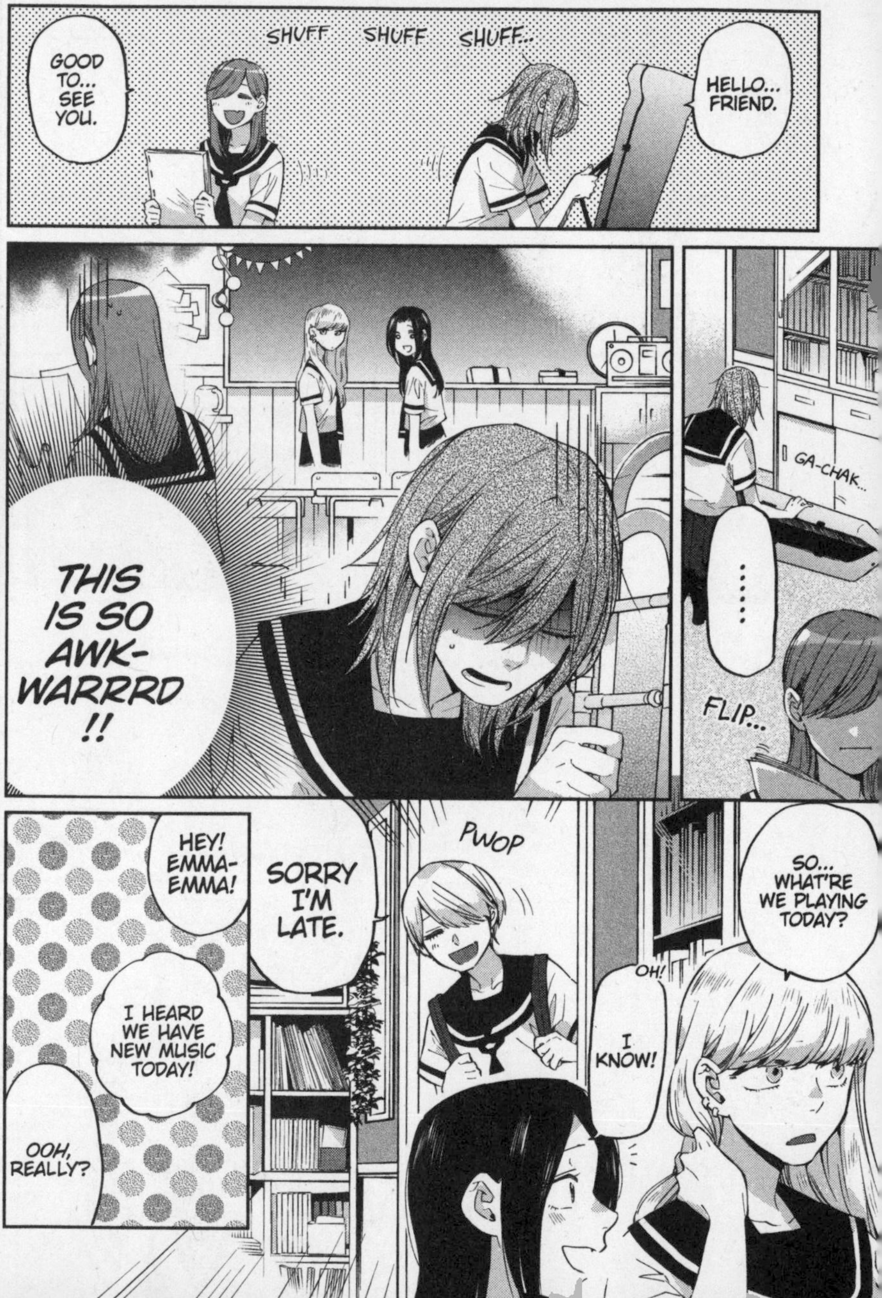
HELLO... FRIEND.
SHUFF SHUFF SHUFF...
GOOD TO... SEE YOU.
GA-CHAK...
......
FLIP...
THIS IS SO AWK-WARRRD!!
SO... WHAT'RE WE PLAYING TODAY?
OH!
I KNOW!
PWOP
SORRY I'M LATE.
HEY! EMMA-EMMA!
I HEARD WE HAVE NEW MUSIC TODAY!
OOH, REALLY?

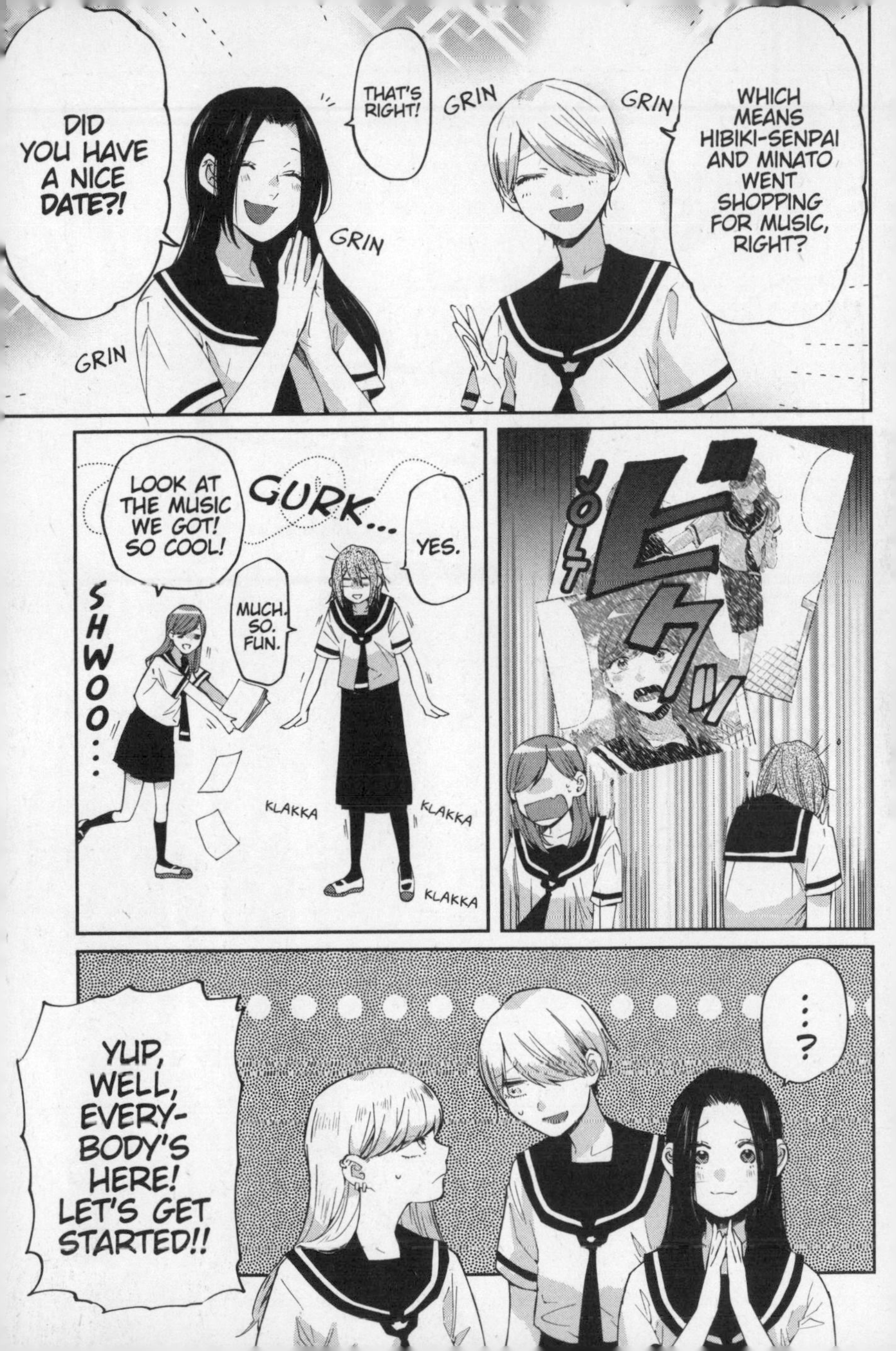
WHICH MEANS HIBIKI-SENPAI AND MINATO WENT SHOPPING FOR MUSIC, RIGHT?
GRIN
THAT'S RIGHT!
GRIN
DID YOU HAVE A NICE DATE?!
GRIN
GRIN
JOLT
YES.
GURK...
LOOK AT THE MUSIC WE GOT! SO COOL!
MUCH. SO. FUN.
SHWOO...
KLAKKA
KLAKKA
KLAKKA
...?
YUP, WELL, EVERY-BODY'S HERE! LET'S GET STARTED!!

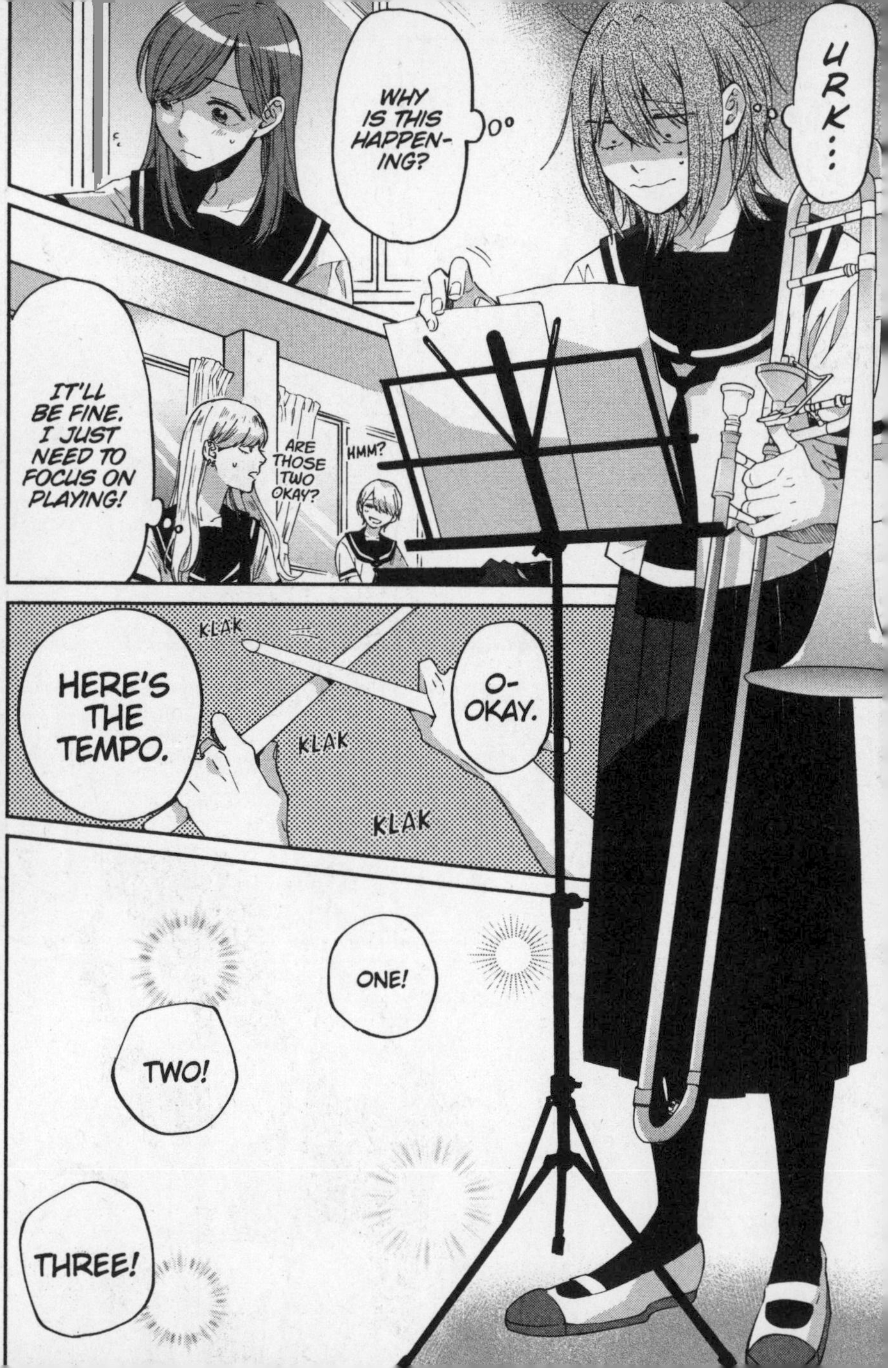
URK...
WHY IS THIS HAPPENING?
HMM?
ARE THOSE TWO OKAY?
IT'LL BE FINE. I JUST NEED TO FOCUS ON PLAYING!
O-OKAY.
KLAK
HERE'S THE TEMPO.
KLAK
KLAK
ONE!
TWO!
THREE!

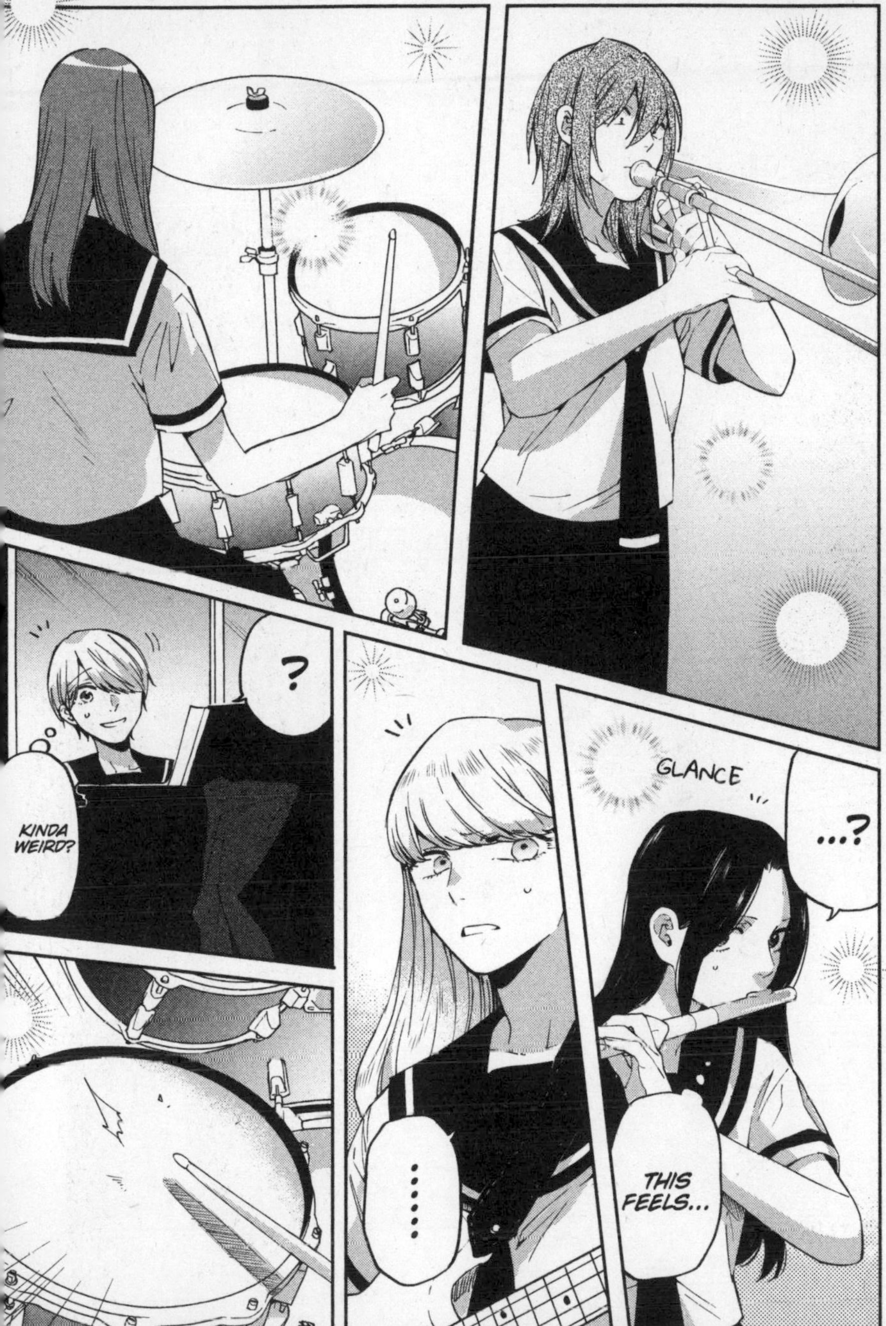
GLANCE
...?
THIS FEELS...
......
?
KINDA WEIRD?

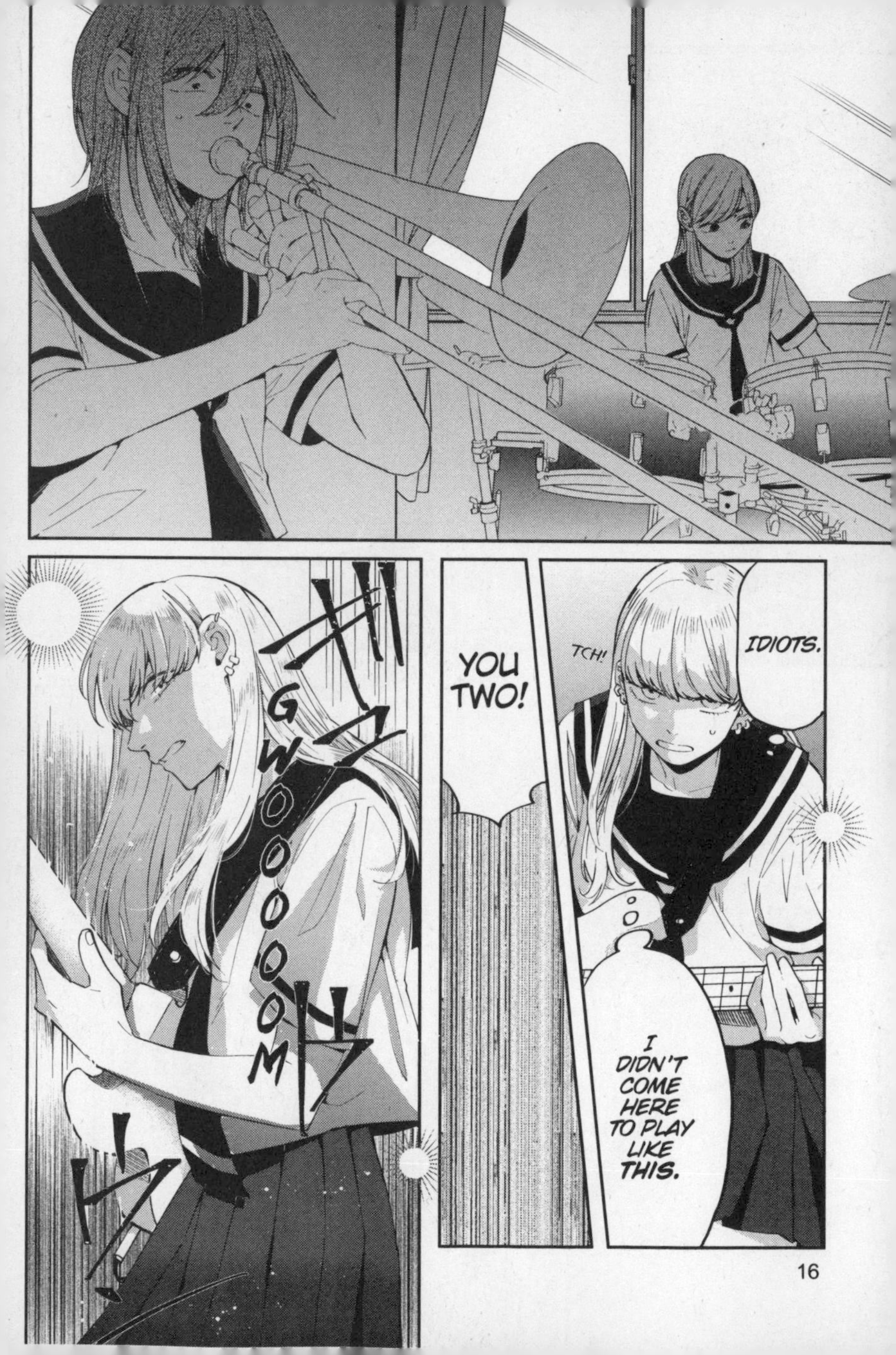
TCH!
IDIOTS.
I DIDN'T COME HERE TO PLAY LIKE THIS.
YOU TWO!
GWOOOOOM

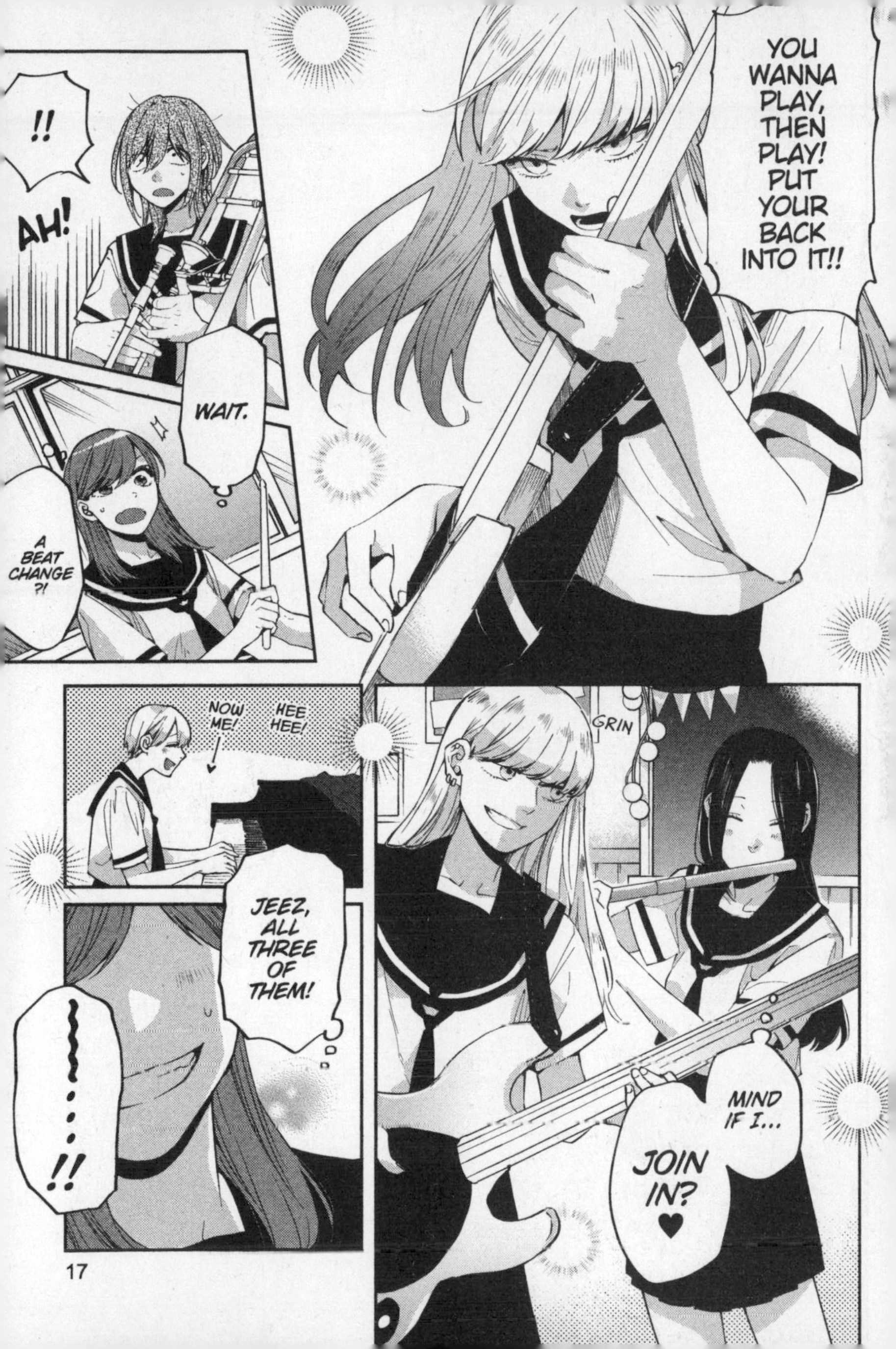
YOU WANNA PLAY, THEN PLAY! PUT YOUR BACK INTO IT!!
!!
AH!
WAIT.
A BEAT CHANGE ?!
GRIN
MIND IF I...
JOIN IN? ♥
HEE HEE!
NOW ME! ♥
JEEZ, ALL THREE OF THEM!
......!!

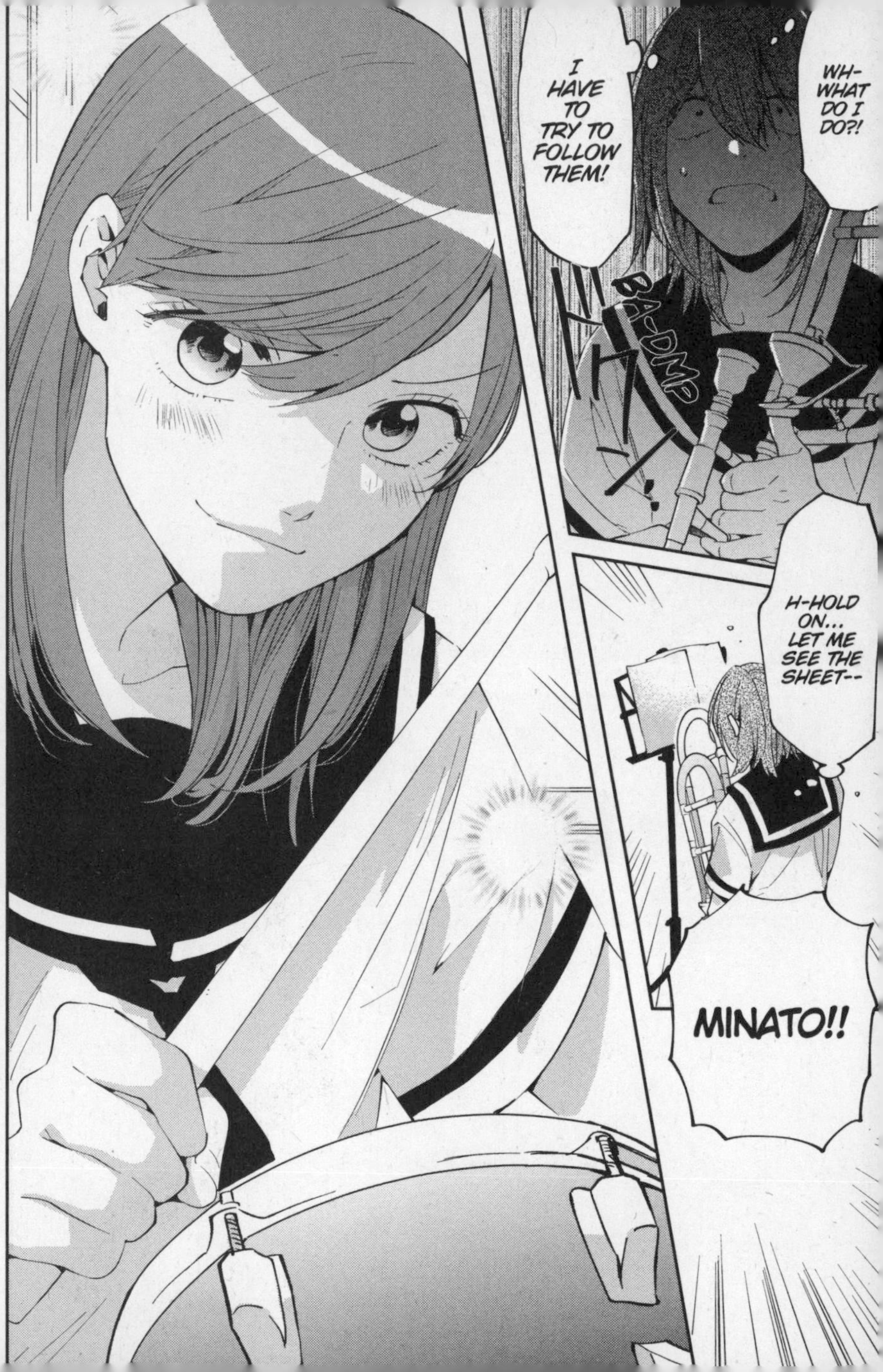
WH-WHAT DO I DO?!
I HAVE TO TRY TO FOLLOW THEM!
BA-DMP
H-HOLD ON... LET ME SEE THE SHEET--
MINATO!!

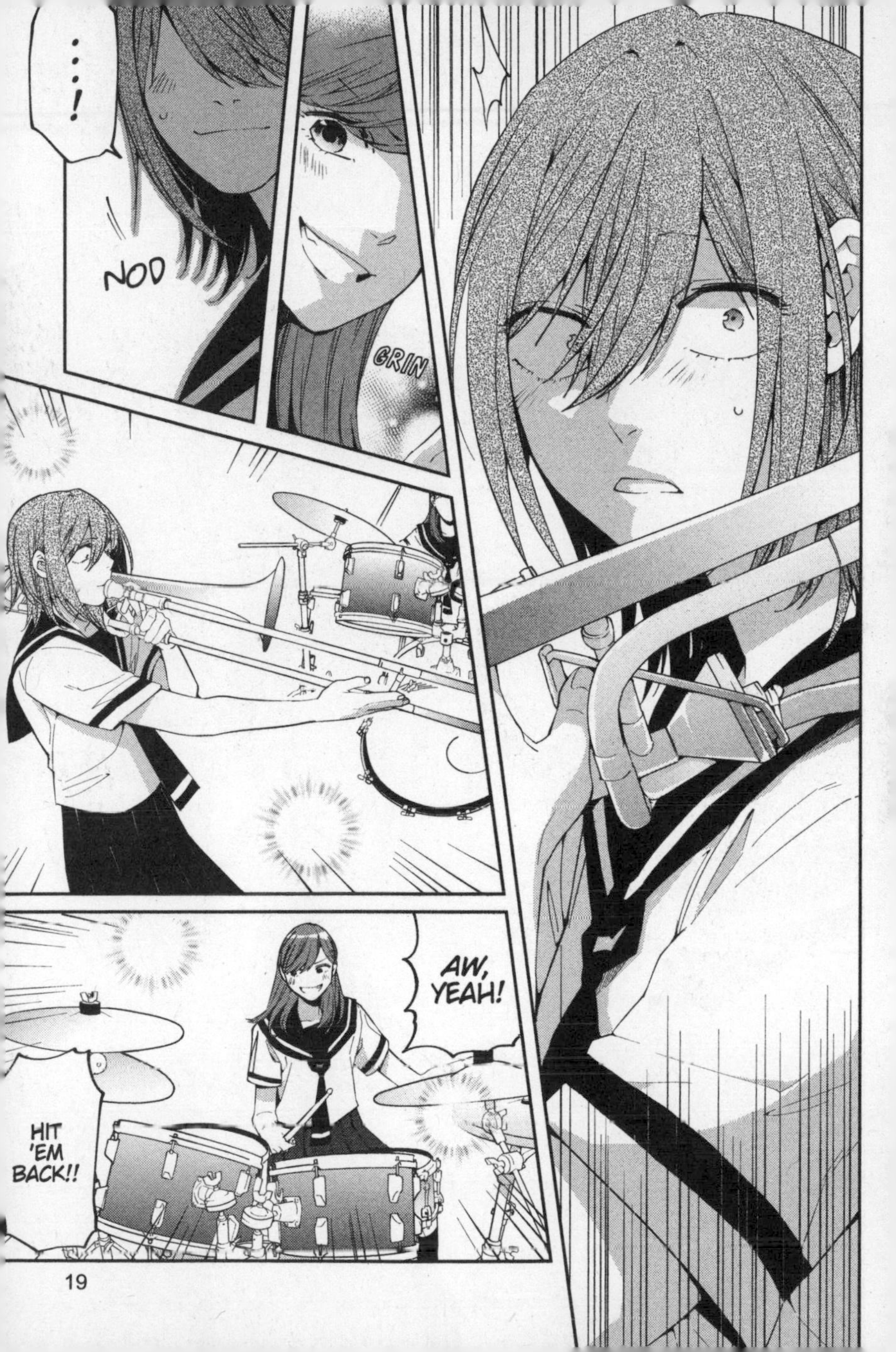
GRIN
...!
NOD
AW, YEAH!
HIT 'EM BACK!!

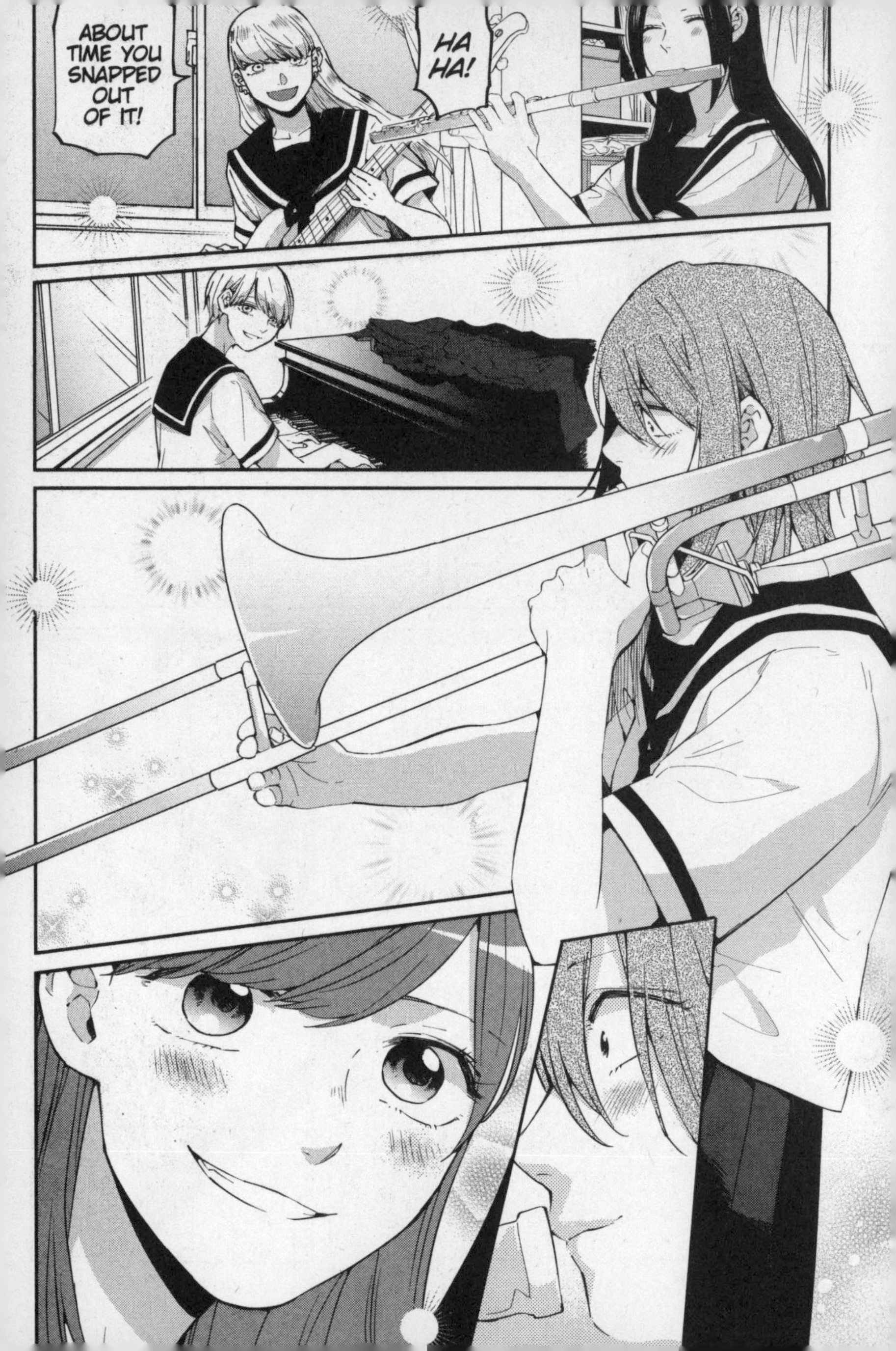
HA HA!
ABOUT TIME YOU SNAPPED OUT OF IT!

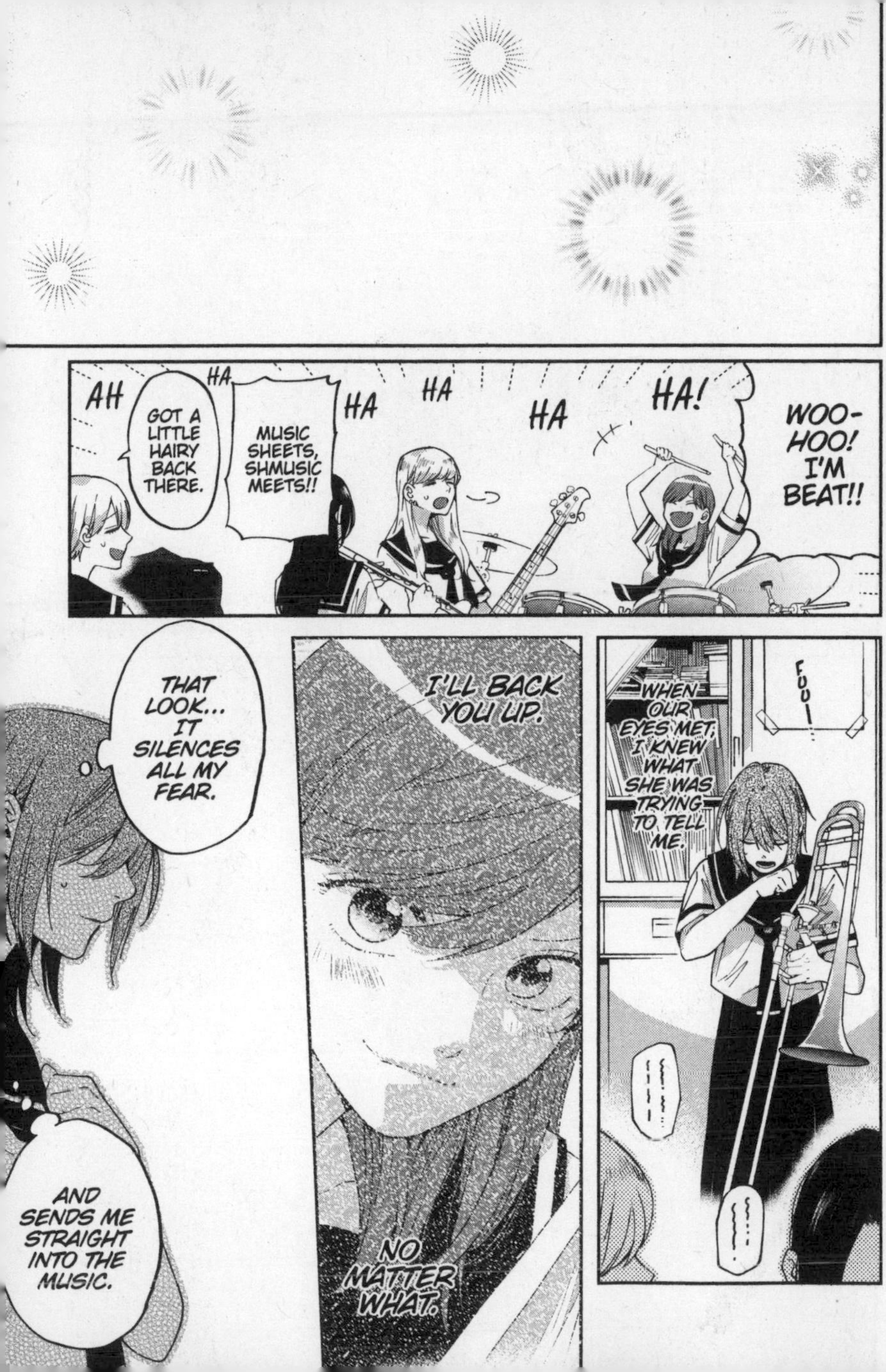
WOO-HOO! I'M BEAT!!
HA!
HA
HA
HA
MUSIC SHEETS, SHMUSIC MEETS!!
HA
GOT A LITTLE HAIRY BACK THERE.
AH
FUU!
WHEN OUR EYES MET, I KNEW WHAT SHE WAS TRYING TO TELL ME.
......
......
I'LL BACK YOU UP.
NO MATTER WHAT.
THAT LOOK... IT SILENCES ALL MY FEAR.
AND SENDS ME STRAIGHT INTO THE MUSIC.

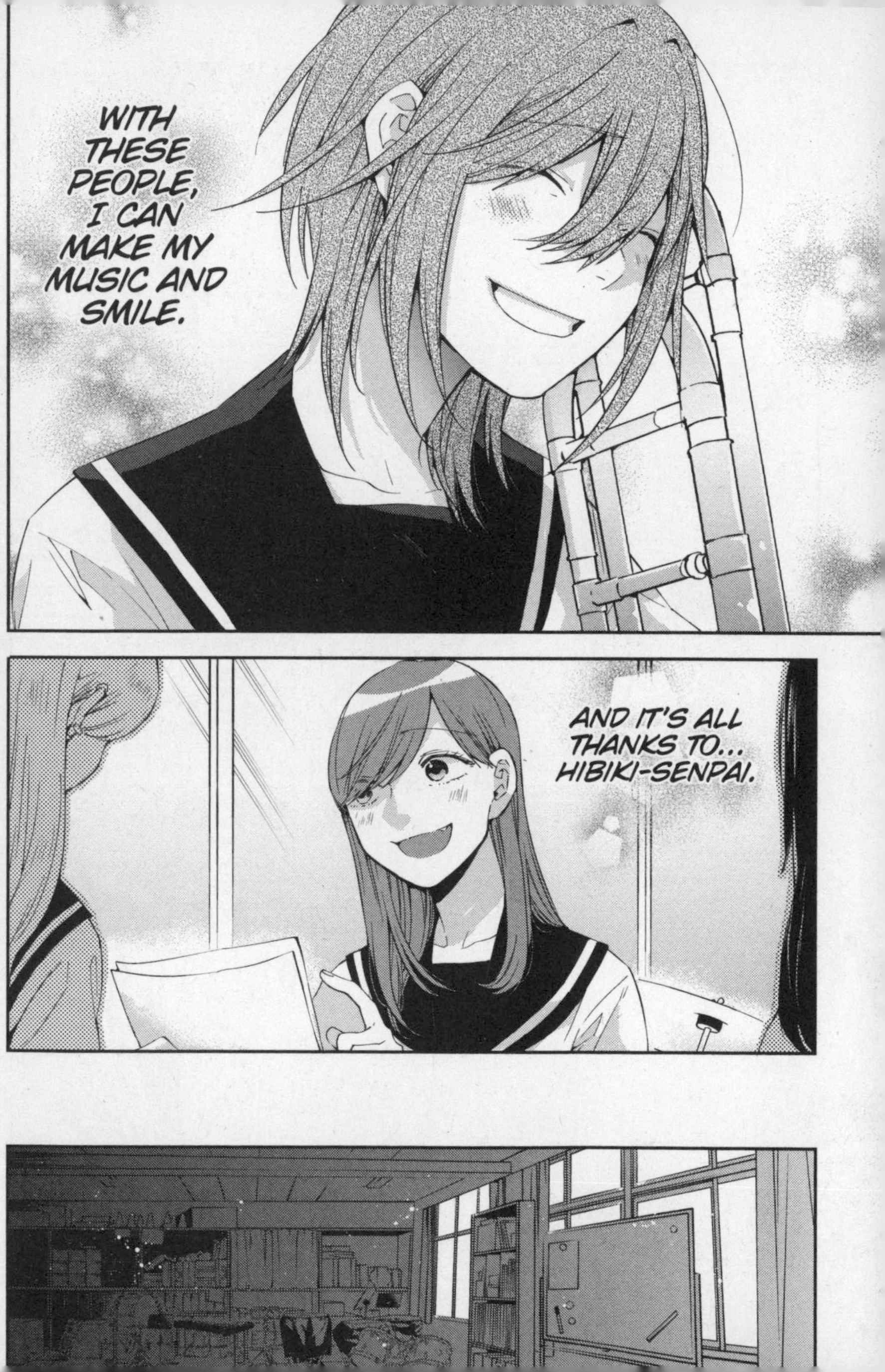
WITH THESE PEOPLE, I CAN MAKE MY MUSIC AND SMILE.
AND IT'S ALL THANKS TO... HIBIKI-SENPAI.

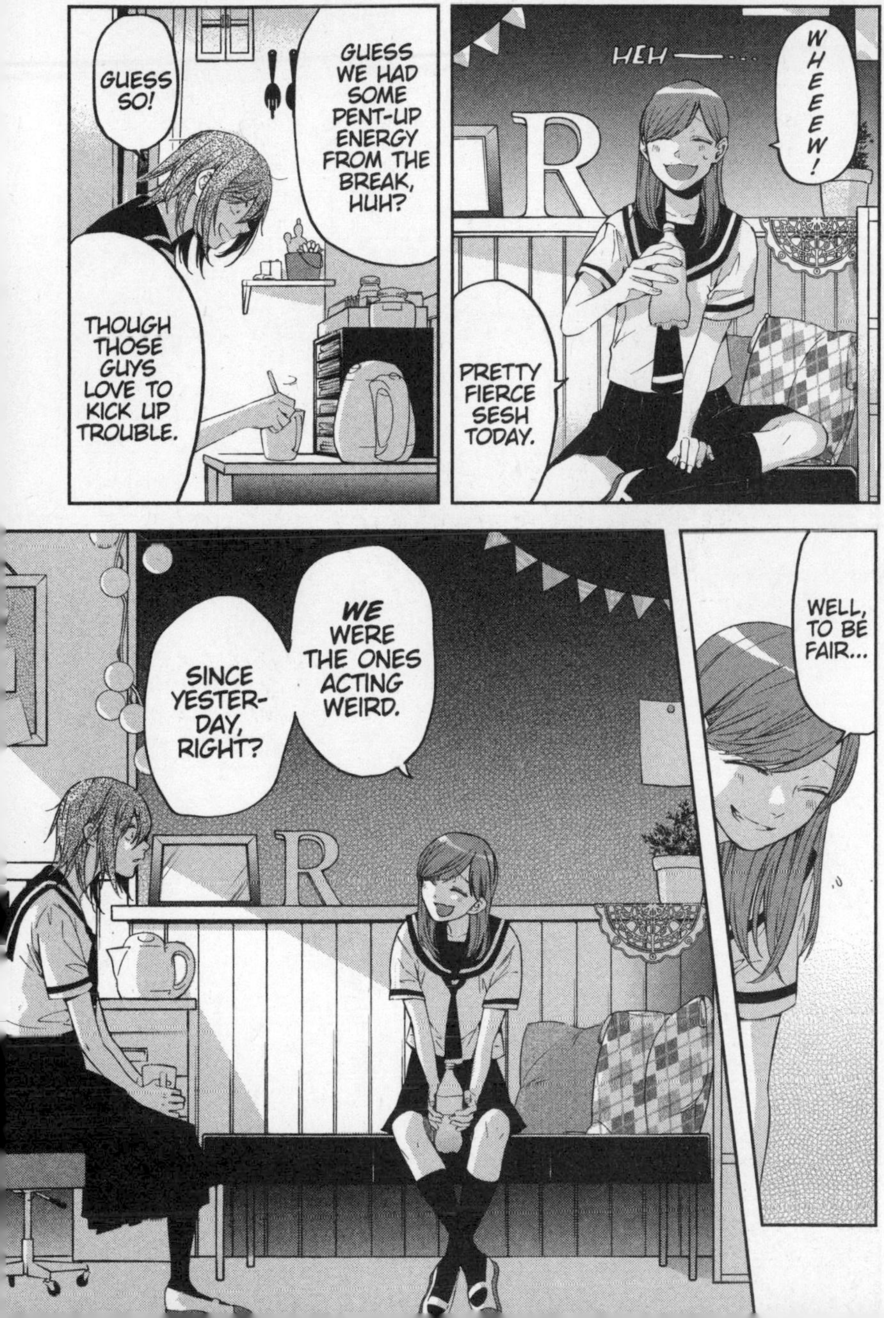
HEH——...
WHEEEW!
PRETTY FIERCE SESH TODAY.
GUESS WE HAD SOME PENT-UP ENERGY FROM THE BREAK, HUH?
GUESS SO!
THOUGH THOSE GUYS LOVE TO KICK UP TROUBLE.
WELL, TO BE FAIR...
WE WERE THE ONES ACTING WEIRD.
SINCE YESTER-DAY, RIGHT?

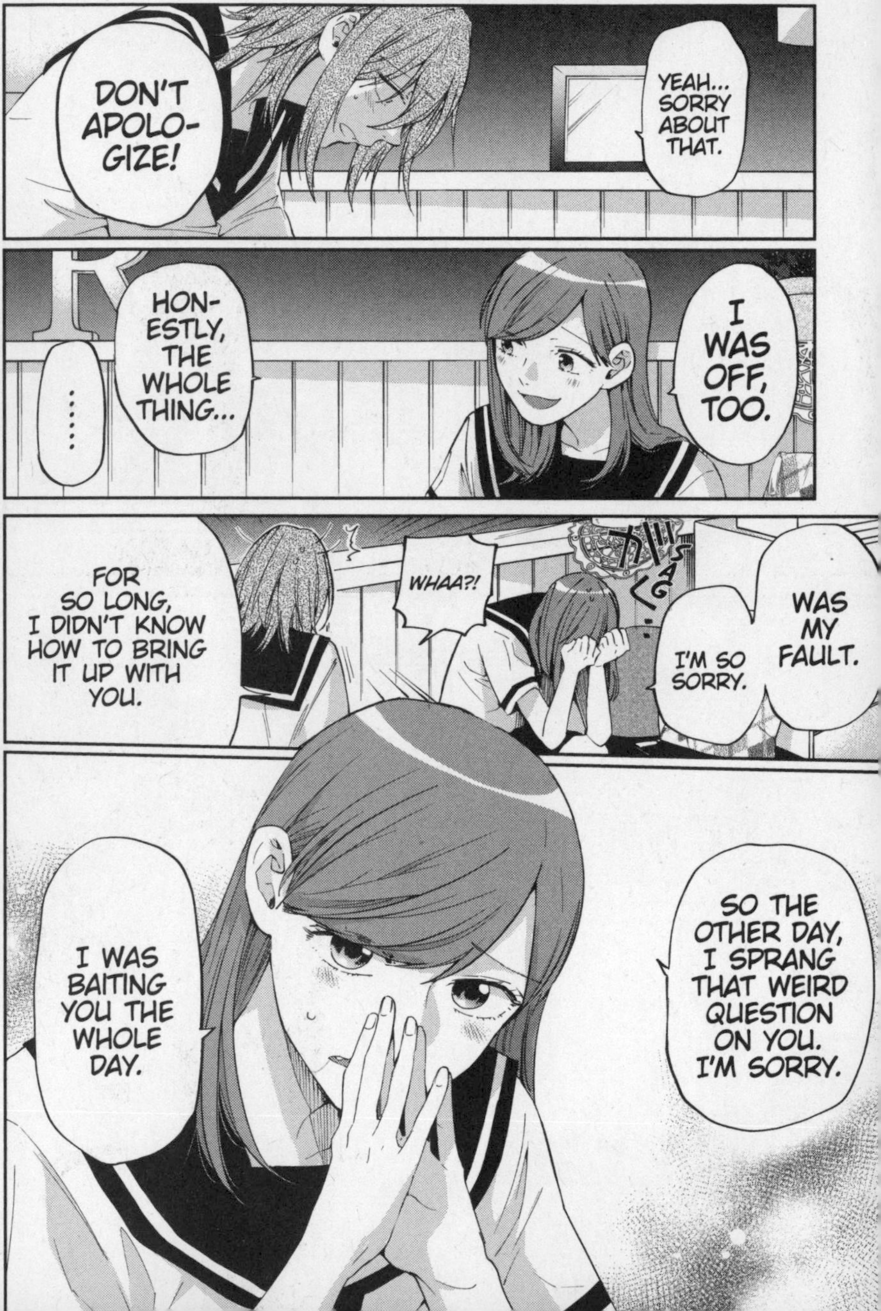
YEAH... SORRY ABOUT THAT.
DON'T APOLO-GIZE!
I WAS OFF, TOO.
HON-ESTLY, THE WHOLE THING...
......
WAS MY FAULT.
I'M SO SORRY.
SAG
WHAA?!
FOR SO LONG, I DIDN'T KNOW HOW TO BRING IT UP WITH YOU.
SO THE OTHER DAY, I SPRANG THAT WEIRD QUESTION ON YOU. I'M SORRY.
I WAS BAITING YOU THE WHOLE DAY.

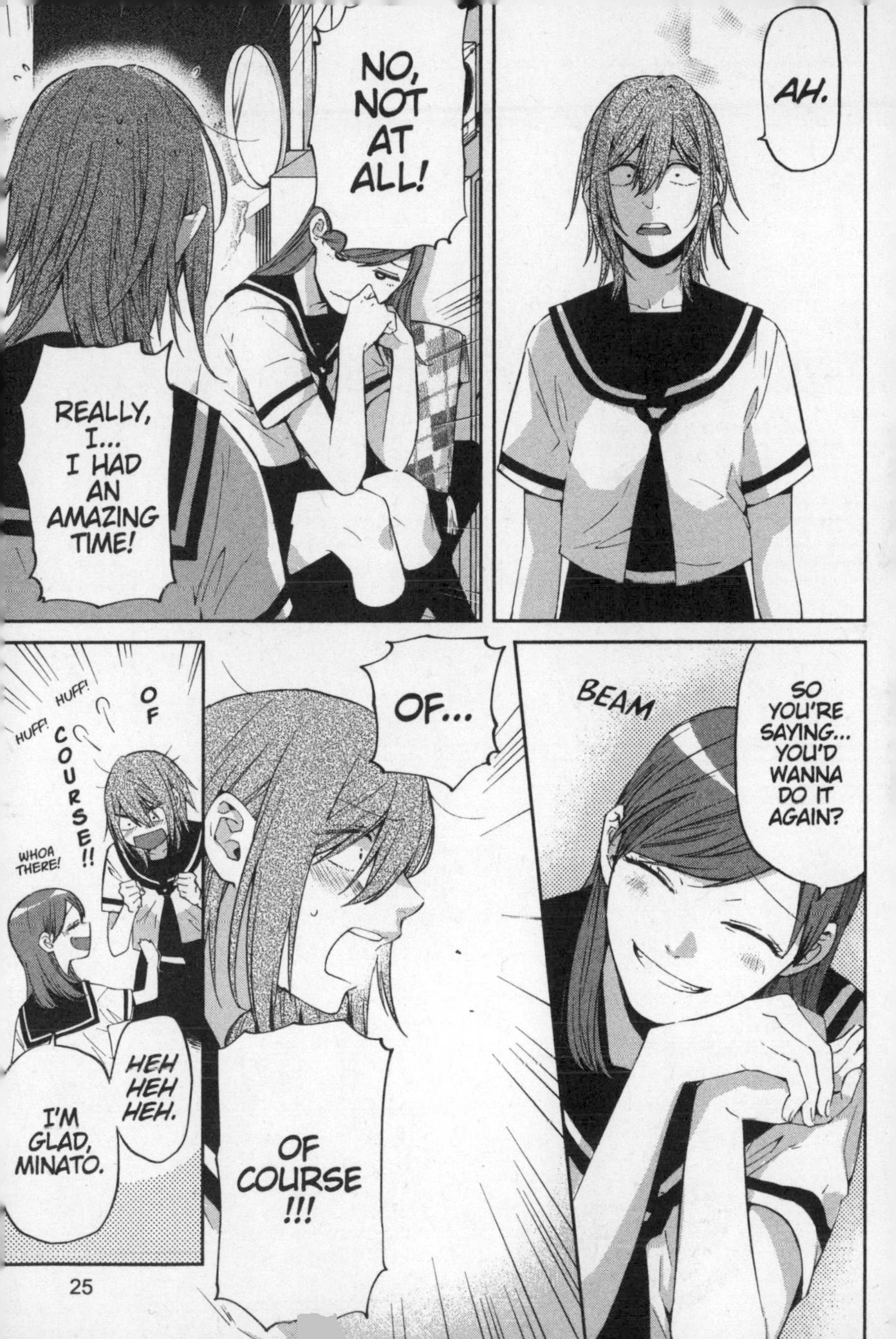
AH.
NO, NOT AT ALL!
REALLY, I... I HAD AN AMAZING TIME!
SO YOU'RE SAYING... YOU'D WANNA DO IT AGAIN?
BEAM
OF...
OF COURSE!!!
OF COURSE!!
HUFF!
HUFF!
WHOA THERE!
HEH HEH HEH.
I'M GLAD, MINATO.

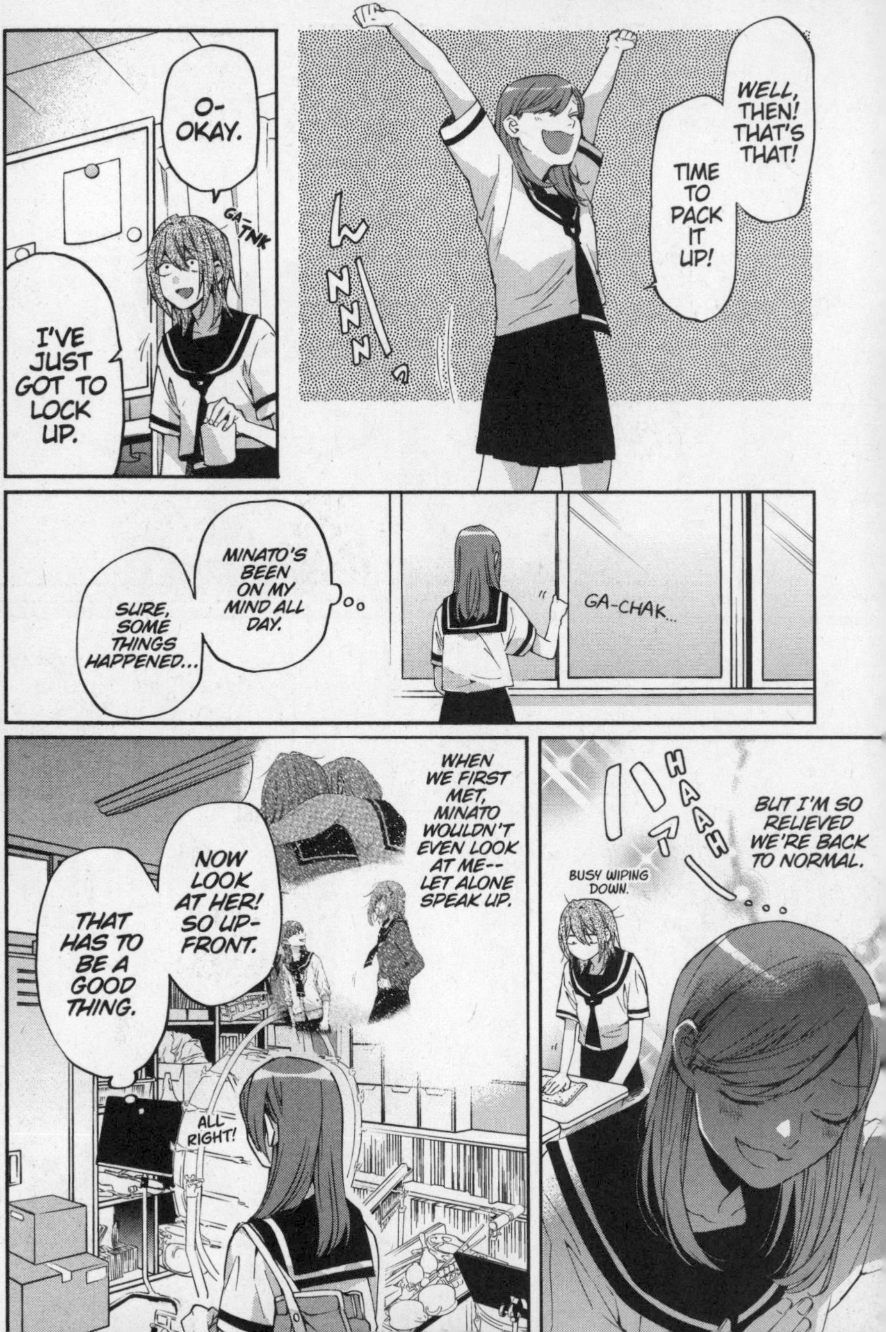
WELL, THEN! THAT'S THAT!
TIME TO PACK IT UP!
WNNN
O-OKAY.
GA-TNK
I'VE JUST GOT TO LOCK UP.
GA-CHAK...
MINATO'S BEEN ON MY MIND ALL DAY.
SURE, SOME THINGS HAPPENED...
HAAAH
BUT I'M SO RELIEVED WE'RE BACK TO NORMAL.
BUSY WIPING DOWN.
WHEN WE FIRST MET, MINATO WOULDN'T EVEN LOOK AT ME-- LET ALONE SPEAK UP.
NOW LOOK AT HER! SO UP-FRONT.
THAT HAS TO BE A GOOD THING.
ALL RIGHT!

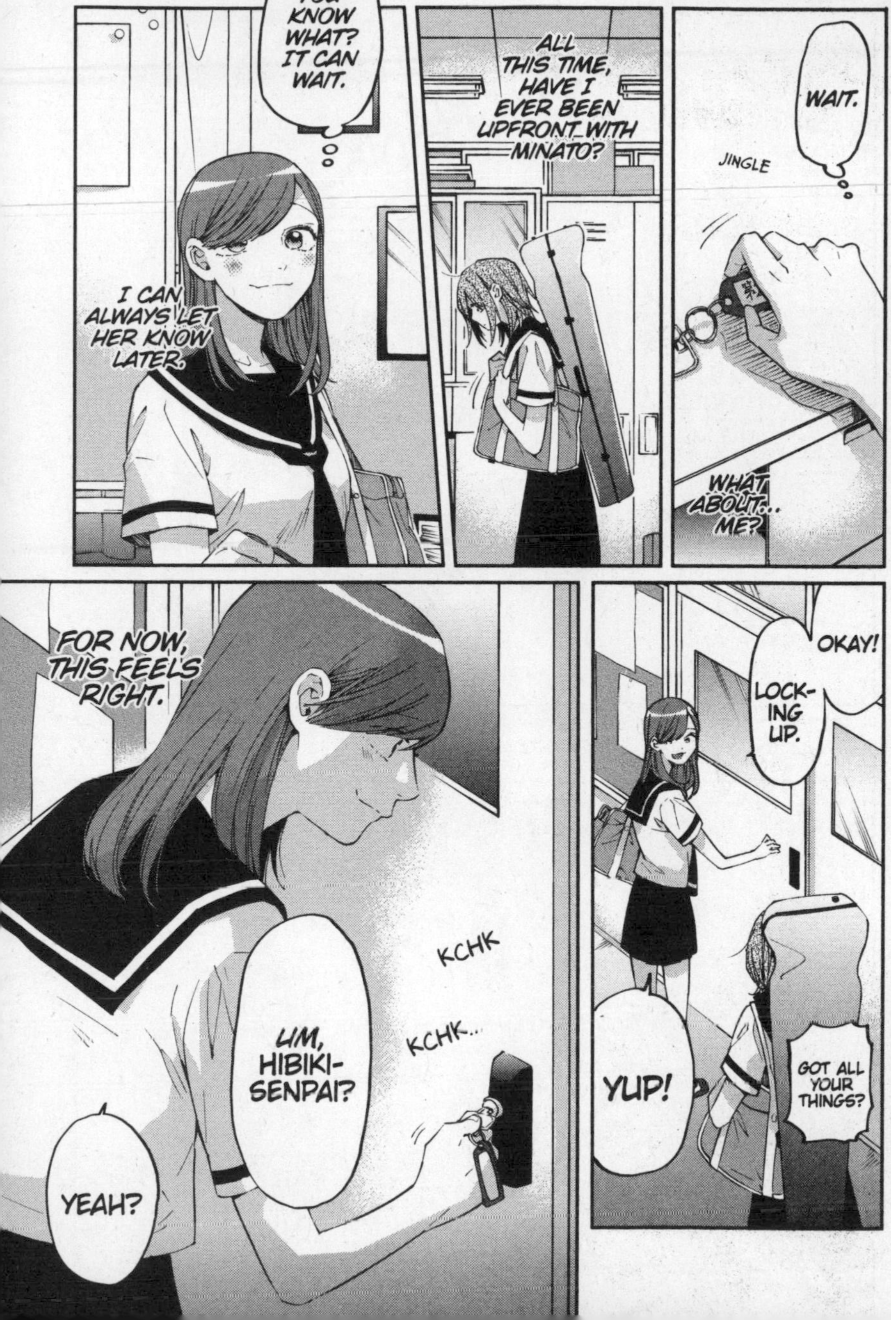

WAIT.
JINGLE
WHAT ABOUT... ME?
ALL THIS TIME, HAVE I EVER BEEN UPFRONT WITH MINATO?
YOU KNOW WHAT? IT CAN WAIT.
I CAN ALWAYS LET HER KNOW LATER.
OKAY!
LOCKING UP.
GOT ALL YOUR THINGS?
YUP!
FOR NOW, THIS FEELS RIGHT.
KCHK
KCHK...
UM, HIBIKI-SENPAI?
YEAH?

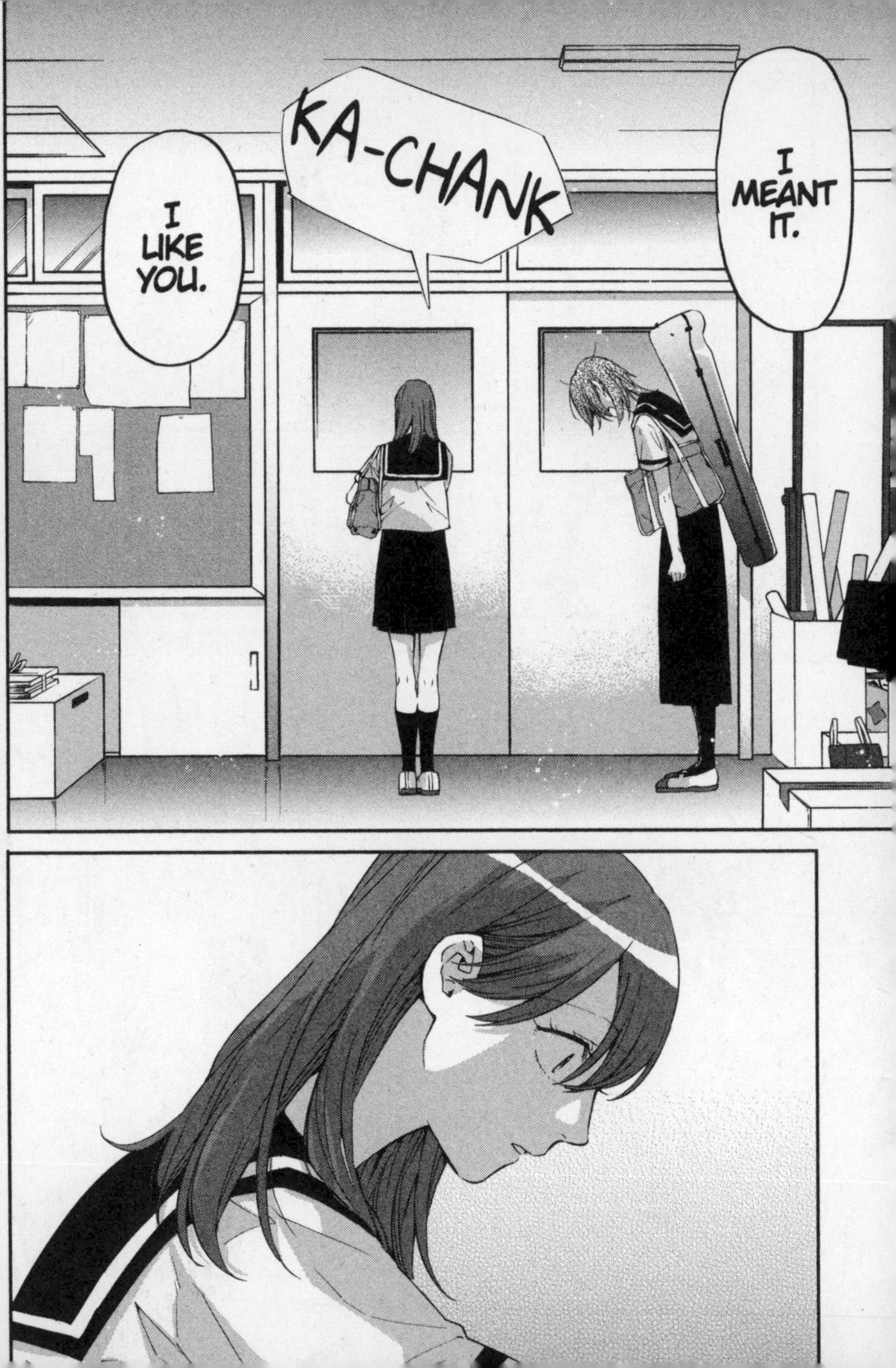
I MEANT IT.
KA-CHANK
I LIKE YOU.

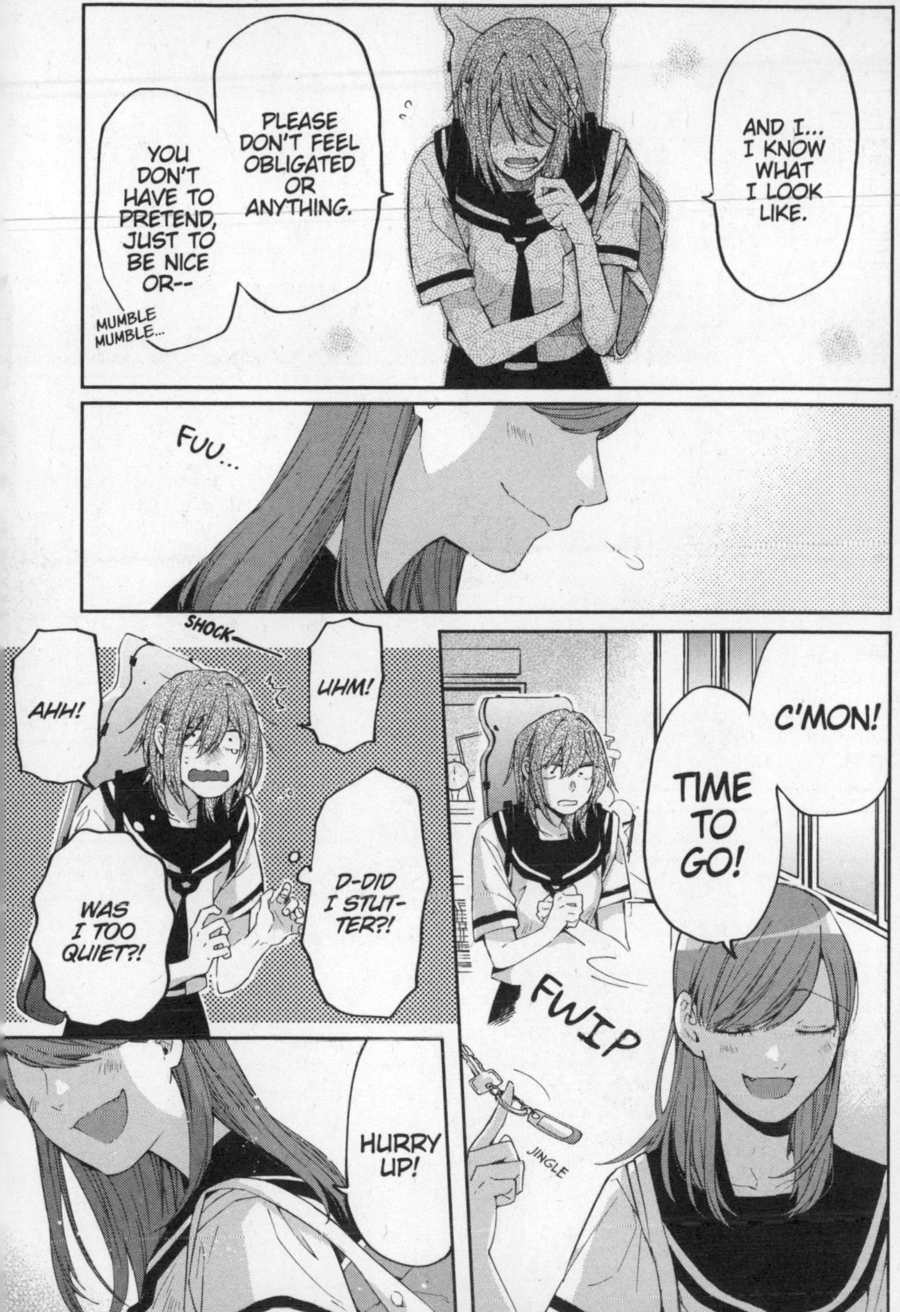
AND I... I KNOW WHAT I LOOK LIKE.
PLEASE DON'T FEEL OBLIGATED OR ANYTHING.
YOU DON'T HAVE TO PRETEND, JUST TO BE NICE OR--
MUMBLE MUMBLE...
FUU...
C'MON!
TIME TO GO!
FWIP
JINGLE
SHOCK
UHM!
AHH!
D-DID I STUTTER?!
WAS I TOO QUIET?!
HURRY UP!

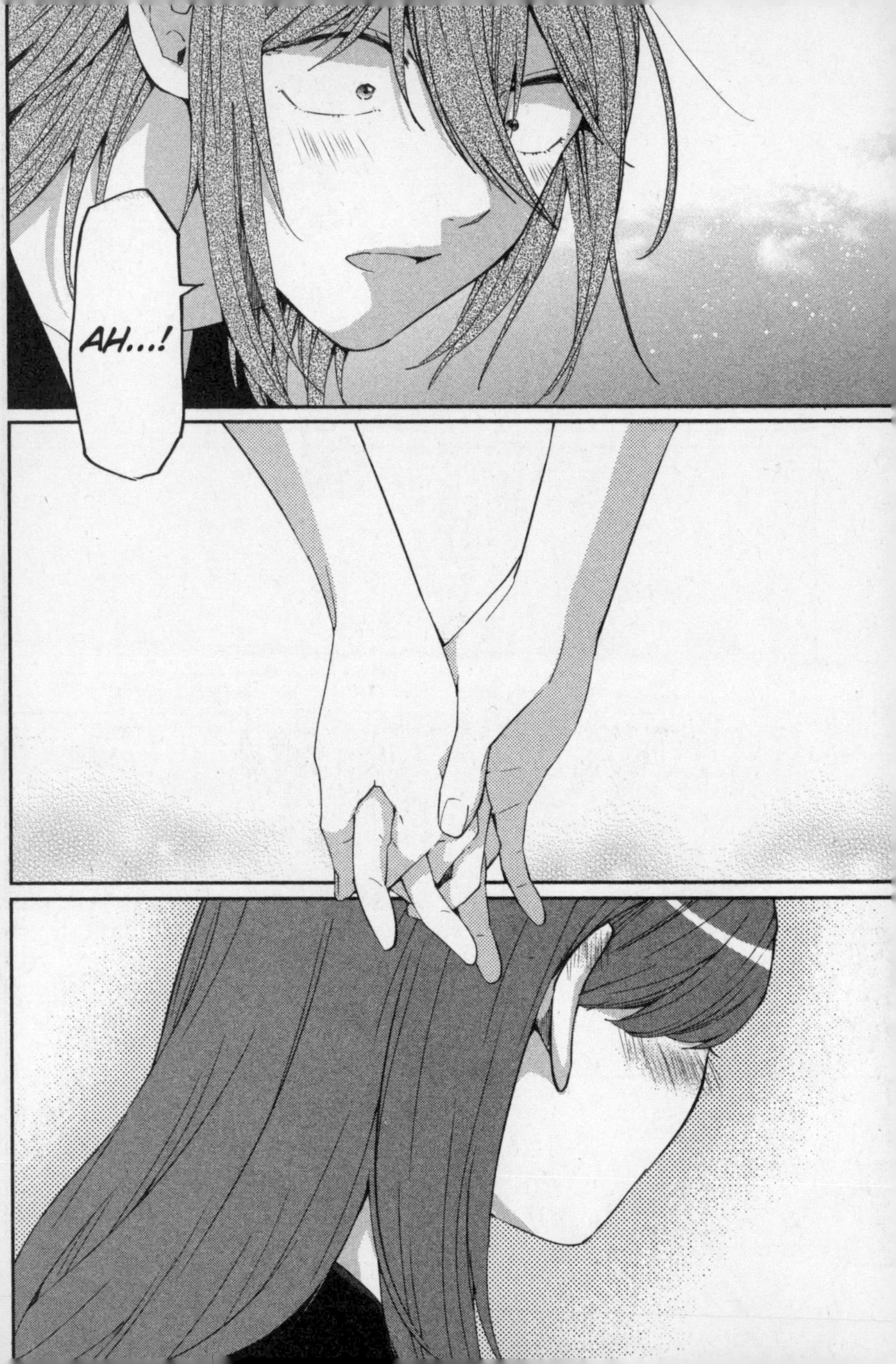
AH...!

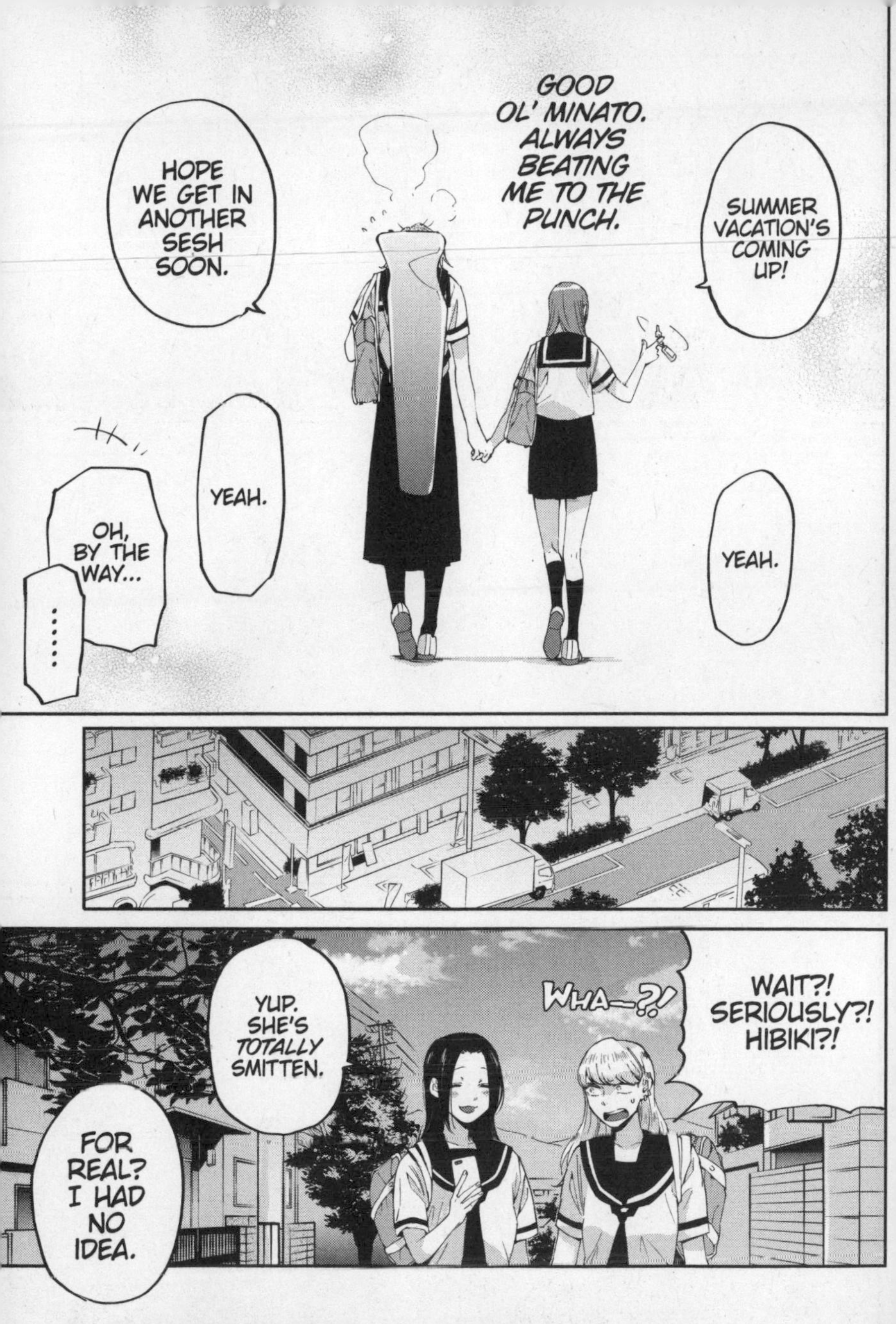
GOOD OL' MINATO. ALWAYS BEATING ME TO THE PUNCH.
SUMMER VACATION'S COMING UP!
HOPE WE GET IN ANOTHER SESH SOON.
YEAH.
YEAH.
OH, BY THE WAY...
......
WAIT?! SERIOUSLY?! HIBIKI?!
WHA—?!
YUP. SHE'S *TOTALLY* SMITTEN.
FOR REAL? I HAD NO IDEA.

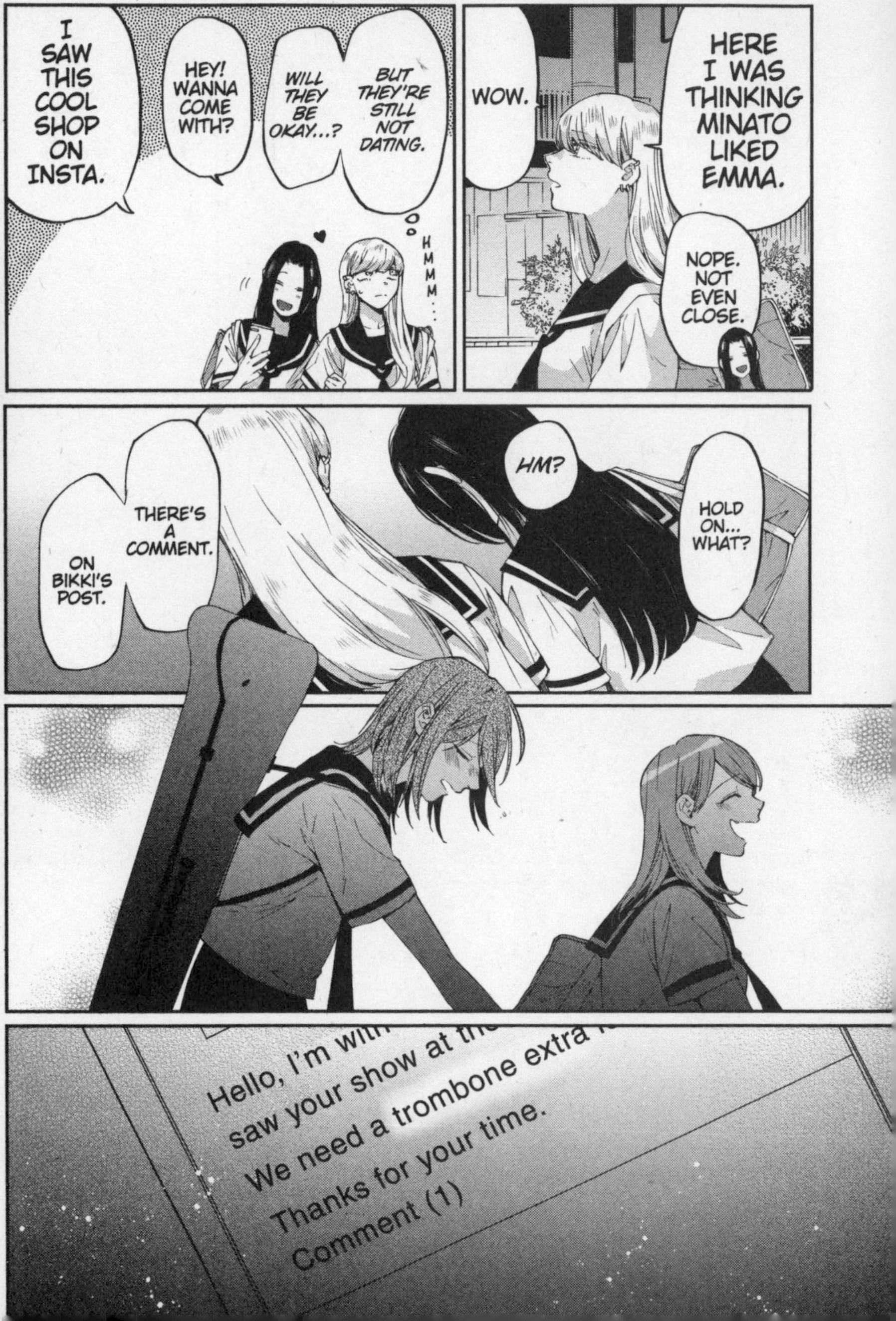
HERE I WAS THINKING MINATO LIKED EMMA.
WOW.
NOPE. NOT EVEN CLOSE.
BUT THEY'RE STILL NOT DATING.
WILL THEY BE OKAY...?
HMMM...
HEY! WANNA COME WITH?
I SAW THIS COOL SHOP ON INSTA.
HOLD ON... WHAT?
HM?
THERE'S A COMMENT.
ON BIKKI'S POST.
Hello, I'm with
saw your show at th
We need a trombone extra
Thanks for your time.
Comment (1)

HELLO, MELAN CHOLIC!

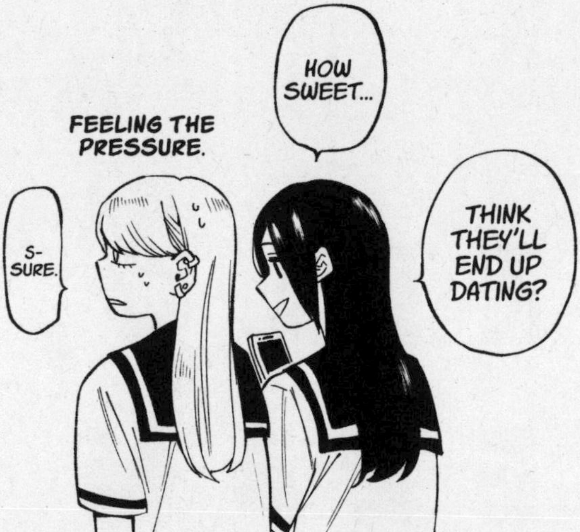
HOW SWEET...
THINK THEY'LL END UP DATING?
FEELING THE PRESSURE.
S-SURE.

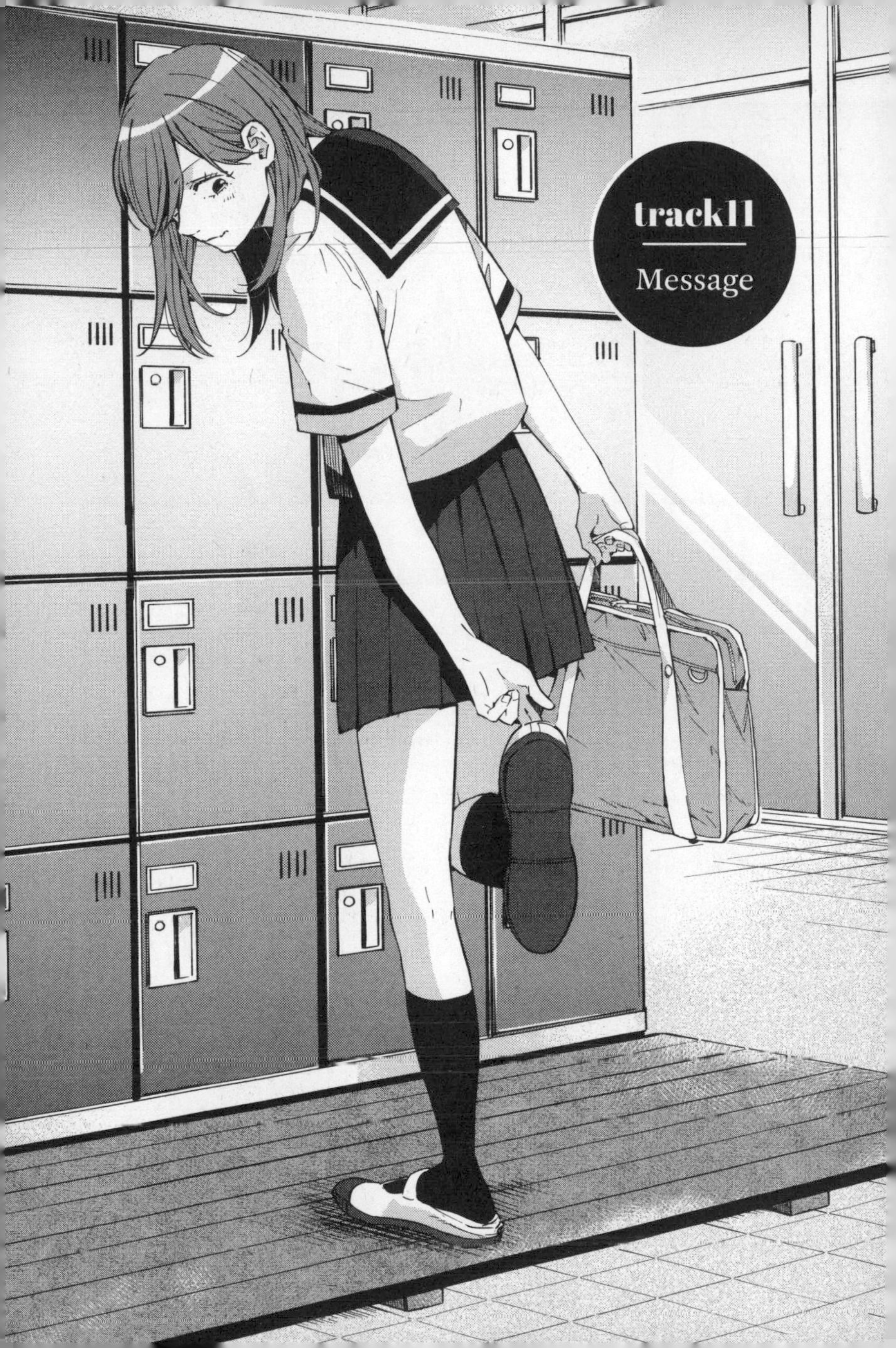
track11
Message

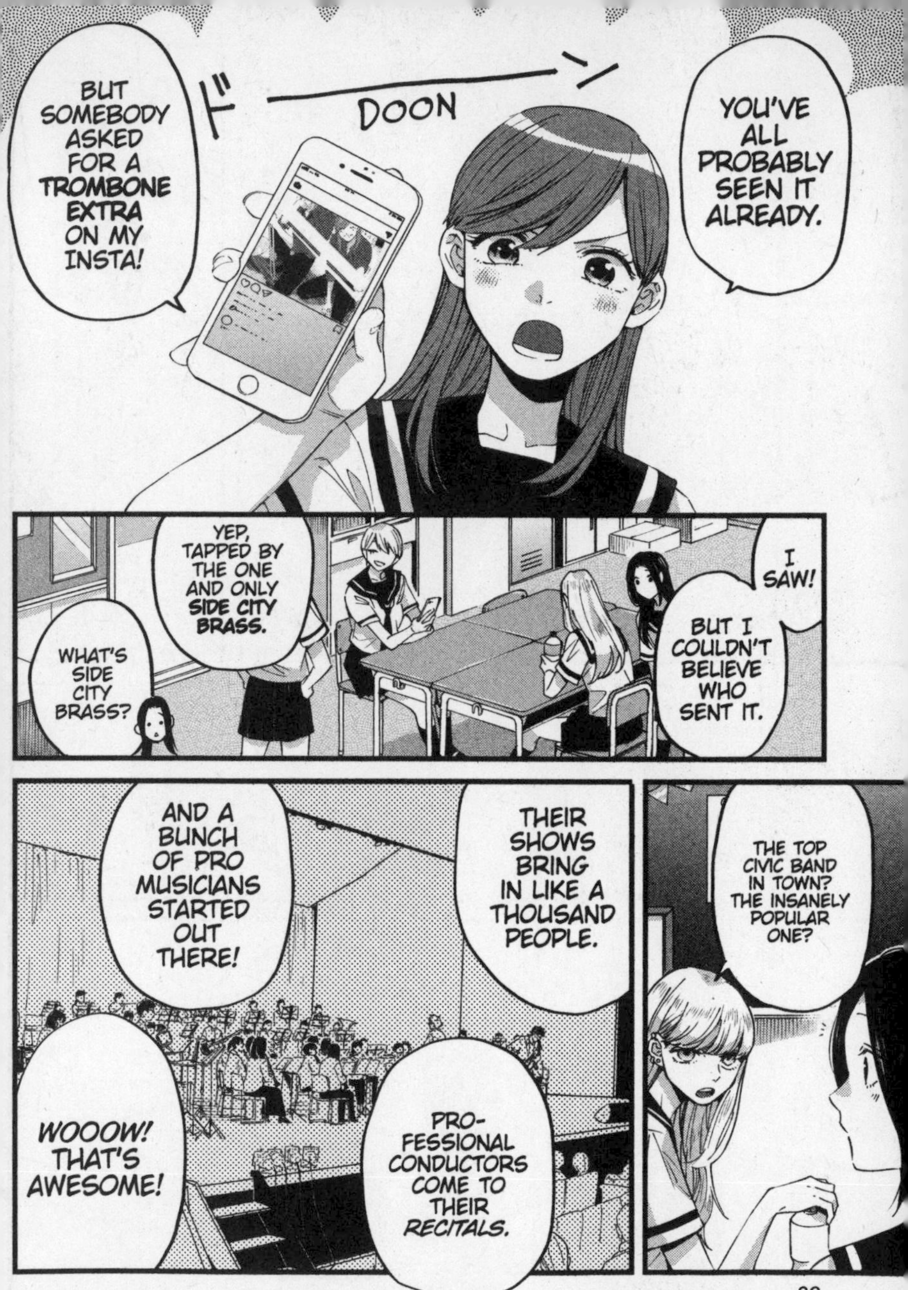
YOU'VE ALL PROBABLY SEEN IT ALREADY.
ドーン
DOON
BUT SOMEBODY ASKED FOR A TROMBONE EXTRA ON MY INSTA!
I SAW!
BUT I COULDN'T BELIEVE WHO SENT IT.
YEP, TAPPED BY THE ONE AND ONLY SIDE CITY BRASS.
WHAT'S SIDE CITY BRASS?
THE TOP CIVIC BAND IN TOWN? THE INSANELY POPULAR ONE?
THEIR SHOWS BRING IN LIKE A THOUSAND PEOPLE.
AND A BUNCH OF PRO MUSICIANS STARTED OUT THERE!
PRO-FESSIONAL CONDUCTORS COME TO THEIR RECITALS.
WOOOW! THAT'S AWESOME!

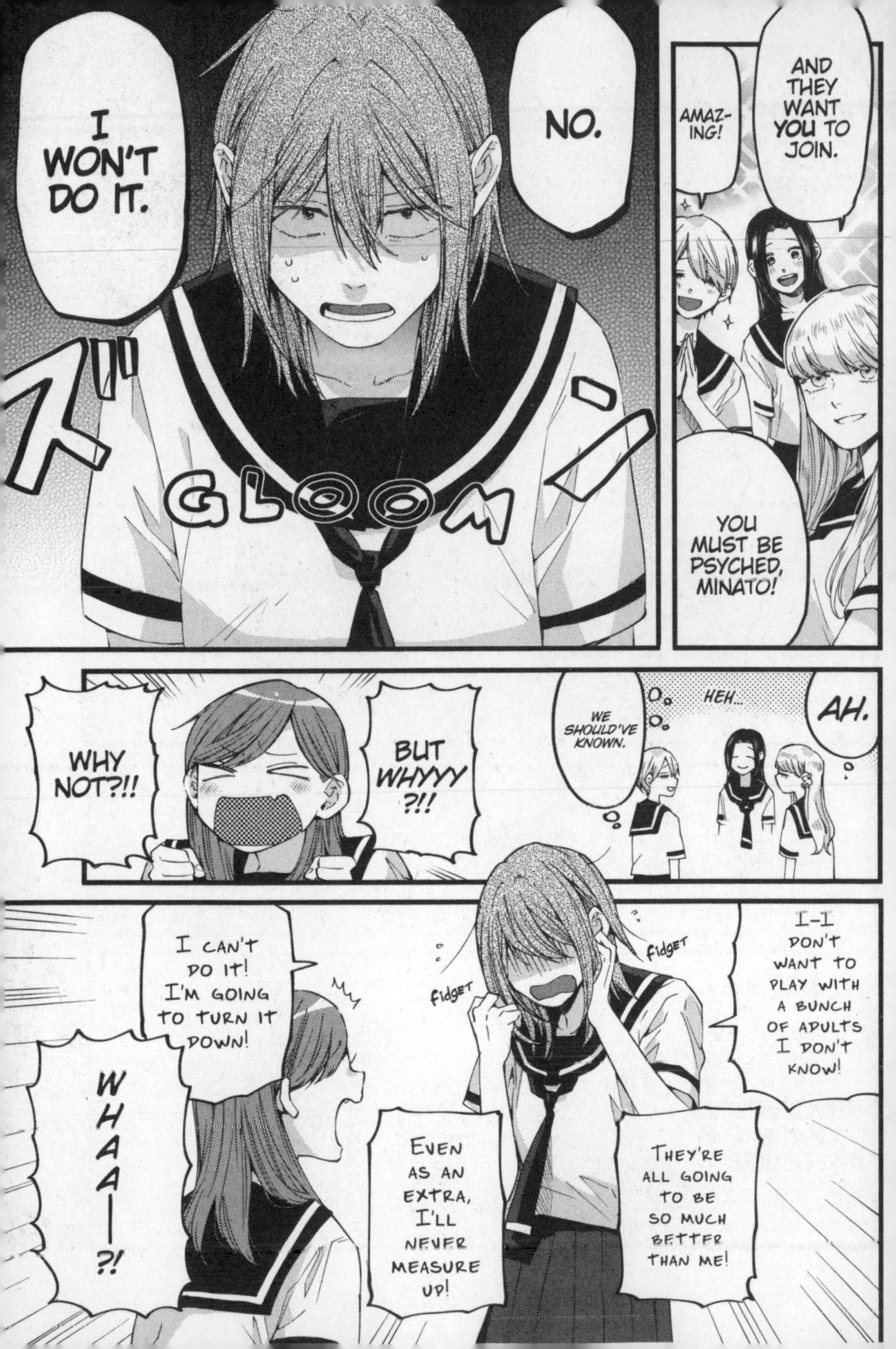
AND THEY WANT YOU TO JOIN.
AMAZ-ING!
YOU MUST BE PSYCHED, MINATO!
NO.
I WON'T DO IT.
GLOOM
AH.
HEH...
WE SHOULD'VE KNOWN.
BUT WHYYY?!!
WHY NOT?!!
I-I DON'T WANT TO PLAY WITH A BUNCH OF ADULTS I DON'T KNOW!
FIDGET
FIDGET
THEY'RE ALL GOING TO BE SO MUCH BETTER THAN ME!
EVEN AS AN EXTRA, I'LL NEVER MEASURE UP!
I CAN'T DO IT! I'M GOING TO TURN IT DOWN!
WHAA—?!

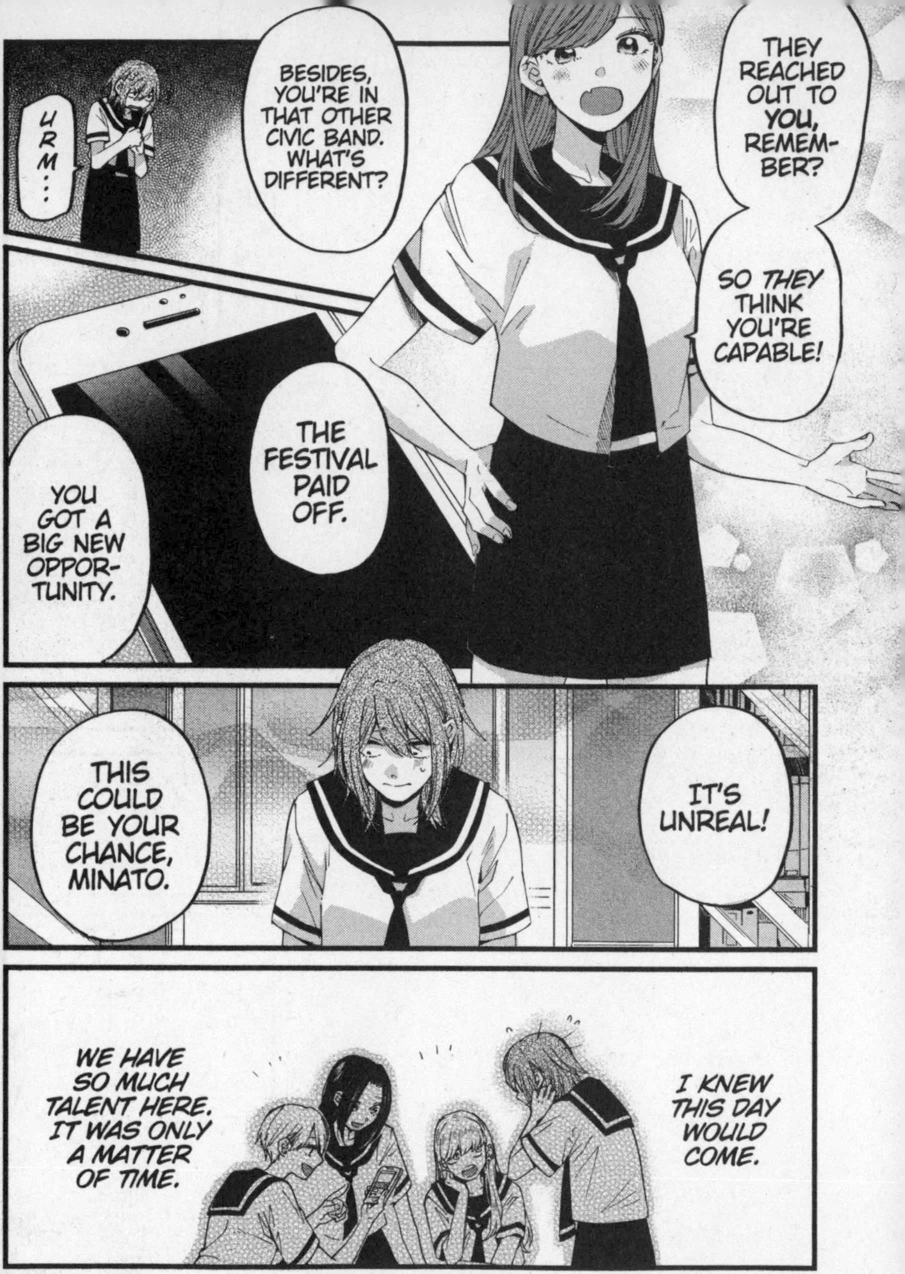
THEY REACHED OUT TO YOU, REMEMBER?
SO THEY THINK YOU'RE CAPABLE!
BESIDES, YOU'RE IN THAT OTHER CIVIC BAND. WHAT'S DIFFERENT?
URM...
THE FESTIVAL PAID OFF.
YOU GOT A BIG NEW OPPORTUNITY.
IT'S UNREAL!
THIS COULD BE YOUR CHANCE, MINATO.
I KNEW THIS DAY WOULD COME.
WE HAVE SO MUCH TALENT HERE. IT WAS ONLY A MATTER OF TIME.

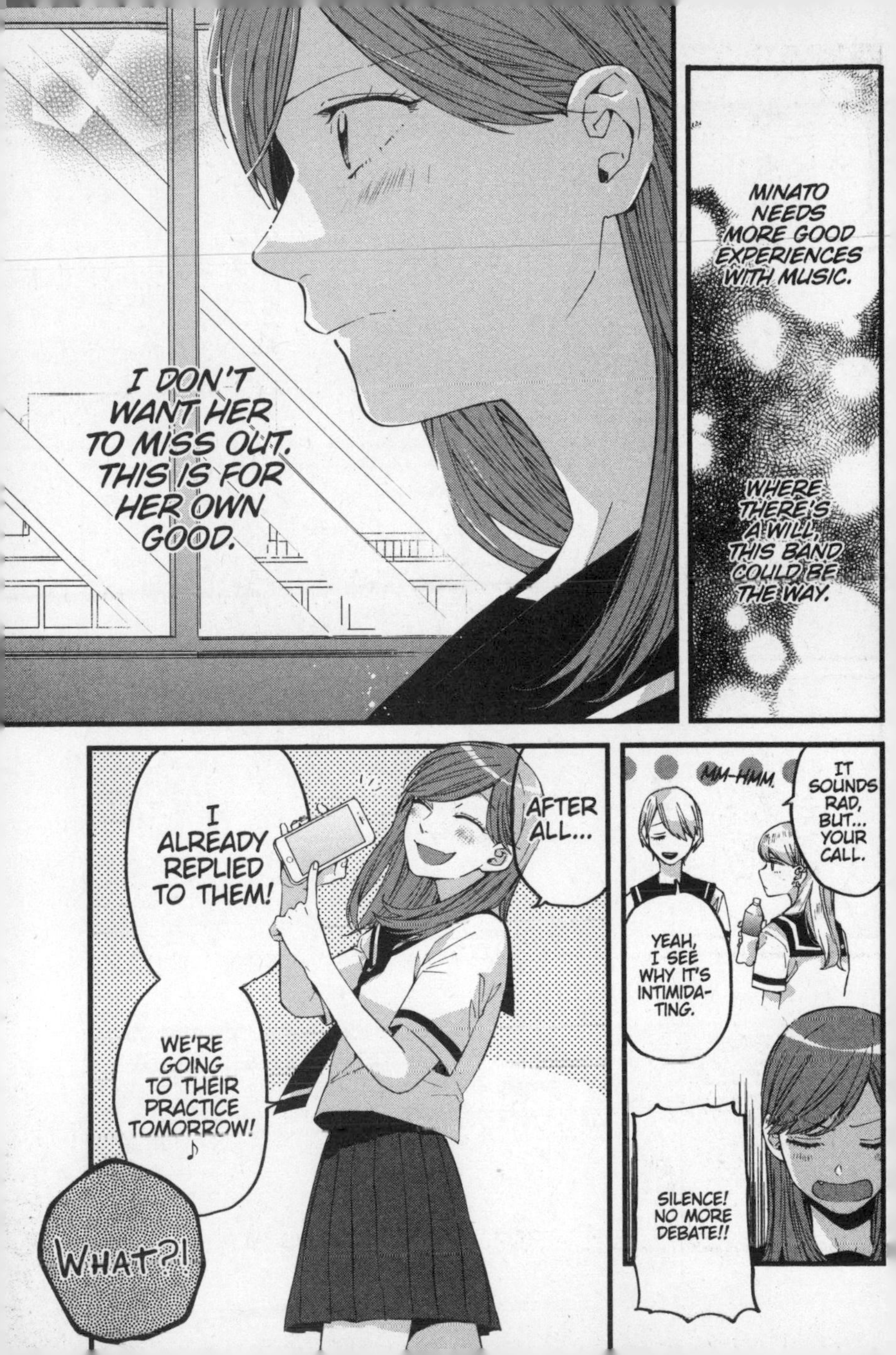
MINATO NEEDS MORE GOOD EXPERIENCES WITH MUSIC.
WHERE THERE'S A WILL, THIS BAND COULD BE THE WAY.
I DON'T WANT HER TO MISS OUT. THIS IS FOR HER OWN GOOD.
MM-HMM.
IT SOUNDS RAD, BUT... YOUR CALL.
YEAH, I SEE WHY IT'S INTIMIDA-TING.
SILENCE! NO MORE DEBATE!!
AFTER ALL...
I ALREADY REPLIED TO THEM!
WE'RE GOING TO THEIR PRACTICE TOMORROW! ♪
WHAT?!

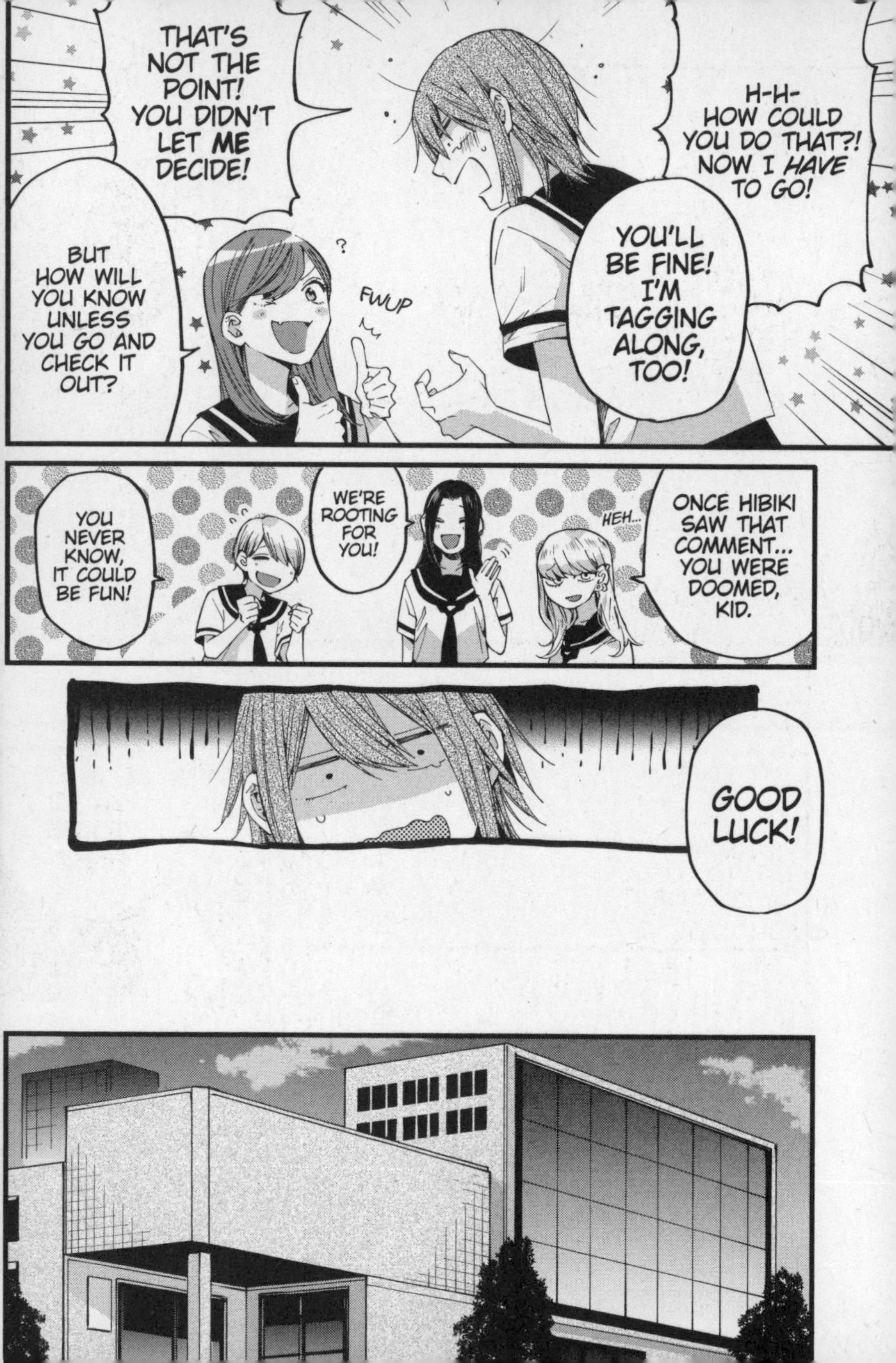
H-H- HOW COULD YOU DO THAT?! NOW I HAVE TO GO!
YOU'LL BE FINE! I'M TAGGING ALONG, TOO!
THAT'S NOT THE POINT! YOU DIDN'T LET ME DECIDE!
FWUP
BUT HOW WILL YOU KNOW UNLESS YOU GO AND CHECK IT OUT?
ONCE HIBIKI SAW THAT COMMENT... YOU WERE DOOMED, KID.
HEH...
WE'RE ROOTING FOR YOU!
YOU NEVER KNOW, IT COULD BE FUN!
GOOD LUCK!

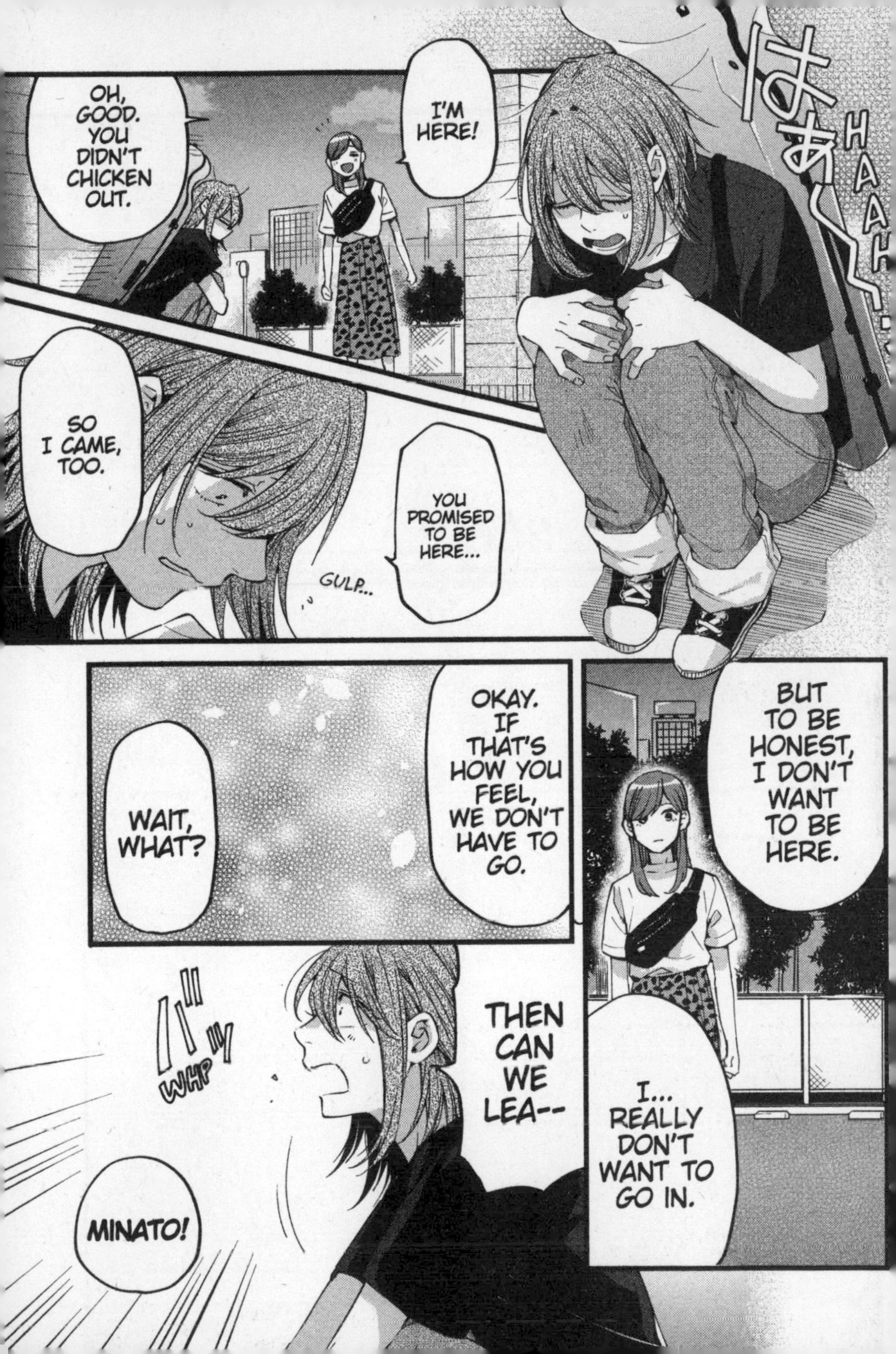
HAAAH...
I'M HERE!
OH, GOOD. YOU DIDN'T CHICKEN OUT.
YOU PROMISED TO BE HERE...
GULP...
SO I CAME, TOO.
BUT TO BE HONEST, I DON'T WANT TO BE HERE.
OKAY. IF THAT'S HOW YOU FEEL, WE DON'T HAVE TO GO.
WAIT, WHAT?
I... REALLY DON'T WANT TO GO IN.
THEN CAN WE LEA--
WHP
MINATO!

PAFF

I'M SORRY FOR BEING SO PUSHY.

FOR BOTH OF US.

BUT I THINK IT'D BE A MISTAKE TO SAY NO WITHOUT EVEN *SEEING* THEM.

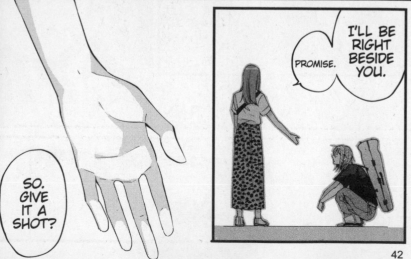

I'LL BE RIGHT BESIDE YOU.

PROMISE.

SO. GIVE IT A SHOT?

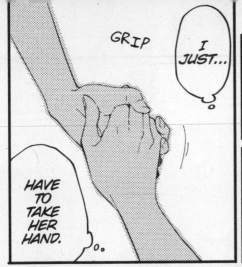

FUU
I JUST...
GRIP
HAVE TO TAKE HER HAND.
FINE. I'LL TRY IT. FOR TODAY.
BUT I STILL DON'T THINK I'M GONNA JOIN!
I KNOW, I KNOW.
AFTERWARDS, I'LL BUY YOU ICE CREAM.
Rehearsal Room #1

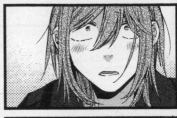

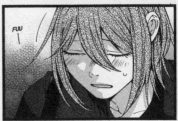

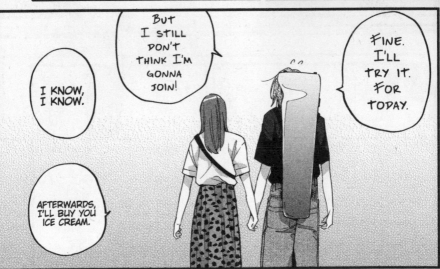

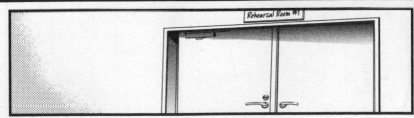

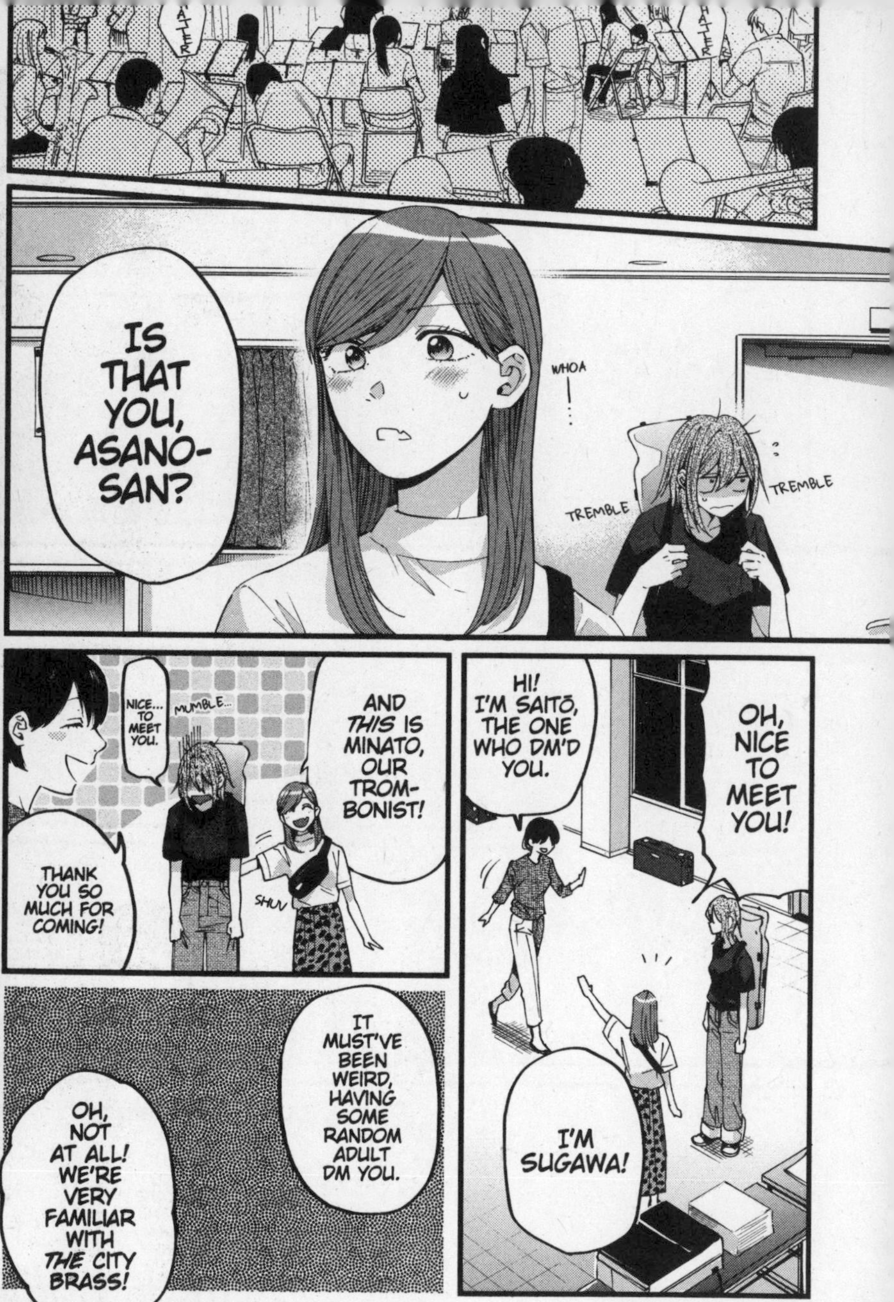
IS THAT YOU, ASANO-SAN?
WHOA
TREMBLE
TREMBLE
OH, NICE TO MEET YOU!
HI! I'M SAITŌ, THE ONE WHO DM'D YOU.
I'M SUGAWA!
AND *THIS* IS MINATO, OUR TROMBONIST!
NICE... TO MEET YOU.
MUMBLE...
SHUV
THANK YOU SO MUCH FOR COMING!
IT MUST'VE BEEN WEIRD, HAVING SOME RANDOM ADULT DM YOU.
OH, NOT AT ALL! WE'RE VERY FAMILIAR WITH *THE* CITY BRASS!

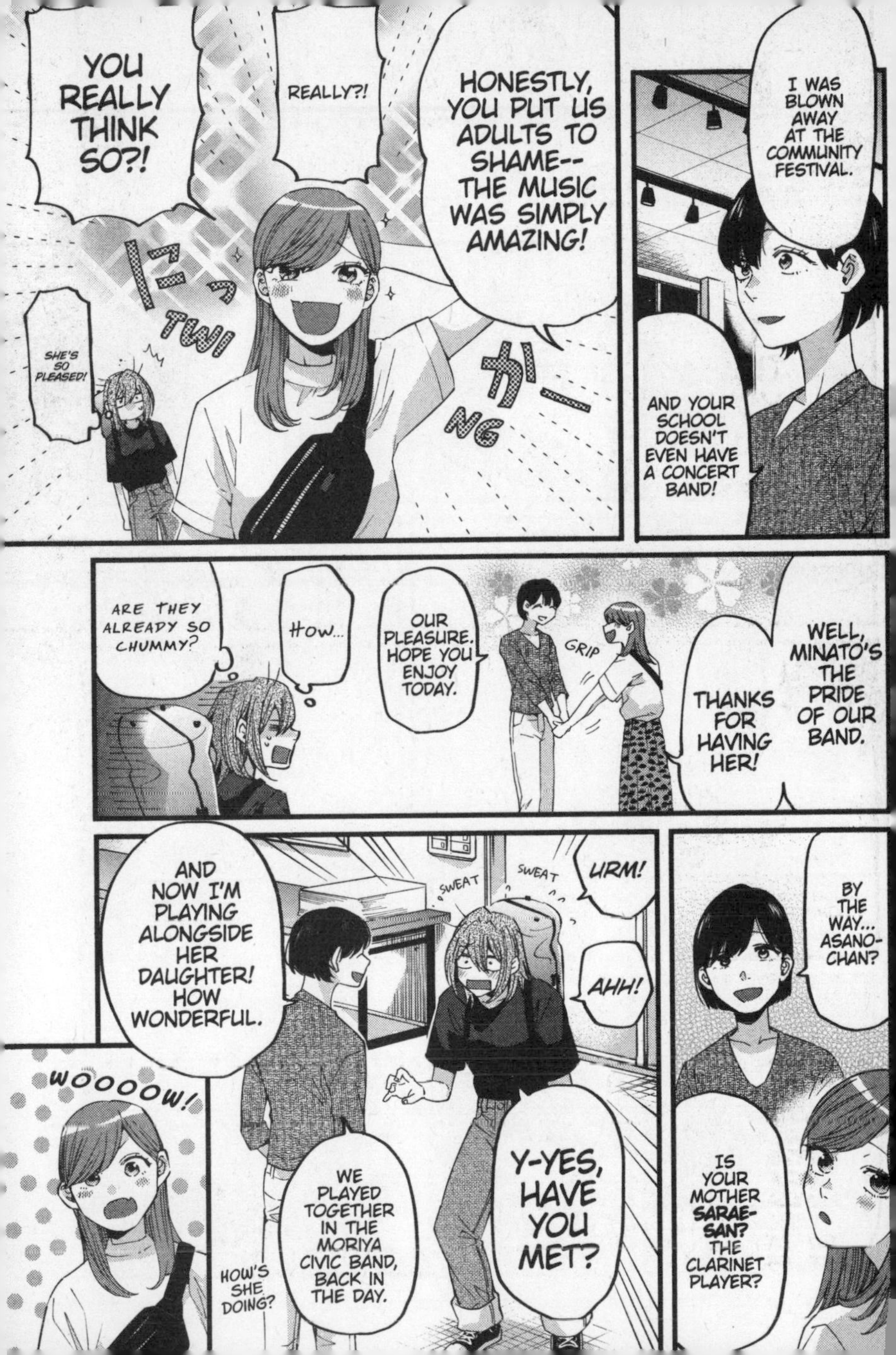
I WAS BLOWN AWAY AT THE COMMUNITY FESTIVAL.
AND YOUR SCHOOL DOESN'T EVEN HAVE A CONCERT BAND!
HONESTLY, YOU PUT US ADULTS TO SHAME-- THE MUSIC WAS SIMPLY AMAZING!
かー
NG
REALLY?!
YOU REALLY THINK SO?!
にっ
TWI
SHE'S SO PLEASED!
WELL, MINATO'S THE PRIDE OF OUR BAND.
THANKS FOR HAVING HER!
GRIP
OUR PLEASURE. HOPE YOU ENJOY TODAY.
HOW...
ARE THEY ALREADY SO CHUMMY?
BY THE WAY... ASANO-CHAN?
IS YOUR MOTHER SARAE-SAN? THE CLARINET PLAYER?
URM!
AHH!
SWEAT
SWEAT
Y-YES, HAVE YOU MET?
WE PLAYED TOGETHER IN THE MORIYA CIVIC BAND, BACK IN THE DAY.
HOW'S SHE DOING?
AND NOW I'M PLAYING ALONGSIDE HER DAUGHTER! HOW WONDERFUL.
WOOOOOW!

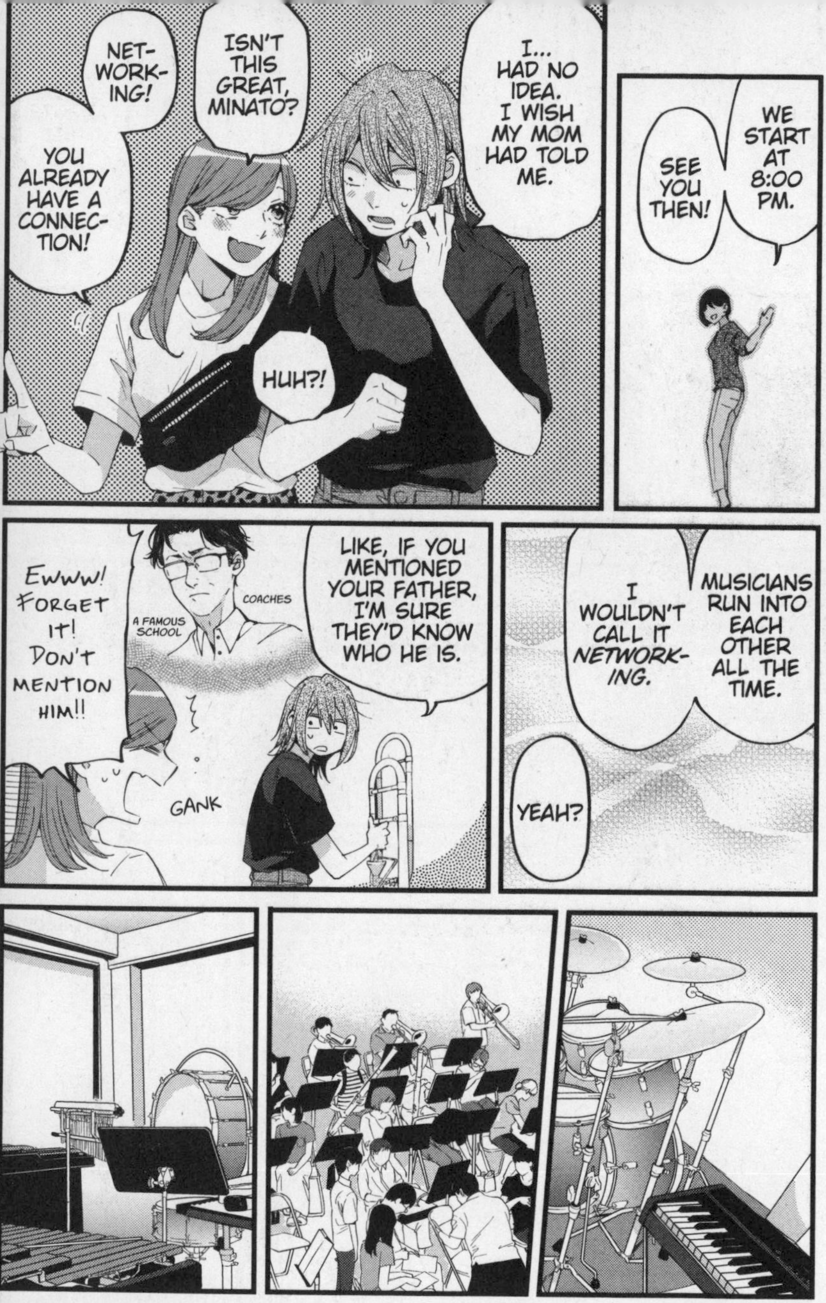

WE START AT 8:00 PM.
SEE YOU THEN!
I... HAD NO IDEA. I WISH MY MOM HAD TOLD ME.
ISN'T THIS GREAT, MINATO?
NET-WORK-ING!
YOU ALREADY HAVE A CONNEC-TION!
HUH?!
MUSICIANS RUN INTO EACH OTHER ALL THE TIME.
I WOULDN'T CALL IT *NETWORK-ING.*
YEAH?
LIKE, IF YOU MENTIONED YOUR FATHER, I'M SURE THEY'D KNOW WHO HE IS.
COACHES
A FAMOUS SCHOOL
Ewww! Forget it! Don't mention him!!
GANK

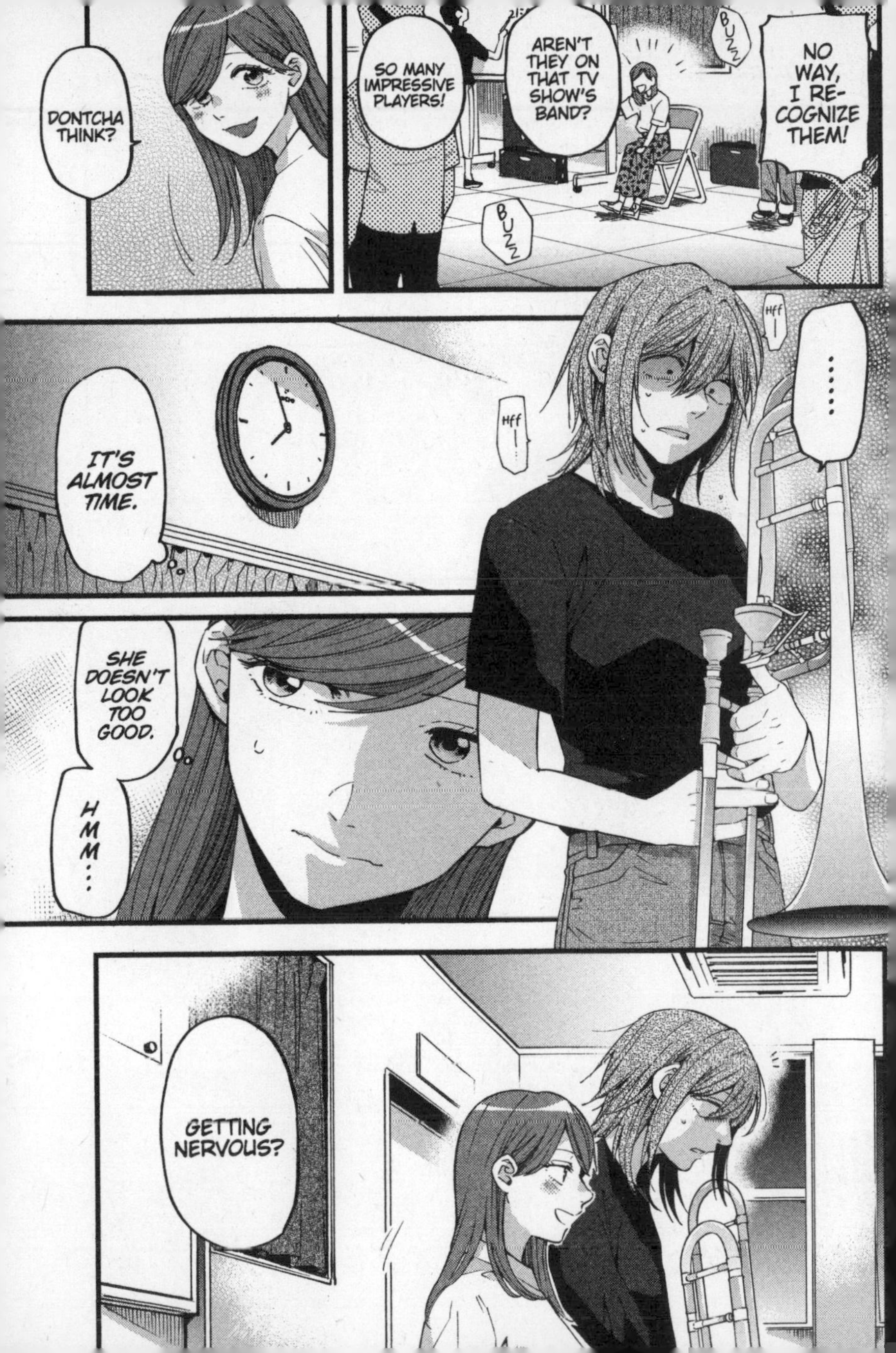
BUZZ
NO WAY, I RE-COGNIZE THEM!
AREN'T THEY ON THAT TV SHOW'S BAND?
SO MANY IMPRESSIVE PLAYERS!
BUZZ
DONTCHA THINK?
......
Hff
Hff
IT'S ALMOST TIME.
SHE DOESN'T LOOK TOO GOOD.
HMM...
GETTING NERVOUS?

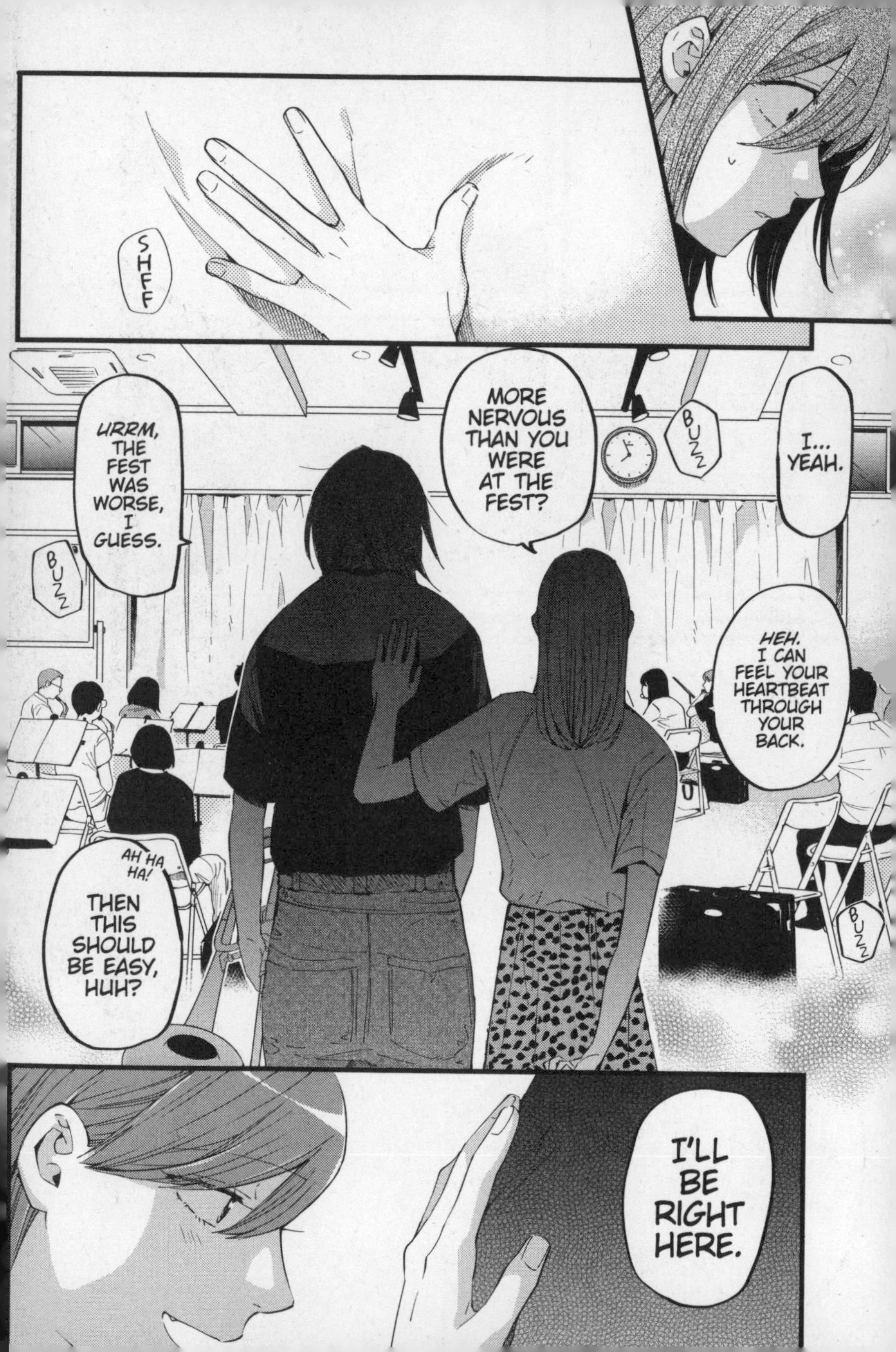
SHFF
I... YEAH.
BUZZ
MORE NERVOUS THAN YOU WERE AT THE FEST?
URRM, THE FEST WAS WORSE, I GUESS.
BUZZ
HEH. I CAN FEEL YOUR HEARTBEAT THROUGH YOUR BACK.
BUZZ
AH HA HA!
THEN THIS SHOULD BE EASY, HUH?
I'LL BE RIGHT HERE.

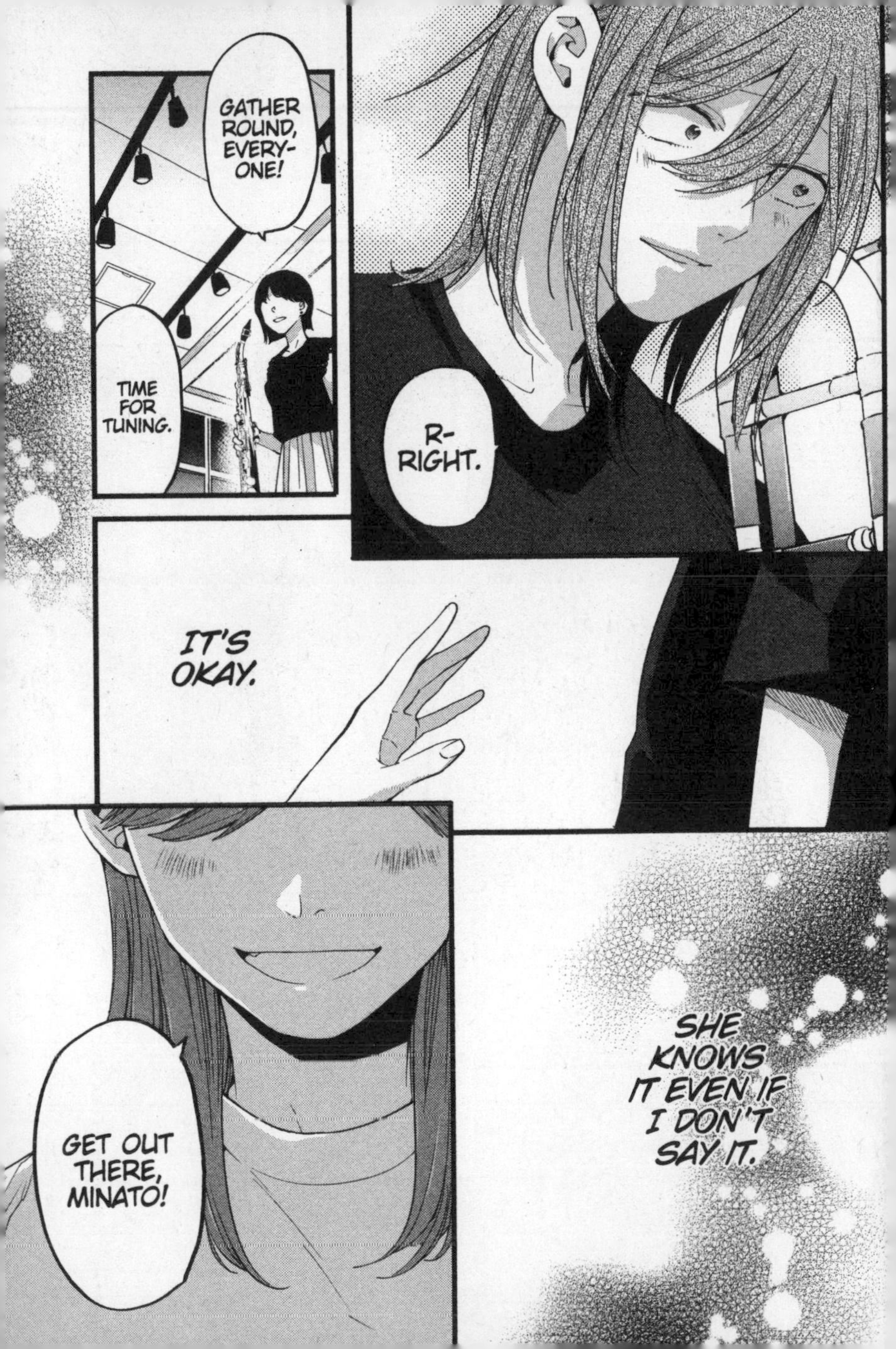
R-RIGHT.
GATHER ROUND, EVERY-ONE!
TIME FOR TUNING.
IT'S OKAY.
SHE KNOWS IT EVEN IF I DON'T SAY IT.
GET OUT THERE, MINATO!

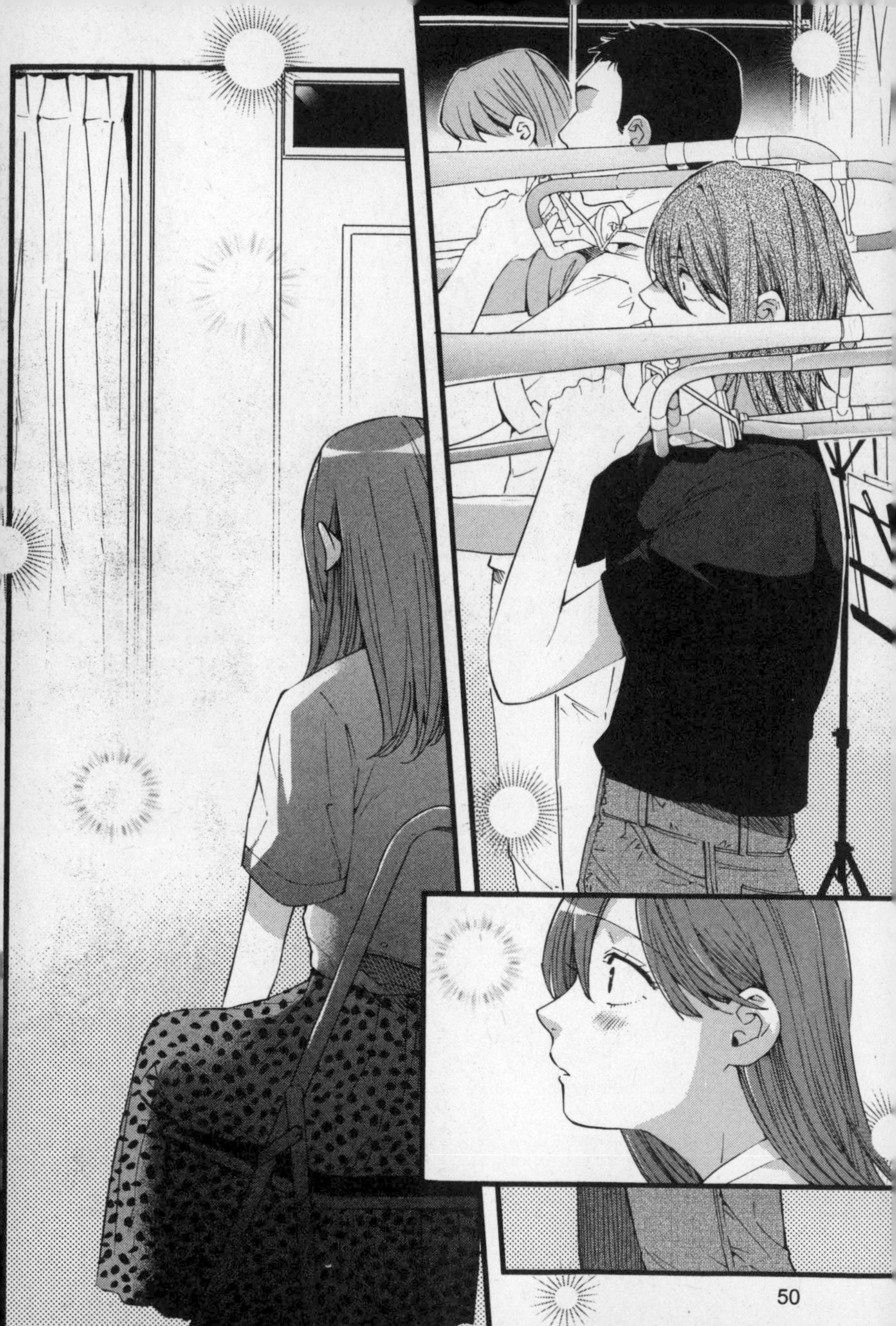

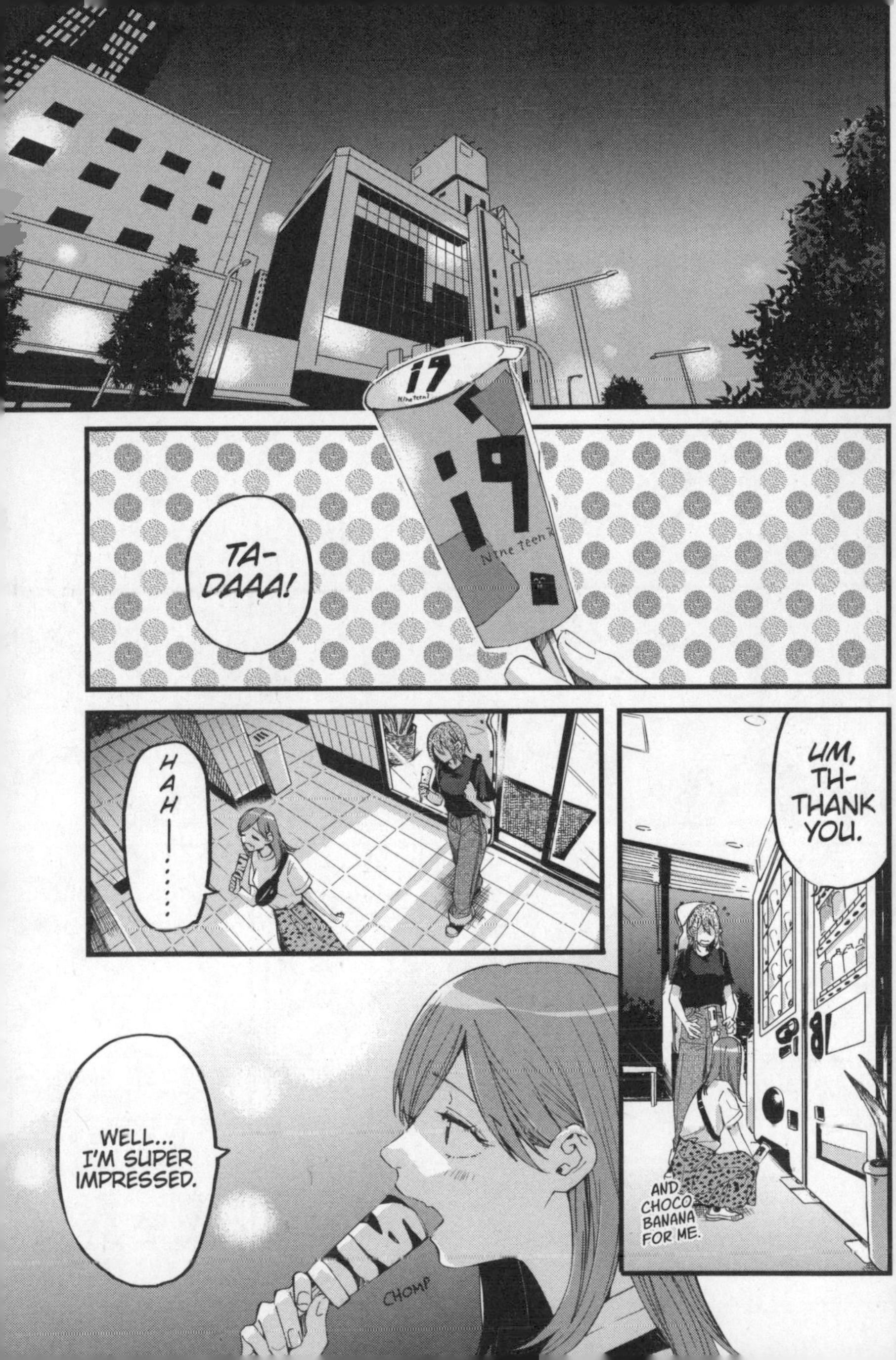
TA-DAAA!
UM, TH-THANK YOU.
AND CHOCO BANANA FOR ME.
HAH—......
WELL... I'M SUPER IMPRESSED.
CHOMP

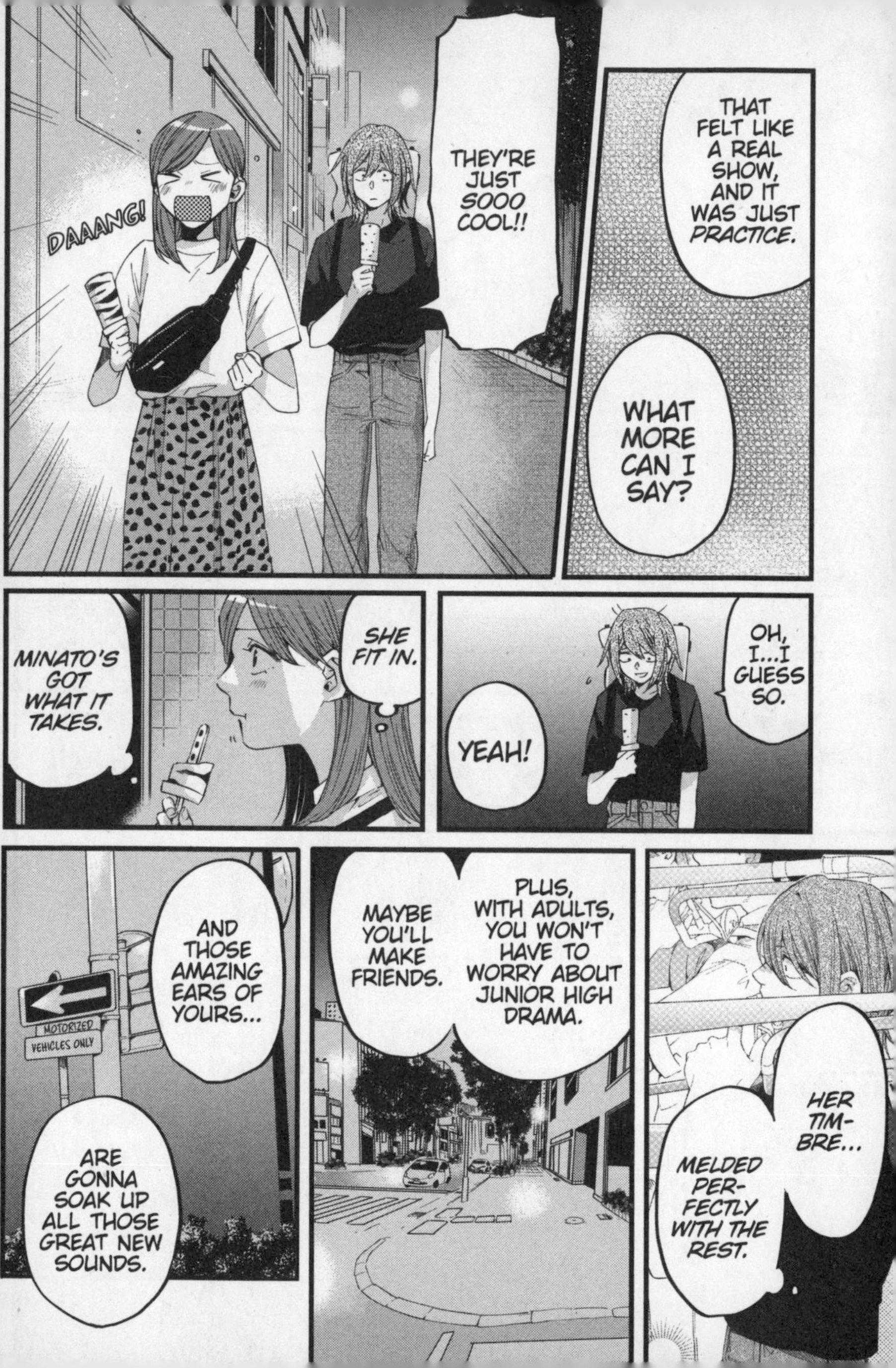
THAT FELT LIKE A REAL SHOW, AND IT WAS JUST PRACTICE.
WHAT MORE CAN I SAY?
THEY'RE JUST SOOO COOL!!
DAAANG!
OH, I...I GUESS SO.
YEAH!
SHE FIT IN.
MINATO'S GOT WHAT IT TAKES.
HER TIMBRE...
MELDED PERFECTLY WITH THE REST.
PLUS, WITH ADULTS, YOU WON'T HAVE TO WORRY ABOUT JUNIOR HIGH DRAMA.
MAYBE YOU'LL MAKE FRIENDS.
AND THOSE AMAZING EARS OF YOURS...
MOTORIZED
VEHICLES ONLY
ARE GONNA SOAK UP ALL THOSE GREAT NEW SOUNDS.

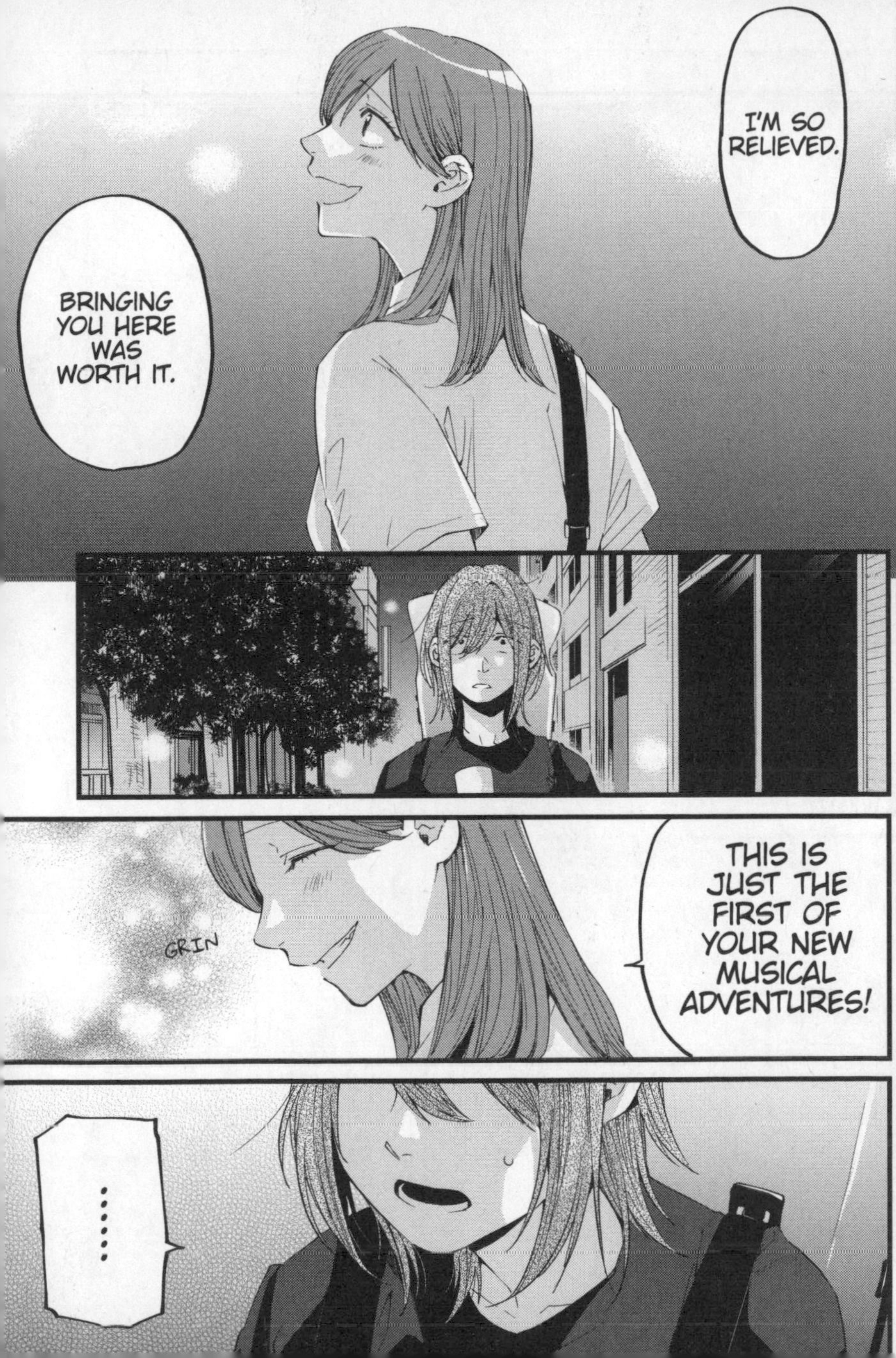
I'M SO RELIEVED.
BRINGING YOU HERE WAS WORTH IT.
THIS IS JUST THE FIRST OF YOUR NEW MUSICAL ADVENTURES!
GRIN
......

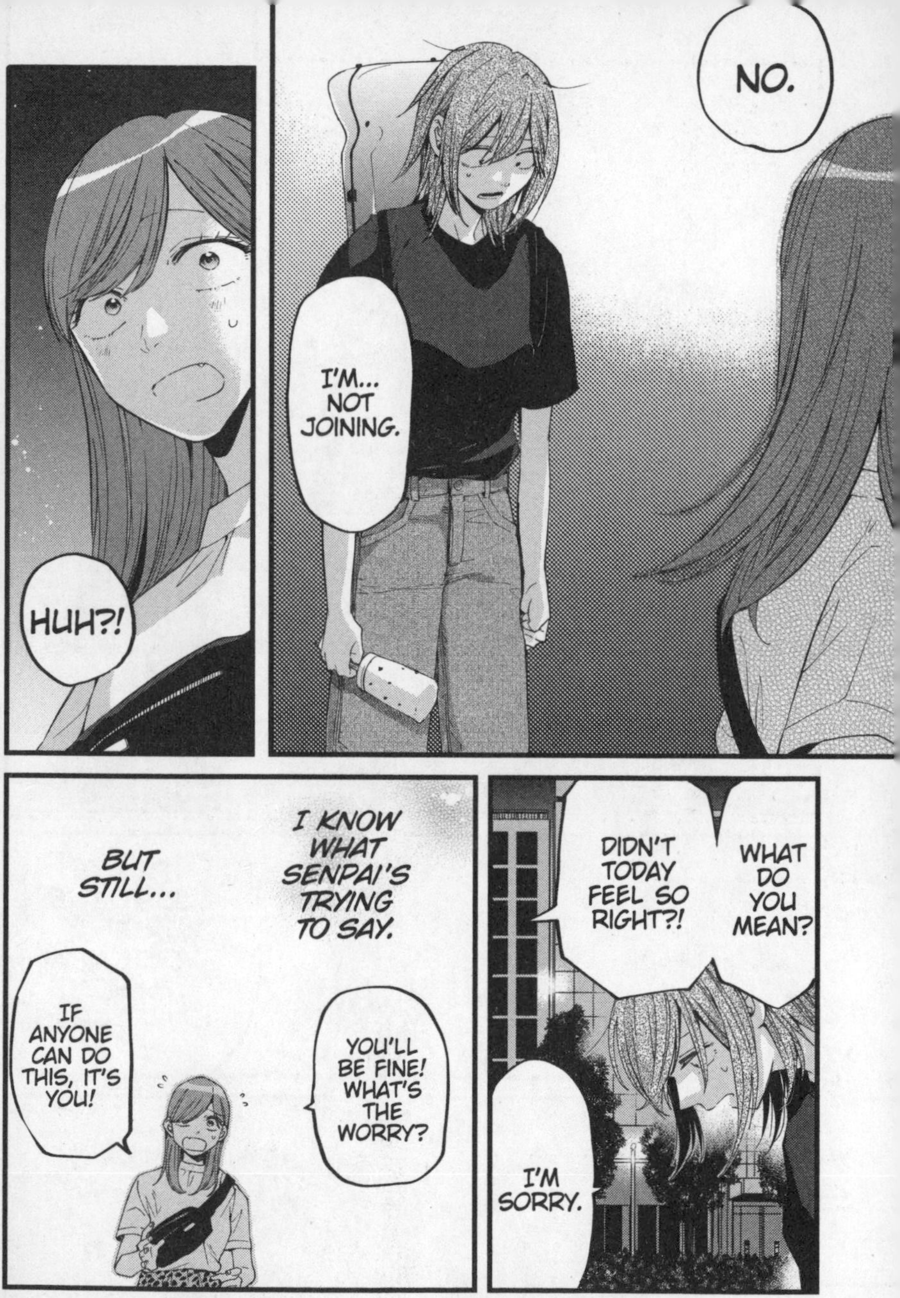
NO.
I'M... NOT JOINING.
HUH?!
WHAT DO YOU MEAN?
DIDN'T TODAY FEEL SO RIGHT?!
I'M SORRY.
I KNOW WHAT SENPAI'S TRYING TO SAY.
BUT STILL...
YOU'LL BE FINE! WHAT'S THE WORRY?
IF ANYONE CAN DO THIS, IT'S YOU!

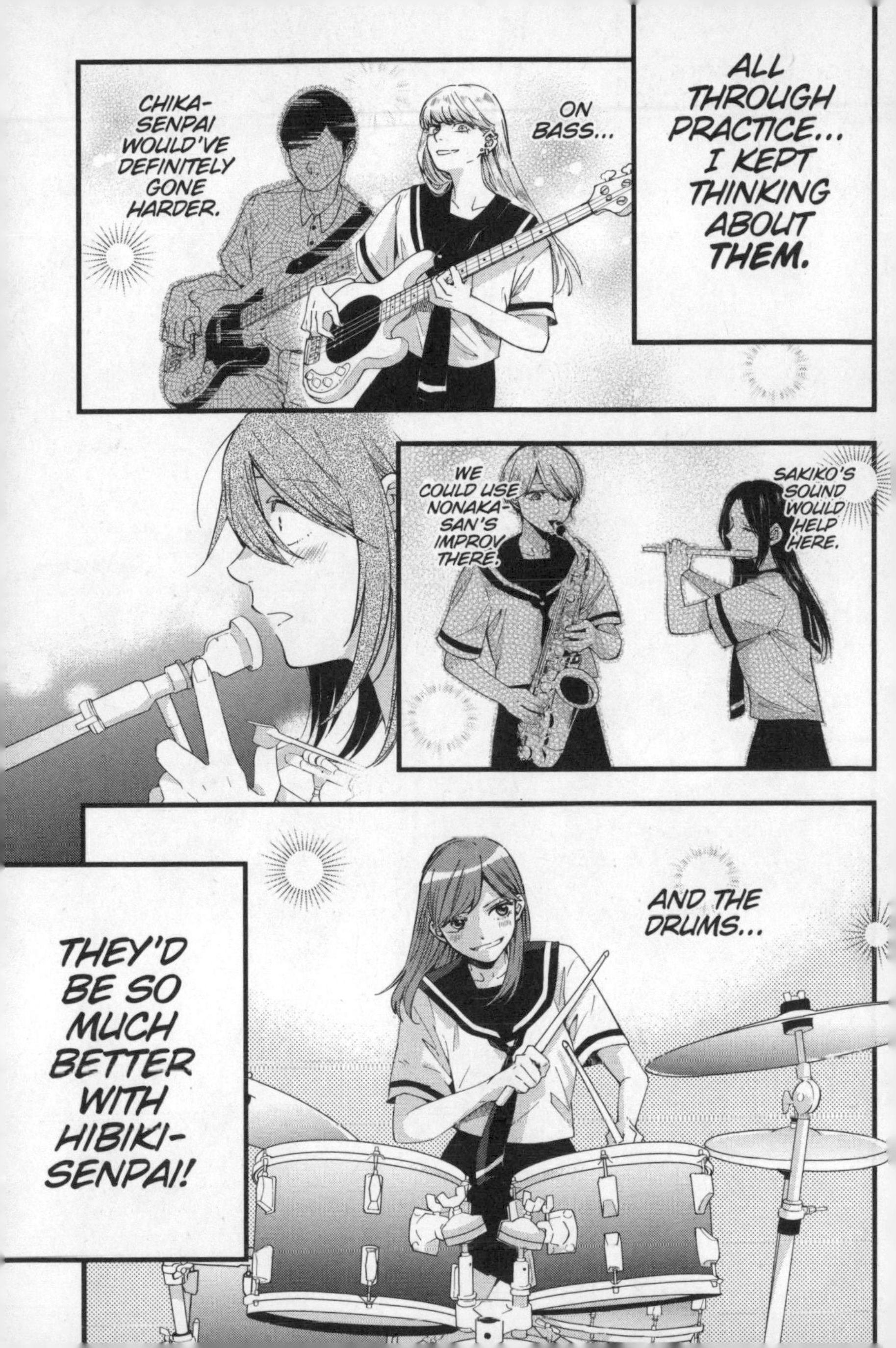
ALL THROUGH PRACTICE... I KEPT THINKING ABOUT THEM.
ON BASS...
CHIKA-SENPAI WOULD'VE DEFINITELY GONE HARDER.
SAKIKO'S SOUND WOULD HELP HERE.
WE COULD USE NONAKA-SAN'S IMPROV THERE.
AND THE DRUMS...
THEY'D BE SO MUCH BETTER WITH HIBIKI-SENPAI!

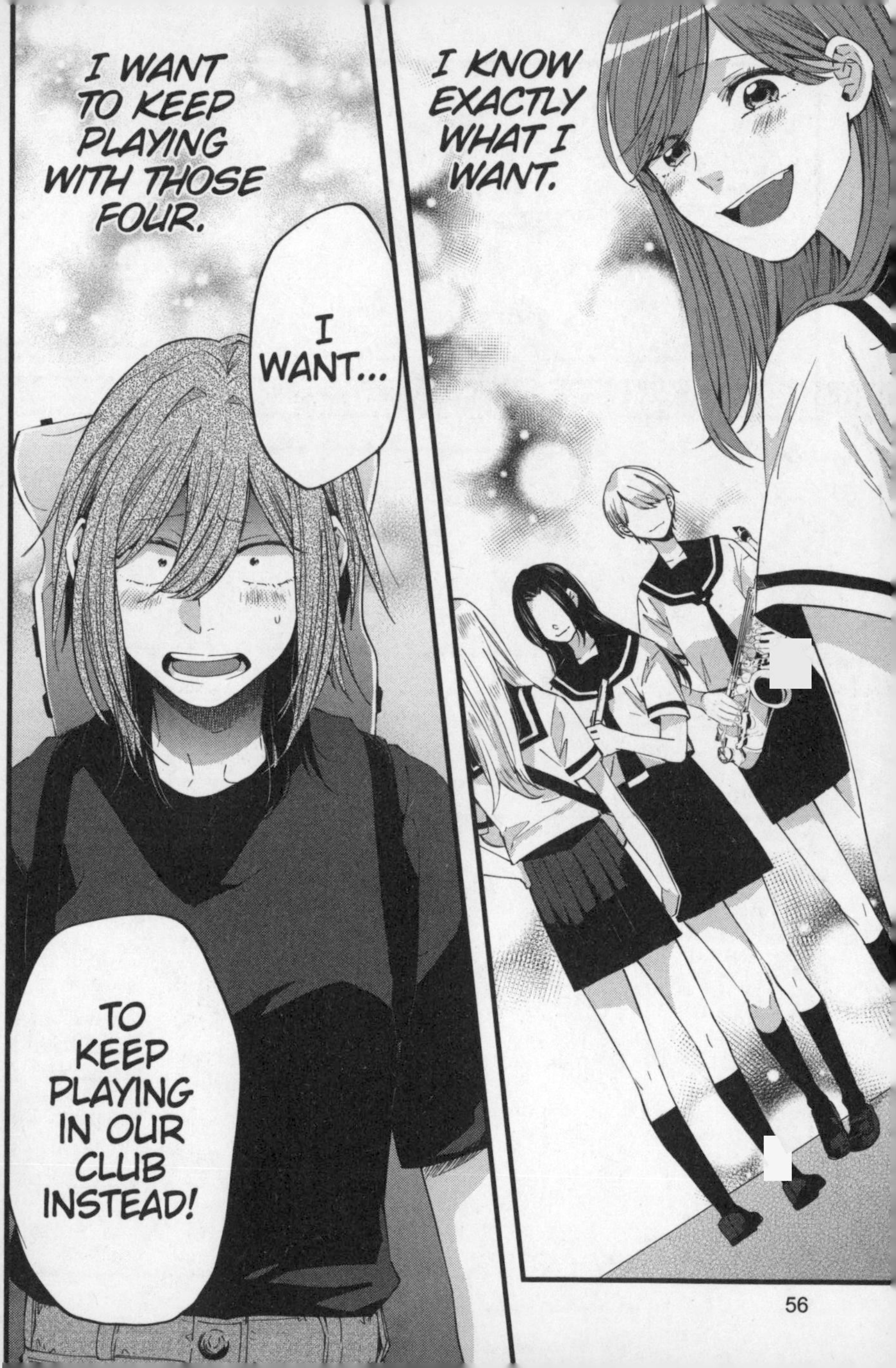
I KNOW EXACTLY WHAT I WANT.
I WANT TO KEEP PLAYING WITH THOSE FOUR.
I WANT...
TO KEEP PLAYING IN OUR CLUB INSTEAD!

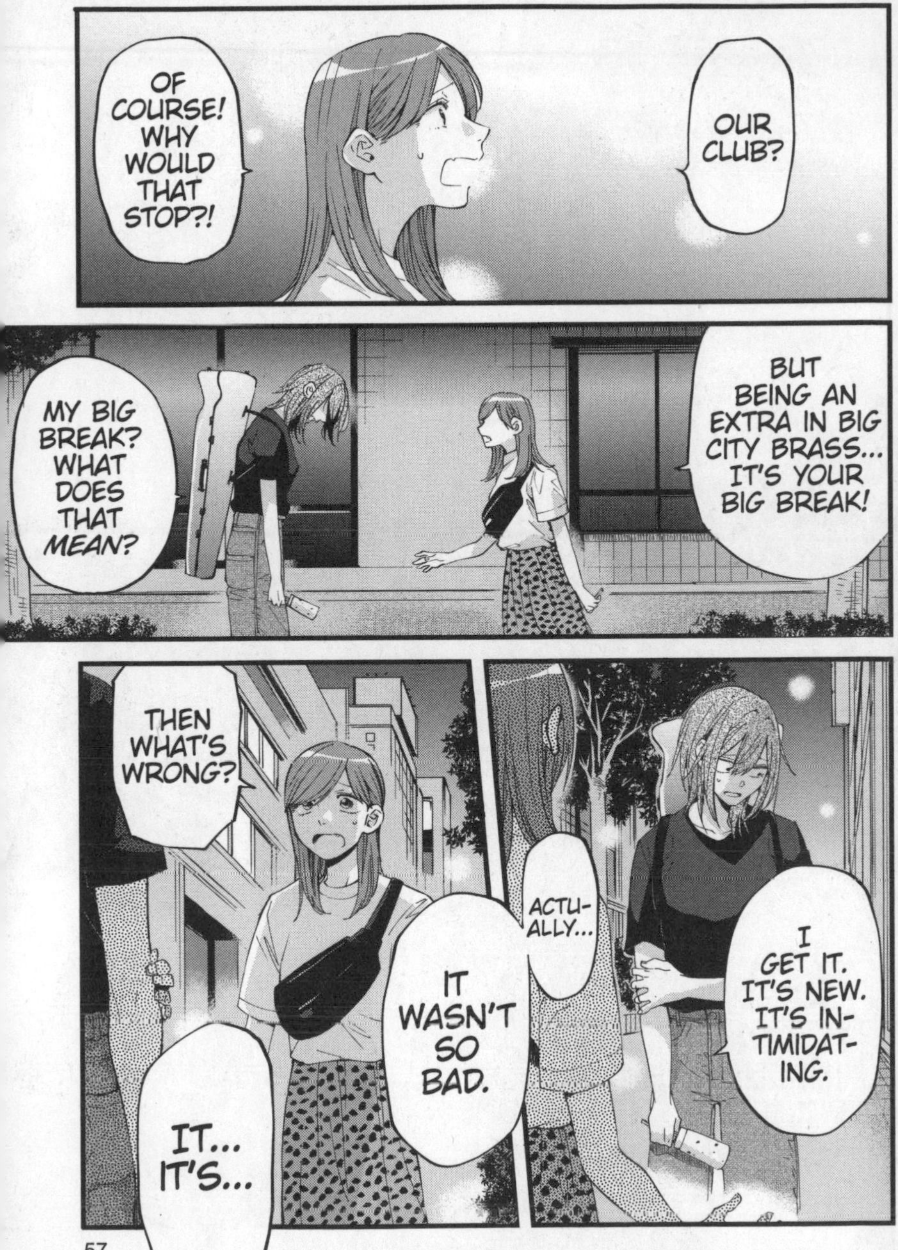
OUR CLUB?
OF COURSE! WHY WOULD THAT STOP?!
BUT BEING AN EXTRA IN BIG CITY BRASS... IT'S YOUR BIG BREAK!
MY BIG BREAK? WHAT DOES THAT *MEAN*?
I GET IT. IT'S NEW. IT'S IN-TIMIDAT-ING.
ACTU-ALLY...
IT WASN'T SO BAD.
THEN WHAT'S WRONG?
IT... IT'S...

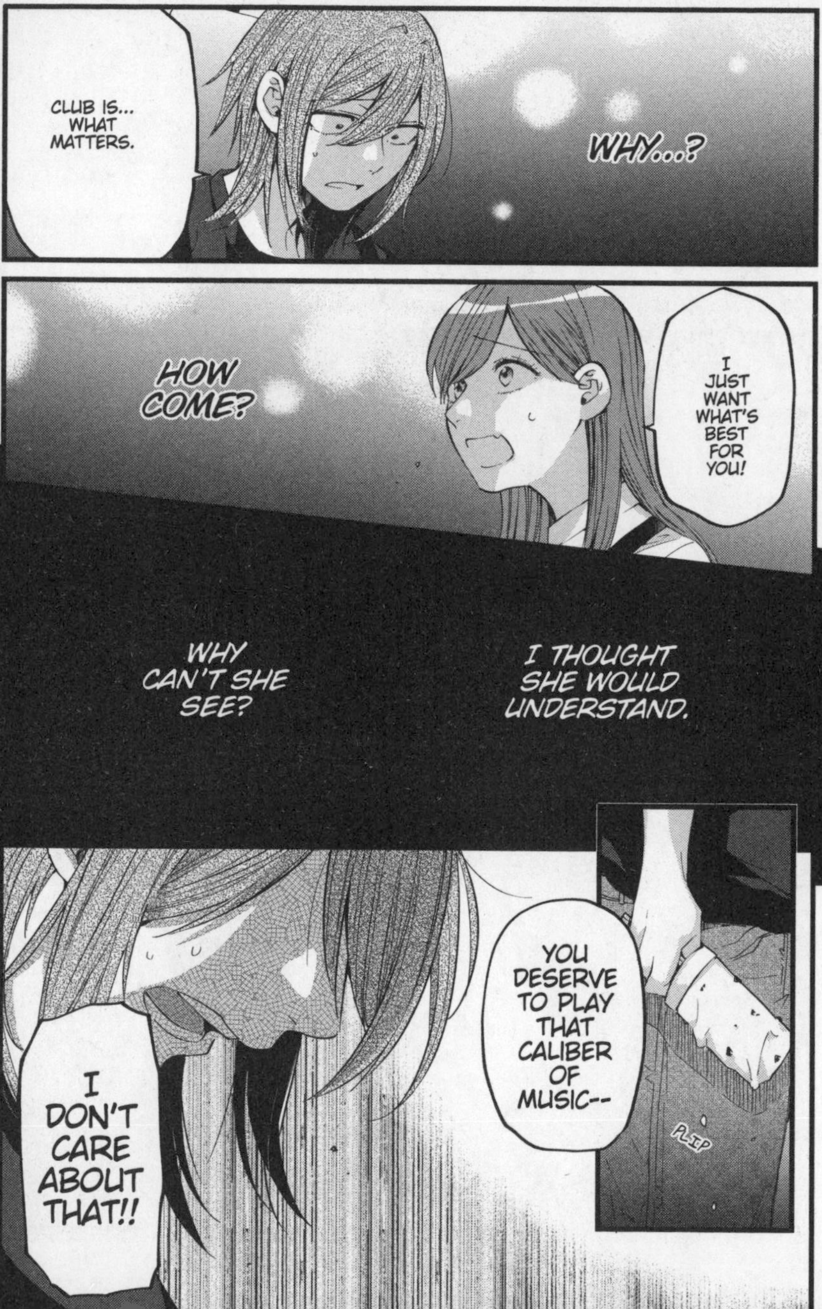
WHY...?
CLUB IS... WHAT MATTERS.
I JUST WANT WHAT'S BEST FOR YOU!
HOW COME?
I THOUGHT SHE WOULD UNDERSTAND.
WHY CAN'T SHE SEE?
YOU DESERVE TO PLAY THAT CALIBER OF MUSIC--
PLIP
I DON'T CARE ABOUT THAT!!

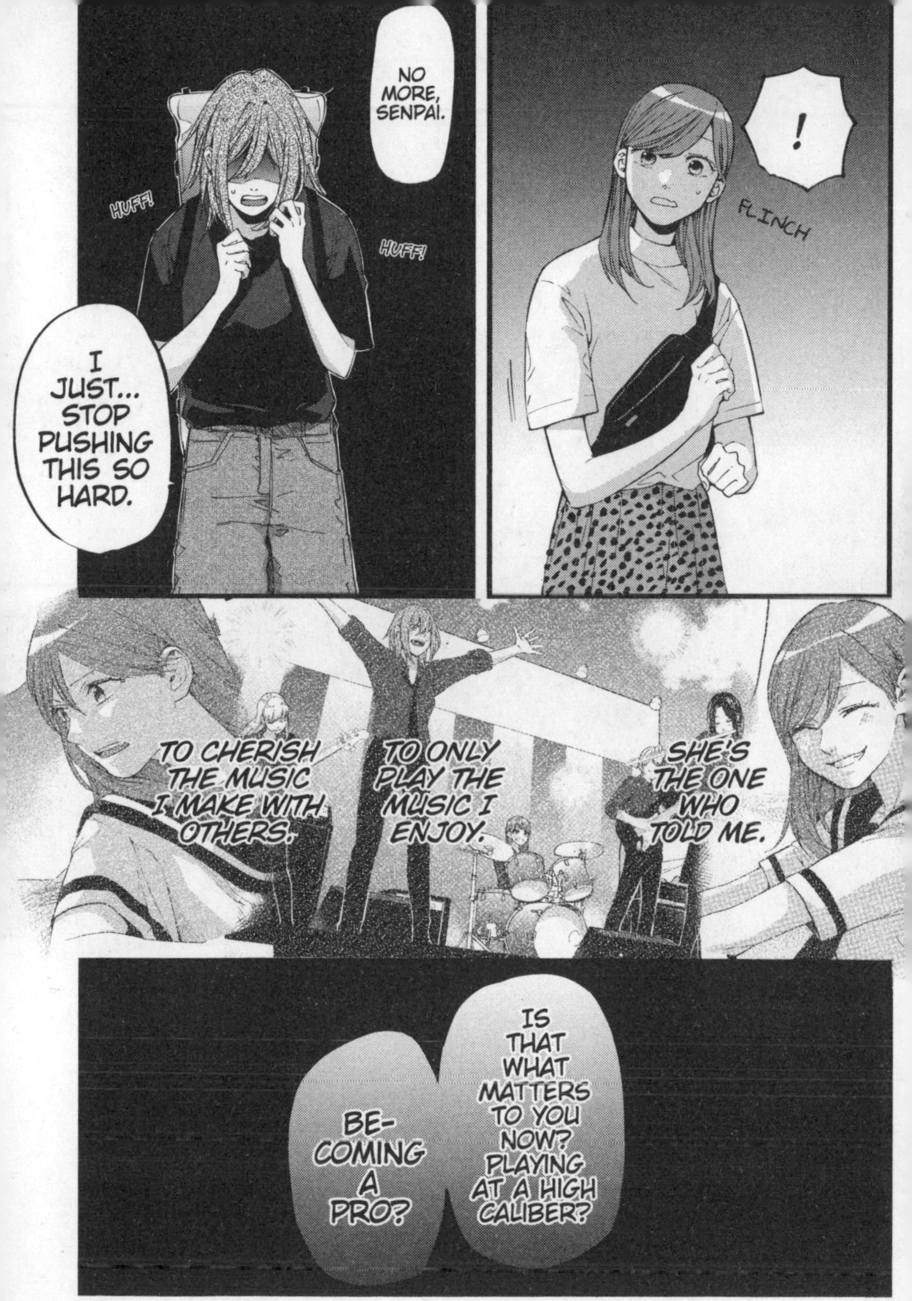
!
FLINCH
NO MORE, SENPAI.
HUFF!
HUFF!
I JUST... STOP PUSHING THIS SO HARD.
SHE'S THE ONE WHO TOLD ME.
TO ONLY PLAY THE MUSIC I ENJOY.
TO CHERISH THE MUSIC I MAKE WITH OTHERS.
IS THAT WHAT MATTERS TO YOU NOW? PLAYING AT A HIGH CALIBER?
BE-COMING A PRO?

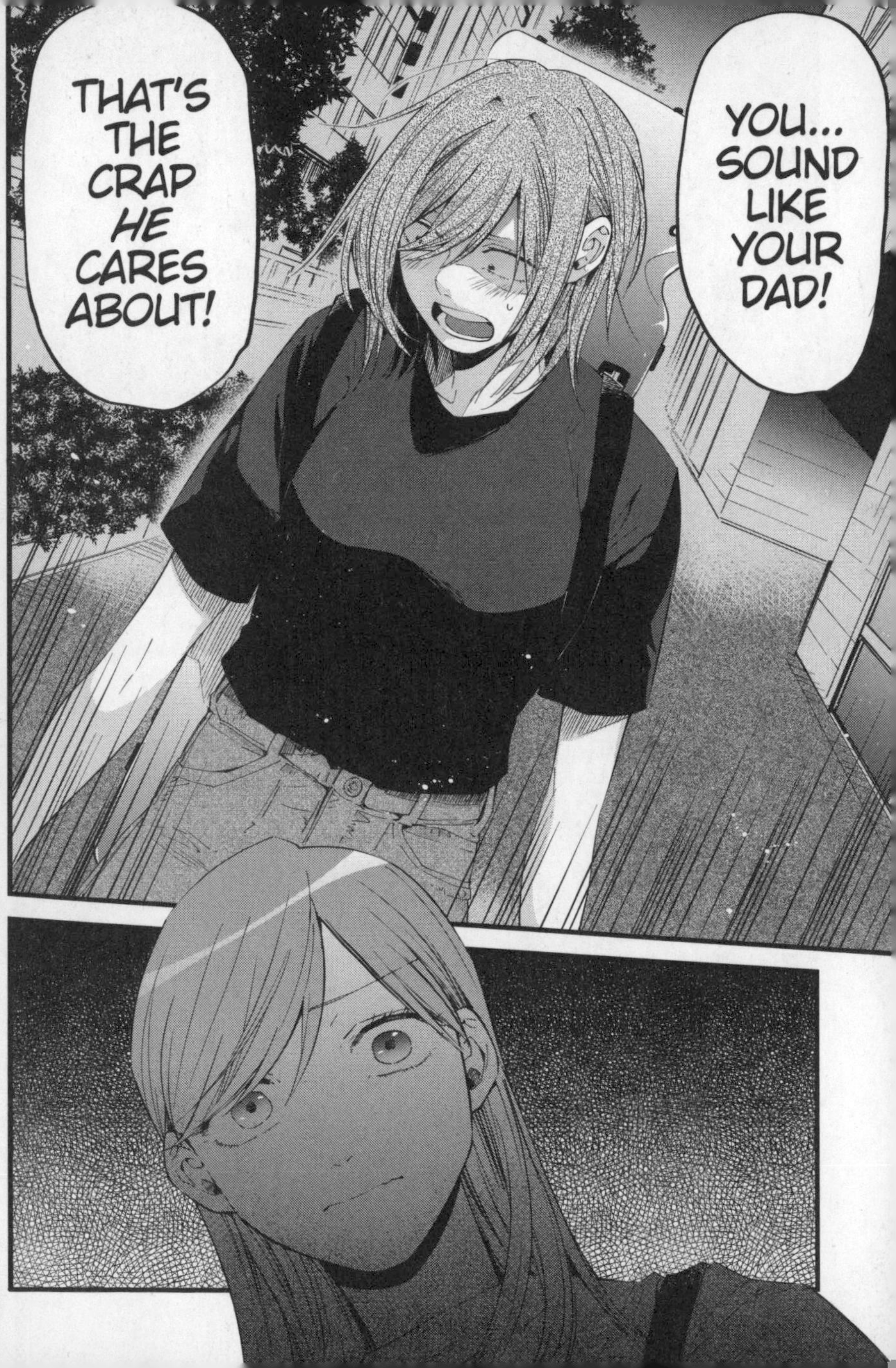
YOU... SOUND LIKE YOUR DAD!
THAT'S THE CRAP *HE* CARES ABOUT!

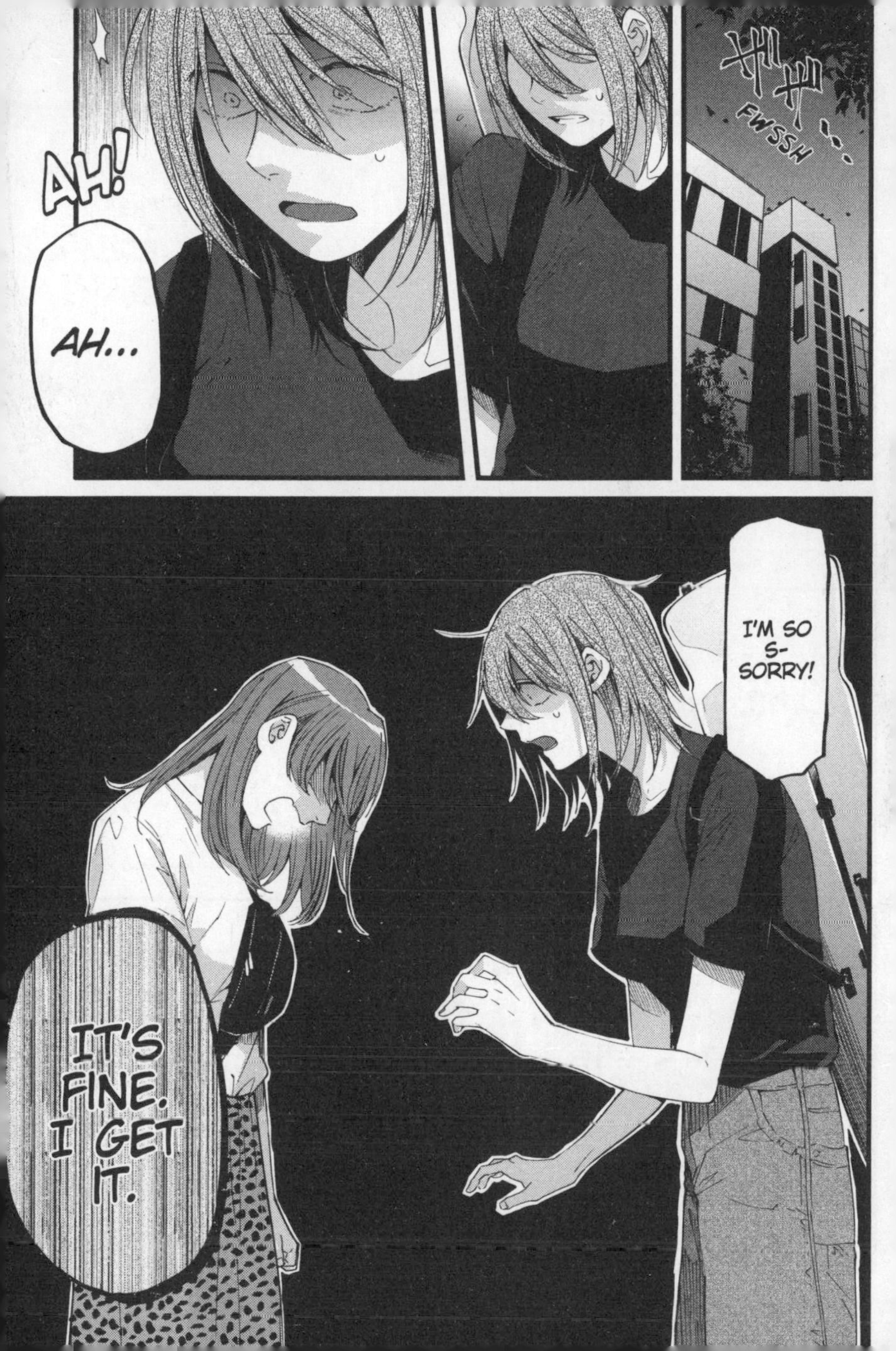
FWSSH
AH!
AH...
I'M SO S-SORRY!
IT'S FINE. I GET IT.

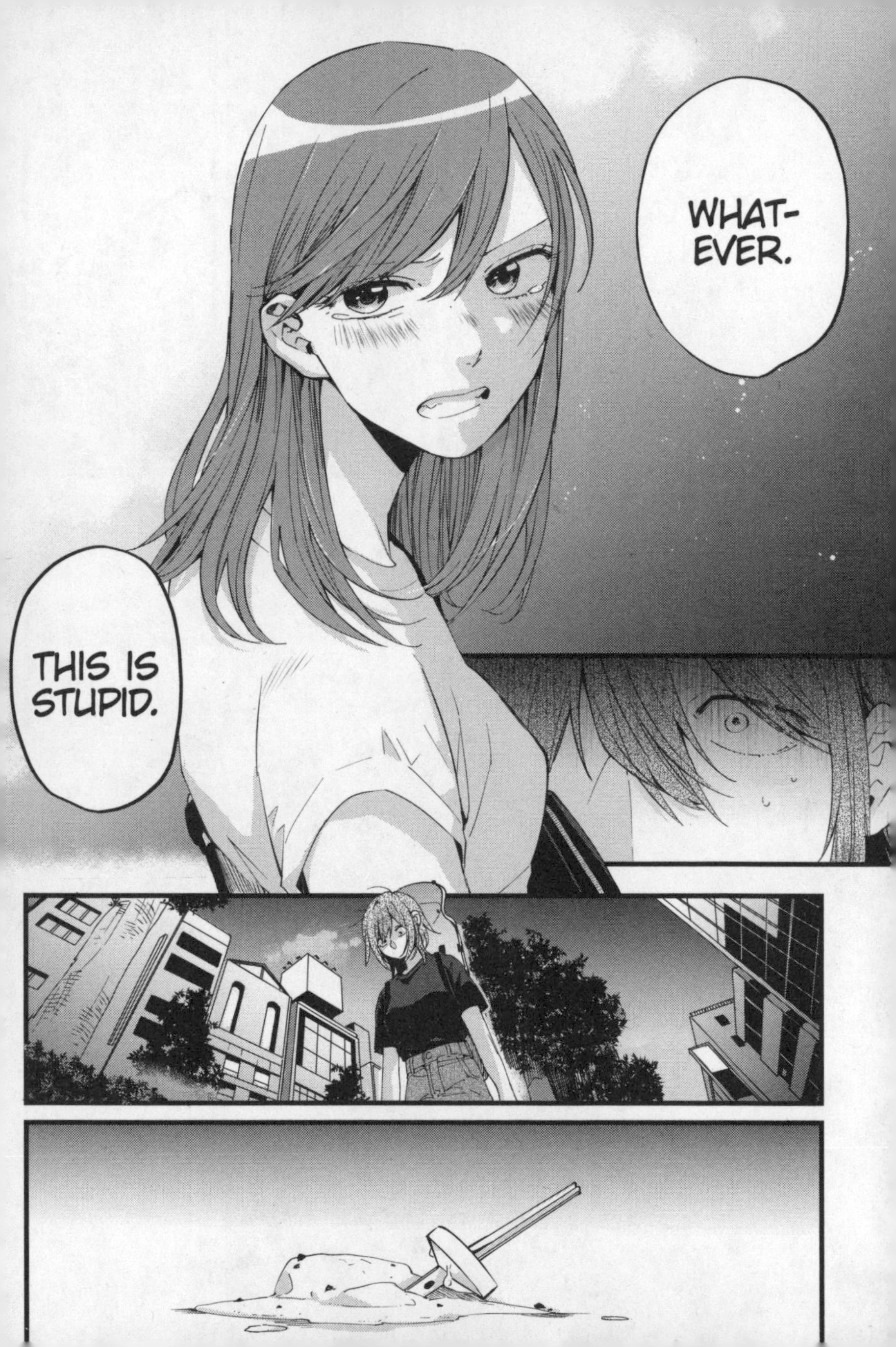
WHAT-EVER.
THIS IS STUPID.

HELLO, MELAN CHOLIC!

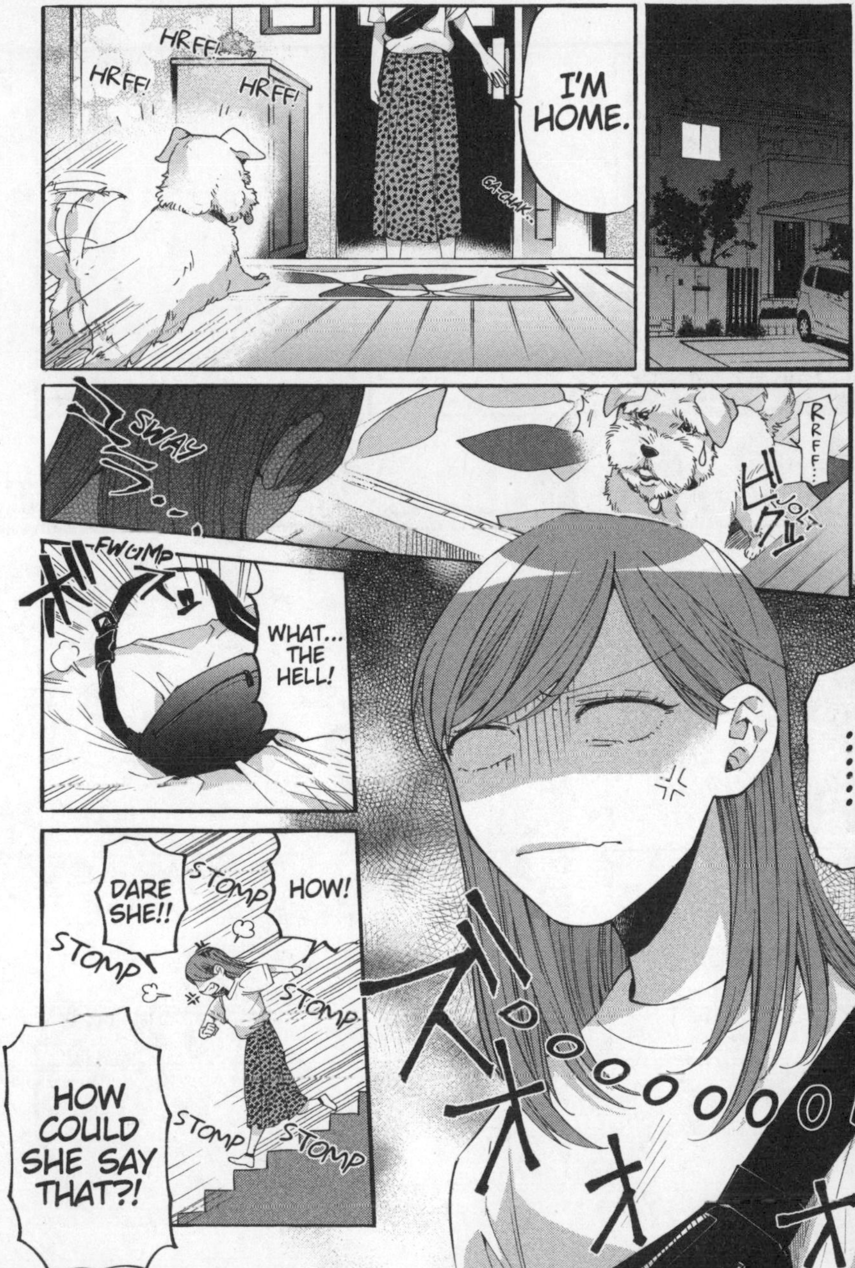
I'M HOME.
GA-CHAK...
HRFF!
HRFF!
HRFF!
RRFF...
JOLT
SWAY
......
DOOOOOOO
FWUMP
WHAT... THE HELL!
HOW!
DARE SHE!!
STOMP
STOMP
STOMP
STOMP
STOMP
STOMP
HOW COULD SHE SAY THAT?!

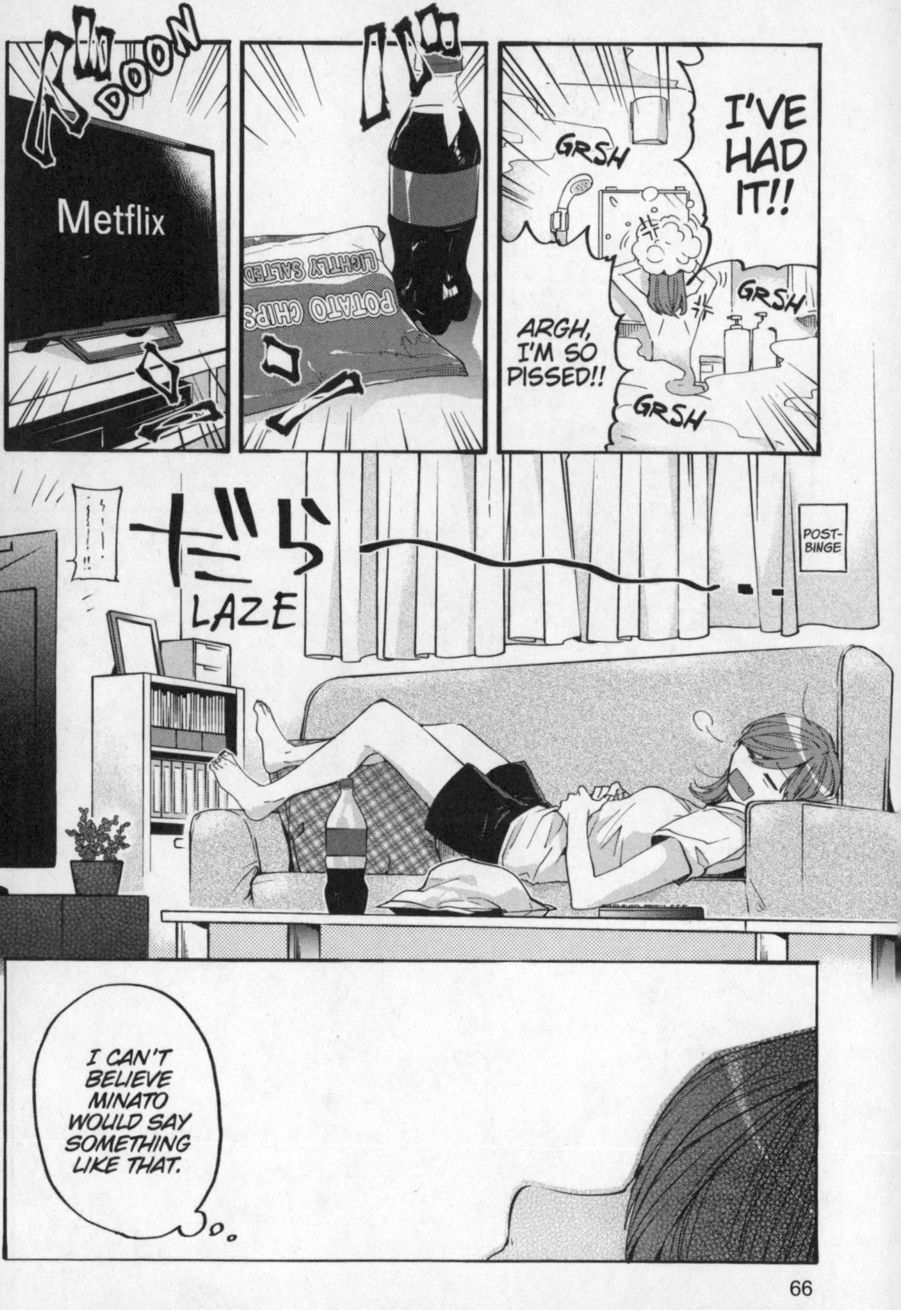
I'VE HAD IT!!
GRSH
GRSH
ARGH, I'M SO PISSED!!
GRSH
LIGHTLY SALTED
POTATO CHIPS
Metflix
DOON
…!!
だら
LAZE
POST-BINGE
I CAN'T BELIEVE MINATO WOULD SAY SOMETHING LIKE THAT.

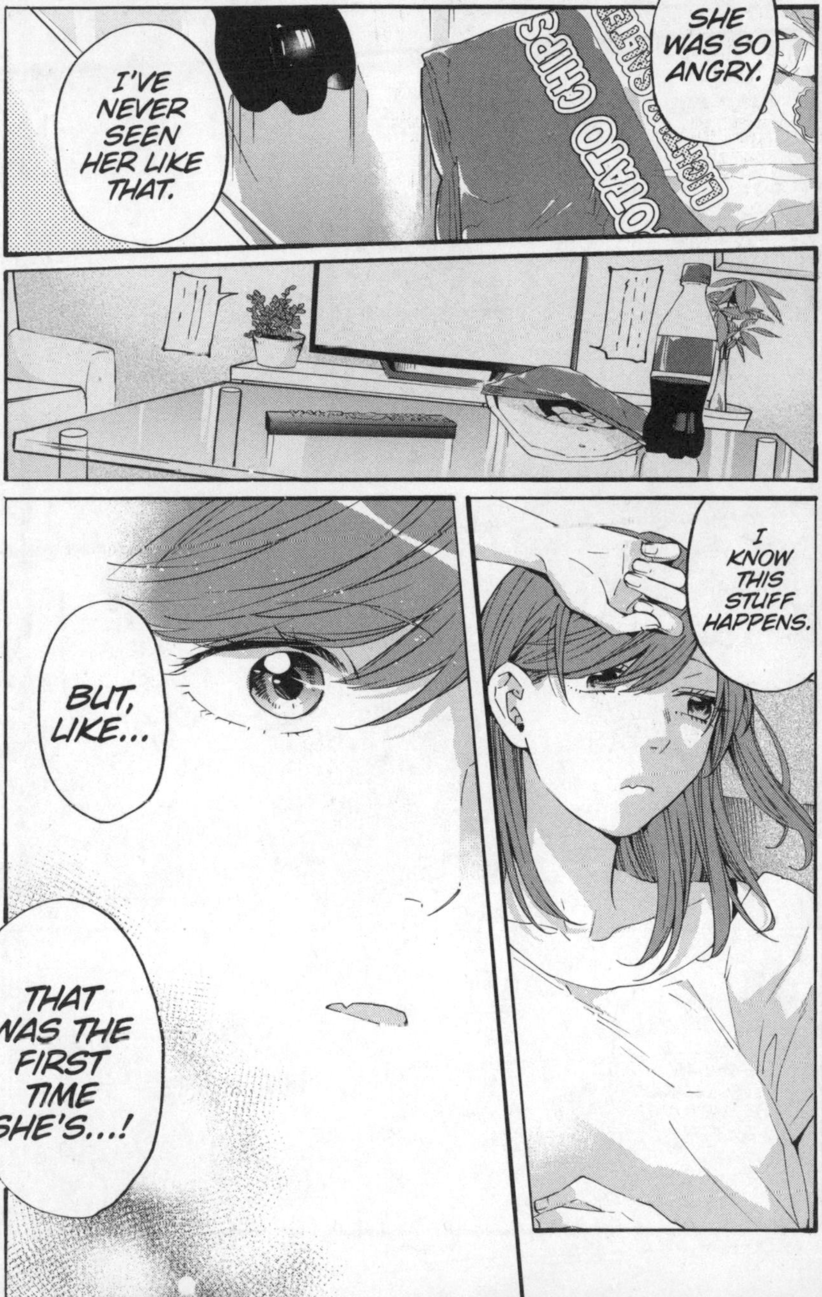
SHE WAS SO ANGRY.
I'VE NEVER SEEN HER LIKE THAT.
I KNOW THIS STUFF HAPPENS.
BUT, LIKE...
THAT WAS THE FIRST TIME SHE'S...!

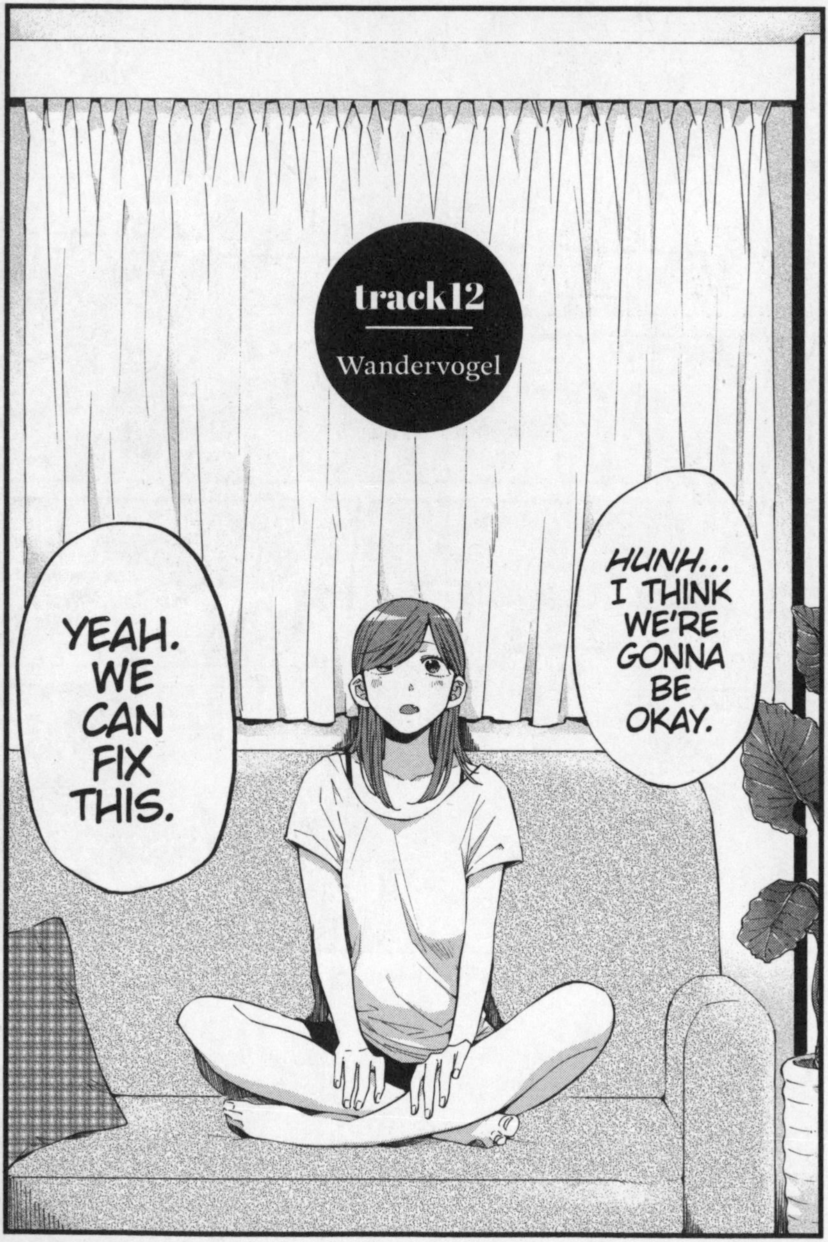
track12
Wandervogel
HUNH... I THINK WE'RE GONNA BE OKAY.
YEAH. WE CAN FIX THIS.

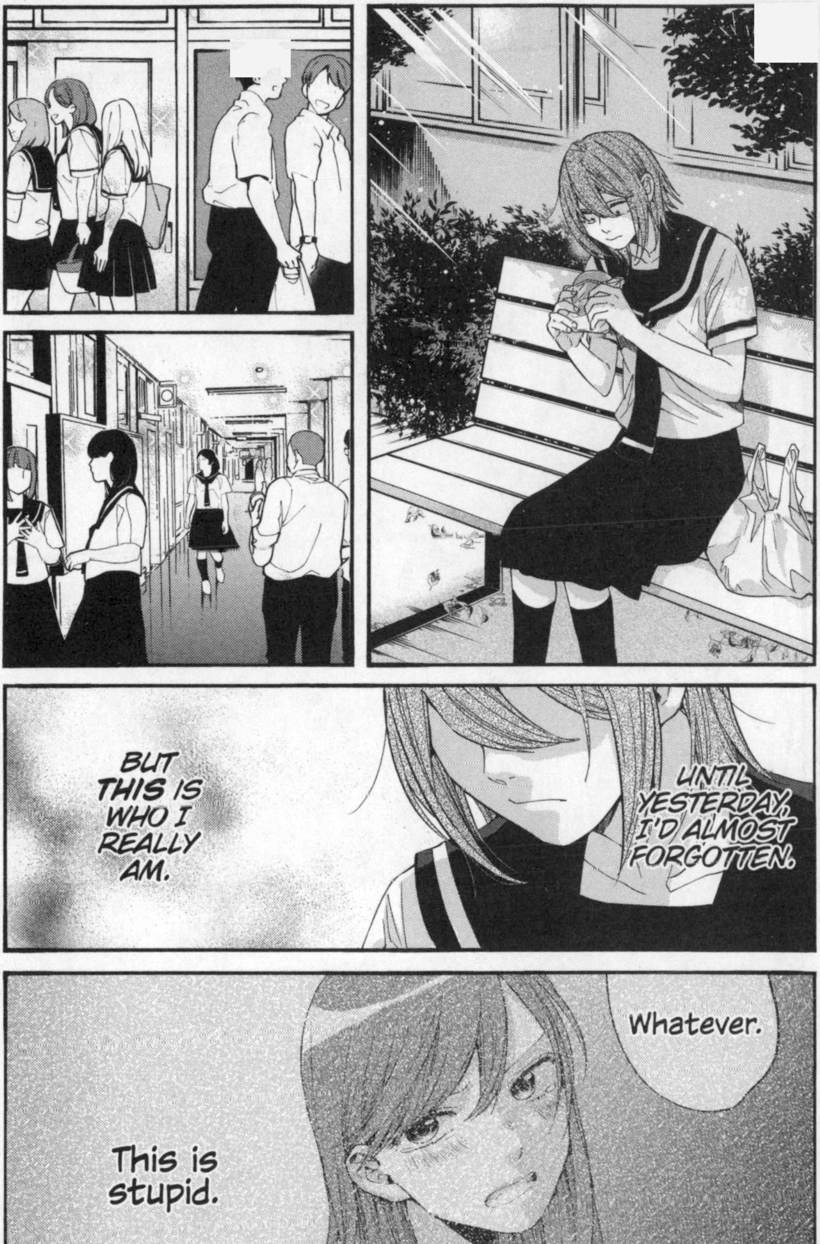
UNTIL YESTERDAY, I'D ALMOST FORGOTTEN.
BUT THIS IS WHO I REALLY AM.
Whatever.
This is stupid.

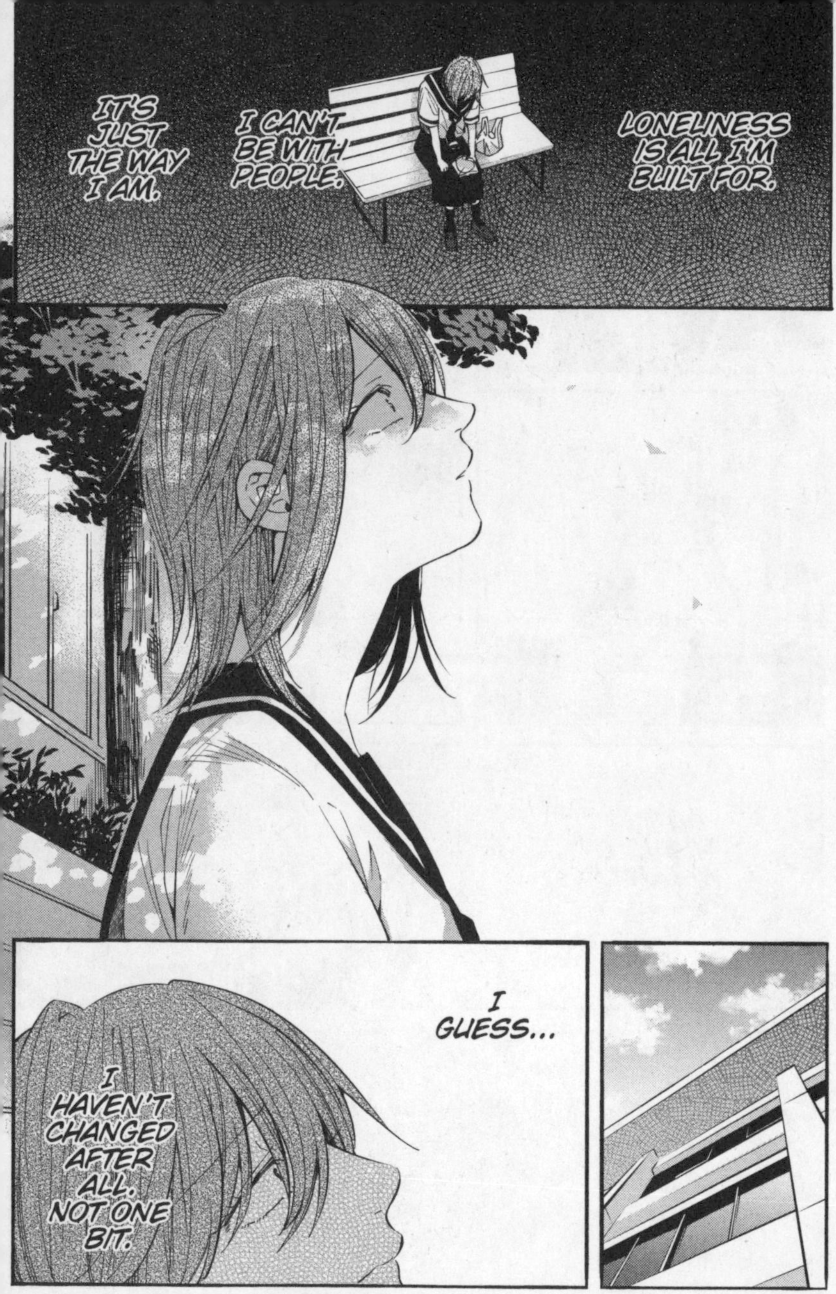
LONELINESS IS ALL I'M BUILT FOR.
I CAN'T BE WITH PEOPLE.
IT'S JUST THE WAY I AM.
I GUESS...
I HAVEN'T CHANGED AFTER ALL. NOT ONE BIT.

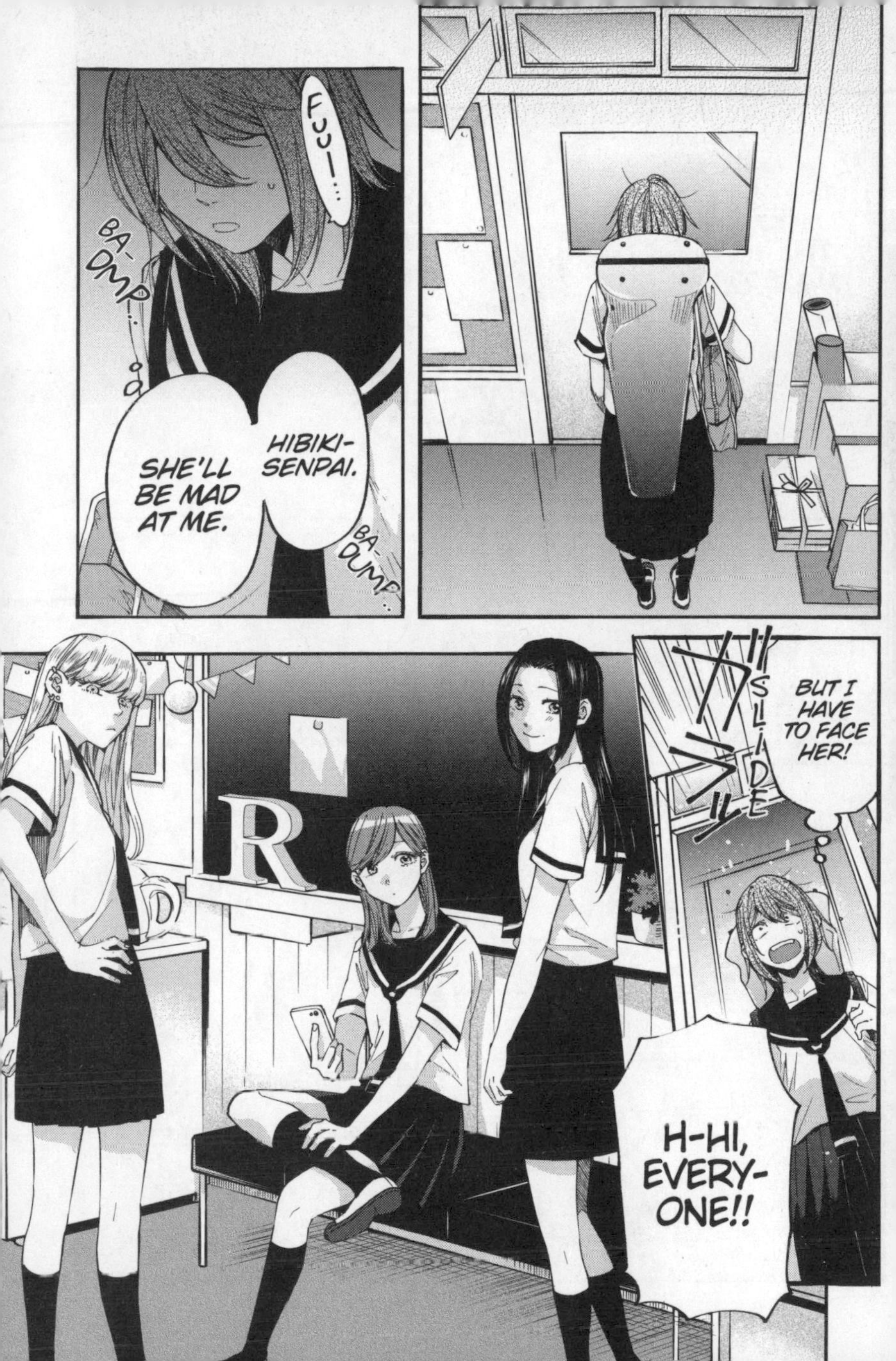
FUJI...
BA-DMP...
HIBIKI-SENPAI.
SHE'LL BE MAD AT ME.
BA-DUMP...
SLIDE
BUT I HAVE TO FACE HER!
H-HI, EVERY-ONE!!

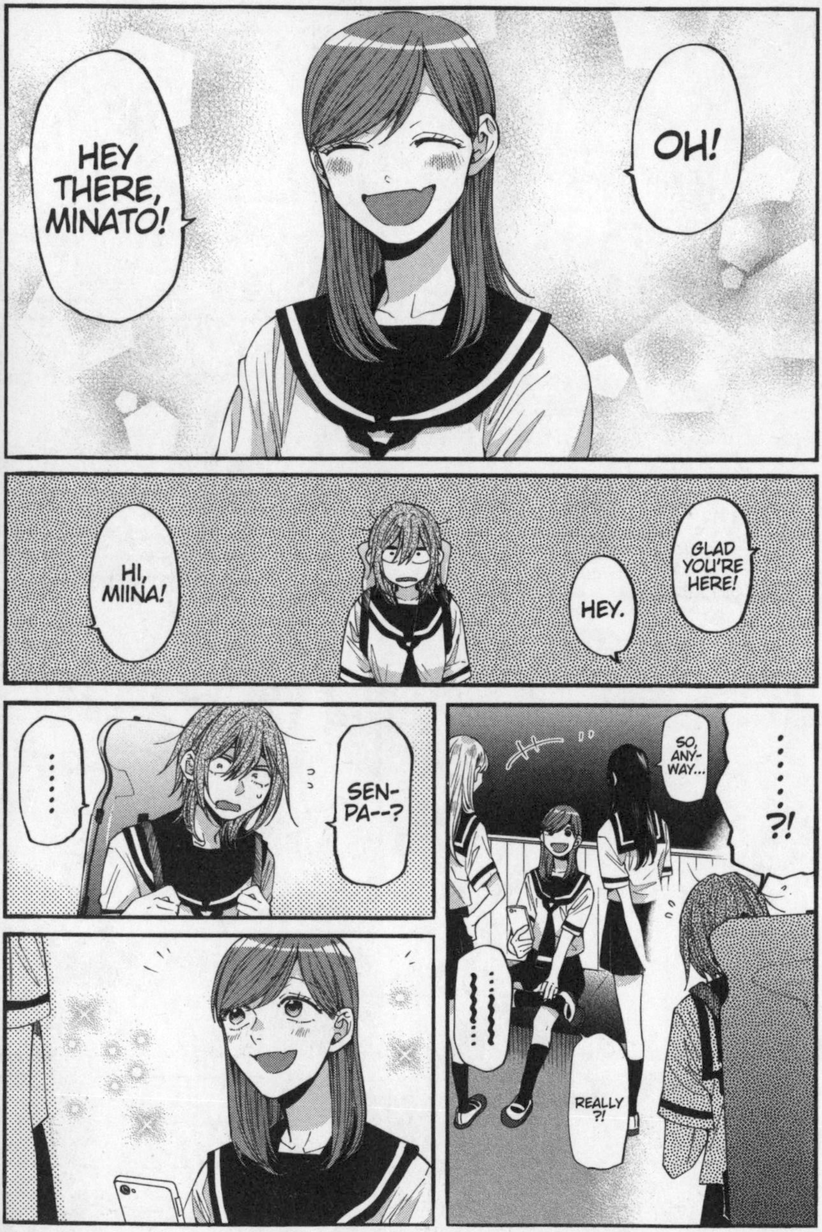
OH!
HEY THERE, MINATO!
GLAD YOU'RE HERE!
HEY.
HI, MIINA!
......?!
SO, ANY-WAY...
......
REALLY?!
SEN-PA--?
......

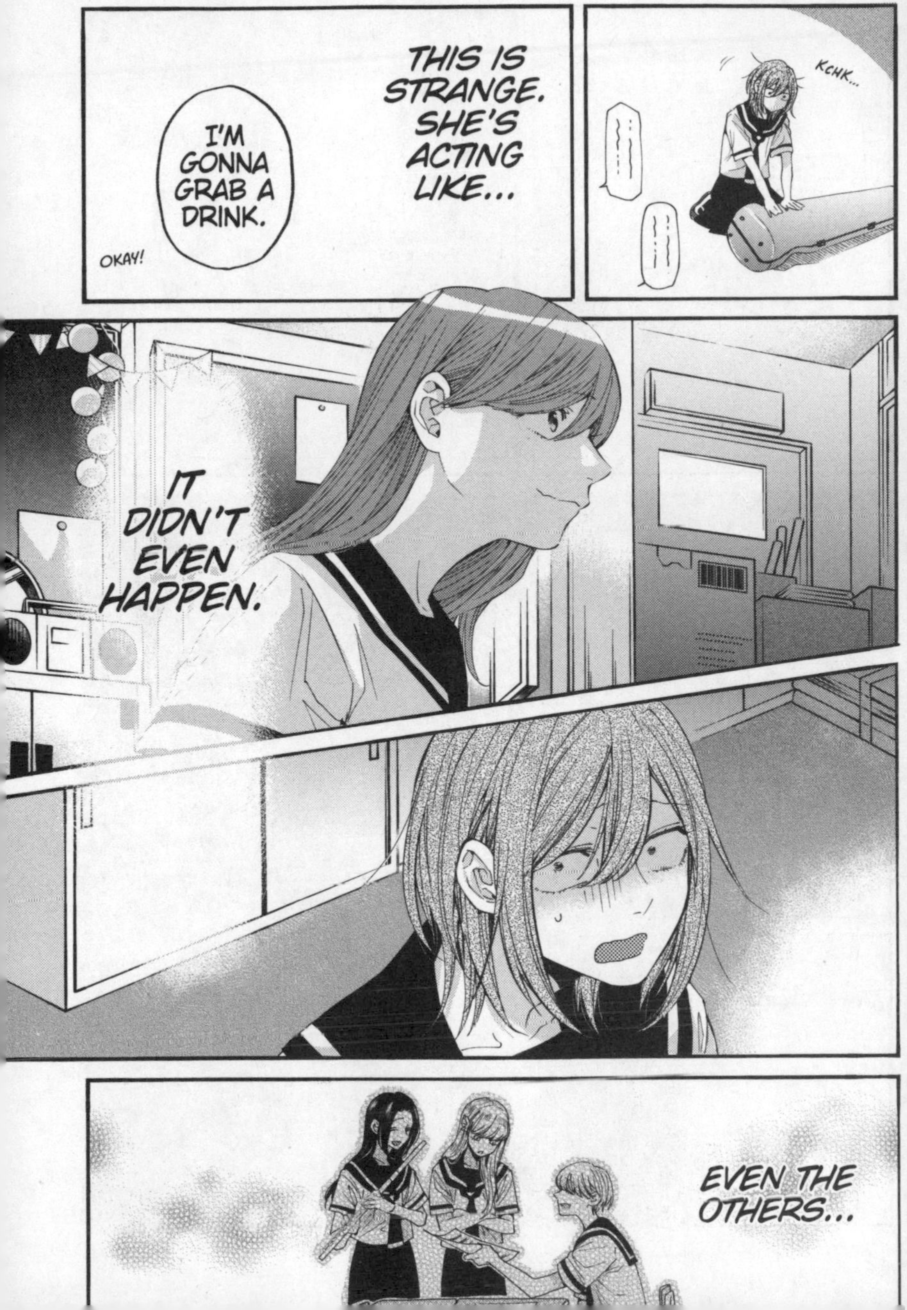
KCHK...
...
...
THIS IS STRANGE. SHE'S ACTING LIKE...
I'M GONNA GRAB A DRINK.
OKAY!
IT DIDN'T EVEN HAPPEN.
EVEN THE OTHERS...

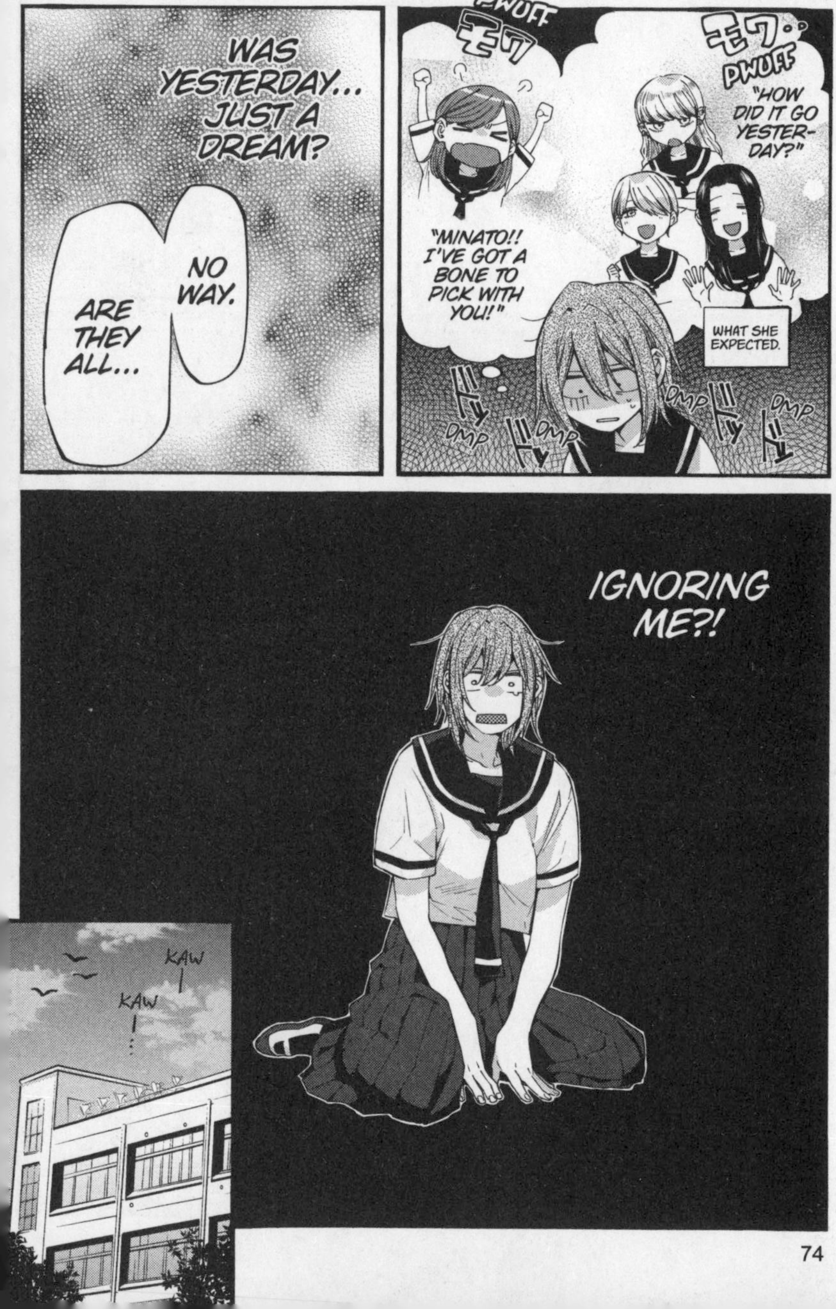
PWUFF
モワ
モワ・。
PWUFF
"HOW DID IT GO YESTER-DAY?"
"MINATO!! I'VE GOT A BONE TO PICK WITH YOU!"
WHAT SHE EXPECTED.
DMP
DMP
DMP
DMP
WAS YESTERDAY... JUST A DREAM?
NO WAY.
ARE THEY ALL...
IGNORING ME?!
KAW
KAW

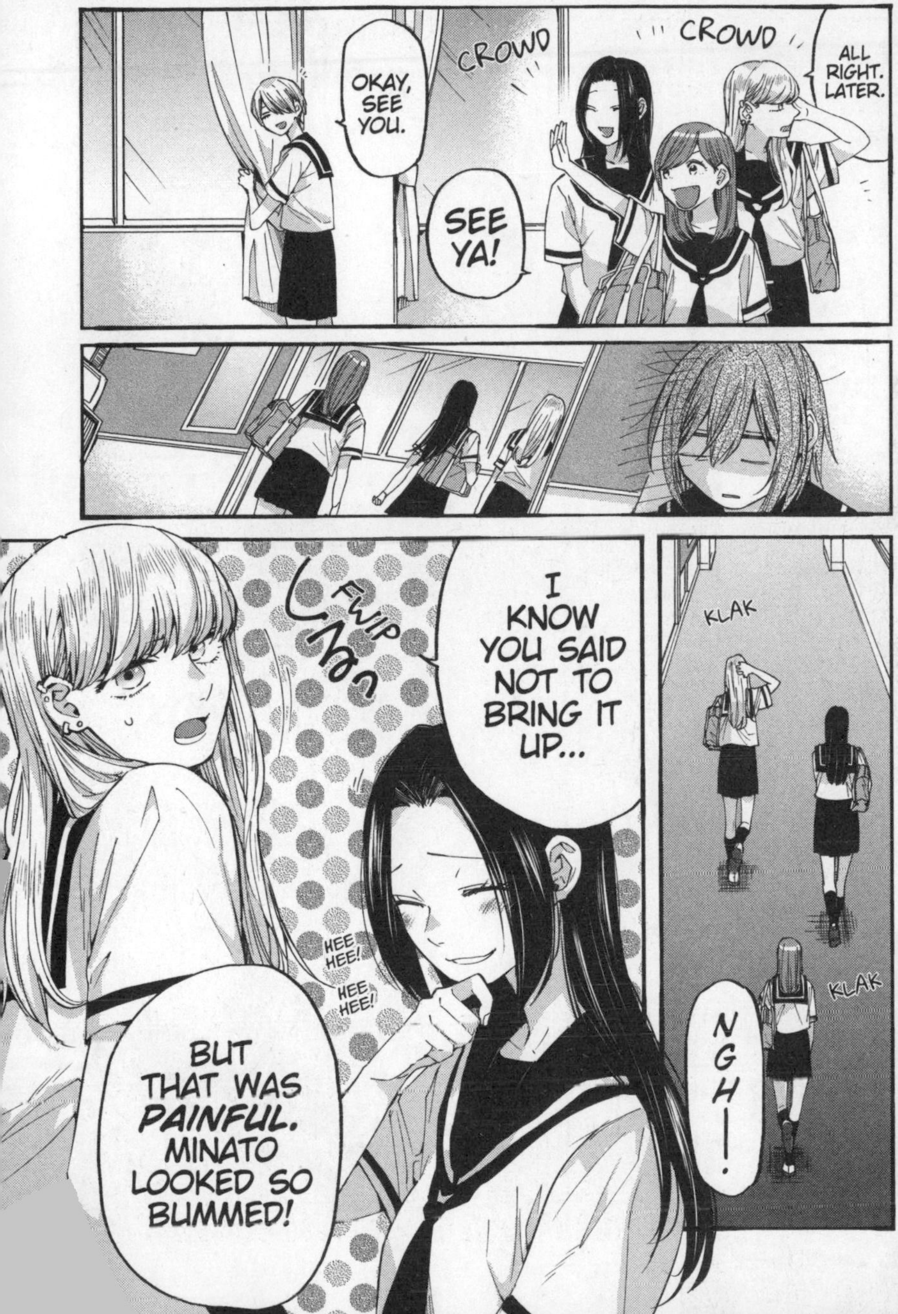
ALL RIGHT. LATER.
CROWD
CROWD
OKAY, SEE YOU.
SEE YA!
KLAK
KLAK
NGH!
I KNOW YOU SAID NOT TO BRING IT UP...
FWIP
HEE HEE!
HEE HEE!
BUT THAT WAS *PAINFUL.* MINATO LOOKED SO BUMMED!

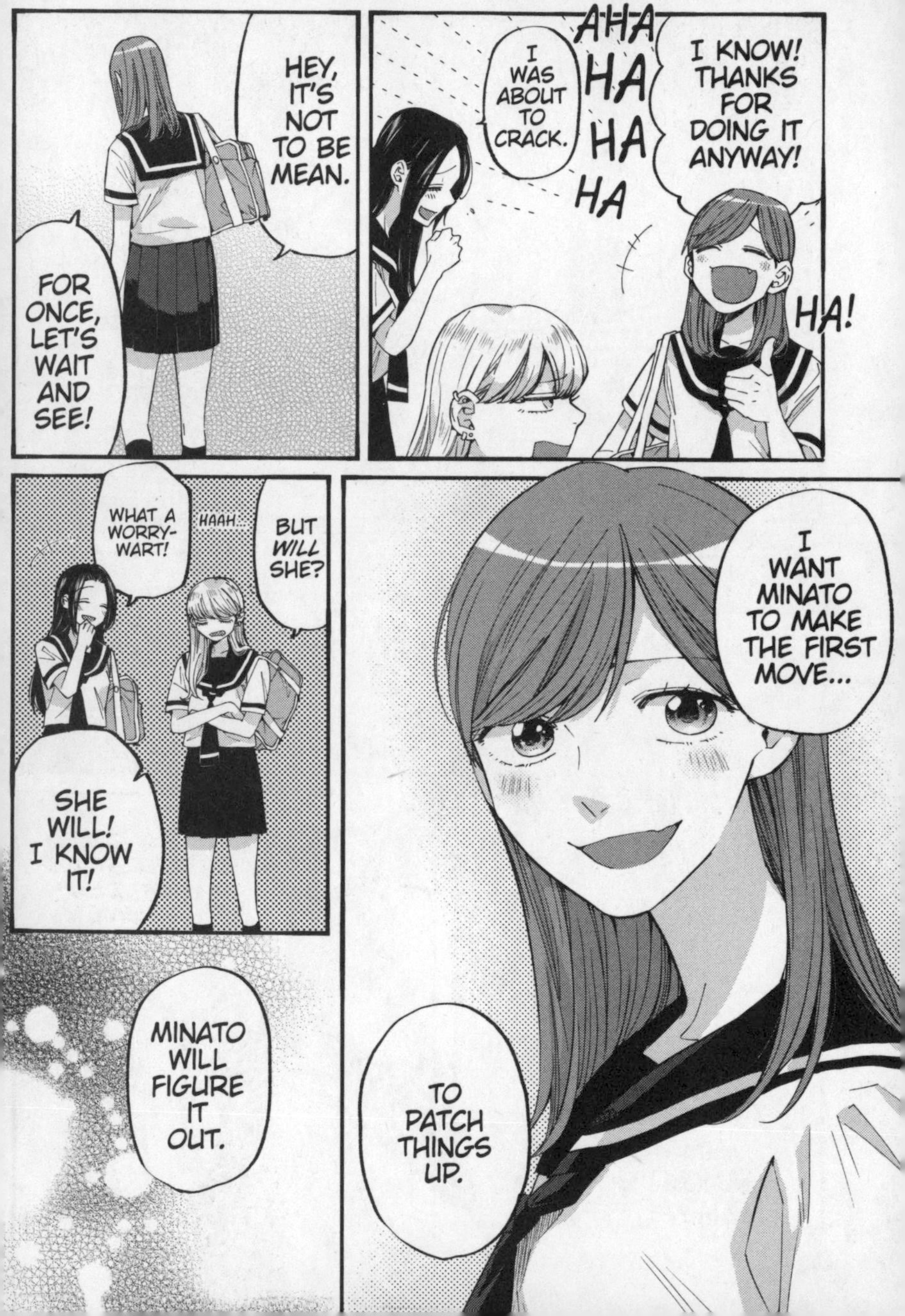
I KNOW! THANKS FOR DOING IT ANYWAY!
AHA HA HA HA
I WAS ABOUT TO CRACK.
HA!
HEY, IT'S NOT TO BE MEAN.
FOR ONCE, LET'S WAIT AND SEE!
I WANT MINATO TO MAKE THE FIRST MOVE...
TO PATCH THINGS UP.
BUT *WILL* SHE?
HAAH...
WHAT A WORRY-WART!
SHE WILL! I KNOW IT!
MINATO WILL FIGURE IT OUT.

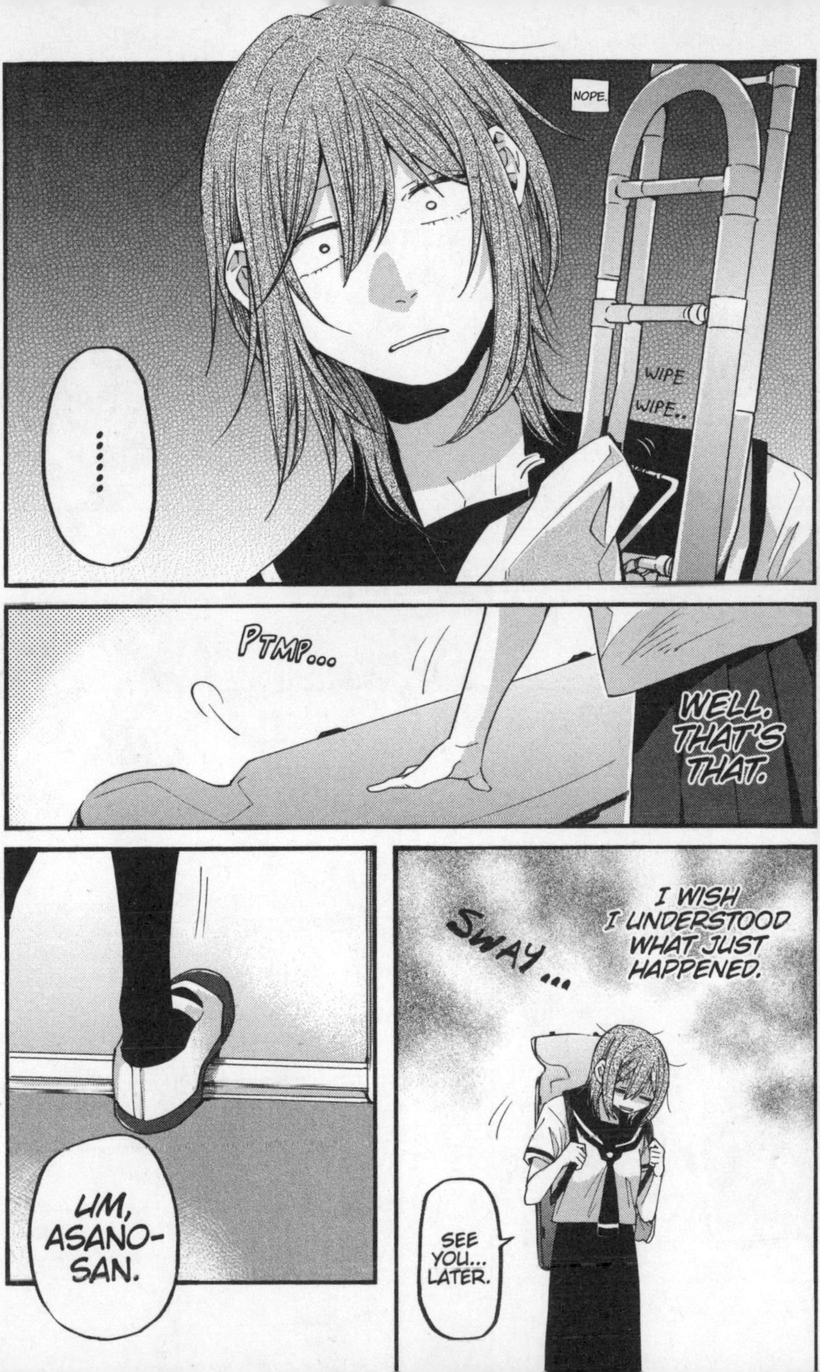
NOPE.
WIPE WIPE..
......
WELL. THAT'S THAT.
PTMP...
I WISH I UNDERSTOOD WHAT JUST HAPPENED.
SWAY...
SEE YOU... LATER.
UM, ASANO-SAN.

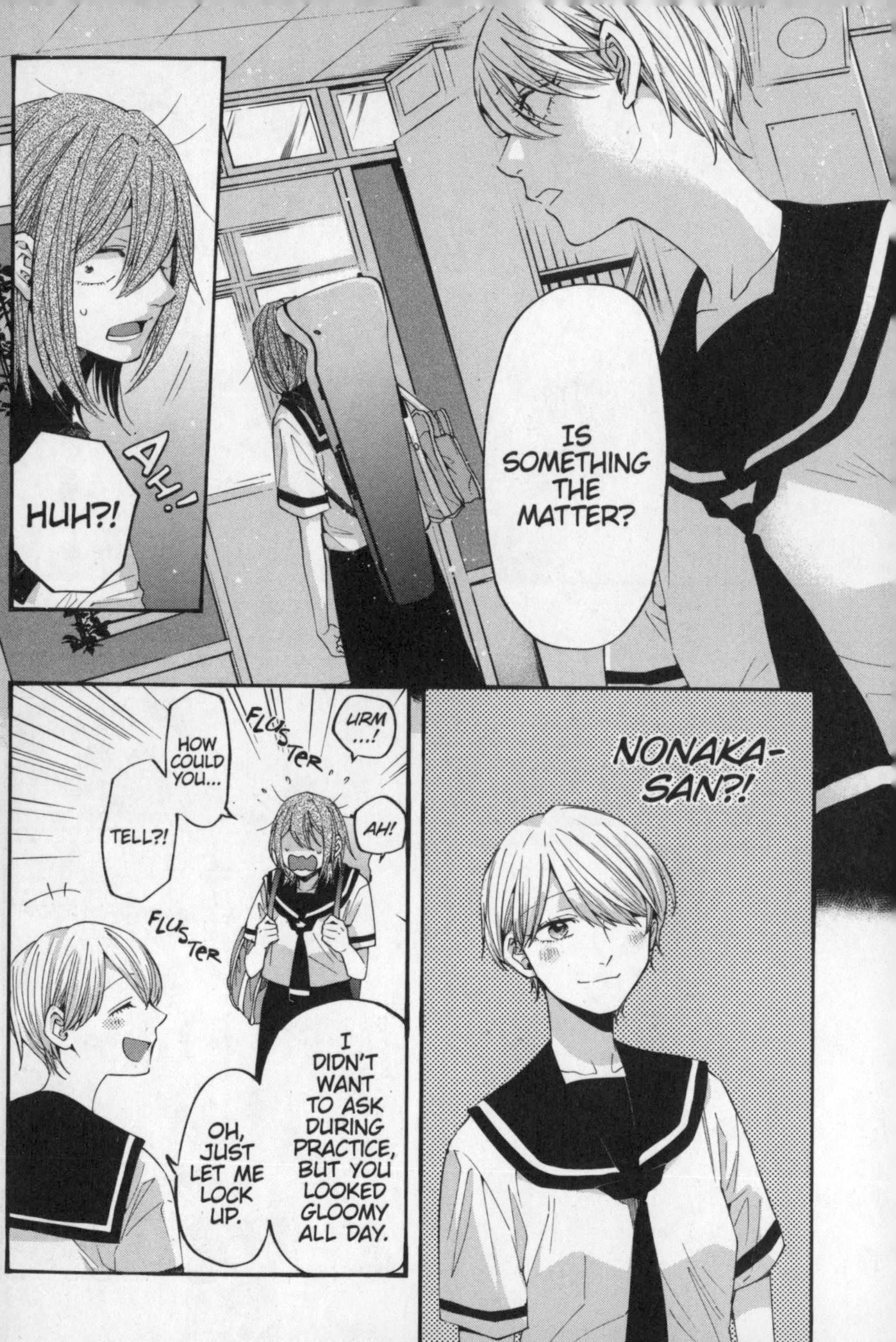
IS SOMETHING THE MATTER?
AH!
HUH?!
NONAKA-SAN?!
URM ...!
FLUSTER
HOW COULD YOU...
AH!
TELL?!
FLUSTER
I DIDN'T WANT TO ASK DURING PRACTICE, BUT YOU LOOKED GLOOMY ALL DAY.
OH, JUST LET ME LOCK UP.

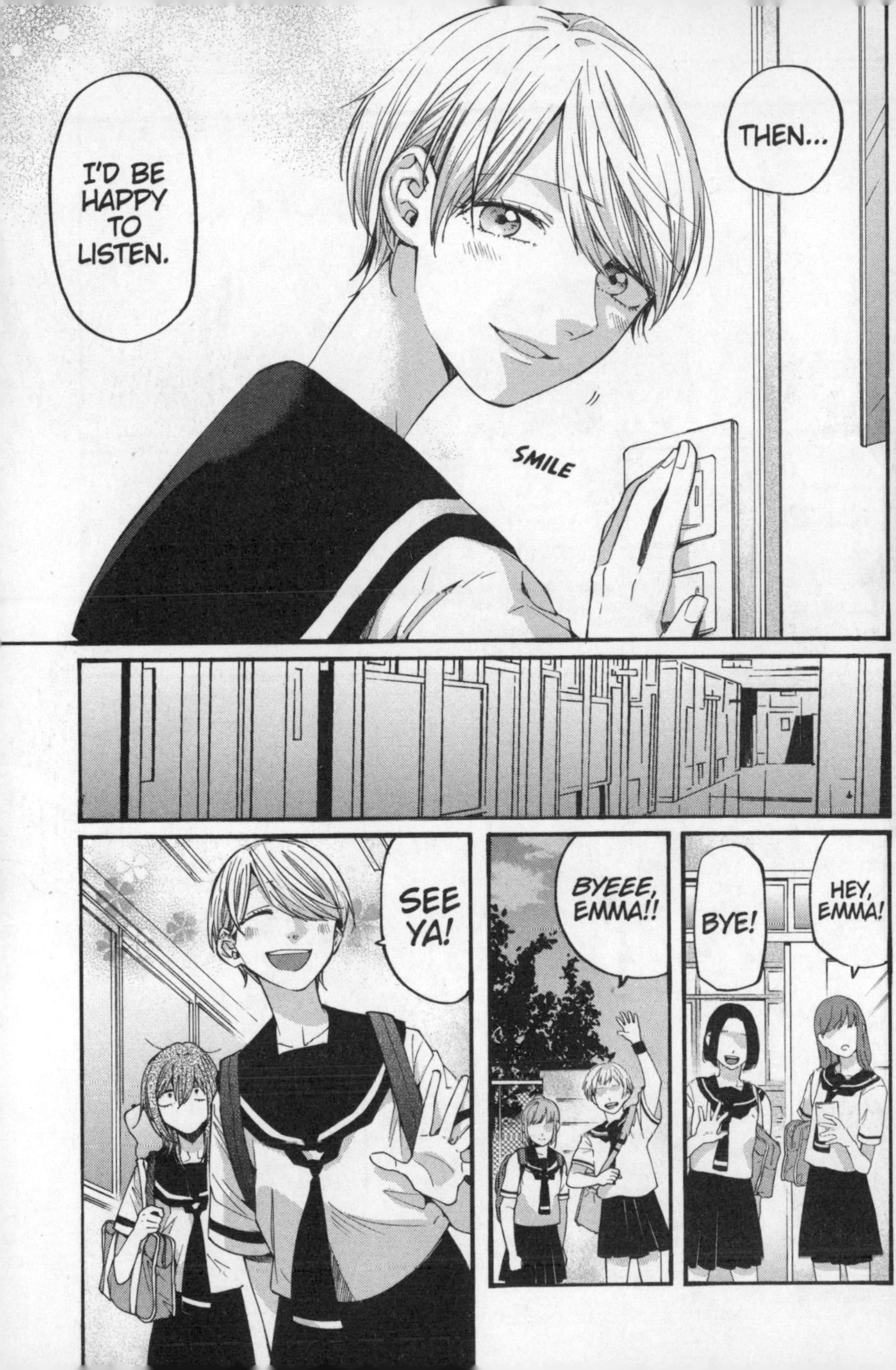
THEN...
I'D BE HAPPY TO LISTEN.
SMILE
HEY, EMMA!
BYE!
BYEEE, EMMA!!
SEE YA!

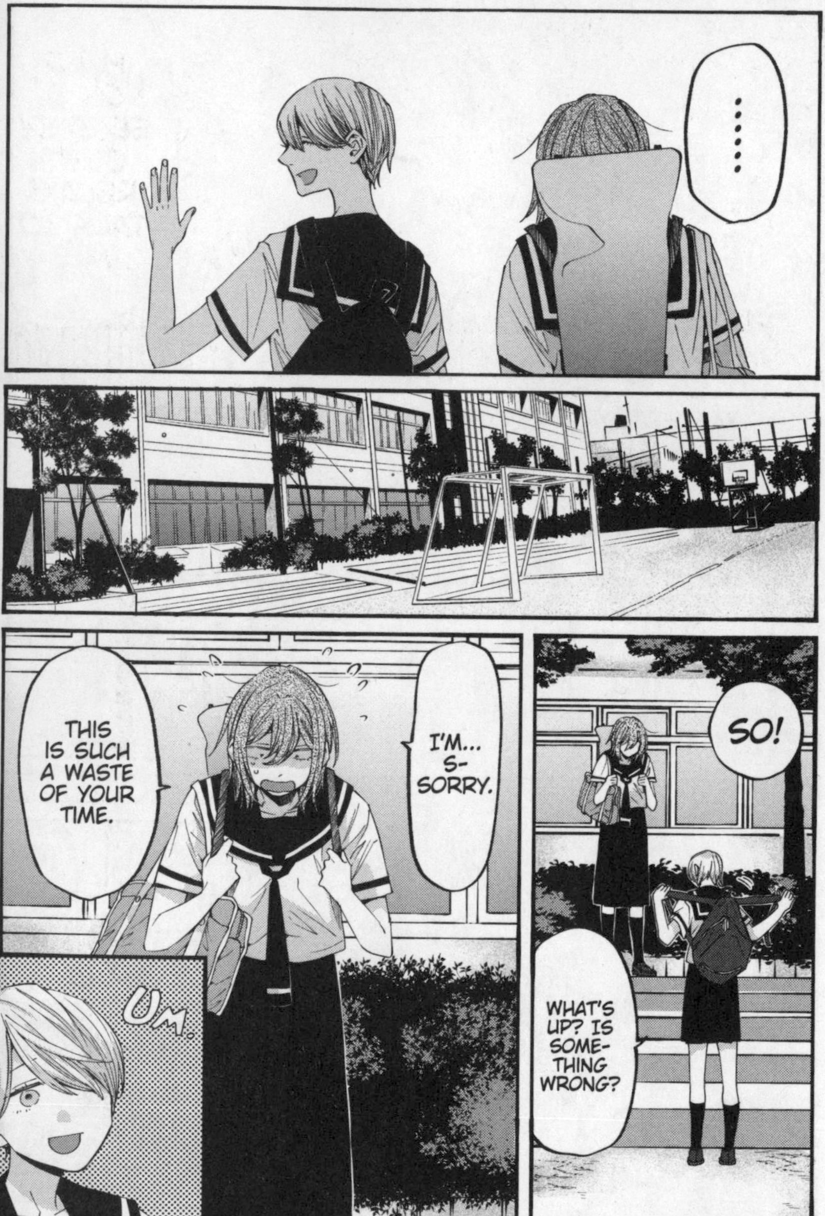
……
SO!
WHAT'S UP? IS SOMETHING WRONG?
I'M... S-SORRY.
THIS IS SUCH A WASTE OF YOUR TIME.
UM.

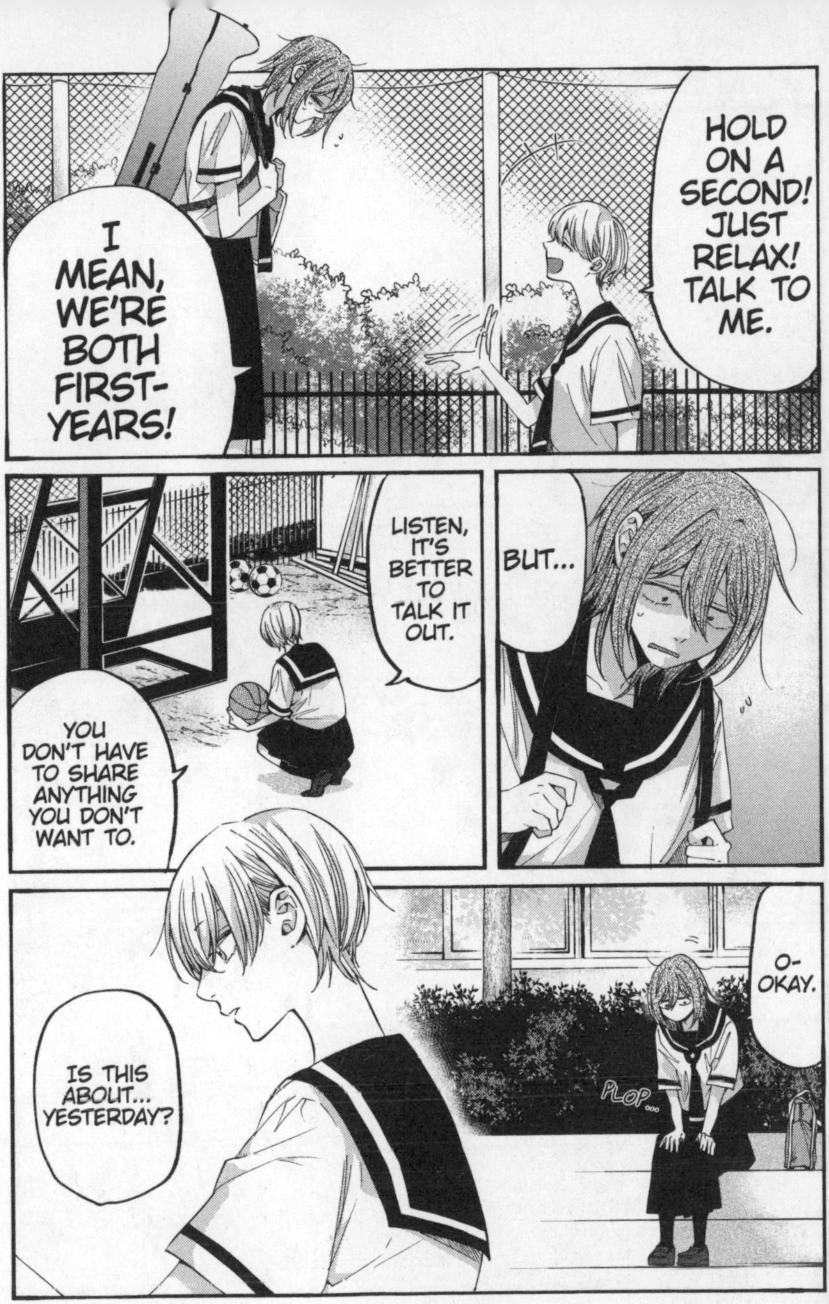
HOLD ON A SECOND! JUST RELAX! TALK TO ME.
I MEAN, WE'RE BOTH FIRST-YEARS!
BUT...
LISTEN, IT'S BETTER TO TALK IT OUT.
YOU DON'T HAVE TO SHARE ANYTHING YOU DON'T WANT TO.
O-OKAY.
PLOP...
IS THIS ABOUT... YESTERDAY?

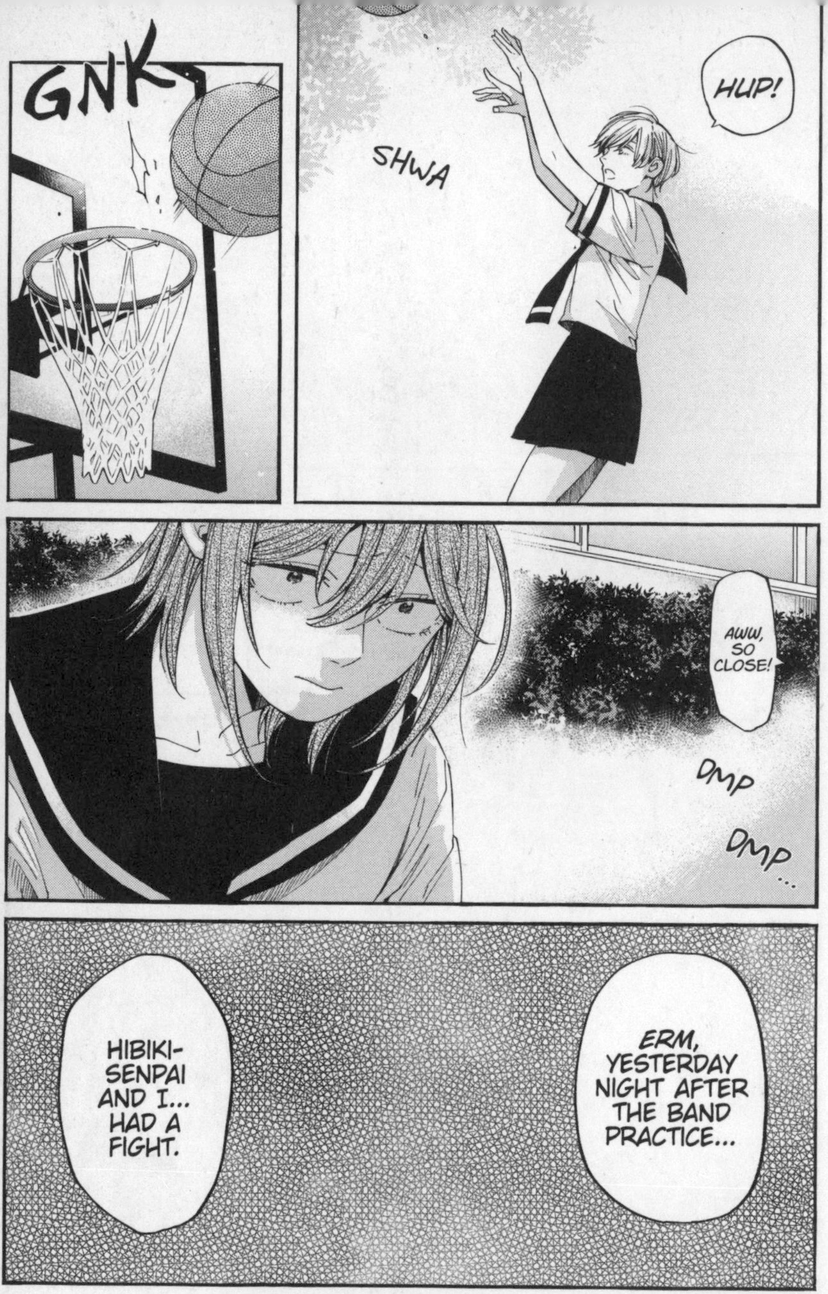
HUP!
SHWA
GNK
AWW, SO CLOSE!
DMP
DMP...
ERM, YESTERDAY NIGHT AFTER THE BAND PRACTICE...
HIBIKI-SENPAI AND I... HAD A FIGHT.

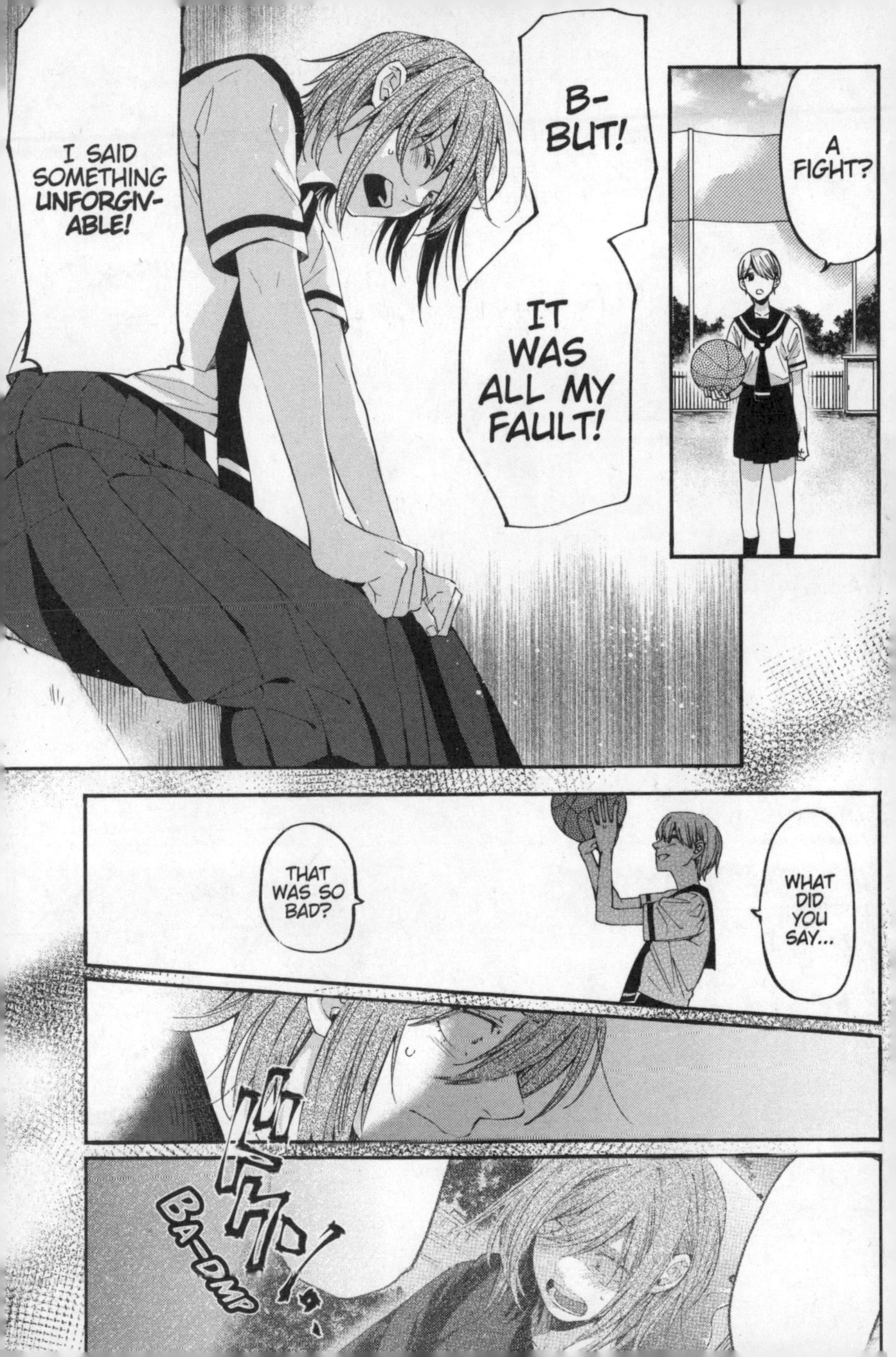
A FIGHT?
B-BUT!
IT WAS ALL MY FAULT!
I SAID SOMETHING UNFORGIV-ABLE!
WHAT DID YOU SAY...
THAT WAS SO BAD?
THUMP!
BA-DMP

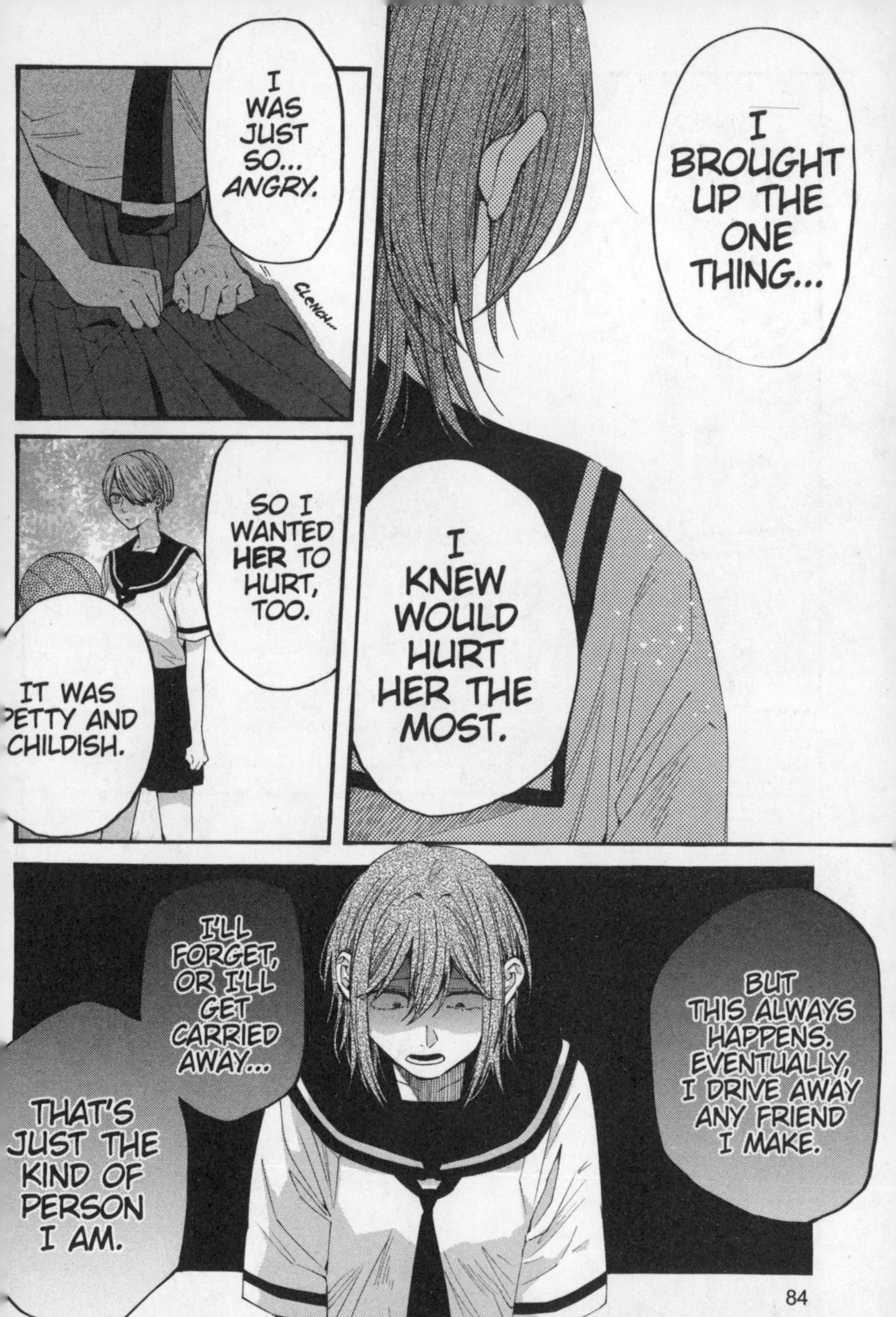
I BROUGHT UP THE ONE THING...
I KNEW WOULD HURT HER THE MOST.
I WAS JUST SO... ANGRY.
CLENCH...
SO I WANTED HER TO HURT, TOO.
IT WAS PETTY AND CHILDISH.
BUT THIS ALWAYS HAPPENS. EVENTUALLY, I DRIVE AWAY ANY FRIEND I MAKE.
I'LL FORGET, OR I'LL GET CARRIED AWAY...
THAT'S JUST THE KIND OF PERSON I AM.

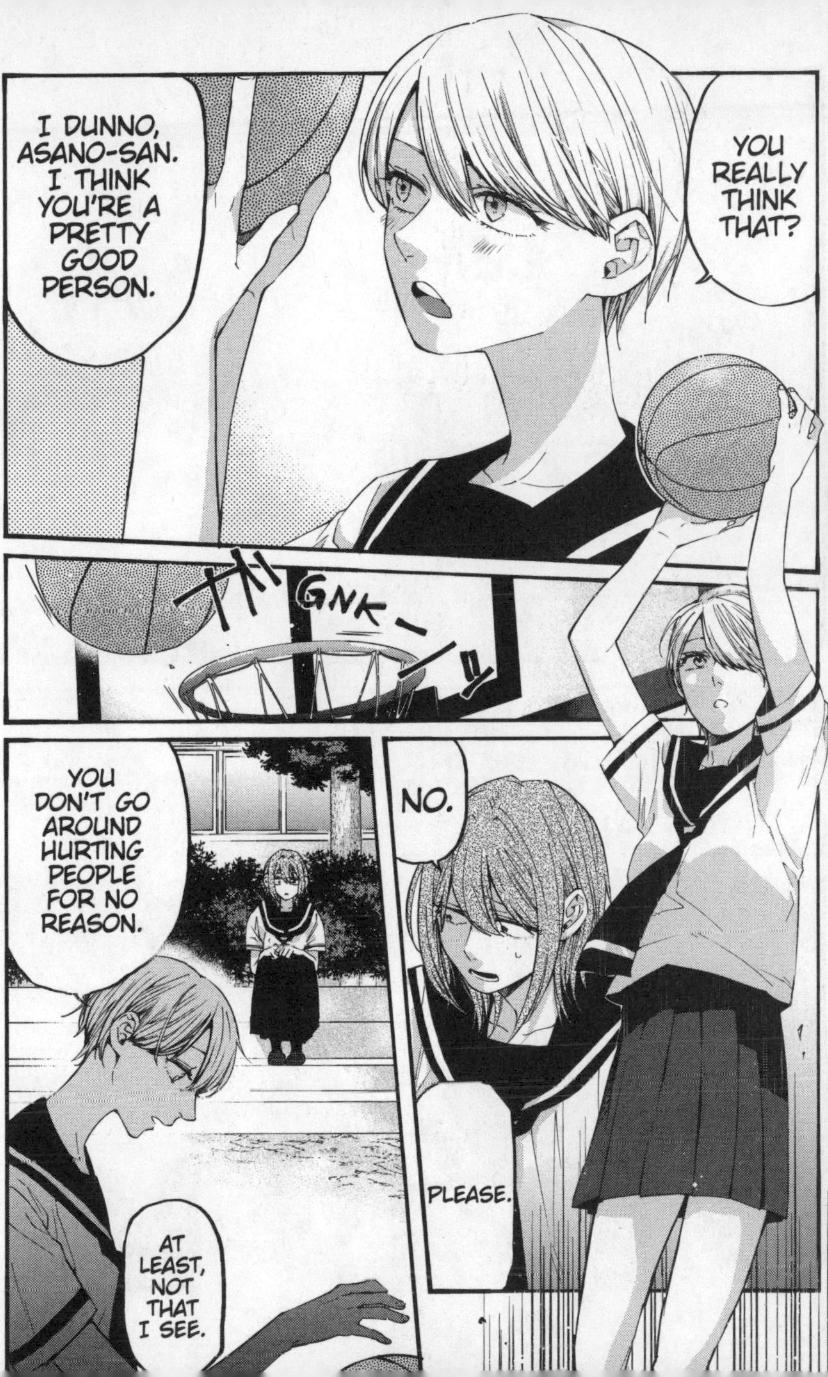
YOU REALLY THINK THAT?
I DUNNO, ASANO-SAN. I THINK YOU'RE A PRETTY GOOD PERSON.
GNK—!!
NO.
PLEASE.
YOU DON'T GO AROUND HURTING PEOPLE FOR NO REASON.
AT LEAST, NOT THAT I SEE.

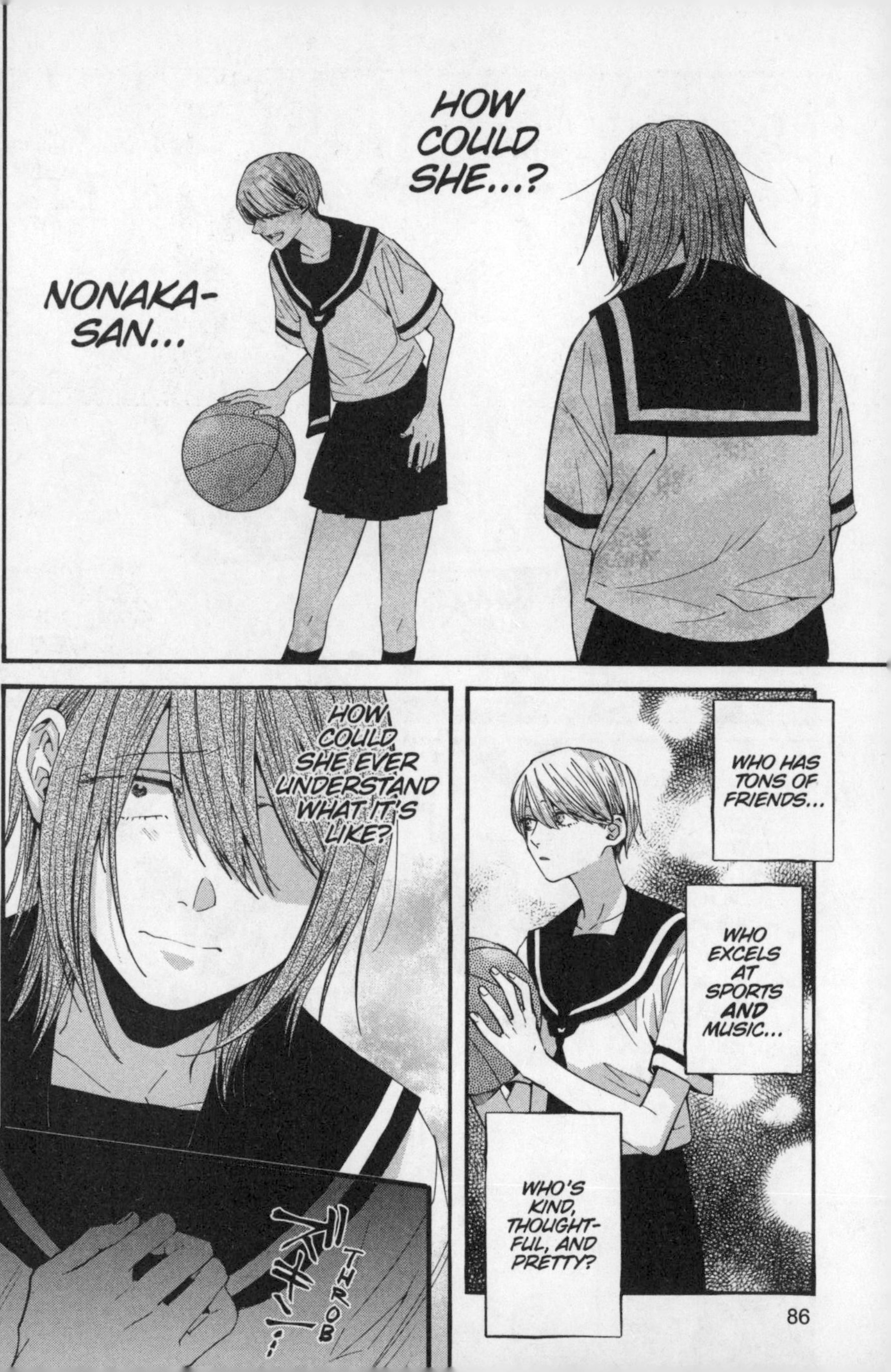
HOW COULD SHE...?
NONAKA-SAN...
WHO HAS TONS OF FRIENDS...
WHO EXCELS AT SPORTS AND MUSIC...
WHO'S KIND, THOUGHT-FUL, AND PRETTY?
HOW COULD SHE EVER UNDERSTAND WHAT IT'S LIKE?
THROB

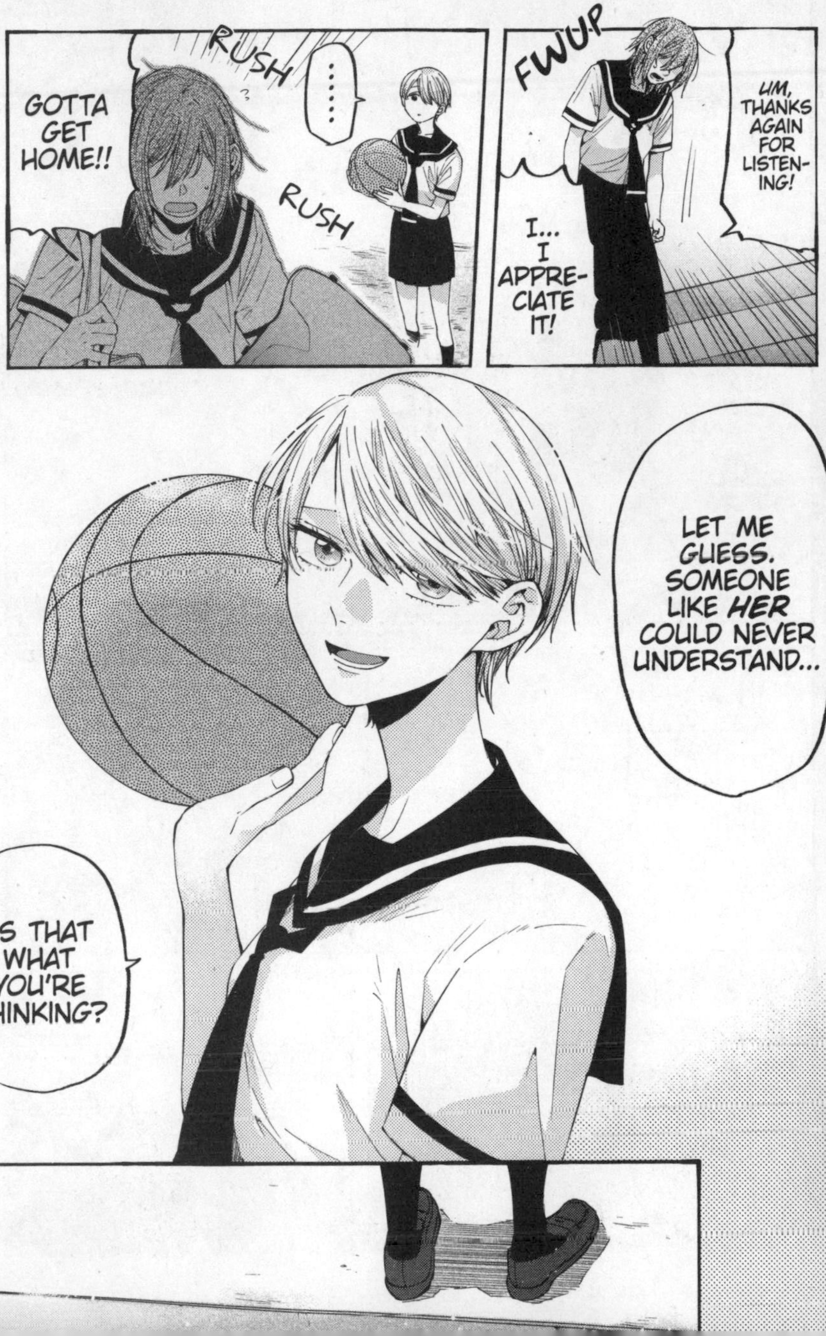
FWUP
UM, THANKS AGAIN FOR LISTENING!
I... I APPRECIATE IT!
RUSH
......
GOTTA GET HOME!!
RUSH
LET ME GUESS. SOMEONE LIKE *HER* COULD NEVER UNDERSTAND...
IS THAT WHAT YOU'RE THINKING?

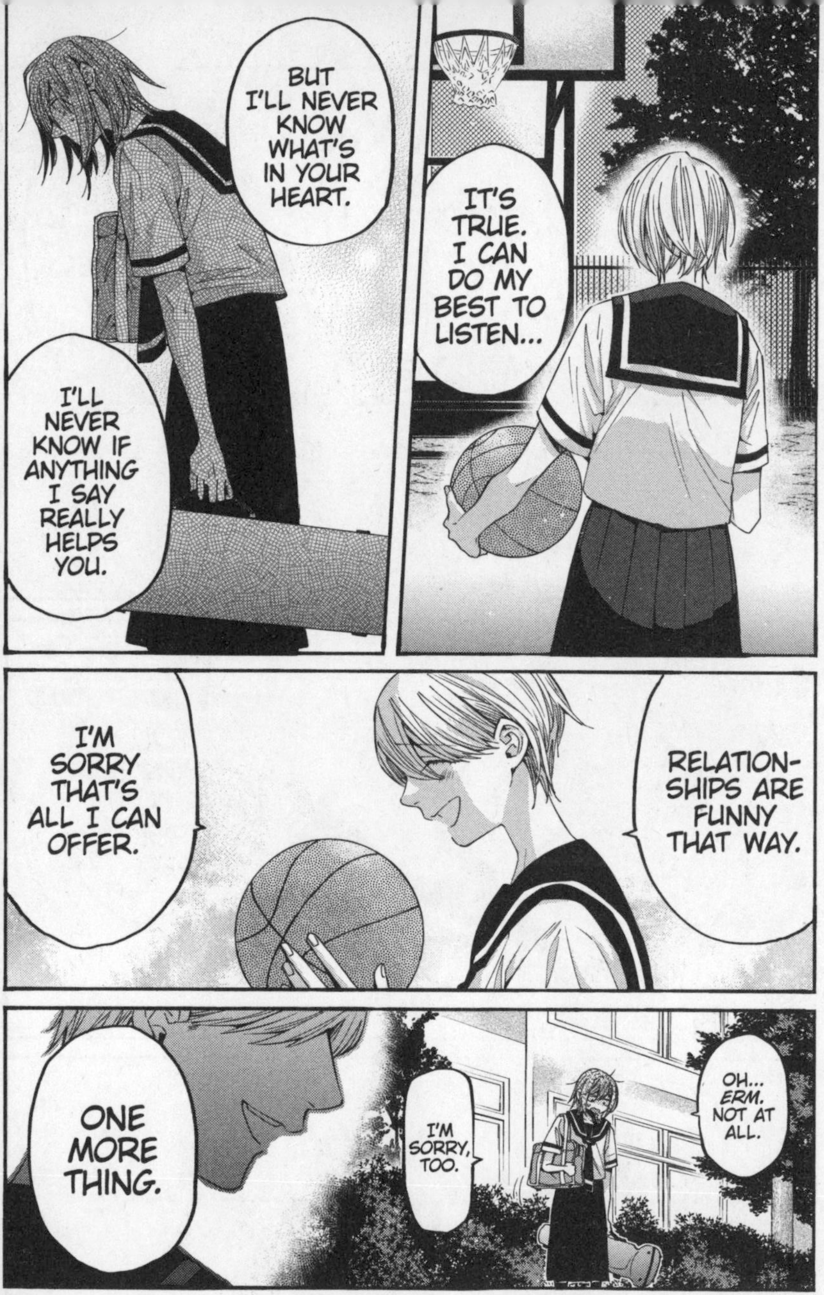
IT'S TRUE. I CAN DO MY BEST TO LISTEN...
BUT I'LL NEVER KNOW WHAT'S IN YOUR HEART.
I'LL NEVER KNOW IF ANYTHING I SAY REALLY HELPS YOU.
RELATION-SHIPS ARE FUNNY THAT WAY.
I'M SORRY THAT'S ALL I CAN OFFER.
OH... *ERM.* NOT AT ALL.
I'M SORRY, TOO.
ONE MORE THING.

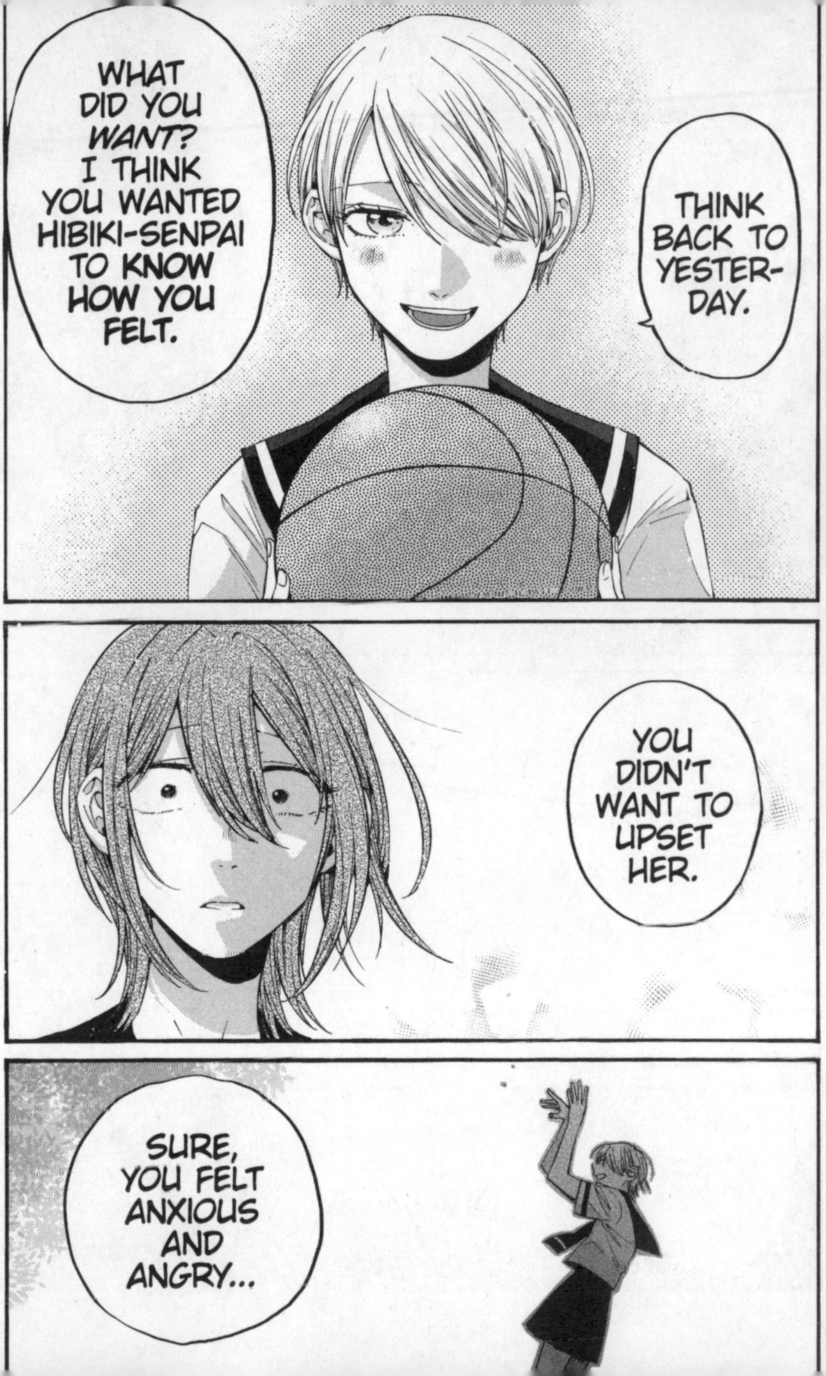
THINK BACK TO YESTER-DAY.
WHAT DID YOU *WANT?* I THINK YOU WANTED HIBIKI-SENPAI TO KNOW HOW YOU FELT.
YOU DIDN'T WANT TO UPSET HER.
SURE, YOU FELT ANXIOUS AND ANGRY...

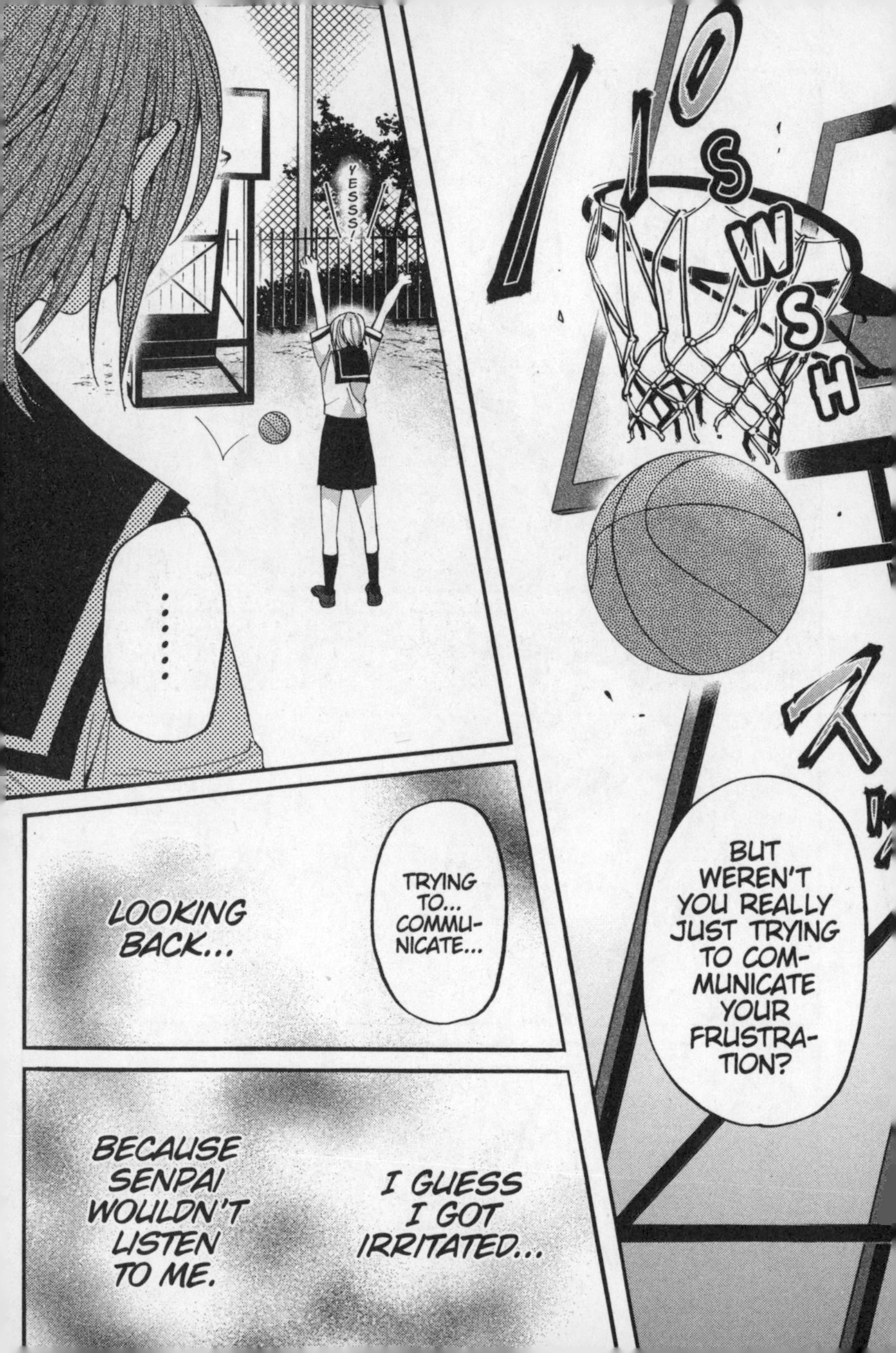
SWISH
BUT WEREN'T YOU REALLY JUST TRYING TO COMMUNICATE YOUR FRUSTRATION?
YESS!
......
LOOKING BACK...
TRYING TO... COMMUNICATE...
I GUESS I GOT IRRITATED...
BECAUSE SENPAI WOULDN'T LISTEN TO ME.

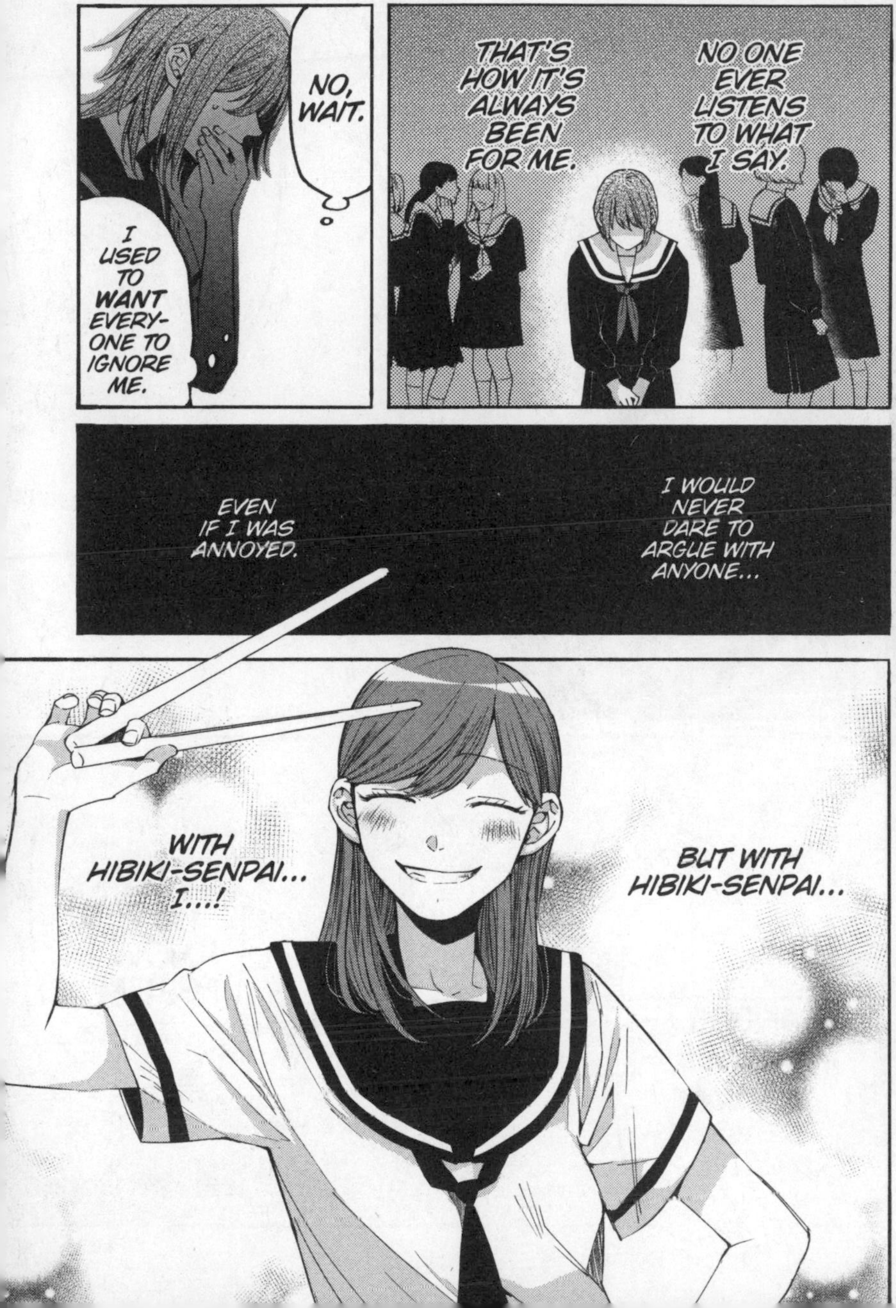
NO ONE EVER LISTENS TO WHAT I SAY.
THAT'S HOW IT'S ALWAYS BEEN FOR ME.
NO, WAIT.
I USED TO WANT EVERYONE TO IGNORE ME.
I WOULD NEVER DARE TO ARGUE WITH ANYONE...
EVEN IF I WAS ANNOYED.
BUT WITH HIBIKI-SENPAI...
WITH HIBIKI-SENPAI... I...!

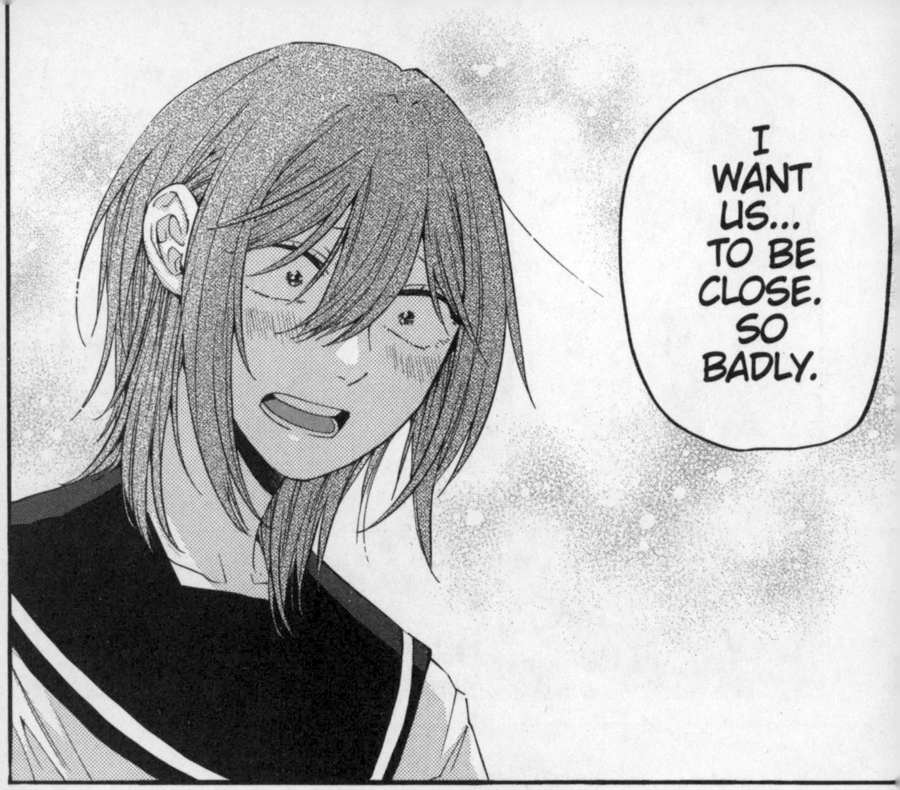
I WANT US... TO BE CLOSE. SO BADLY.

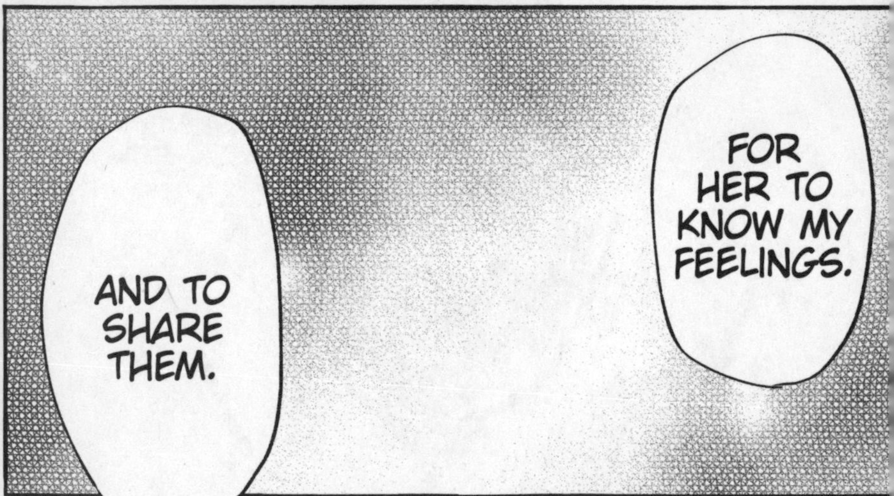
FOR HER TO KNOW MY FEELINGS.
AND TO SHARE THEM.

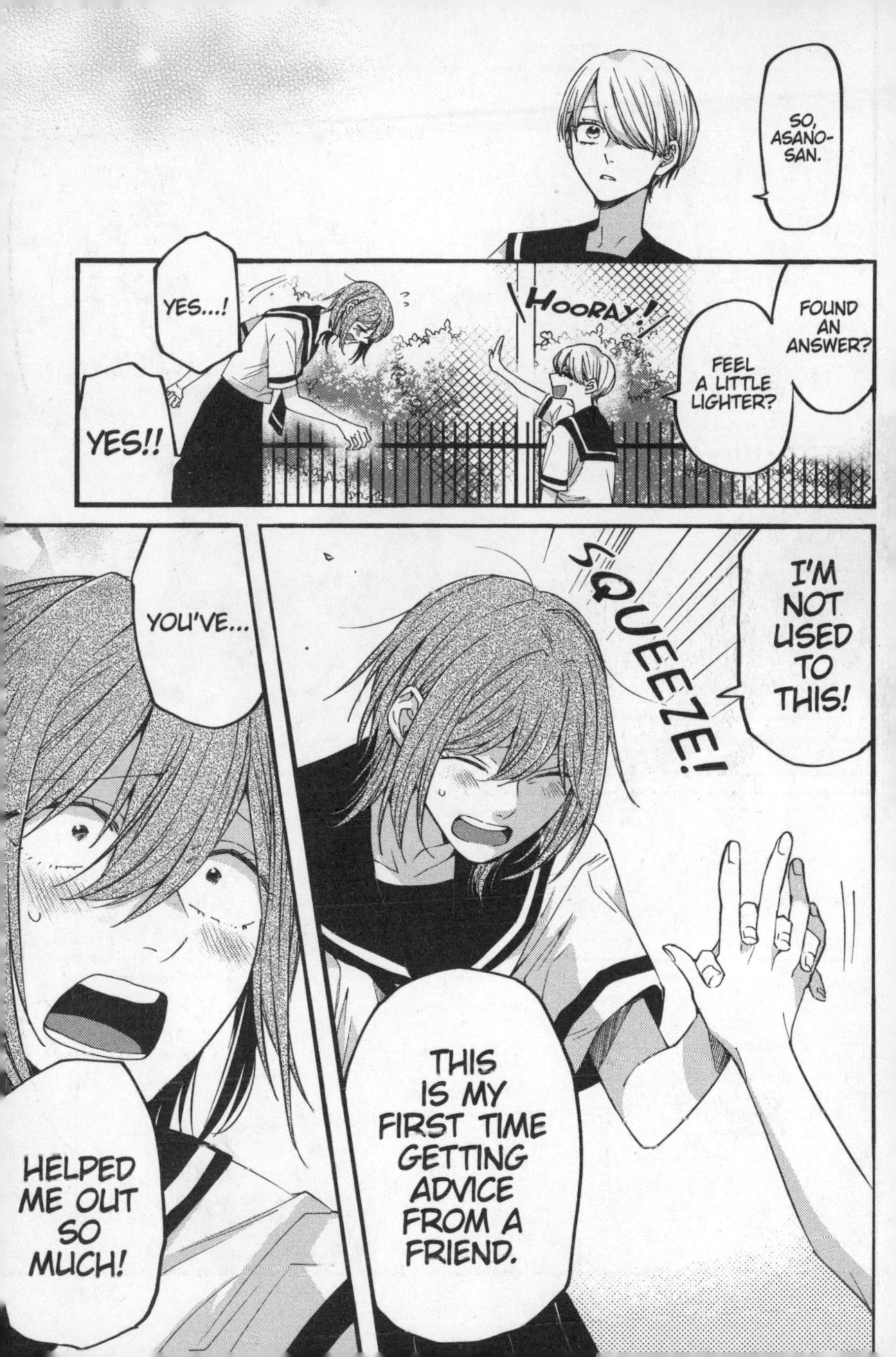
SO, ASANO-SAN.
FOUND AN ANSWER?
FEEL A LITTLE LIGHTER?
HOORAY!
YES...!
YES!!
I'M NOT USED TO THIS!
SQUEEZE!
THIS IS MY FIRST TIME GETTING ADVICE FROM A FRIEND.
YOU'VE...
HELPED ME OUT SO MUCH!

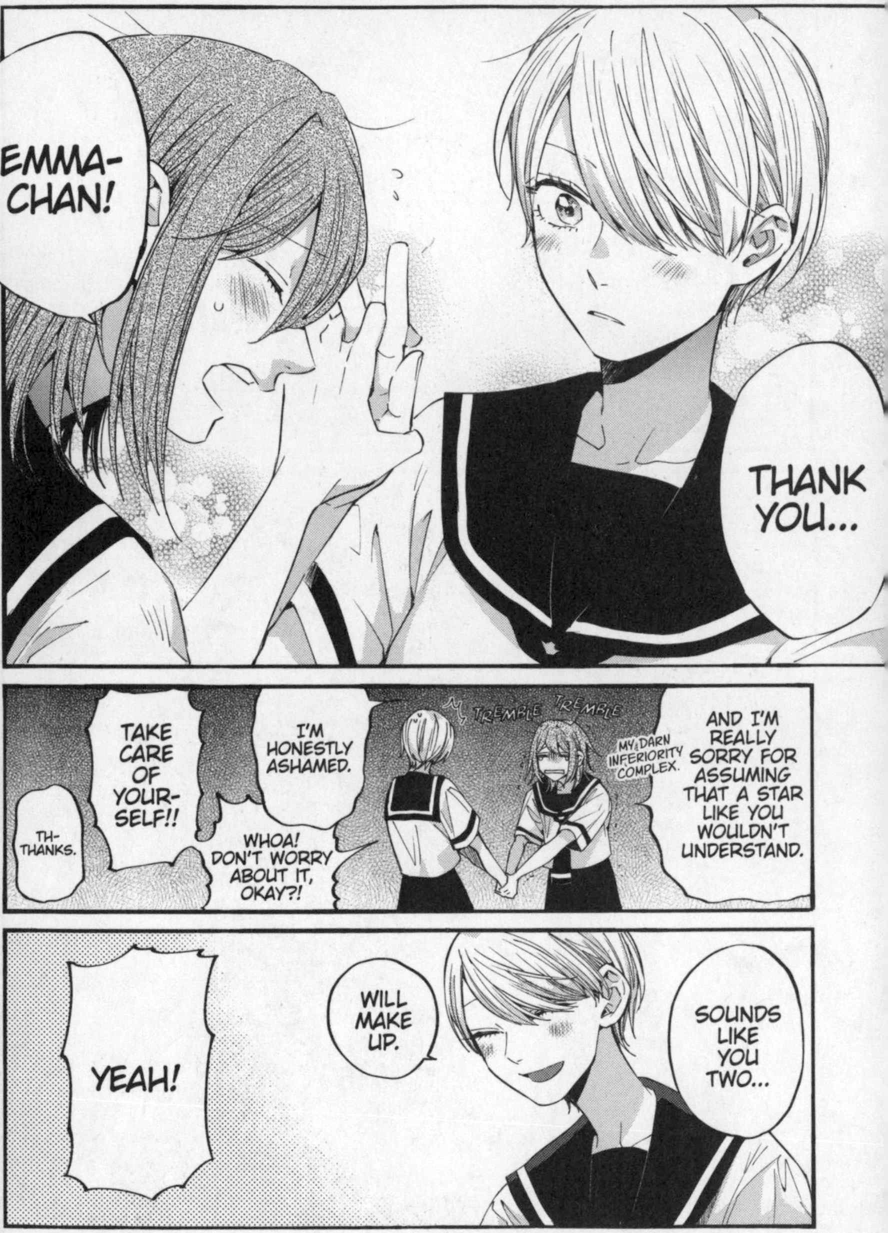
THANK YOU...
EMMA-CHAN!
AND I'M REALLY SORRY FOR ASSUMING THAT A STAR LIKE YOU WOULDN'T UNDERSTAND.
MY DARN INFERIORITY COMPLEX.
TREMBLE TREMBLE
I'M HONESTLY ASHAMED.
WHOA! DON'T WORRY ABOUT IT, OKAY?!
TAKE CARE OF YOURSELF!!
TH-THANKS.
SOUNDS LIKE YOU TWO...
WILL MAKE UP.
YEAH!

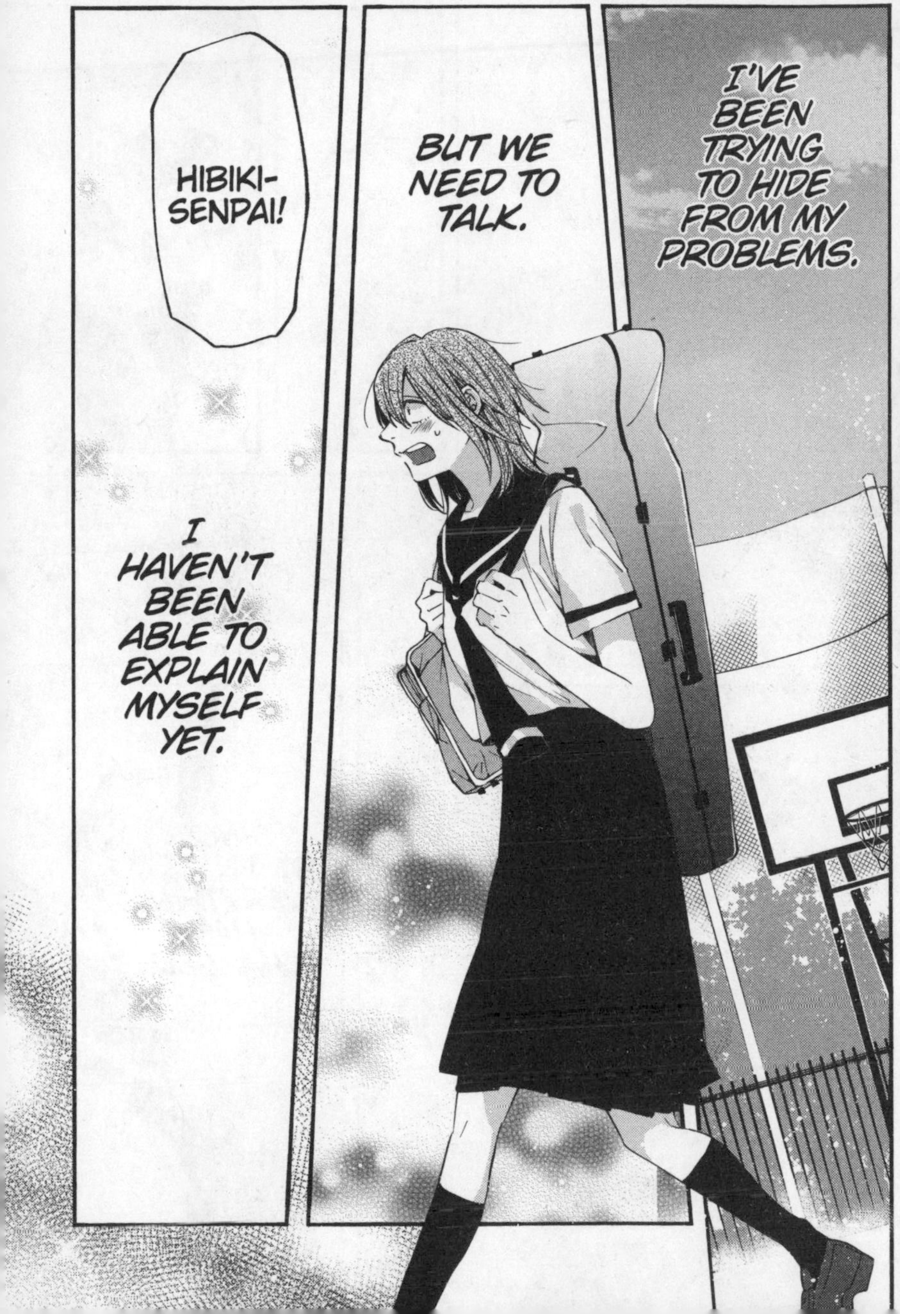
I'VE BEEN TRYING TO HIDE FROM MY PROBLEMS.
BUT WE NEED TO TALK.
HIBIKI-SENPAI!
I HAVEN'T BEEN ABLE TO EXPLAIN MYSELF YET.

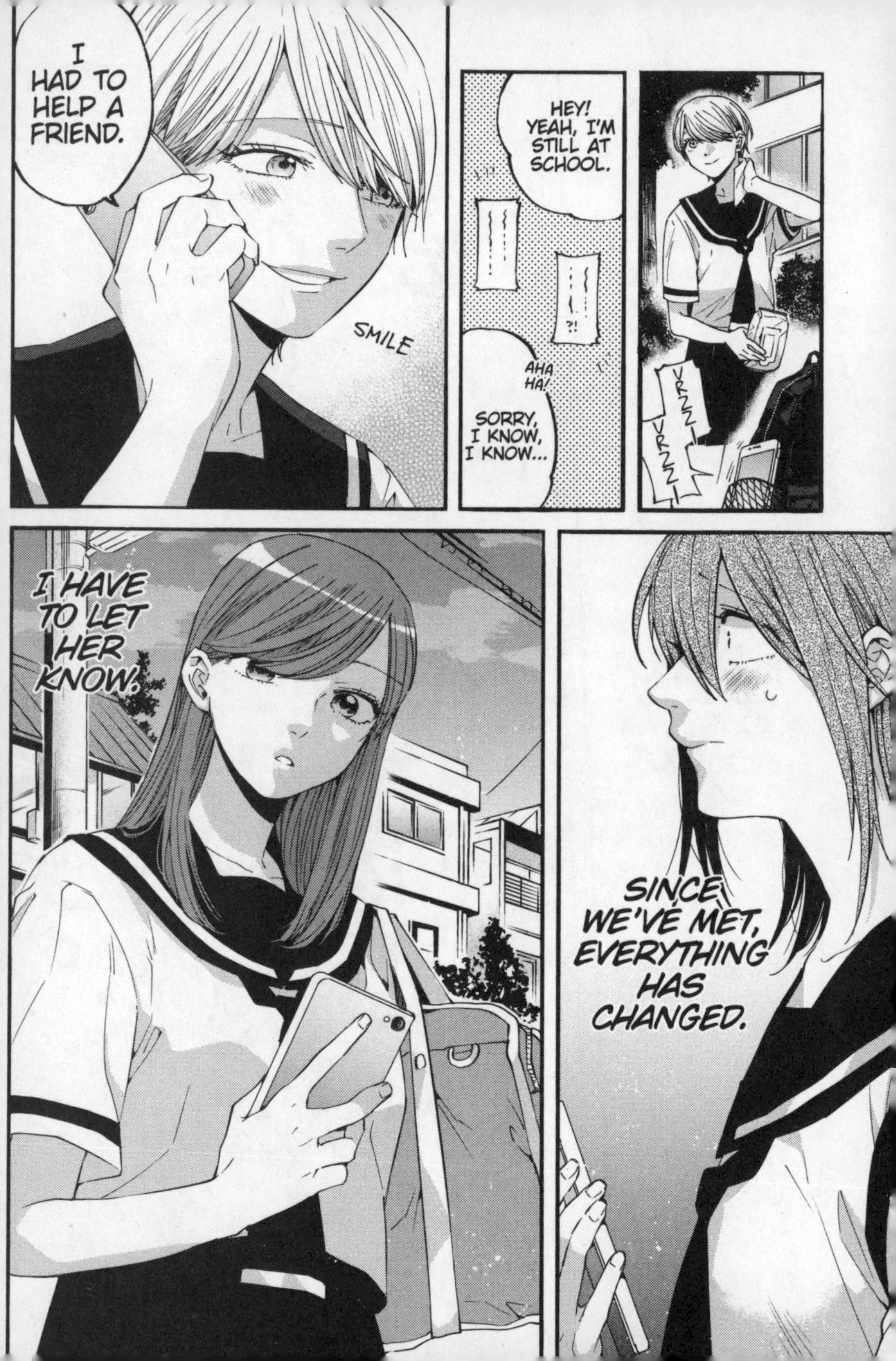
VRZZZ
VRZZZ
HEY! YEAH, I'M STILL AT SCHOOL.
?!
AHA HA!
SORRY, I KNOW, I KNOW...
I HAD TO HELP A FRIEND.
SMILE
SINCE WE'VE MET, EVERYTHING HAS CHANGED.
I HAVE TO LET HER KNOW.

HELLO, MELAN CHOLIC!

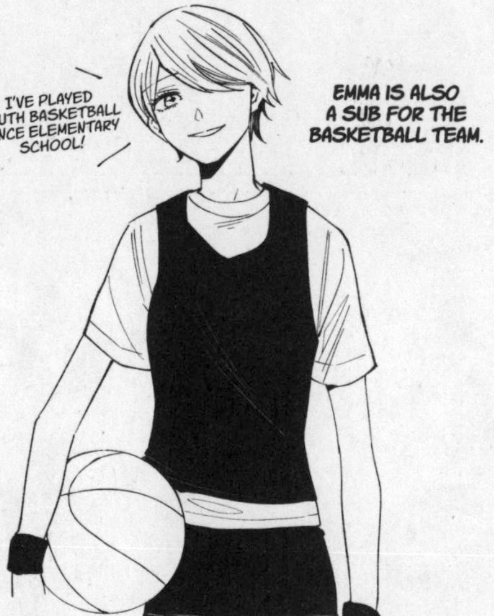
EMMA IS ALSO A SUB FOR THE BASKETBALL TEAM.
I'VE PLAYED YOUTH BASKETBALL SINCE ELEMENTARY SCHOOL!

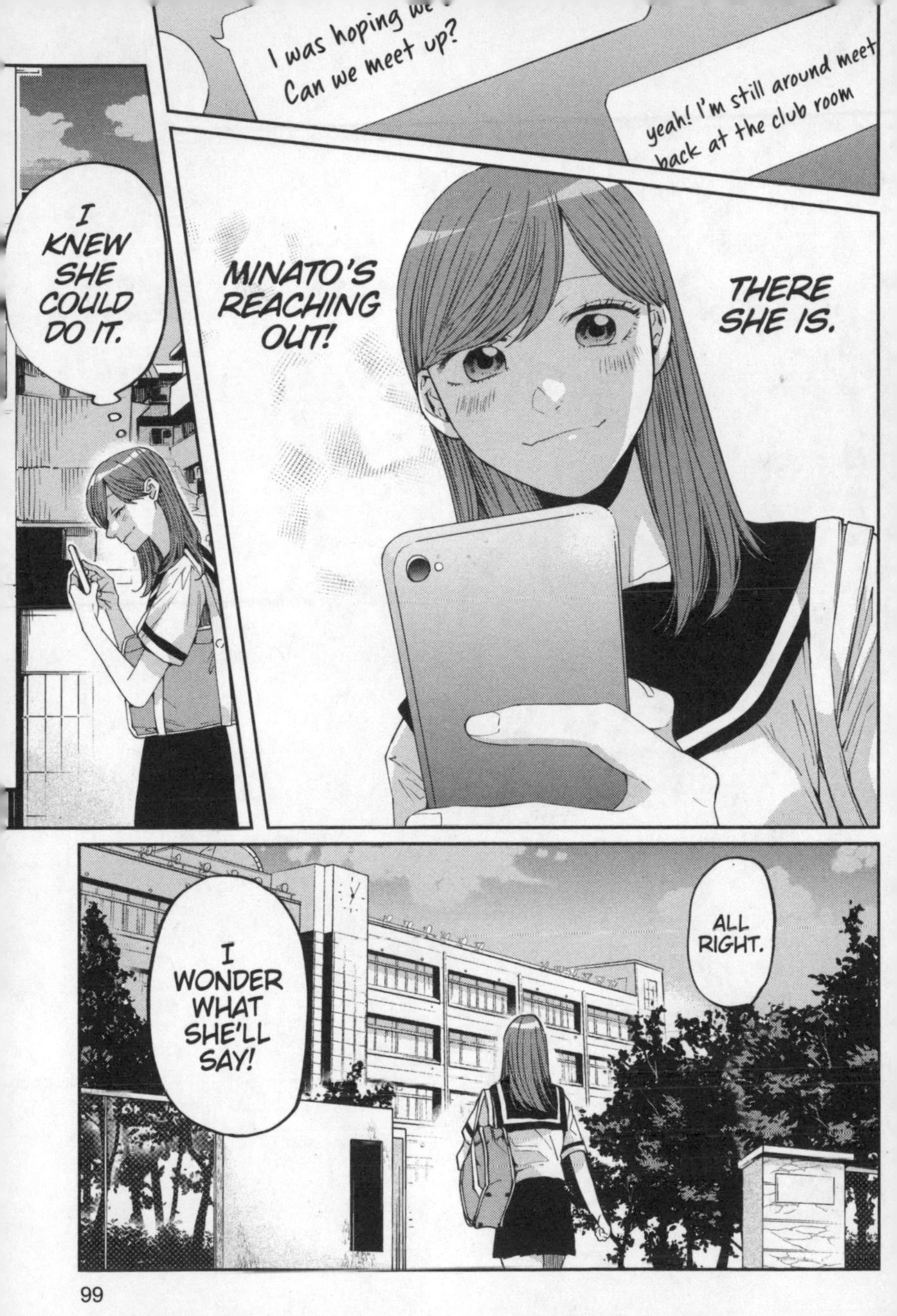
I was hoping we
Can we meet up?
yeah! I'm still around meet back at the club room
I KNEW SHE COULD DO IT.
MINATO'S REACHING OUT!
THERE SHE IS.
I WONDER WHAT SHE'LL SAY!
ALL RIGHT.

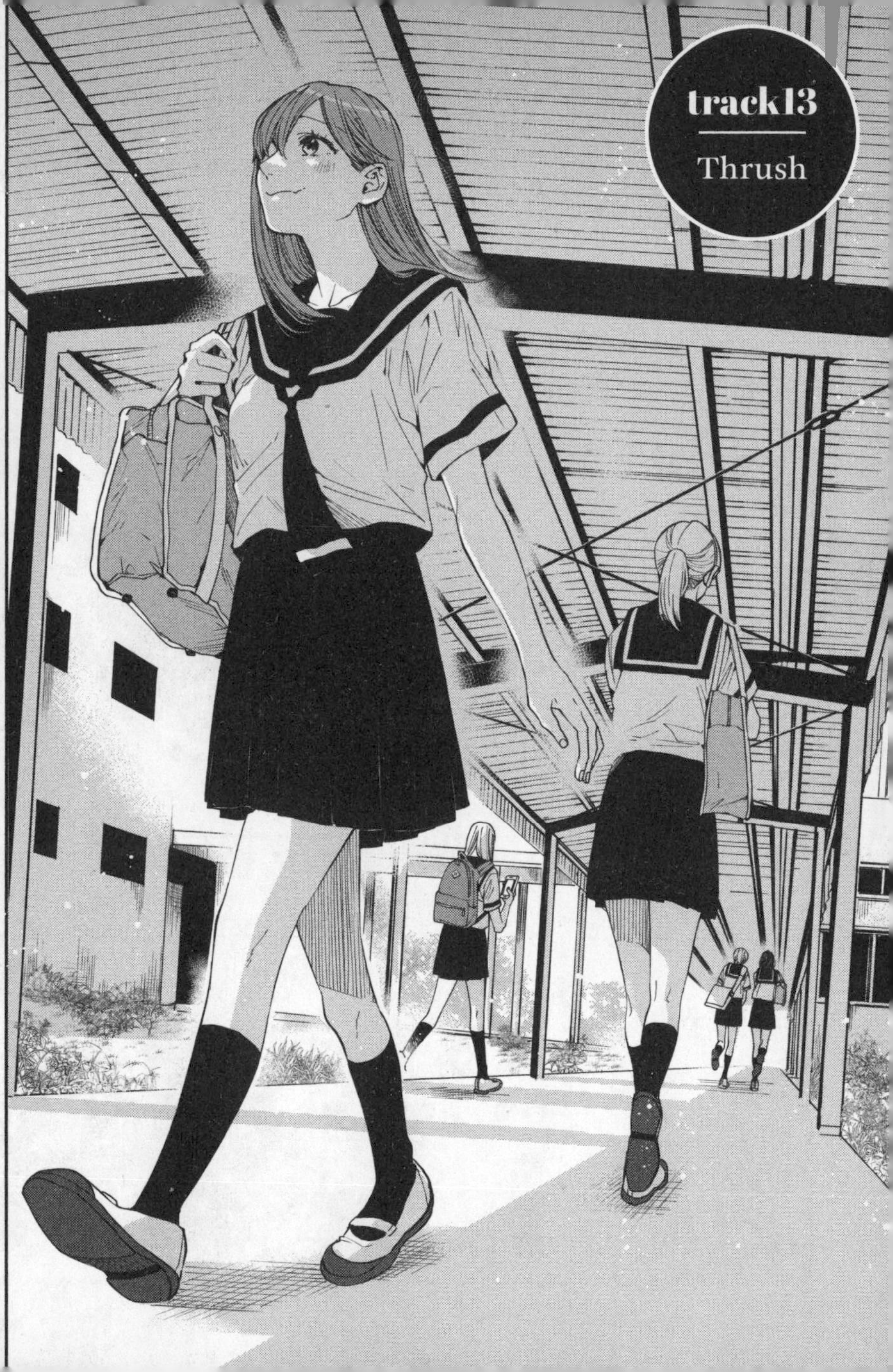
track13
Thrush

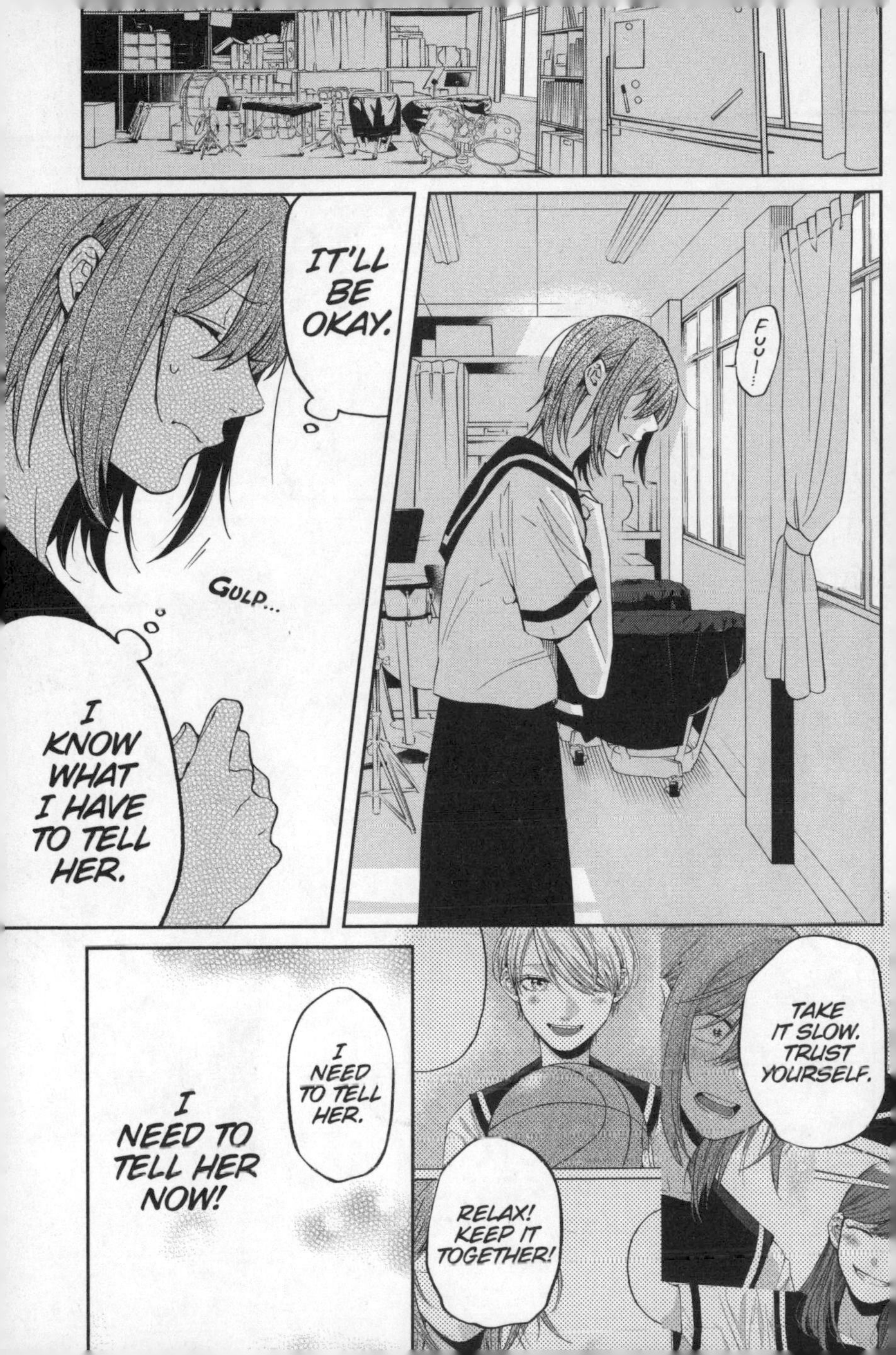
FUU!...
IT'LL BE OKAY.
GULP...
I KNOW WHAT I HAVE TO TELL HER.
TAKE IT SLOW. TRUST YOURSELF.
I NEED TO TELL HER.
RELAX! KEEP IT TOGETHER!
I NEED TO TELL HER NOW!

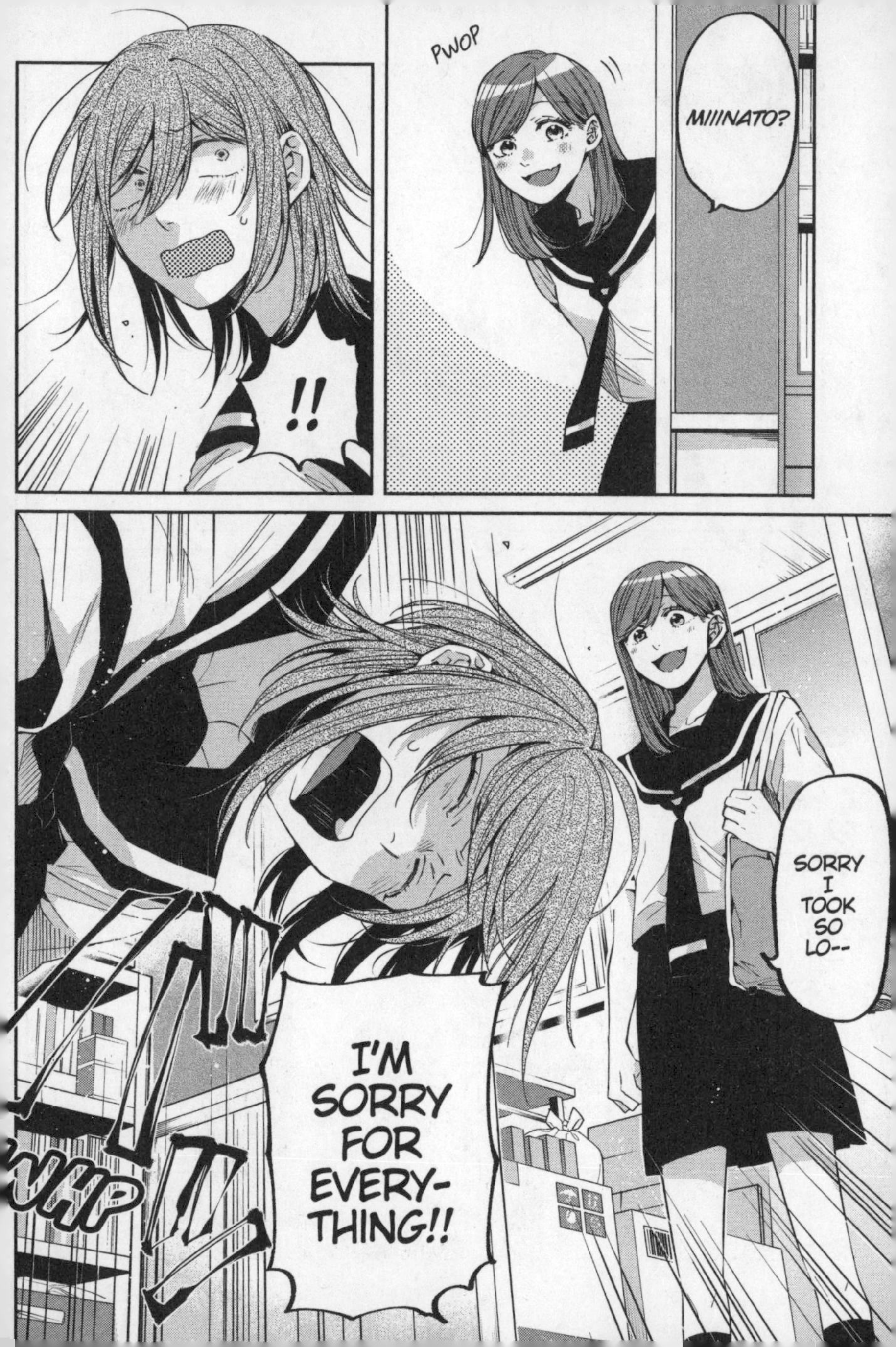
PWOP
MIIINATO?
!!
SORRY I TOOK SO LO--
I'M SORRY FOR EVERY-THING!!

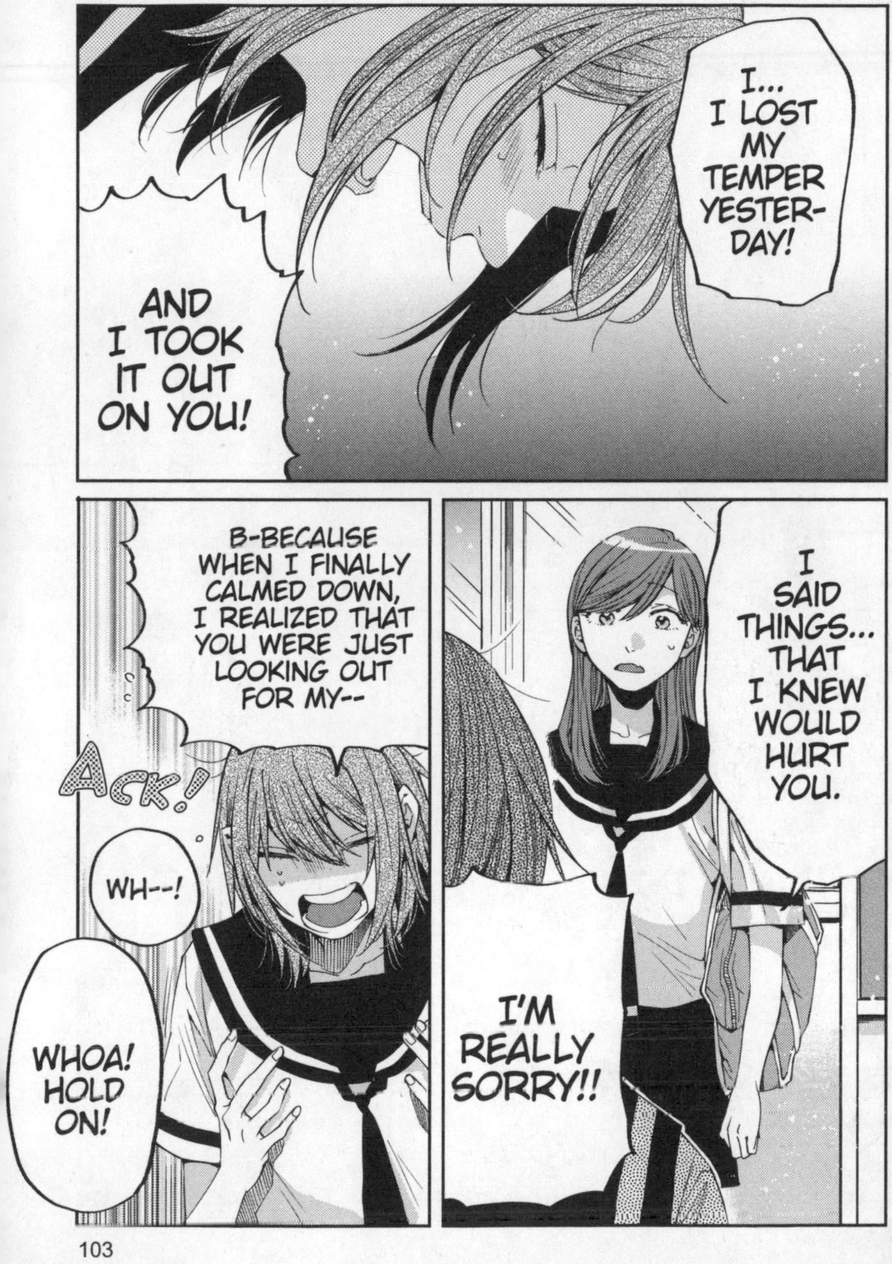
I... I LOST MY TEMPER YESTER-DAY!
AND I TOOK IT OUT ON YOU!
I SAID THINGS... THAT I KNEW WOULD HURT YOU.
I'M REALLY SORRY!!
B-BECAUSE WHEN I FINALLY CALMED DOWN, I REALIZED THAT YOU WERE JUST LOOKING OUT FOR MY--
ACK!
WH--!
WHOA! HOLD ON!

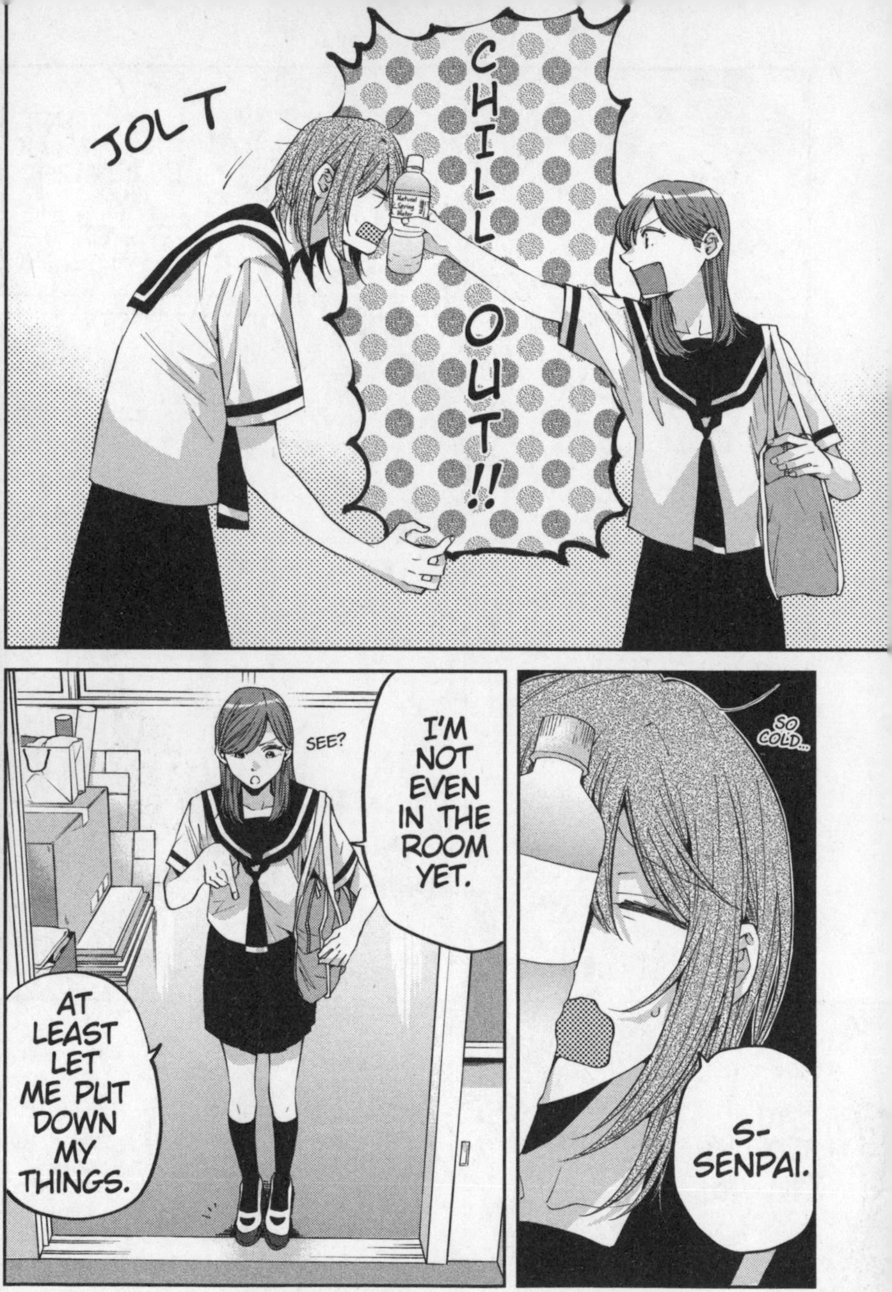
CHILL OUT!!
JOLT
SO COLD...
S-SENPAI.
I'M NOT EVEN IN THE ROOM YET.
SEE?
AT LEAST LET ME PUT DOWN MY THINGS.

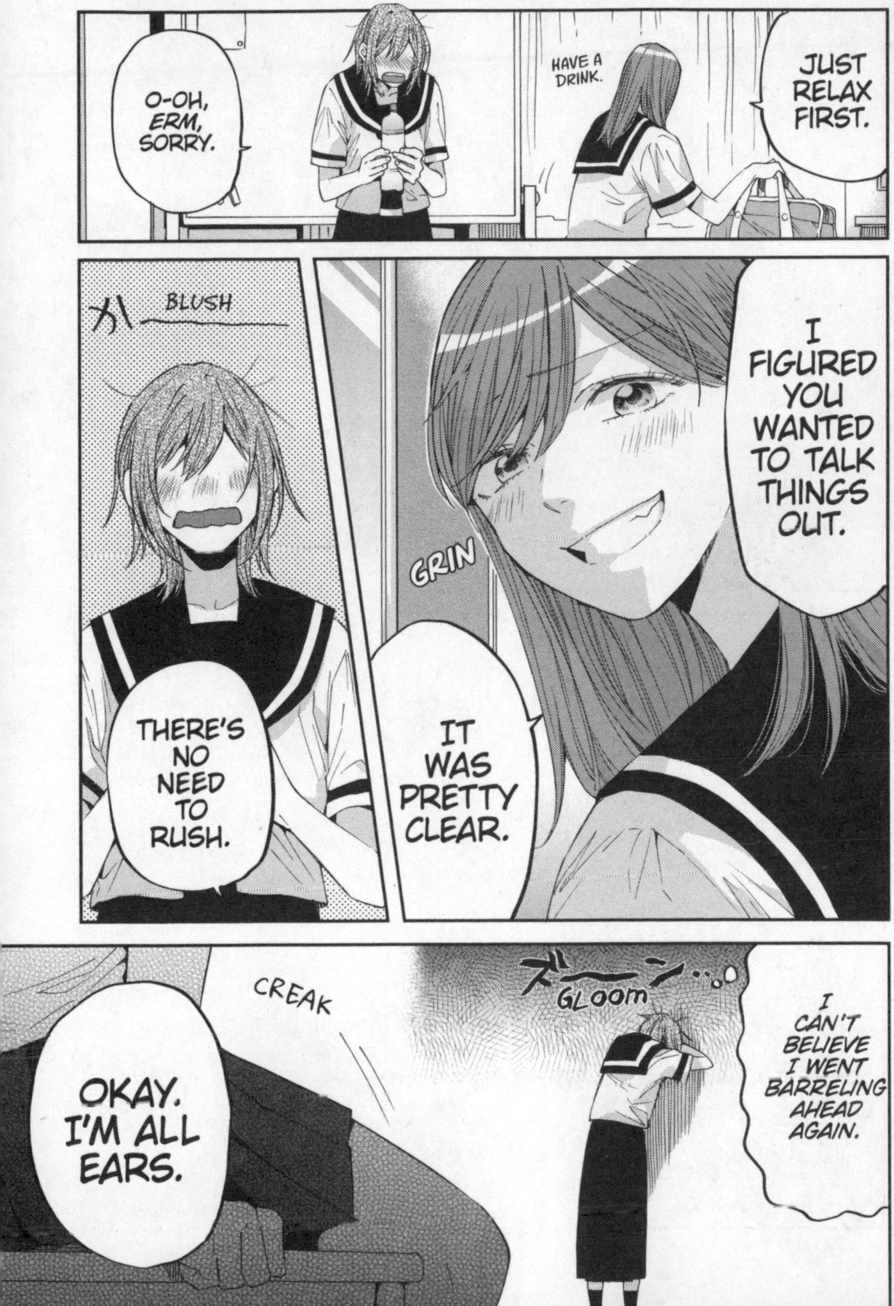
JUST RELAX FIRST.
HAVE A DRINK.
O-OH, ERM, SORRY.
I FIGURED YOU WANTED TO TALK THINGS OUT.
GRIN
IT WAS PRETTY CLEAR.
BLUSH
THERE'S NO NEED TO RUSH.
I CAN'T BELIEVE I WENT BARRELING AHEAD AGAIN.
GLOOM
CREAK
OKAY. I'M ALL EARS.

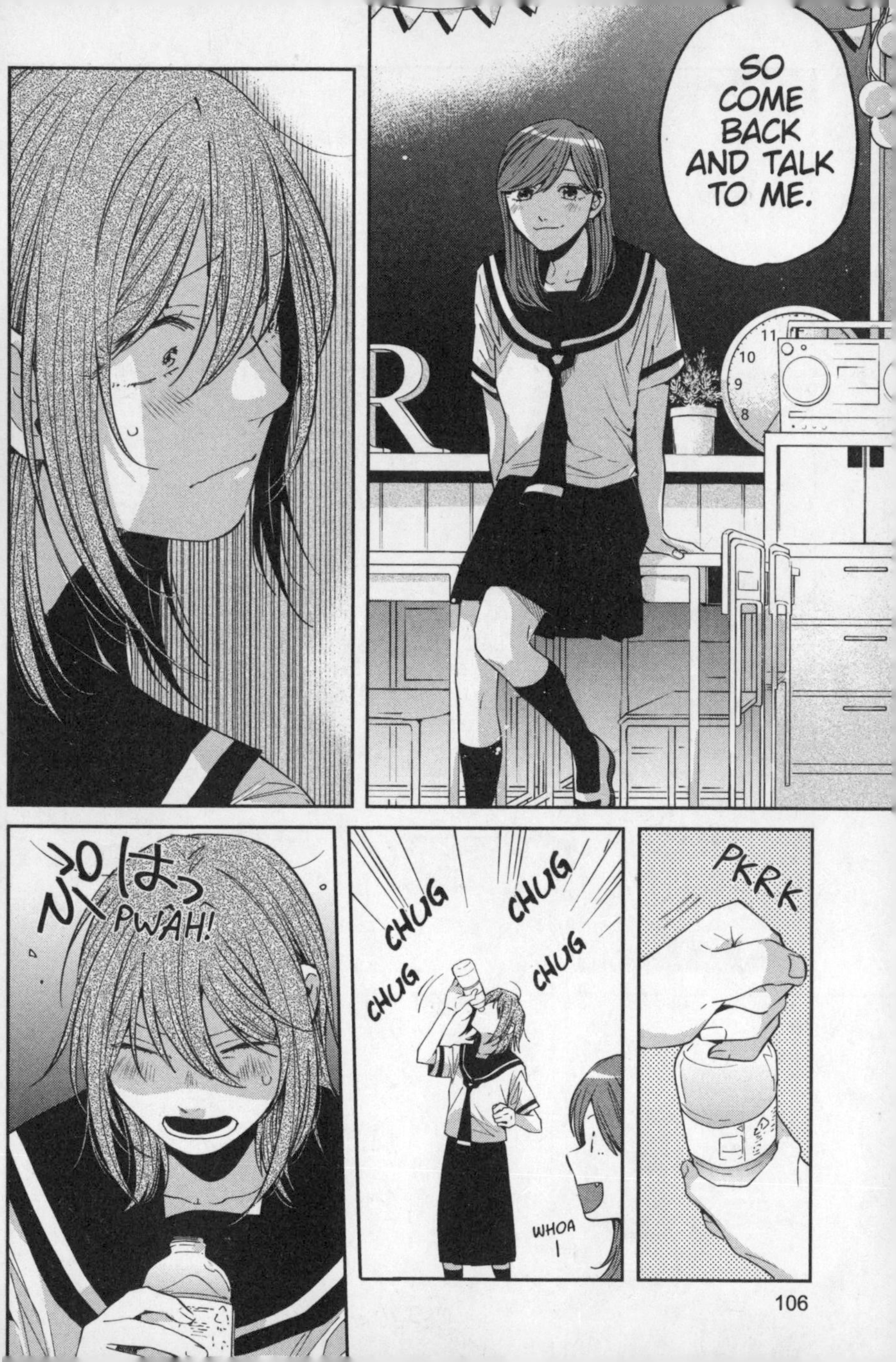
SO COME BACK AND TALK TO ME.
PKRK
CHUG
CHUG
CHUG
CHUG
WHOA
ぷはっ
PWAH!

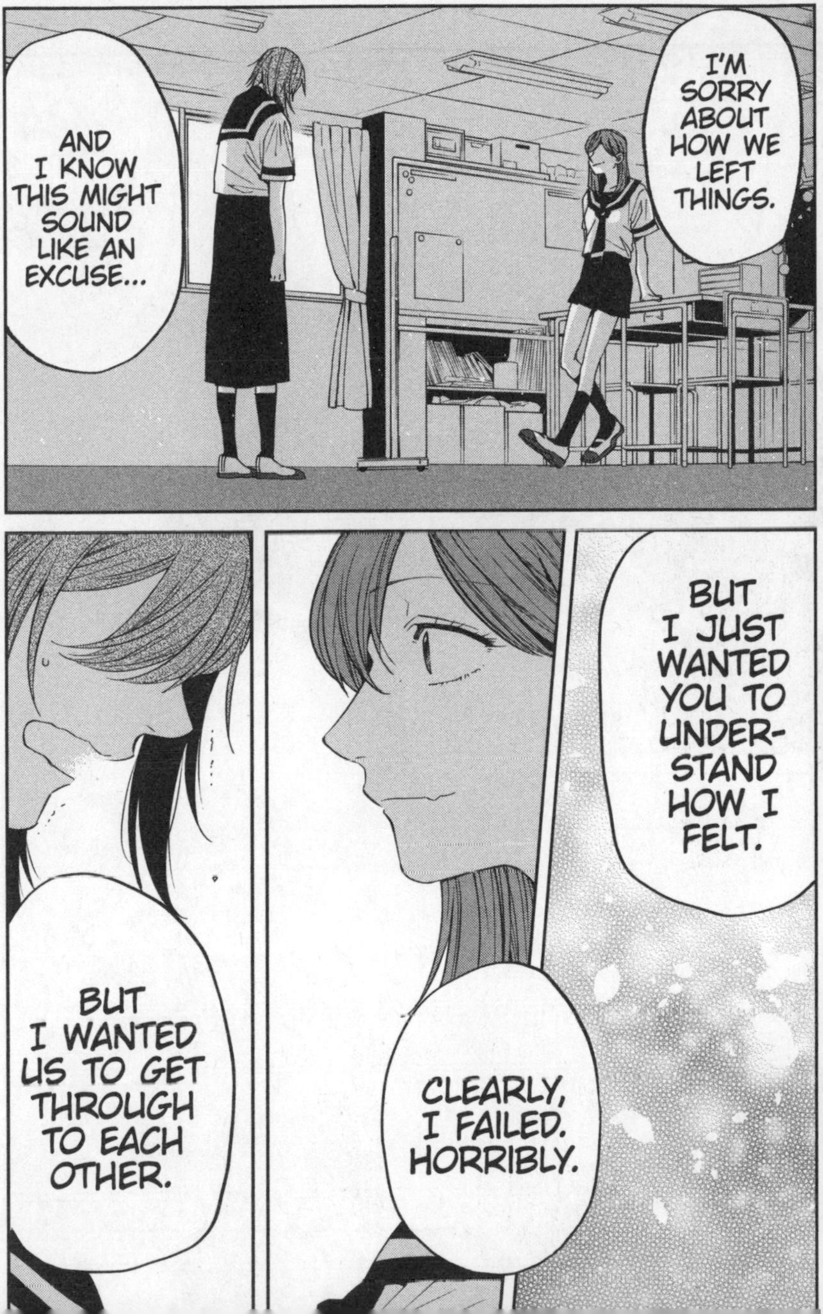
I'M SORRY ABOUT HOW WE LEFT THINGS.
AND I KNOW THIS MIGHT SOUND LIKE AN EXCUSE...
BUT I JUST WANTED YOU TO UNDER-STAND HOW I FELT.
CLEARLY, I FAILED. HORRIBLY.
BUT I WANTED US TO GET THROUGH TO EACH OTHER.

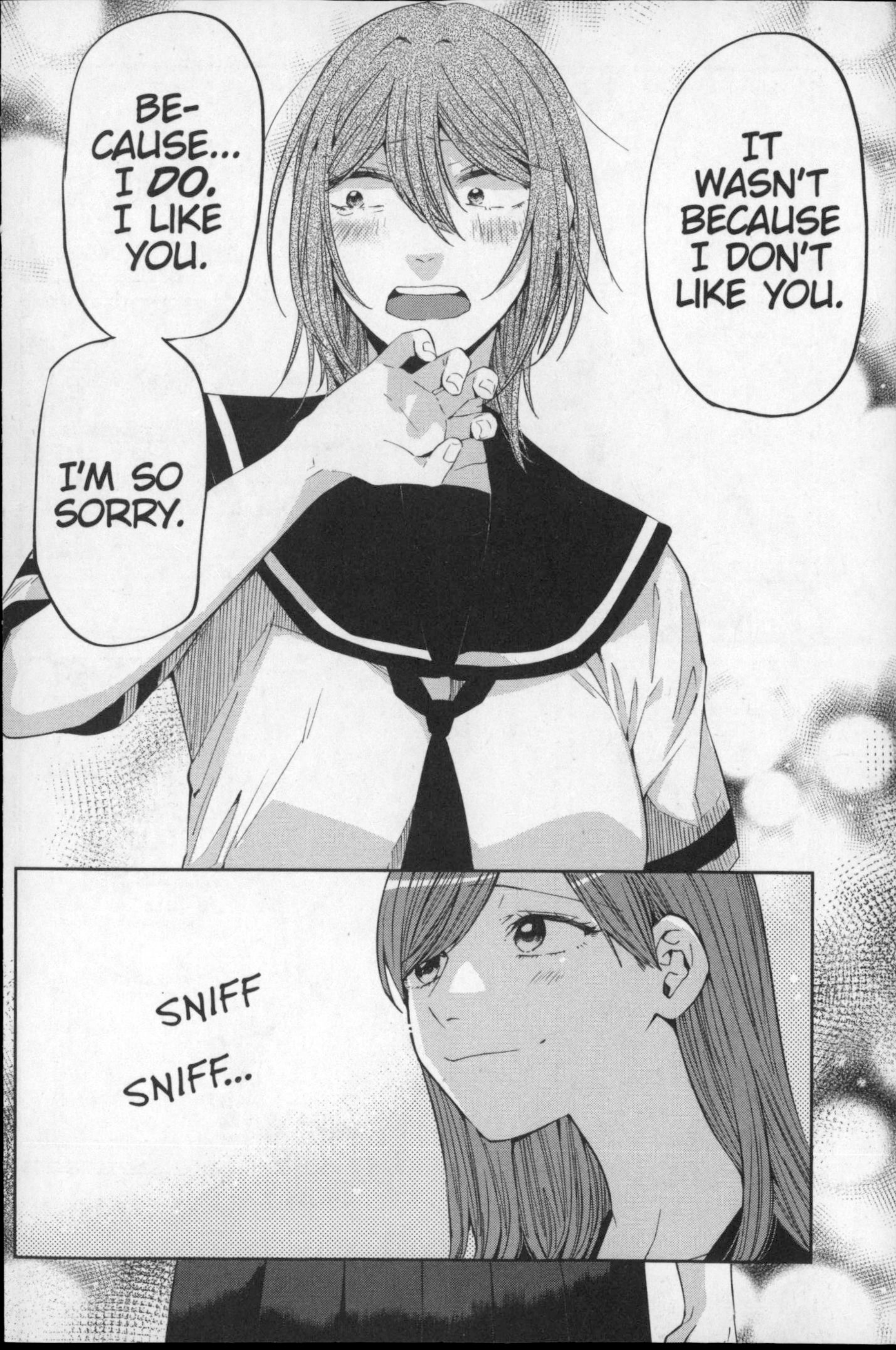
IT WASN'T BECAUSE I DON'T LIKE YOU.
BE-CAUSE... I *DO.* I LIKE YOU.
I'M SO SORRY.
SNIFF
SNIFF...

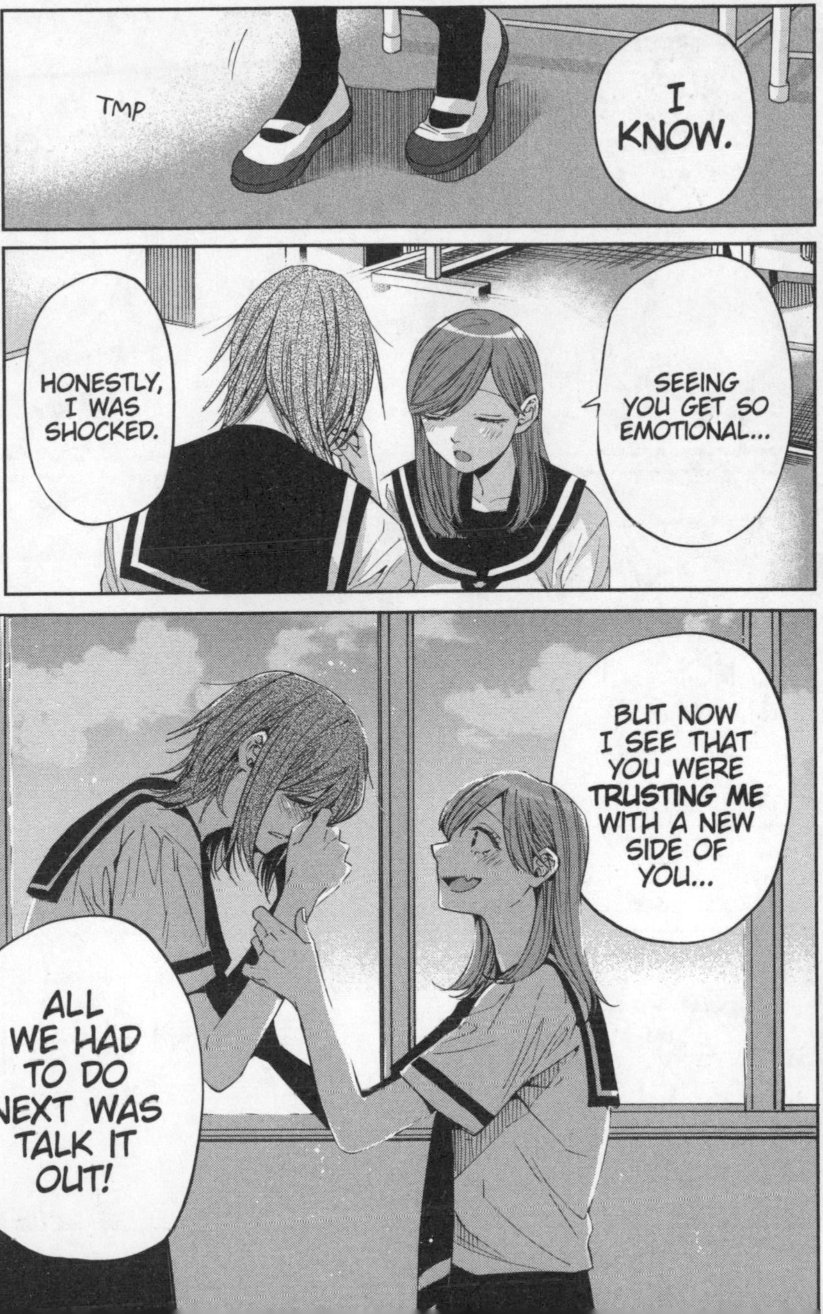
I KNOW.
TMP
SEEING YOU GET SO EMOTIONAL...
HONESTLY, I WAS SHOCKED.
BUT NOW I SEE THAT YOU WERE TRUSTING ME WITH A NEW SIDE OF YOU...
ALL WE HAD TO DO NEXT WAS TALK IT OUT!

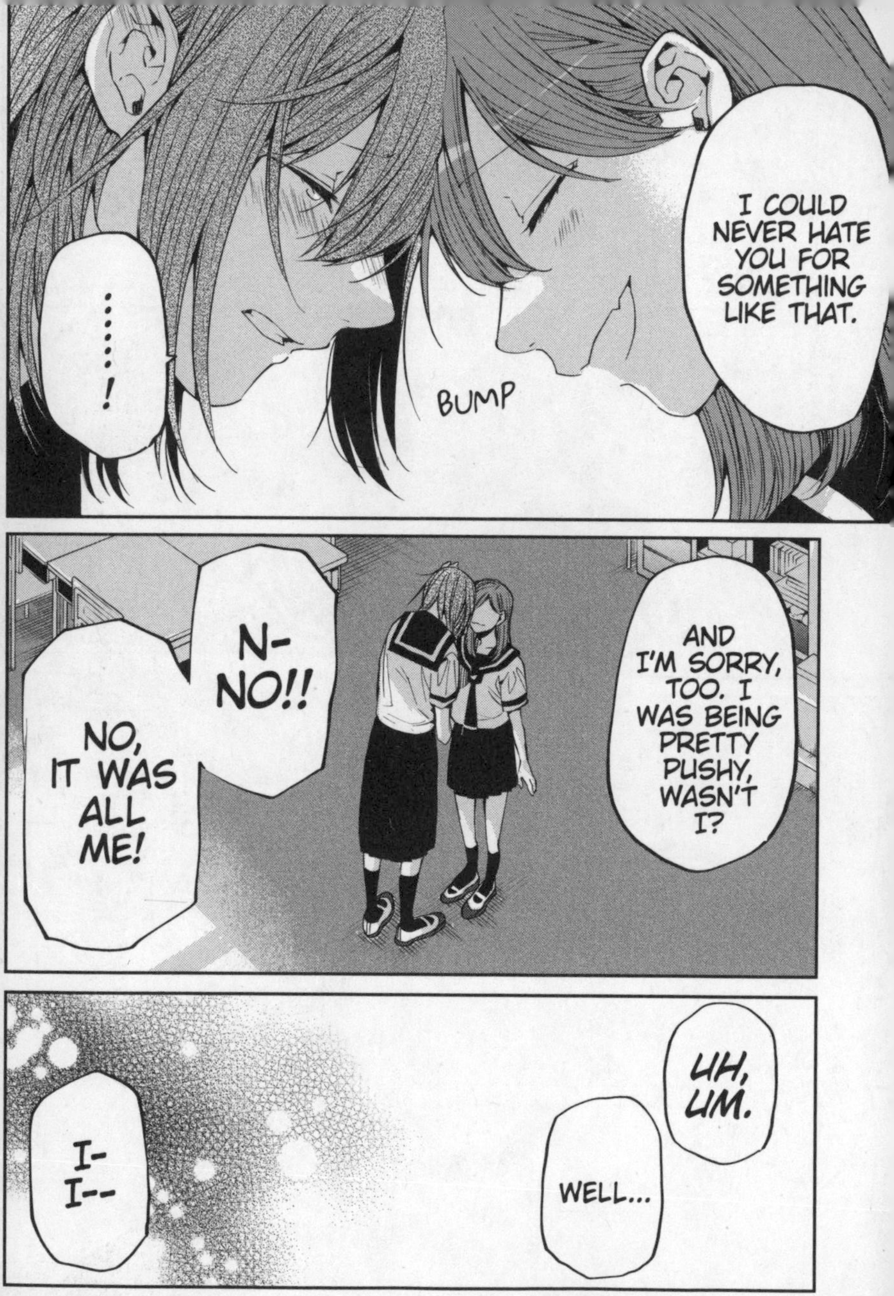
I COULD NEVER HATE YOU FOR SOMETHING LIKE THAT.
BUMP
......!
AND I'M SORRY, TOO. I WAS BEING PRETTY PUSHY, WASN'T I?
N-NO!!
NO, IT WAS ALL ME!
UH, UM.
WELL...
I- I--

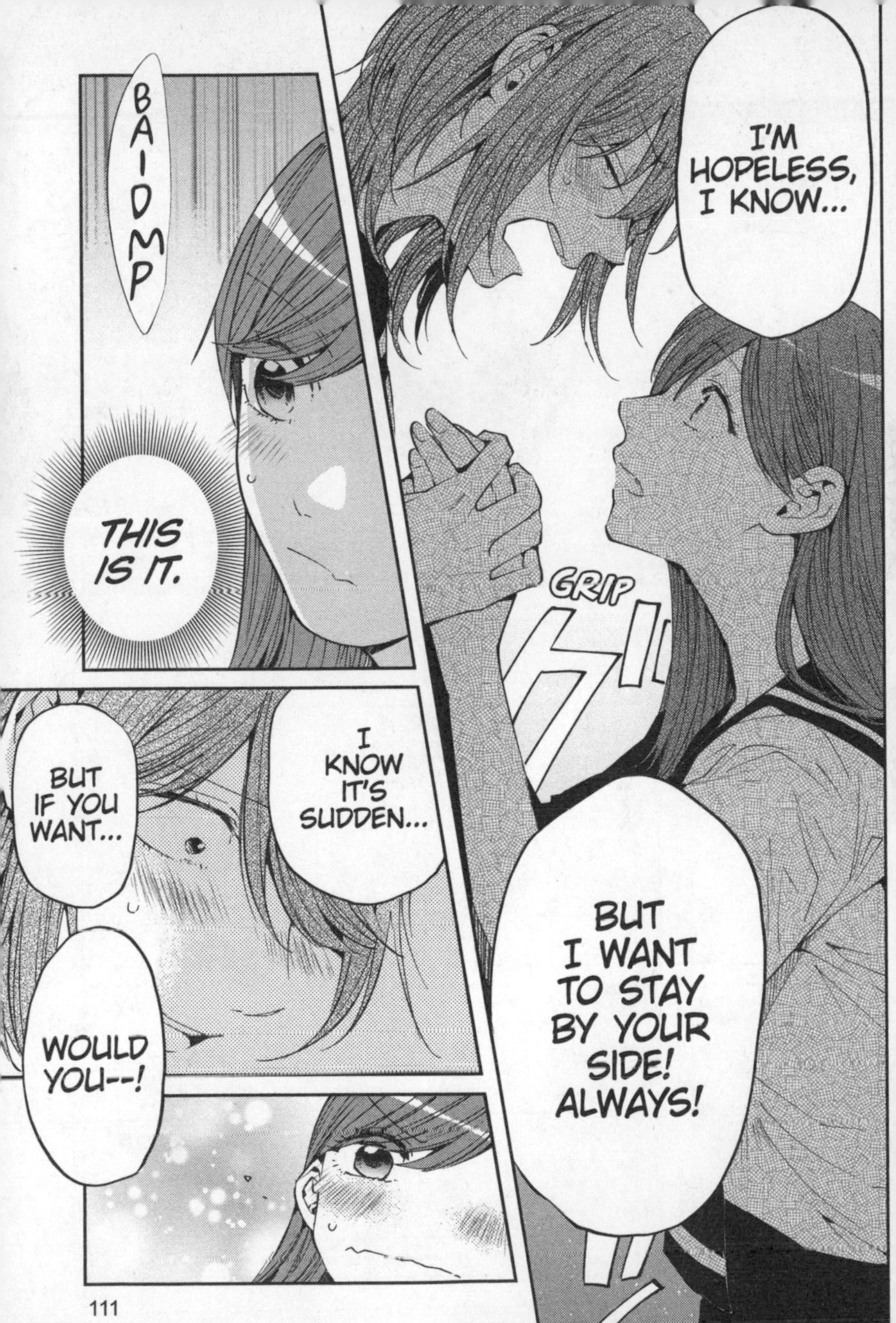
I'M HOPELESS, I KNOW...
GRIP
BUT I WANT TO STAY BY YOUR SIDE! ALWAYS!
BAIDMP
THIS IS IT.
I KNOW IT'S SUDDEN...
BUT IF YOU WANT...
WOULD YOU--!

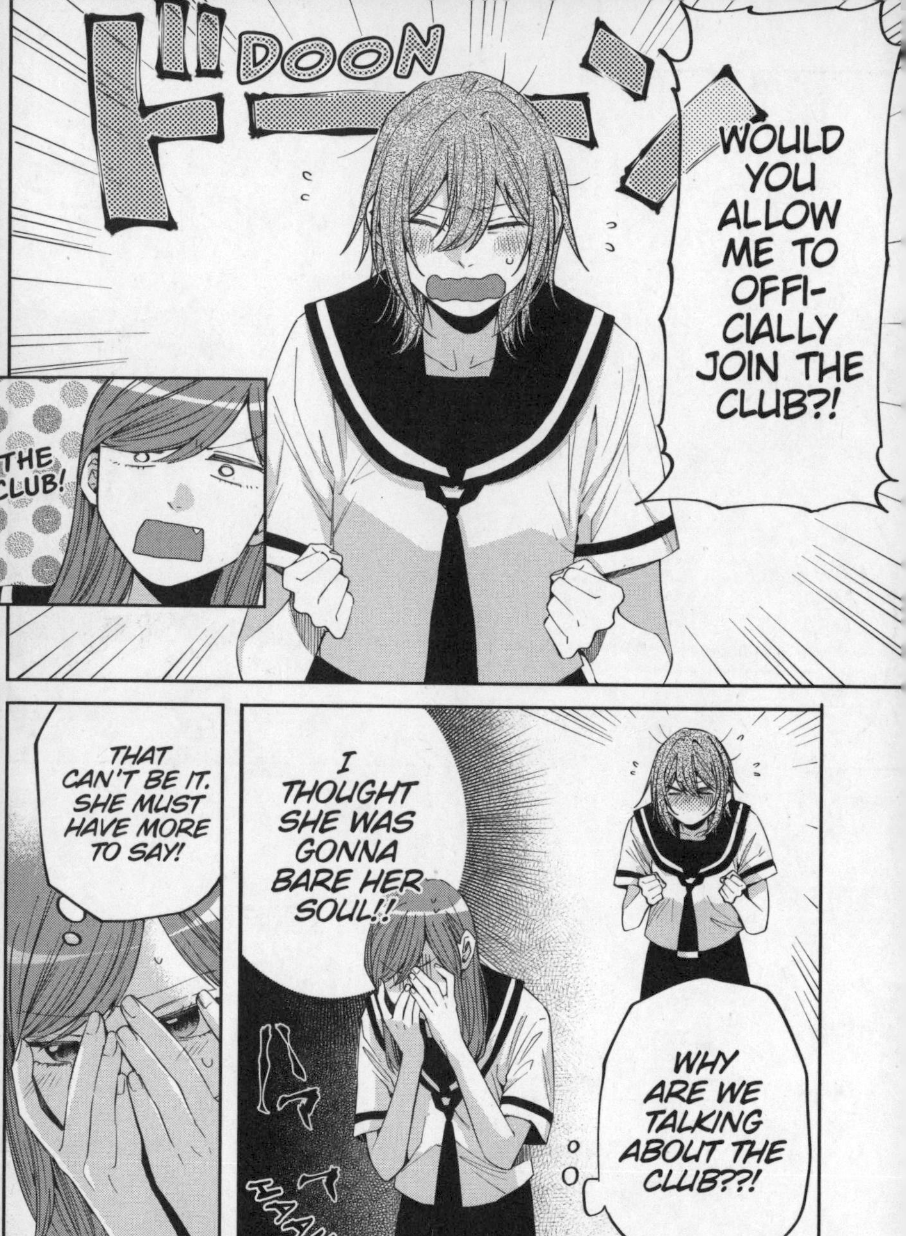
DOOON
WOULD YOU ALLOW ME TO OFFICIALLY JOIN THE CLUB?!
THE CLUB!
I THOUGHT SHE WAS GONNA BARE HER SOUL!!
WHY ARE WE TALKING ABOUT THE CLUB??!
HAAAH...
THAT CAN'T BE IT. SHE MUST HAVE MORE TO SAY!

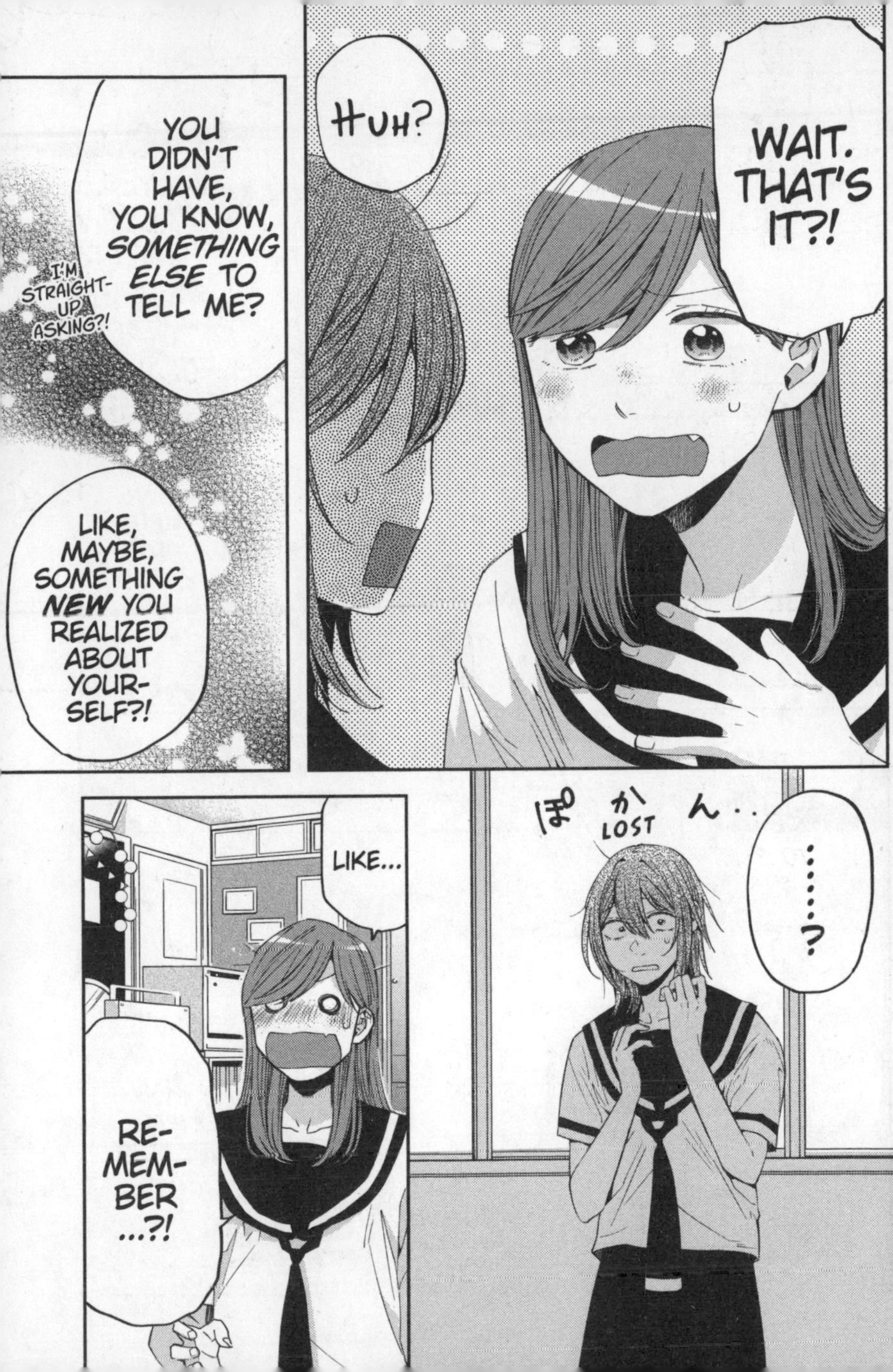
WAIT. THAT'S IT?!
HUH?
YOU DIDN'T HAVE, YOU KNOW, SOMETHING ELSE TO TELL ME?
I'M STRAIGHT-UP ASKING?!
LIKE, MAYBE, SOMETHING NEW YOU REALIZED ABOUT YOUR-SELF?!
ぽかん..
LOST
.....?
LIKE...
RE-MEM-BER...?!

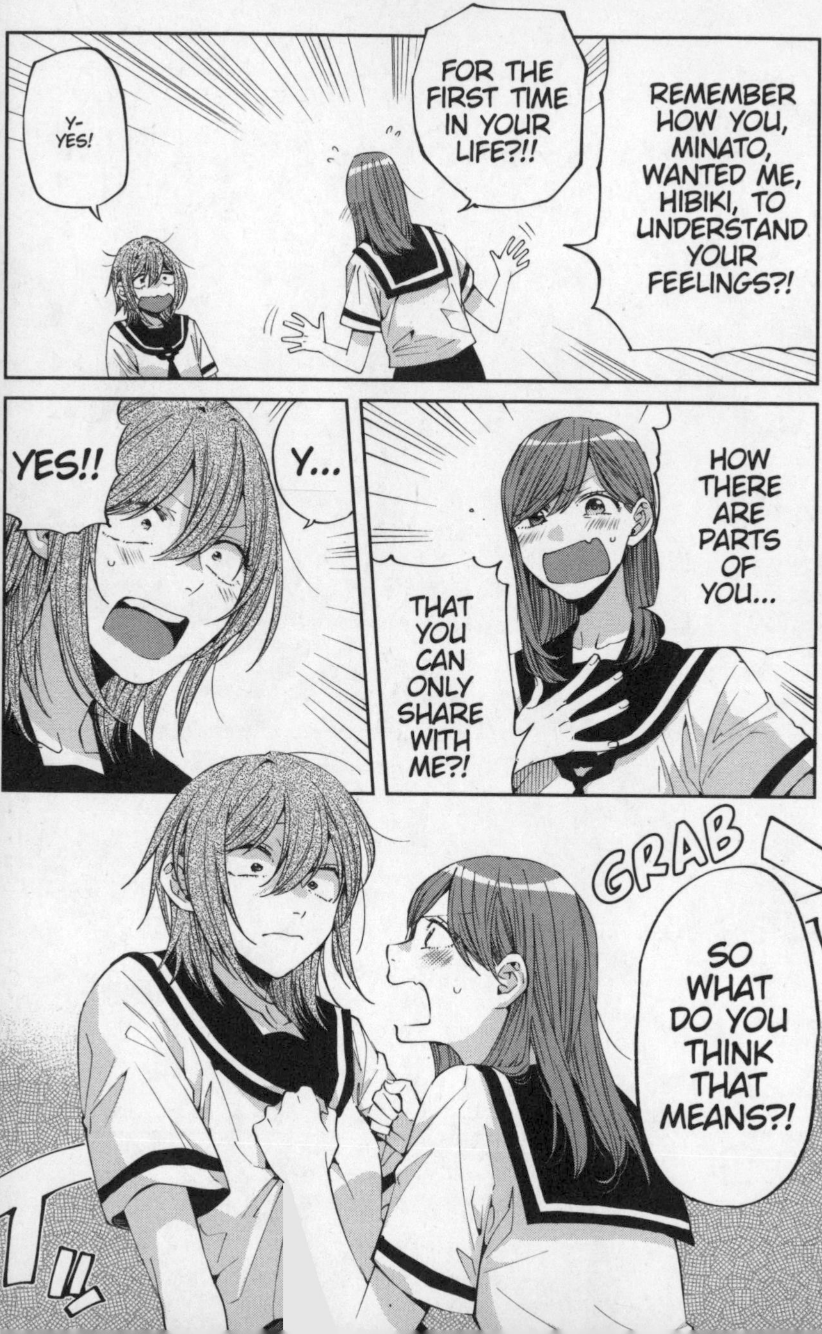
REMEMBER HOW YOU, MINATO, WANTED ME, HIBIKI, TO UNDERSTAND YOUR FEELINGS?!
FOR THE FIRST TIME IN YOUR LIFE?!!
Y- YES!
HOW THERE ARE PARTS OF YOU...
THAT YOU CAN ONLY SHARE WITH ME?!
Y...
YES!!
GRAB
SO WHAT DO YOU THINK THAT MEANS?!

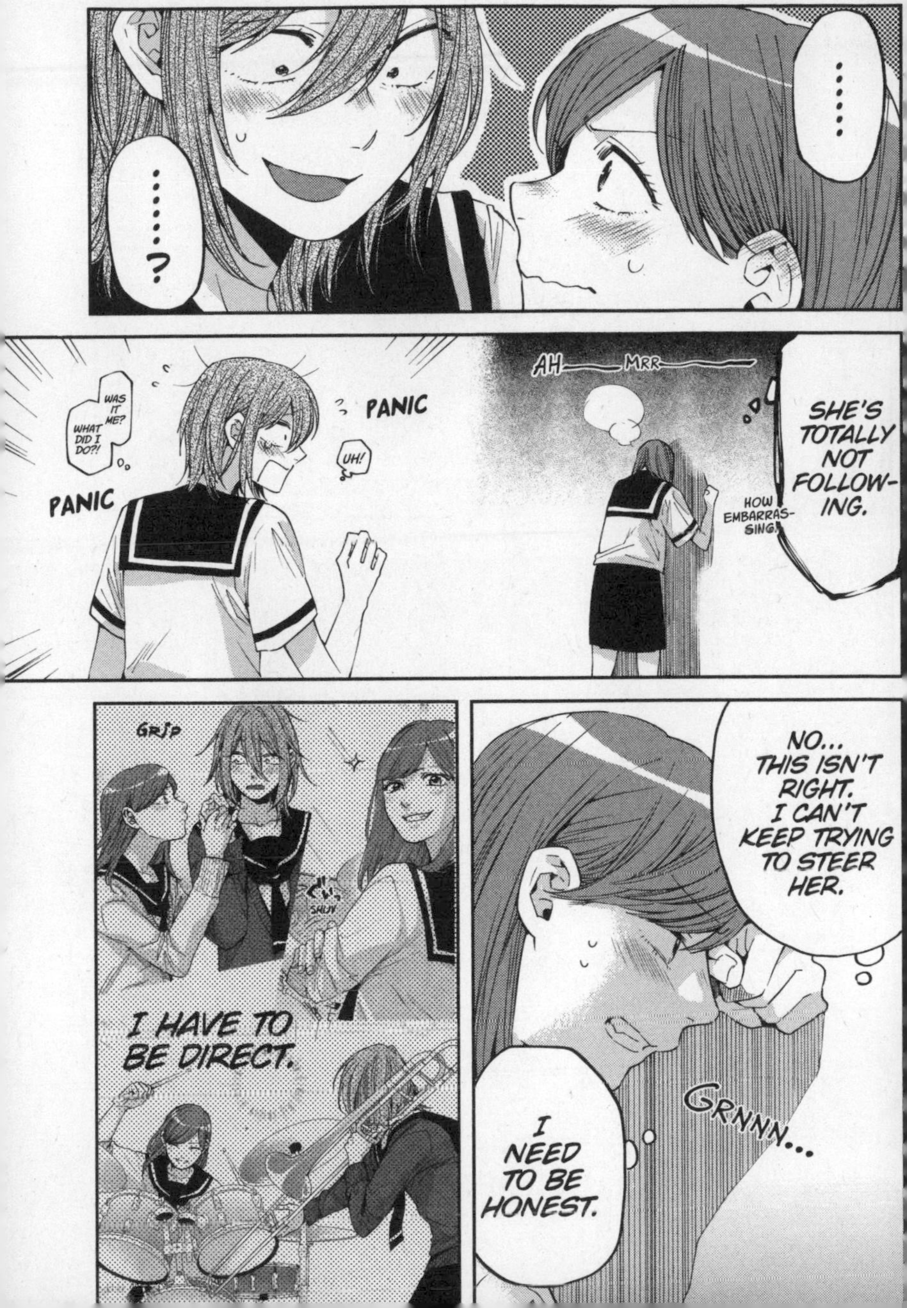
......
......?
SHE'S TOTALLY NOT FOLLOWING.
HOW EMBARRASSING!
AH—— MRR——
PANIC
UH!
WAS IT ME? WHAT DID I DO?!
PANIC
NO... THIS ISN'T RIGHT. I CAN'T KEEP TRYING TO STEER HER.
GRNNN...
I NEED TO BE HONEST.
GRIP
I HAVE TO BE DIRECT.

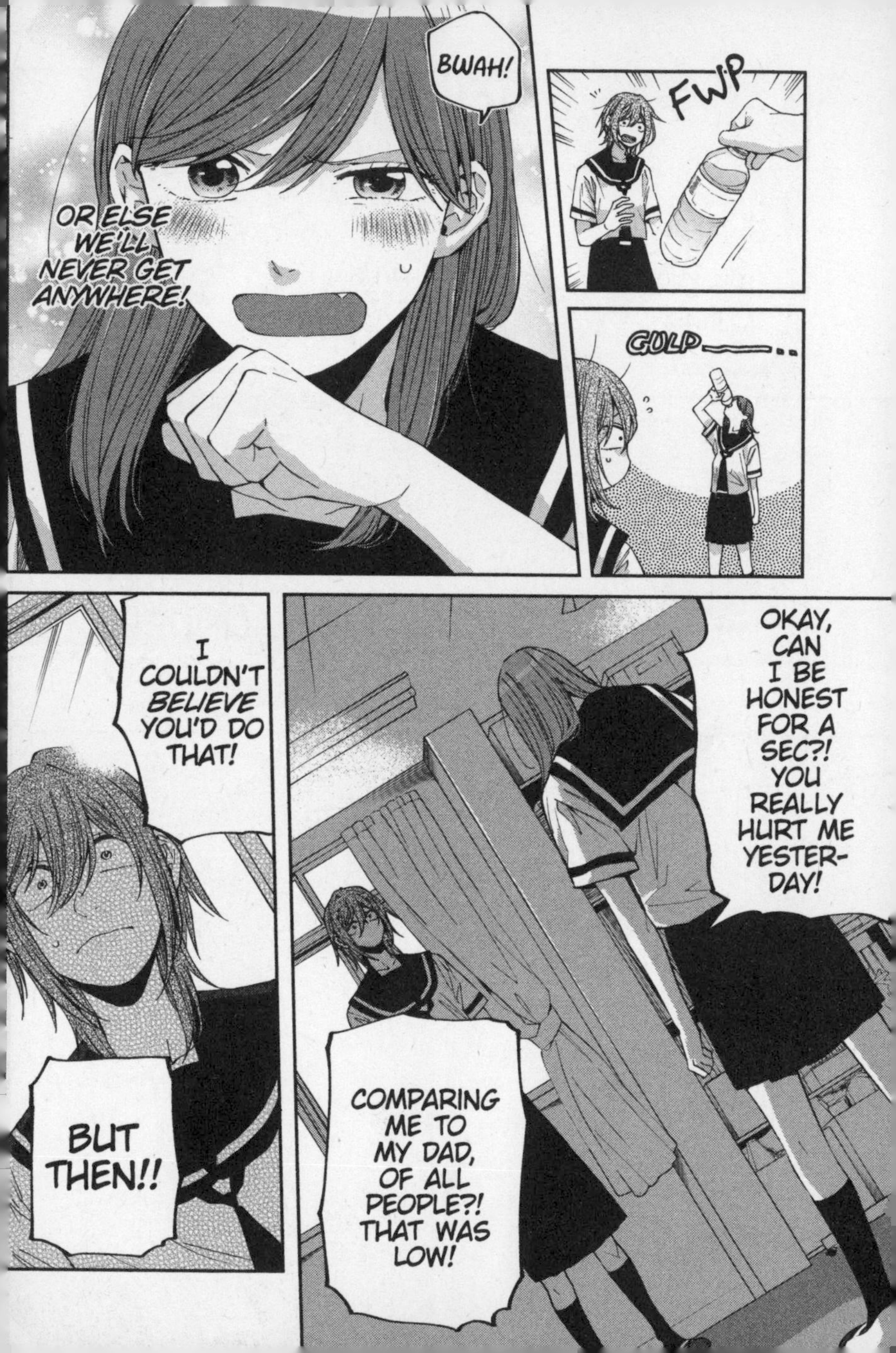
FWP
GULP...
BWAH!
OR ELSE WE'LL NEVER GET ANYWHERE!
OKAY, CAN I BE HONEST FOR A SEC?! YOU REALLY HURT ME YESTER-DAY!
COMPARING ME TO MY DAD, OF ALL PEOPLE?! THAT WAS LOW!
I COULDN'T BELIEVE YOU'D DO THAT!
BUT THEN!!

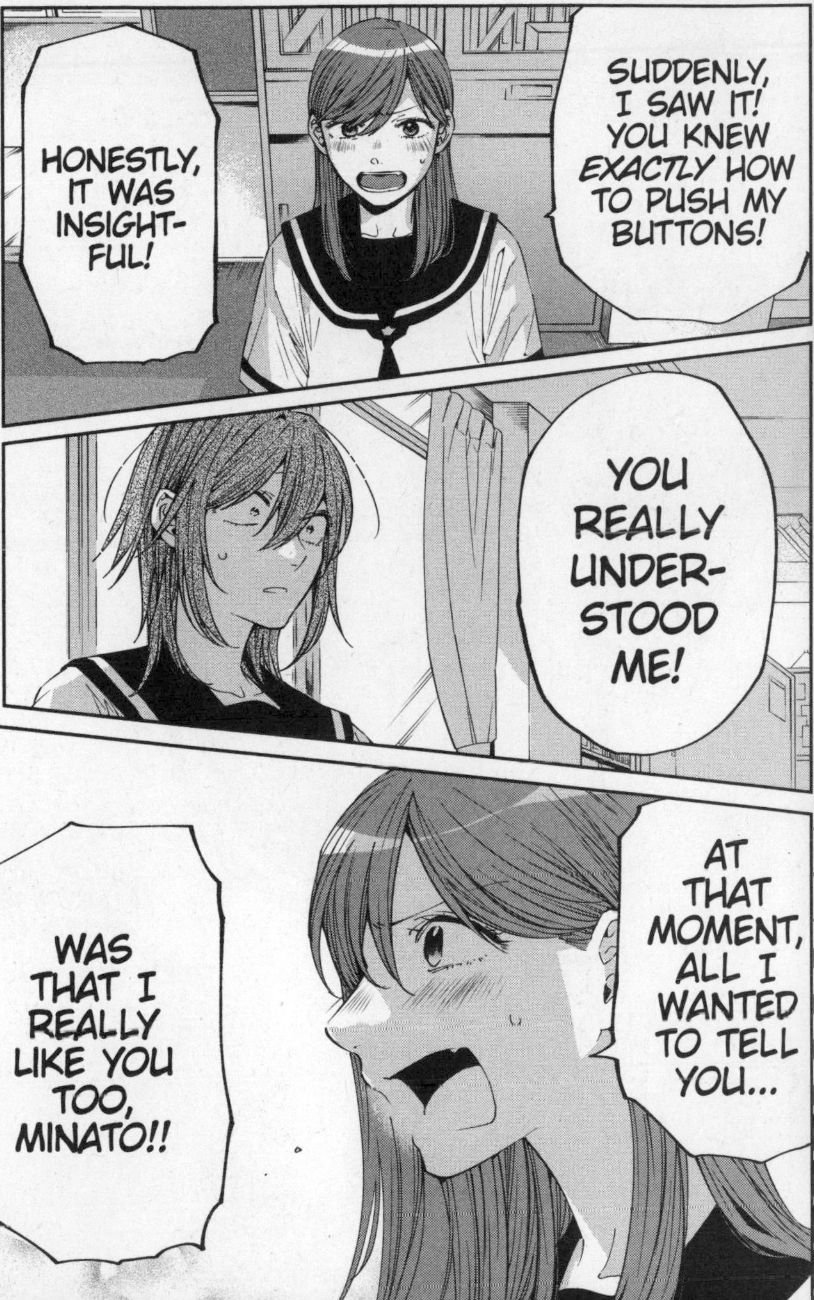
SUDDENLY, I SAW IT! YOU KNEW *EXACTLY* HOW TO PUSH MY BUTTONS!
HONESTLY, IT WAS INSIGHT-FUL!
YOU REALLY UNDER-STOOD ME!
AT THAT MOMENT, ALL I WANTED TO TELL YOU...
WAS THAT I REALLY LIKE YOU TOO, MINATO!!

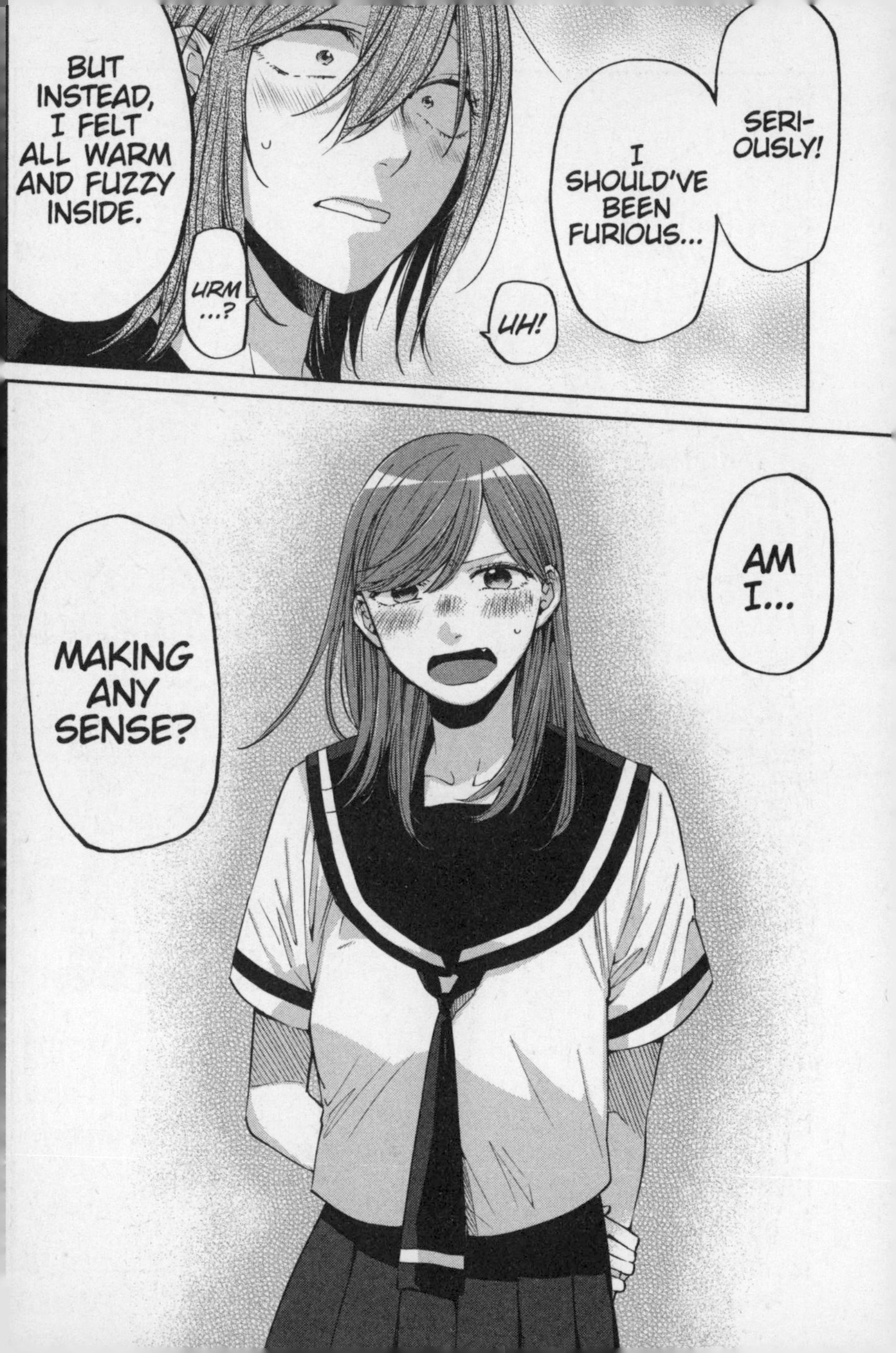
SERI-OUSLY!
I SHOULD'VE BEEN FURIOUS...
UH!
URM ...?
BUT INSTEAD, I FELT ALL WARM AND FUZZY INSIDE.
AM I...
MAKING ANY SENSE?

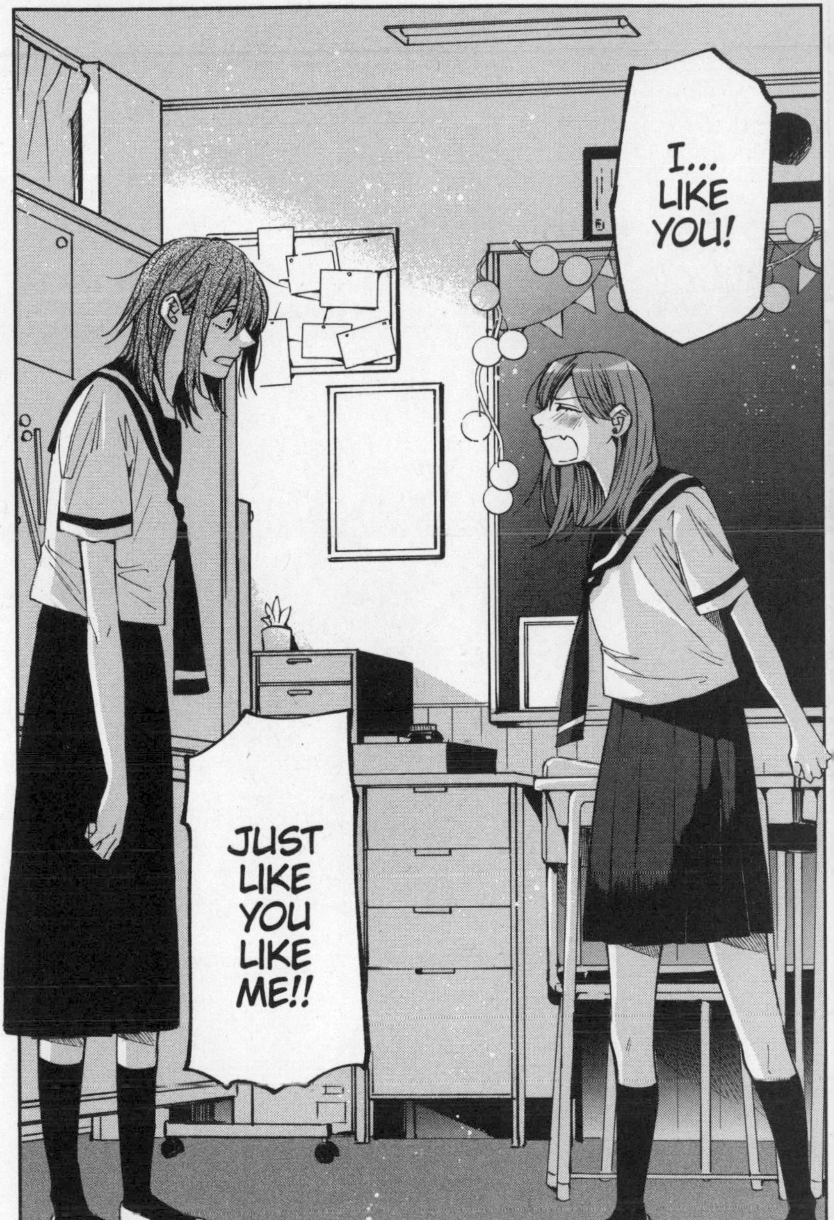
I... LIKE YOU!
JUST LIKE YOU LIKE ME!!

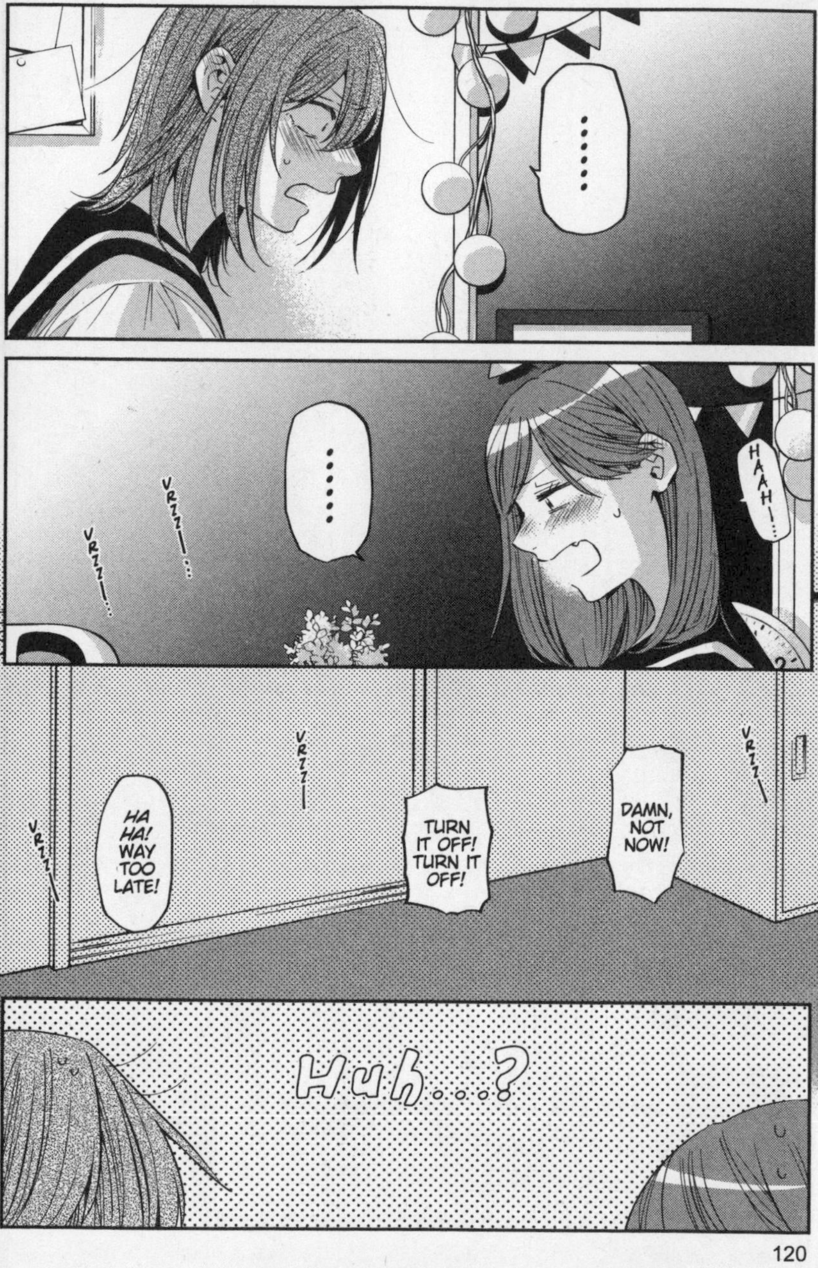
......
HAAH!...
......
VRZZZ—...
VRZZZ—...
VRZZZ—
DAMN, NOT NOW!
TURN IT OFF! TURN IT OFF!
VRZZZ—
HA HA! WAY TOO LATE!
VRZZZ—
Huh...?

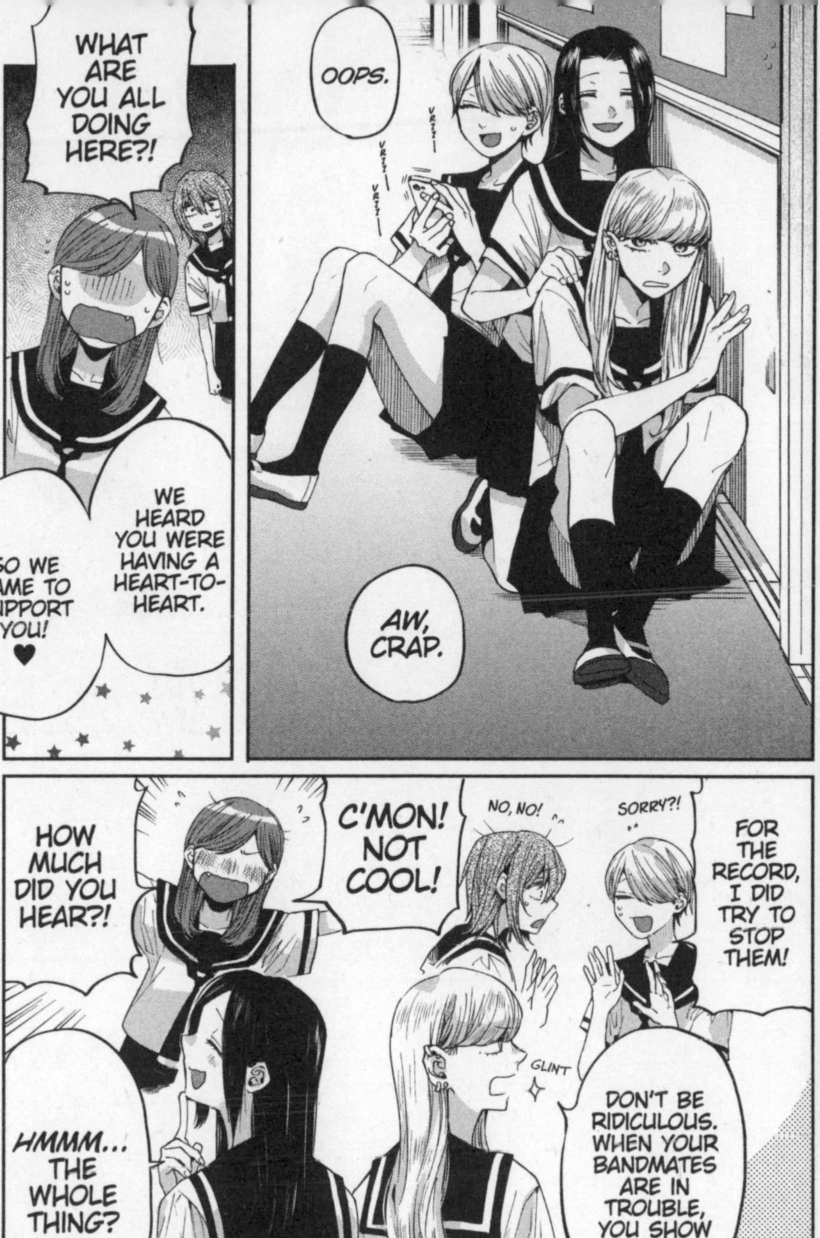
OOPS.
VRZZ
VRZZ
VRZZ
AW, CRAP.
WHAT ARE YOU ALL DOING HERE?!
WE HEARD YOU WERE HAVING A HEART-TO-HEART.
SO WE CAME TO SUPPORT YOU! ♥
FOR THE RECORD, I DID TRY TO STOP THEM!
SORRY?!
NO, NO!
C'MON! NOT COOL!
HOW MUCH DID YOU HEAR?!
DON'T BE RIDICULOUS. WHEN YOUR BANDMATES ARE IN TROUBLE, YOU SHOW UP!
GLINT
HMMM... THE WHOLE THING?

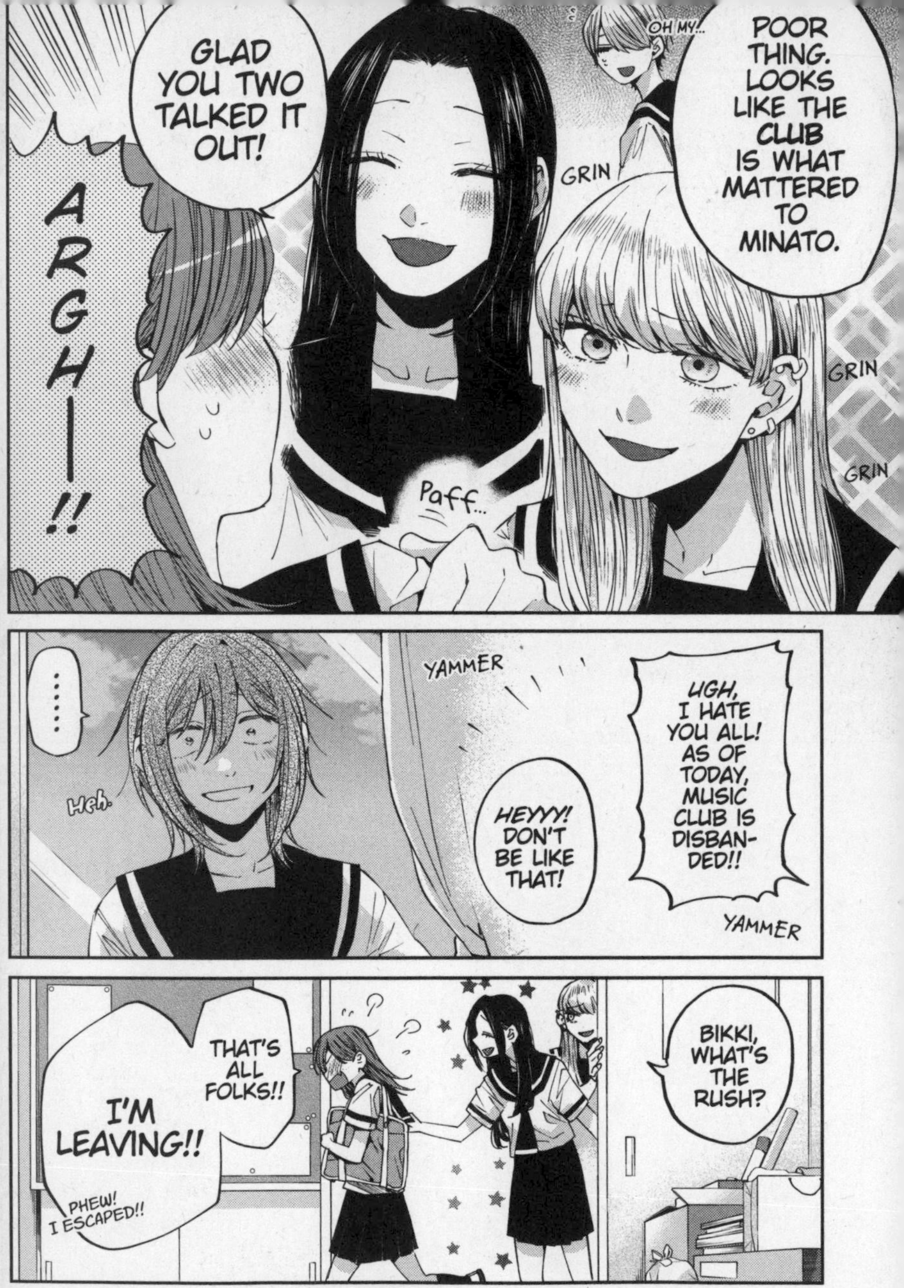
OH MY...
POOR THING. LOOKS LIKE THE CLUB IS WHAT MATTERED TO MINATO.
GRIN
GRIN
GRIN
GLAD YOU TWO TALKED IT OUT!
Paff...
ARGH—!!
UGH, I HATE YOU ALL! AS OF TODAY, MUSIC CLUB IS DISBANDED!!
YAMMER
YAMMER
HEYYY! DON'T BE LIKE THAT!
......
Heh.
BIKKI, WHAT'S THE RUSH?
THAT'S ALL FOLKS!!
I'M LEAVING!!
PHEW! I ESCAPED!!

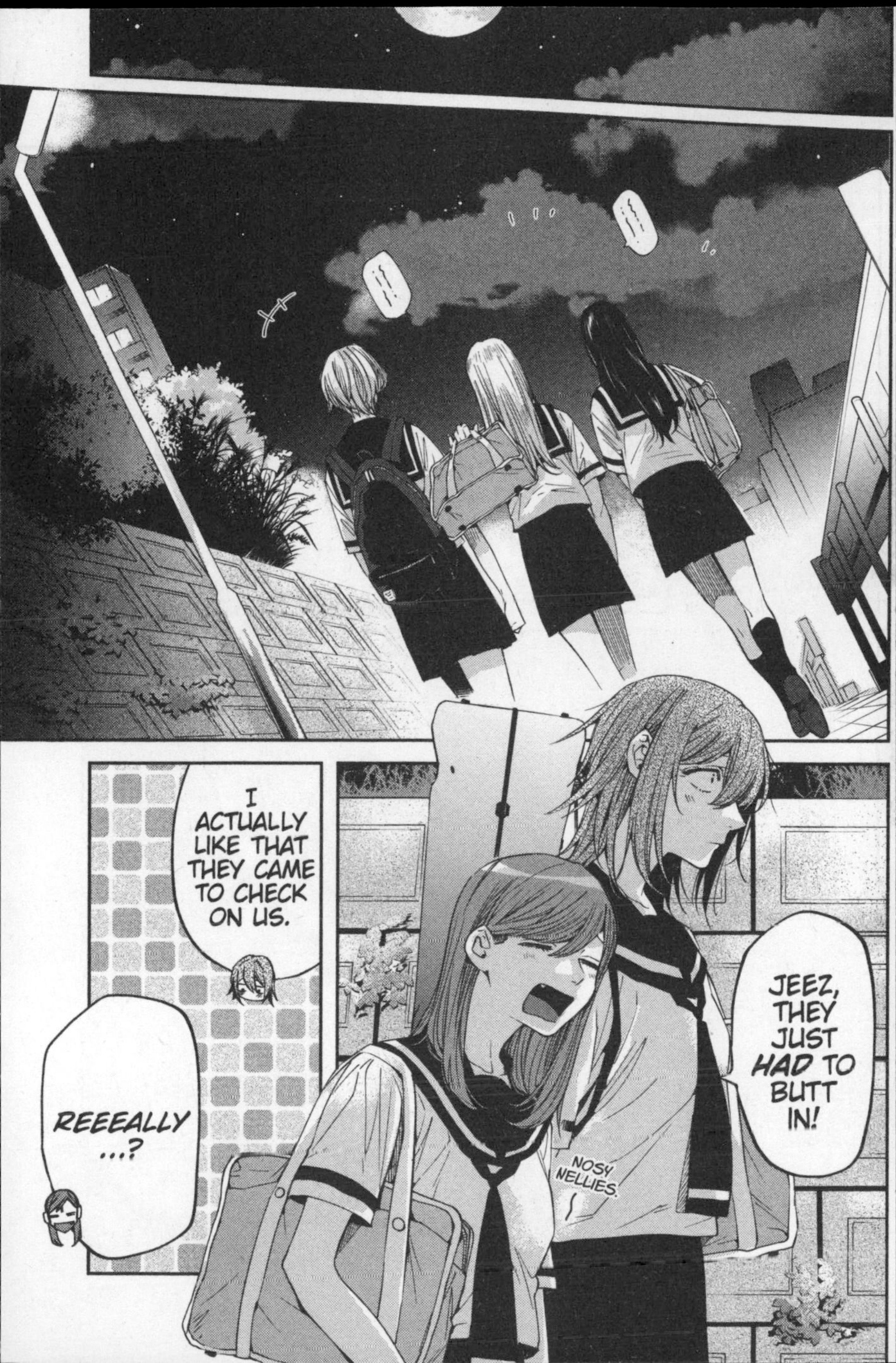
JEEZ, THEY JUST *HAD* TO BUTT IN!
NOSY NELLIES.
I ACTUALLY LIKE THAT THEY CAME TO CHECK ON US.
REEEALLY ...?

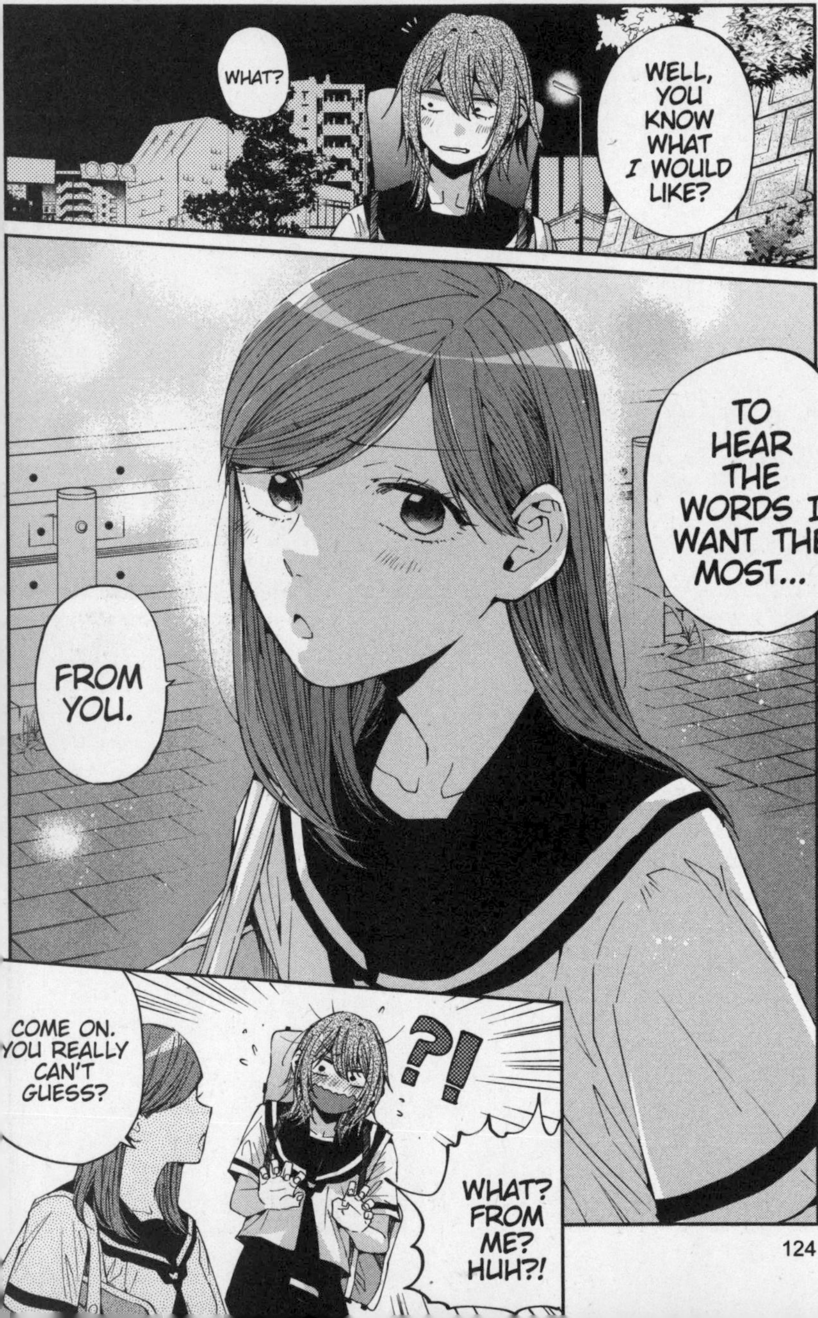
WELL, YOU KNOW WHAT I WOULD LIKE?
WHAT?
TO HEAR THE WORDS I WANT THE MOST...
FROM YOU.
?!
COME ON. YOU REALLY CAN'T GUESS?
WHAT? FROM ME? HUH?!

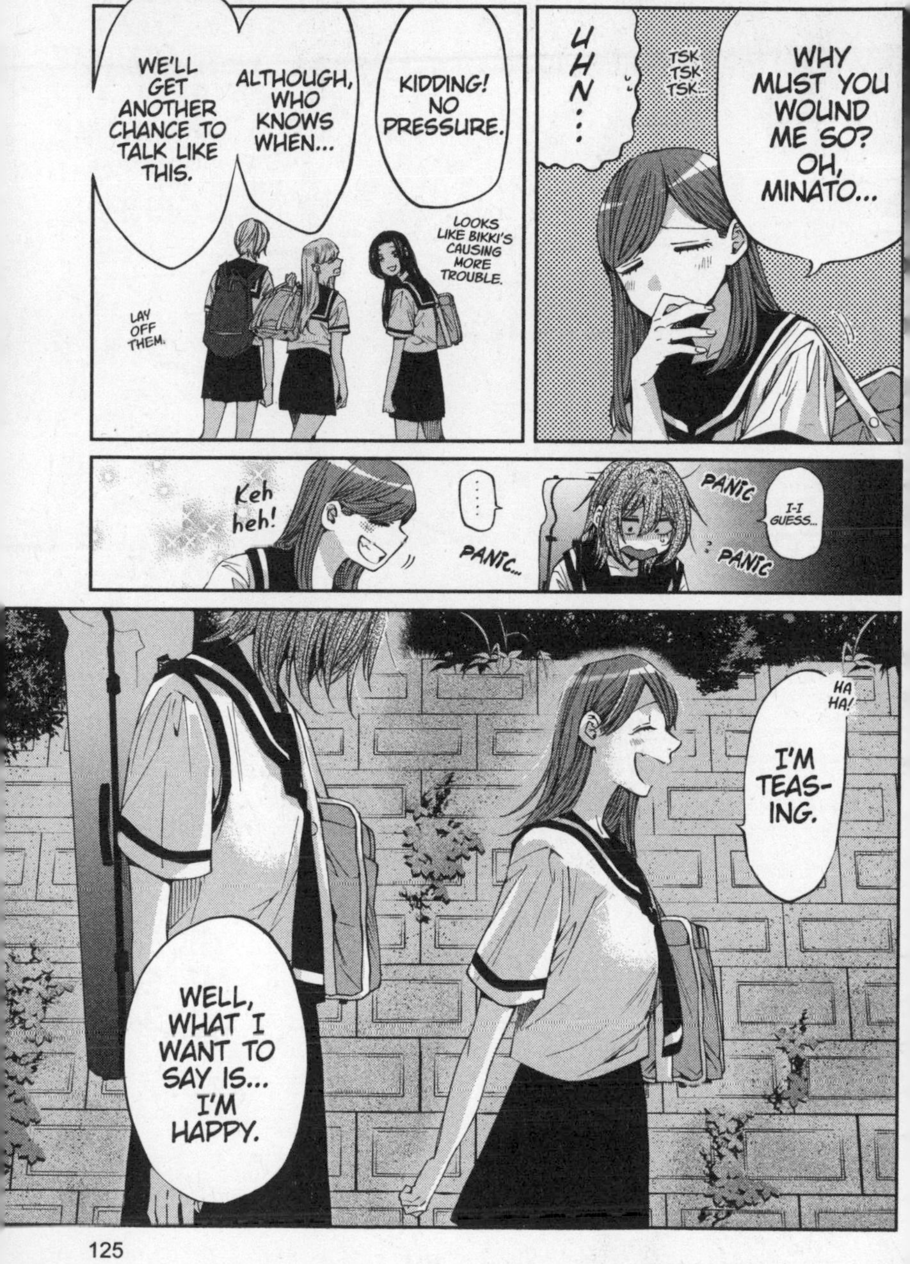
WHY MUST YOU WOUND ME SO? OH, MINATO...
TSK TSK TSK...
UHN...
KIDDING! NO PRESSURE.
ALTHOUGH, WHO KNOWS WHEN...
WE'LL GET ANOTHER CHANCE TO TALK LIKE THIS.
LOOKS LIKE BIKKI'S CAUSING MORE TROUBLE.
LAY OFF THEM.
PANIC
I-I GUESS...
PANIC
......
PANIC...
Keh heh!
HA HA!
I'M TEAS-ING.
WELL, WHAT I WANT TO SAY IS... I'M HAPPY.

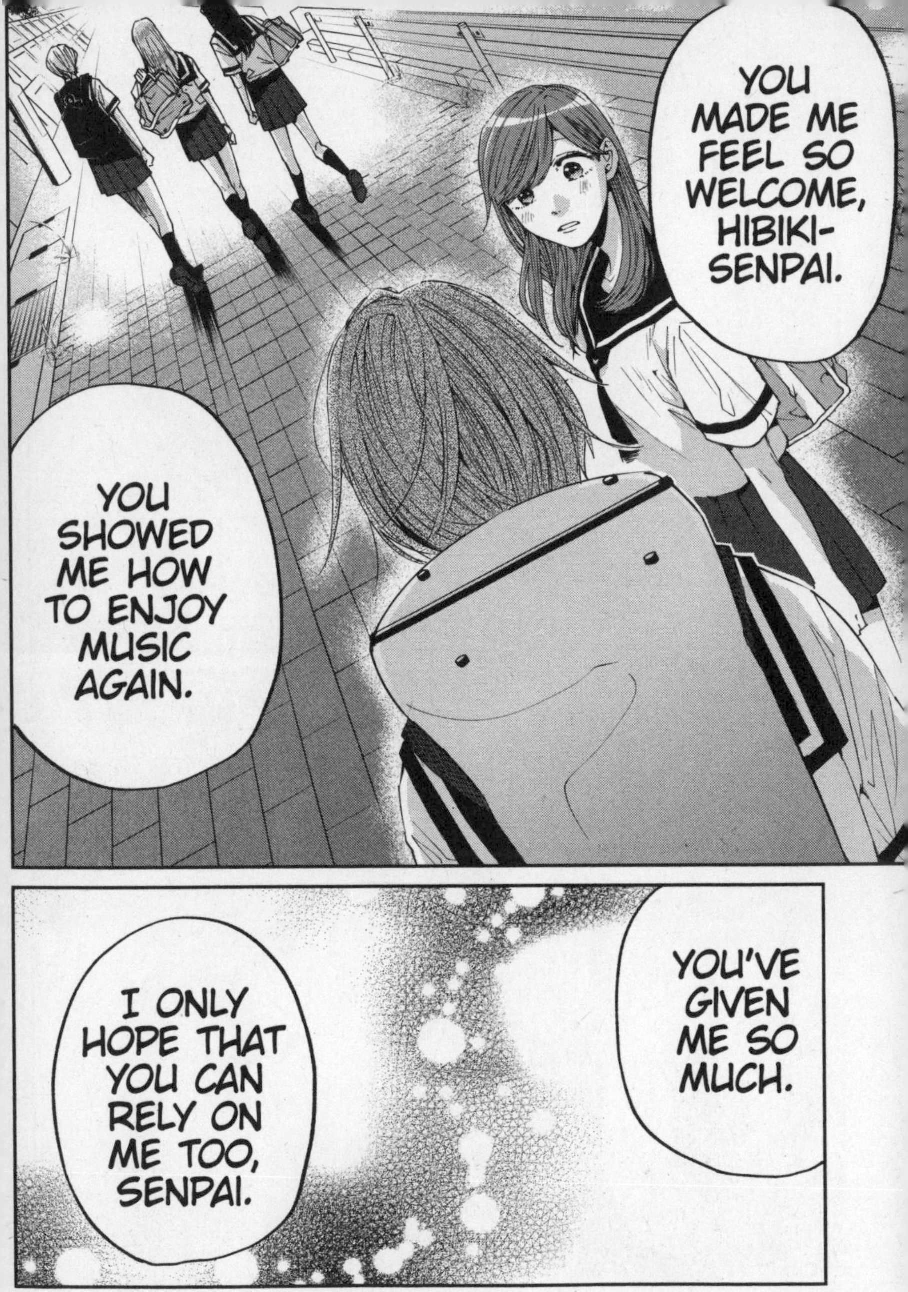
YOU MADE ME FEEL SO WELCOME, HIBIKI-SENPAI.
YOU SHOWED ME HOW TO ENJOY MUSIC AGAIN.
YOU'VE GIVEN ME SO MUCH.
I ONLY HOPE THAT YOU CAN RELY ON ME TOO, SENPAI.

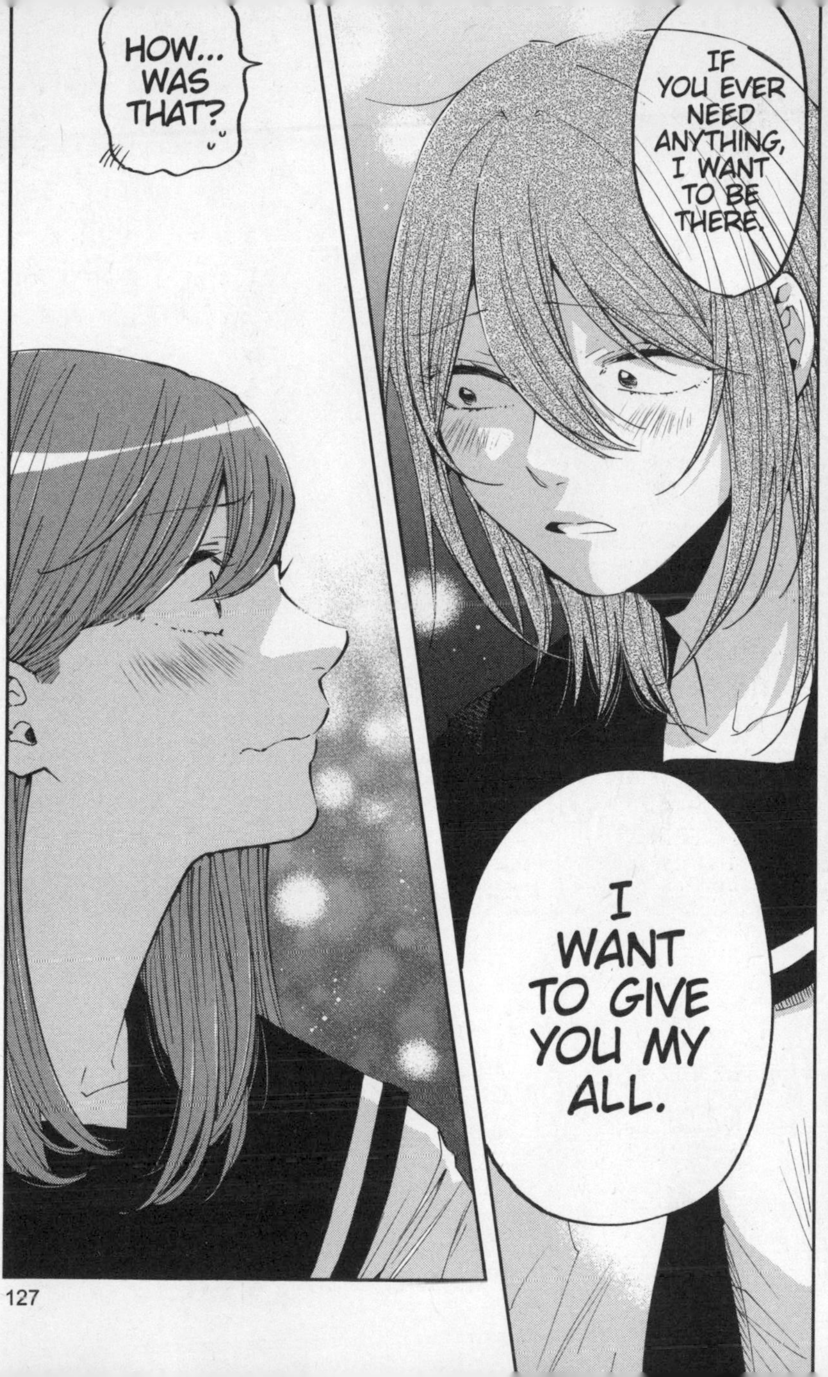
IF YOU EVER NEED ANYTHING, I WANT TO BE THERE.
I WANT TO GIVE YOU MY ALL.
HOW... WAS THAT?

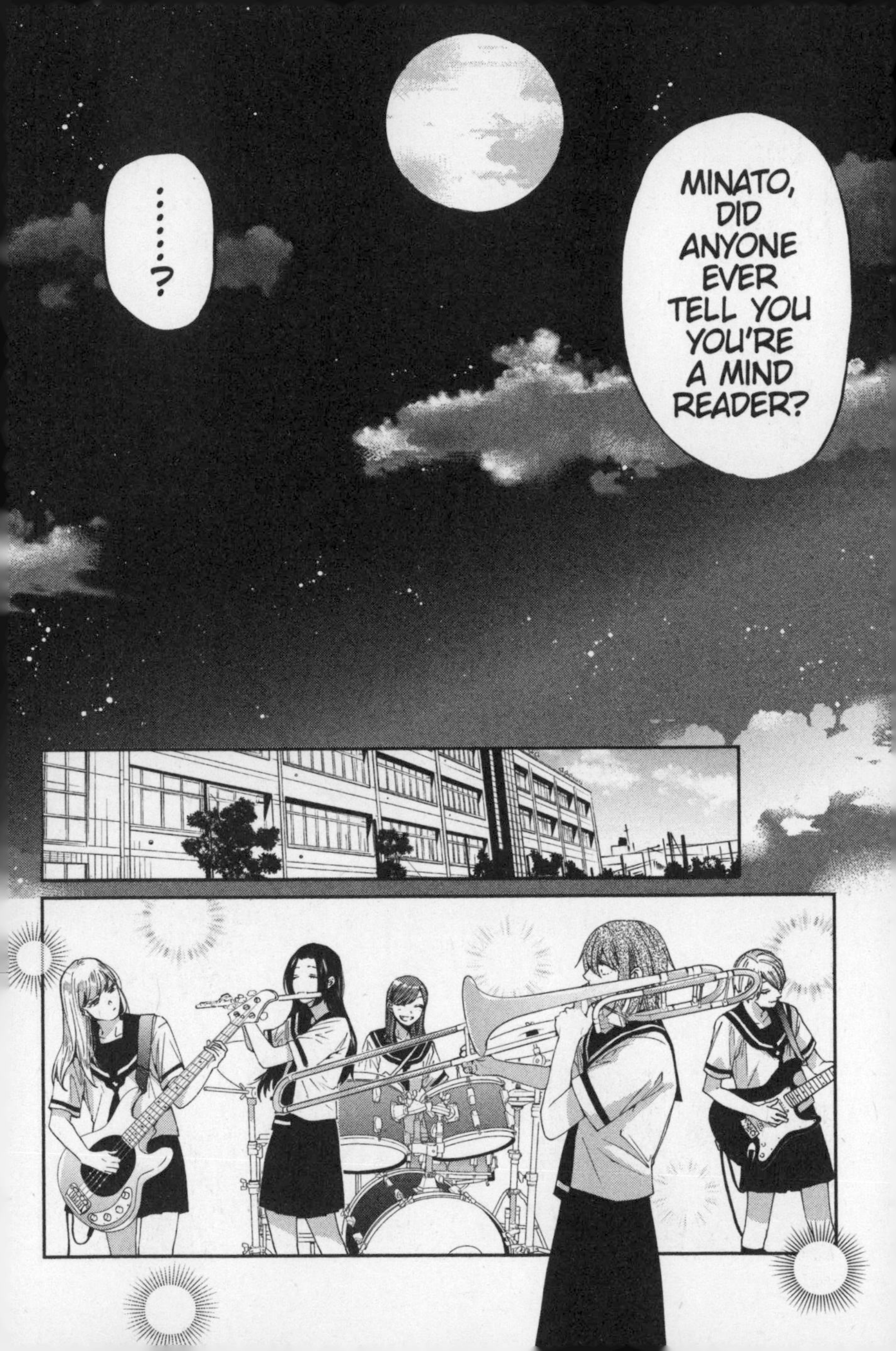
MINATO, DID ANYONE EVER TELL YOU YOU'RE A MIND READER?
.....?

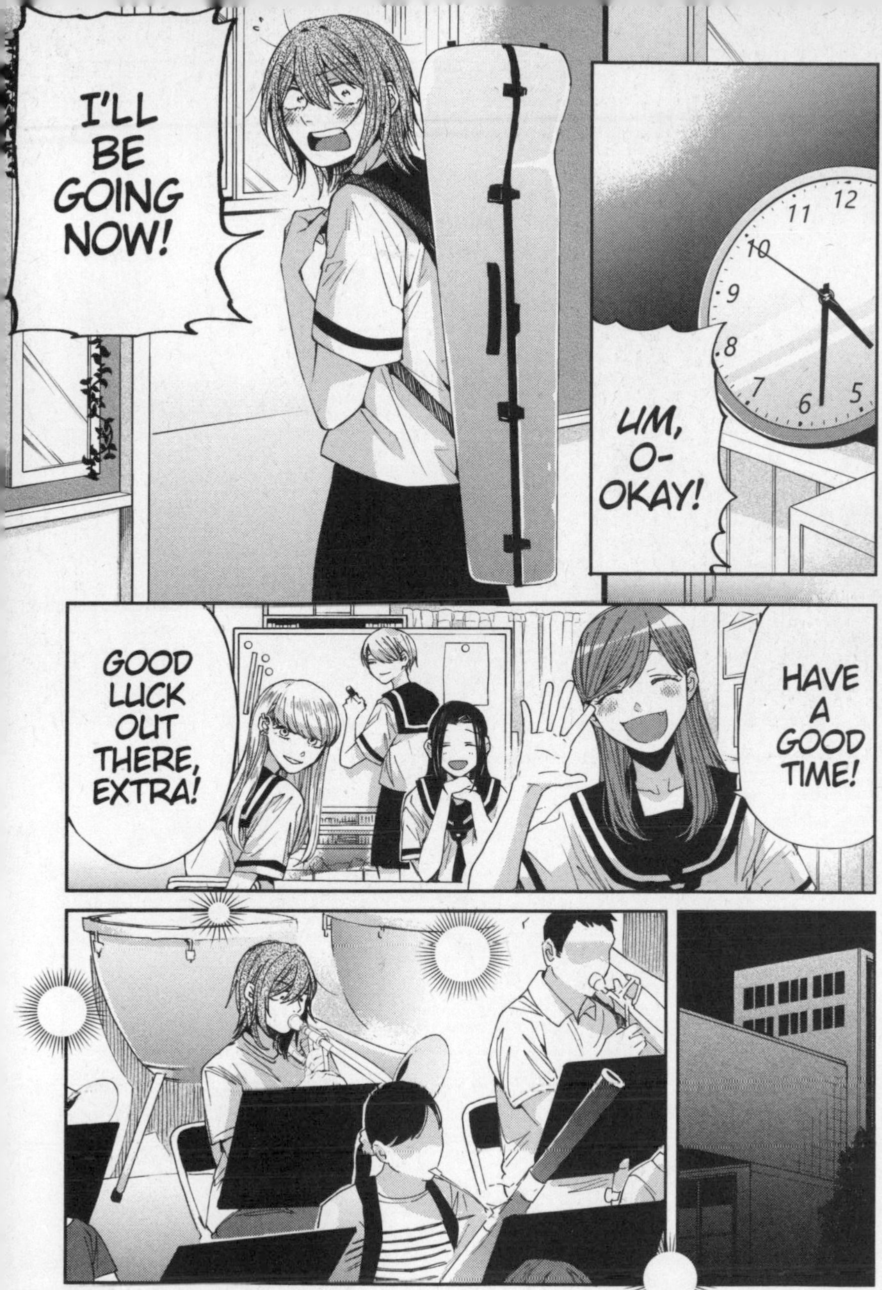
UM, O-OKAY!
I'LL BE GOING NOW!
HAVE A GOOD TIME!
GOOD LUCK OUT THERE, EXTRA!

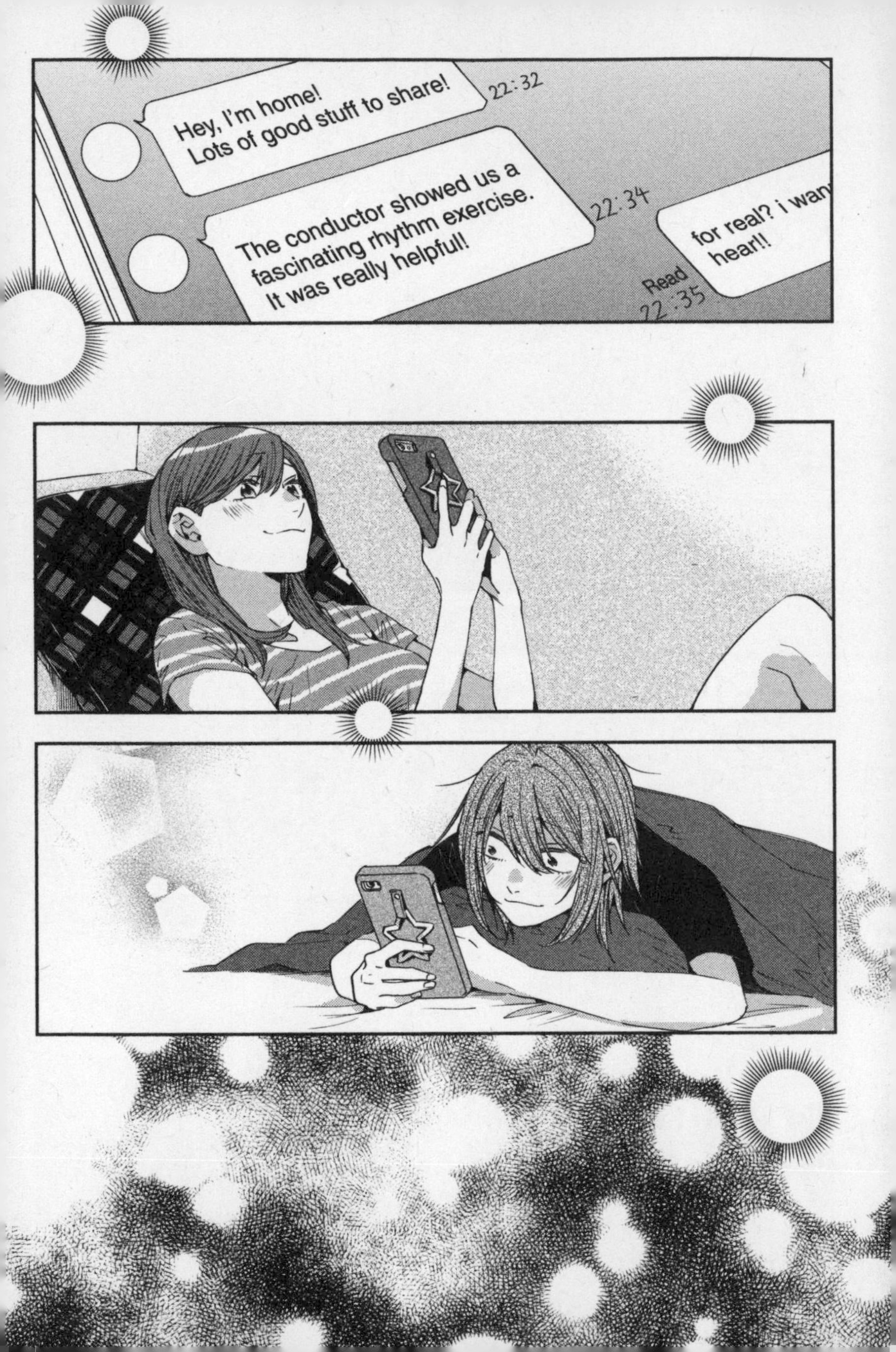
Hey, I'm home!
Lots of good stuff to share!
22:32
The conductor showed us a fascinating rhythm exercise. It was really helpful!
22:34
for real? i wan
hear!!
Read
22:35

HELLO,
MELAN
CHOLIC!

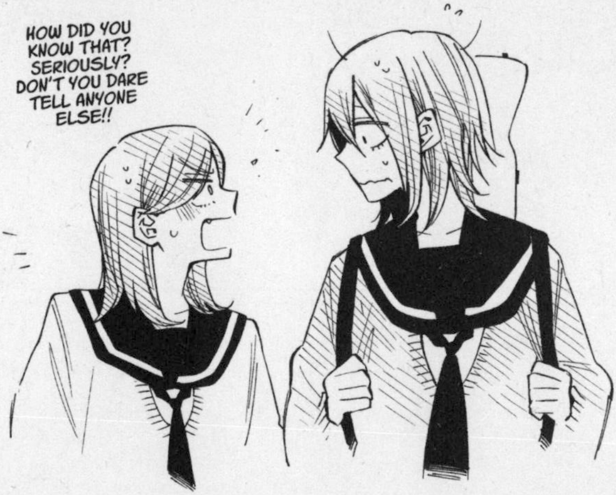
HOW DID YOU KNOW THAT? SERIOUSLY? DON'T YOU DARE TELL ANYONE ELSE!!

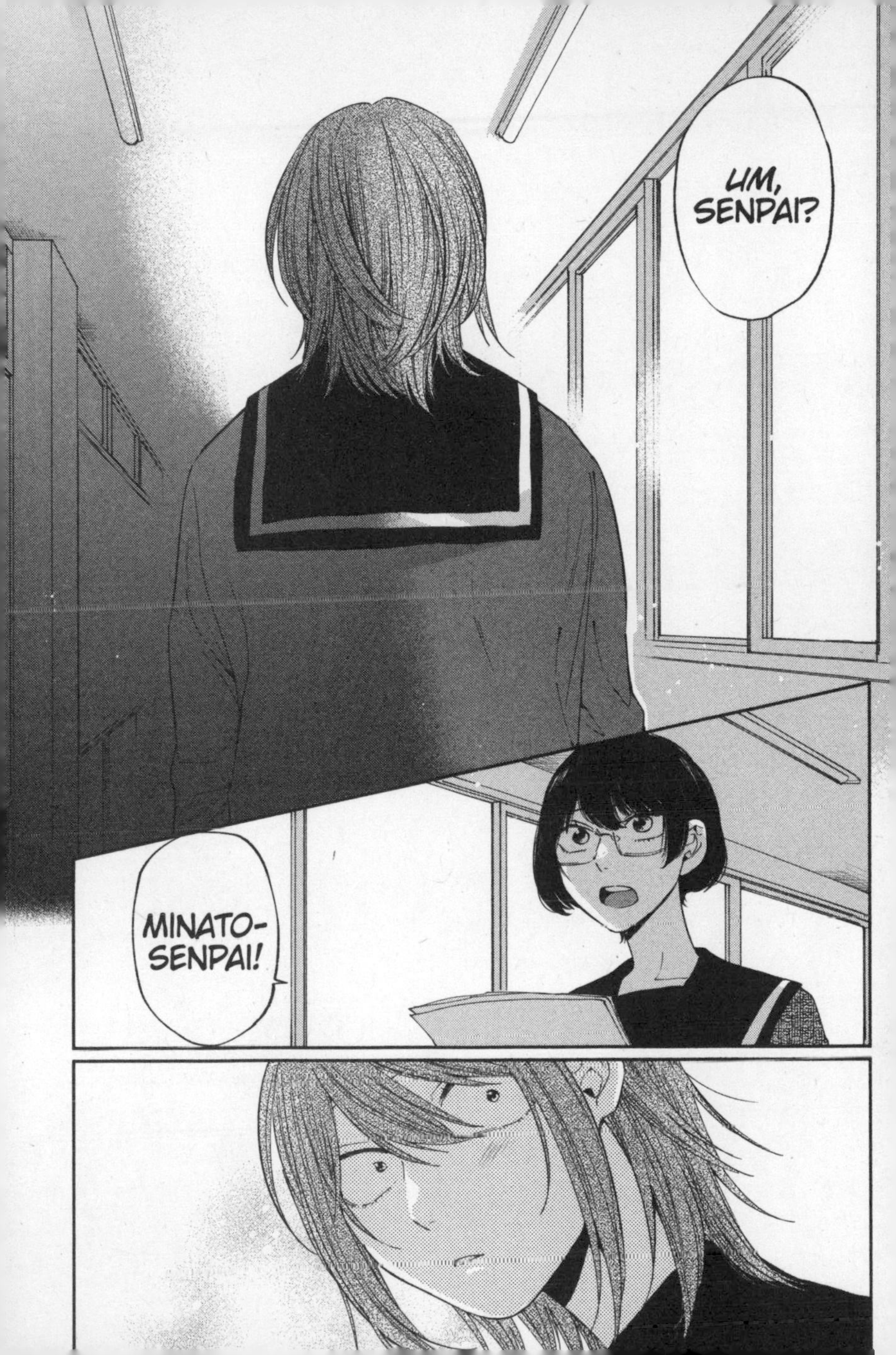
UM, SENPAI?
MINATO-SENPAI!

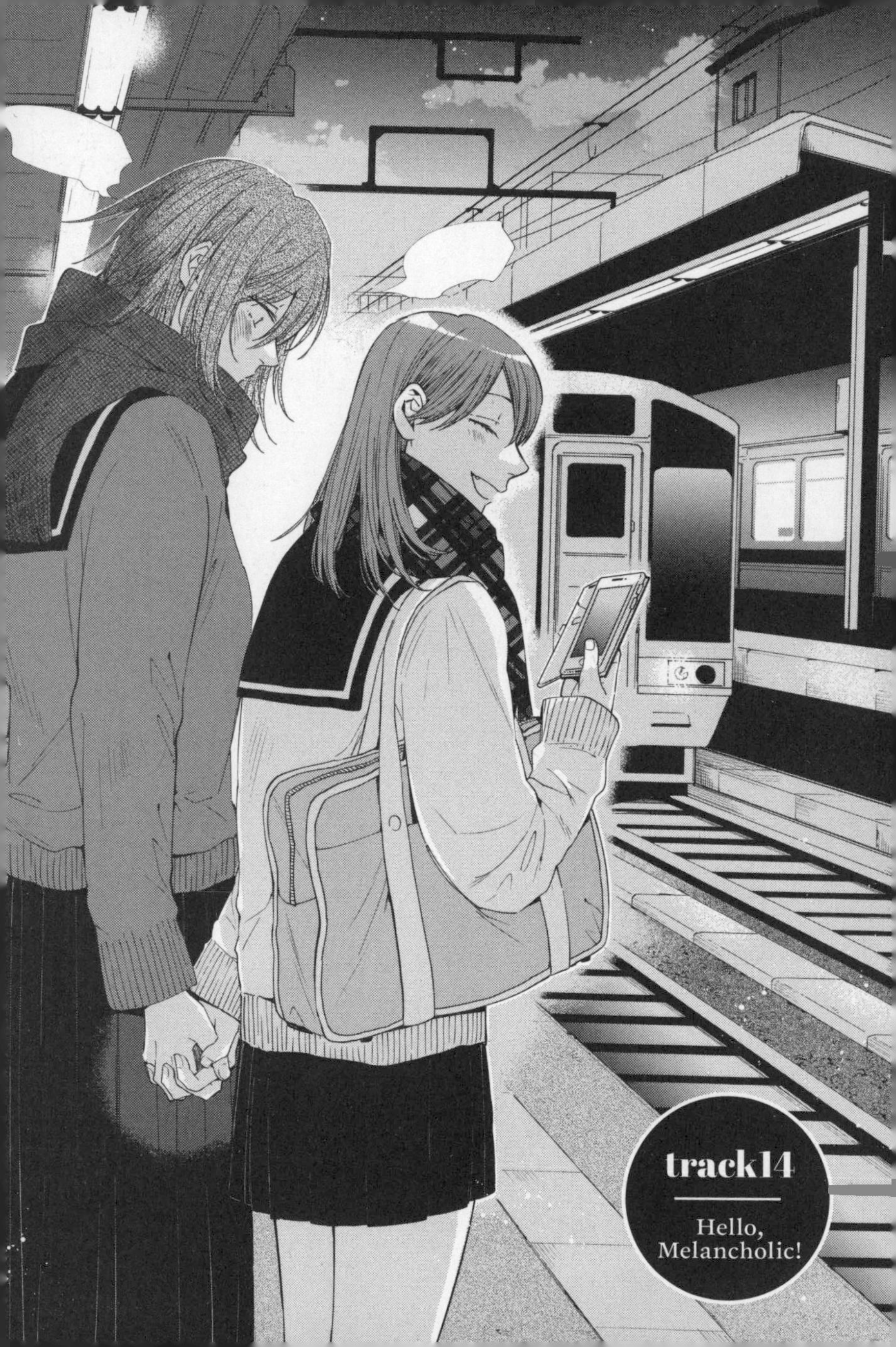
track14
Hello, Melancholic!

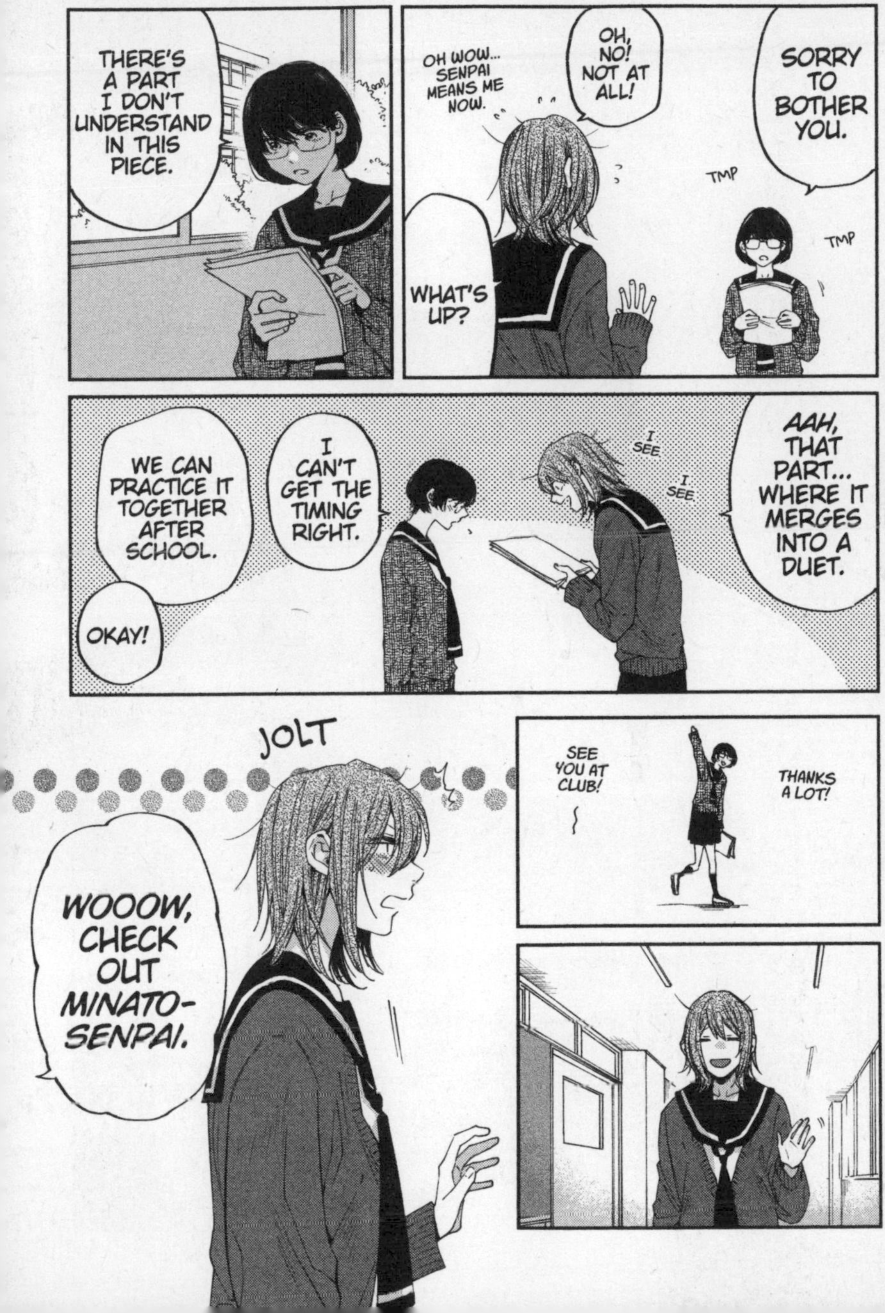
SORRY TO BOTHER YOU.
TMP
TMP
OH, NO! NOT AT ALL!
OH WOW... SENPAI MEANS ME NOW.
WHAT'S UP?
THERE'S A PART I DON'T UNDERSTAND IN THIS PIECE.
AAH, THAT PART... WHERE IT MERGES INTO A DUET.
I SEE.
I SEE.
I CAN'T GET THE TIMING RIGHT.
WE CAN PRACTICE IT TOGETHER AFTER SCHOOL.
OKAY!
THANKS A LOT!
SEE YOU AT CLUB!
JOLT
WOOOW, CHECK OUT MINATO-SENPAI.

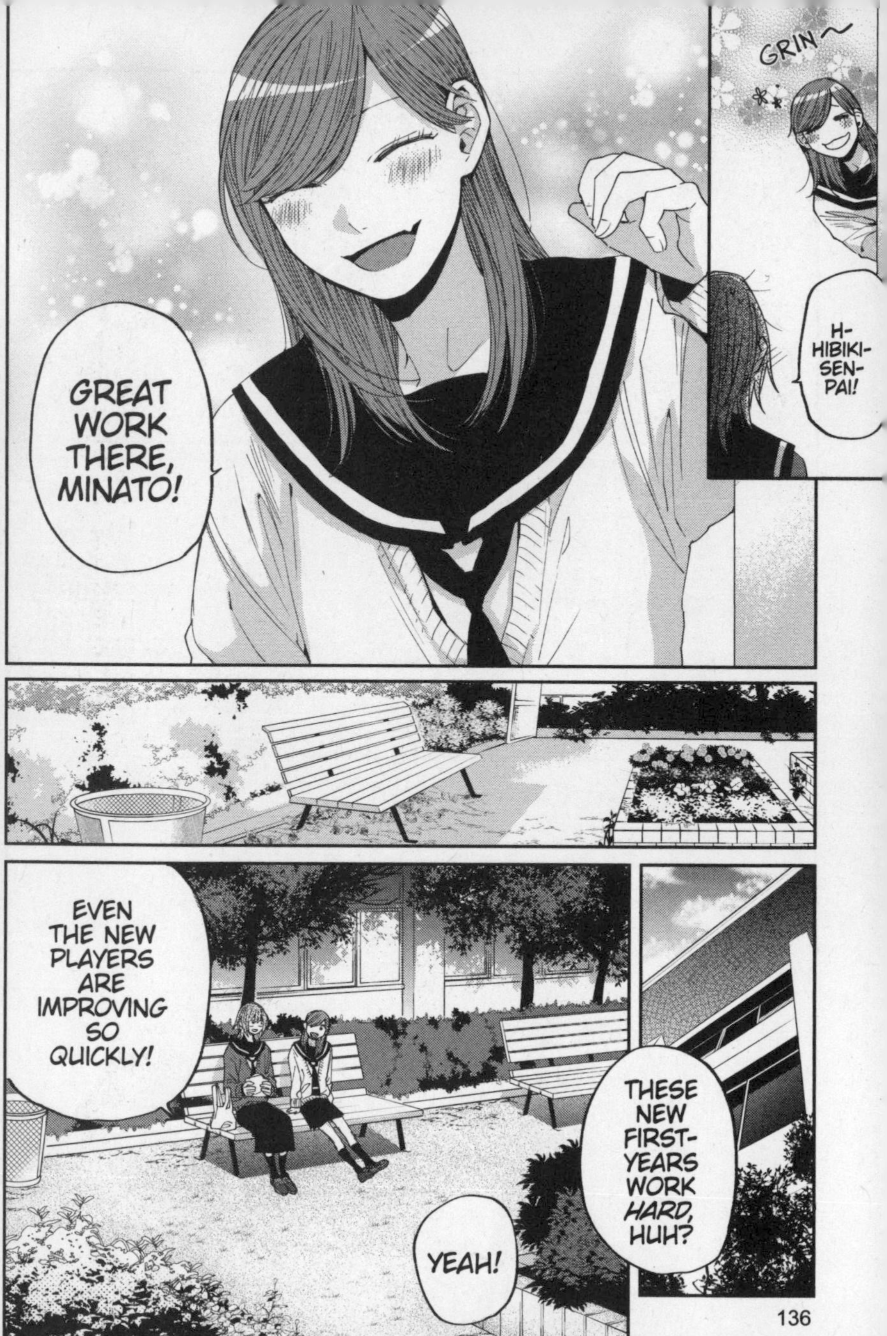
GRIN~
H-HIBIKI-SENPAI!
GREAT WORK THERE, MINATO!
THESE NEW FIRST-YEARS WORK *HARD*, HUH?
YEAH!
EVEN THE NEW PLAYERS ARE IMPROVING SO QUICKLY!

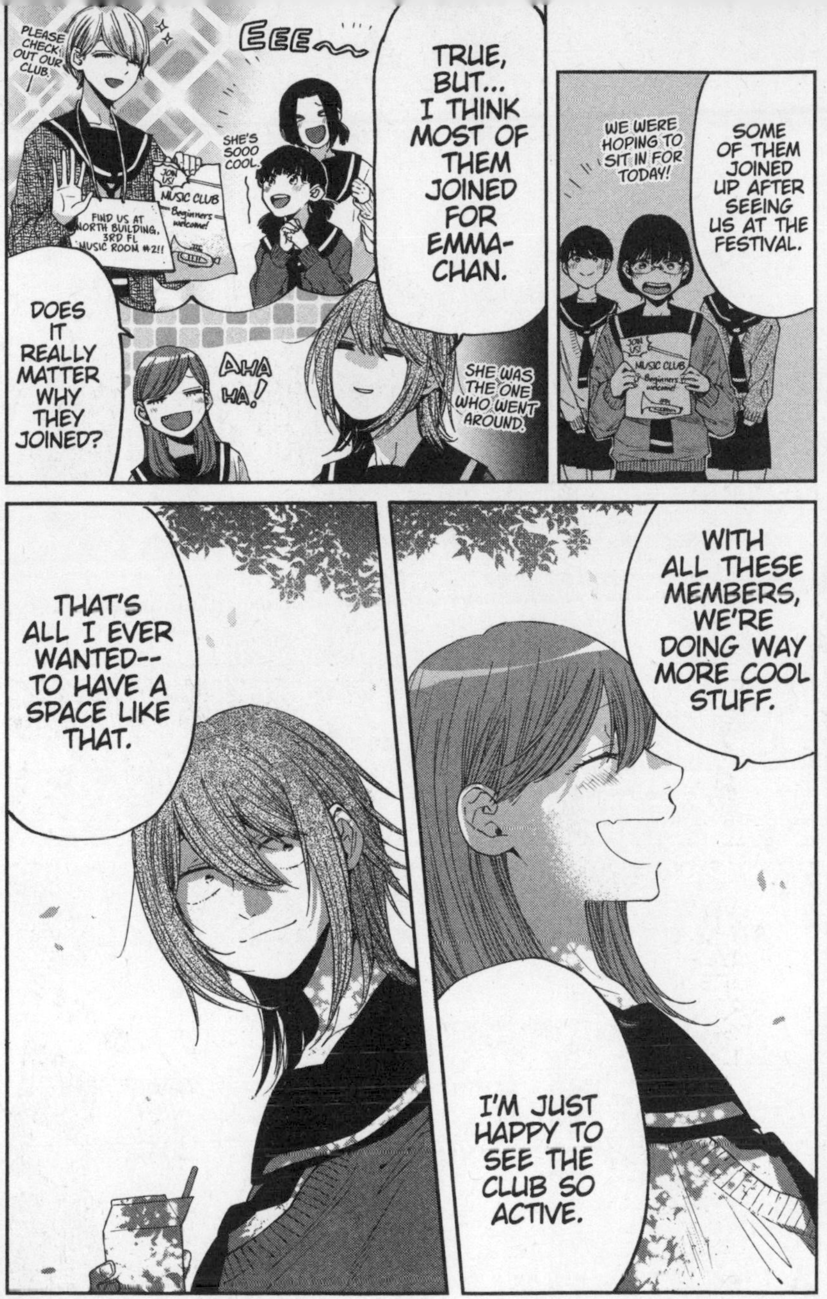
SOME OF THEM JOINED UP AFTER SEEING US AT THE FESTIVAL.
WE WERE HOPING TO SIT IN FOR TODAY!
JOIN US! MUSIC CLUB Beginners welcome!
TRUE, BUT... I THINK MOST OF THEM JOINED FOR EMMA-CHAN.
EEE~~
PLEASE CHECK OUT OUR CLUB.
SHE'S SOOO COOL.
JOIN US! MUSIC CLUB Beginners welcome! FIND US AT NORTH BUILDING, 3RD FL MUSIC ROOM #2!!
SHE WAS THE ONE WHO WENT AROUND.
AHA HA!
DOES IT REALLY MATTER WHY THEY JOINED?
WITH ALL THESE MEMBERS, WE'RE DOING WAY MORE COOL STUFF.
I'M JUST HAPPY TO SEE THE CLUB SO ACTIVE.
THAT'S ALL I EVER WANTED-- TO HAVE A SPACE LIKE THAT.

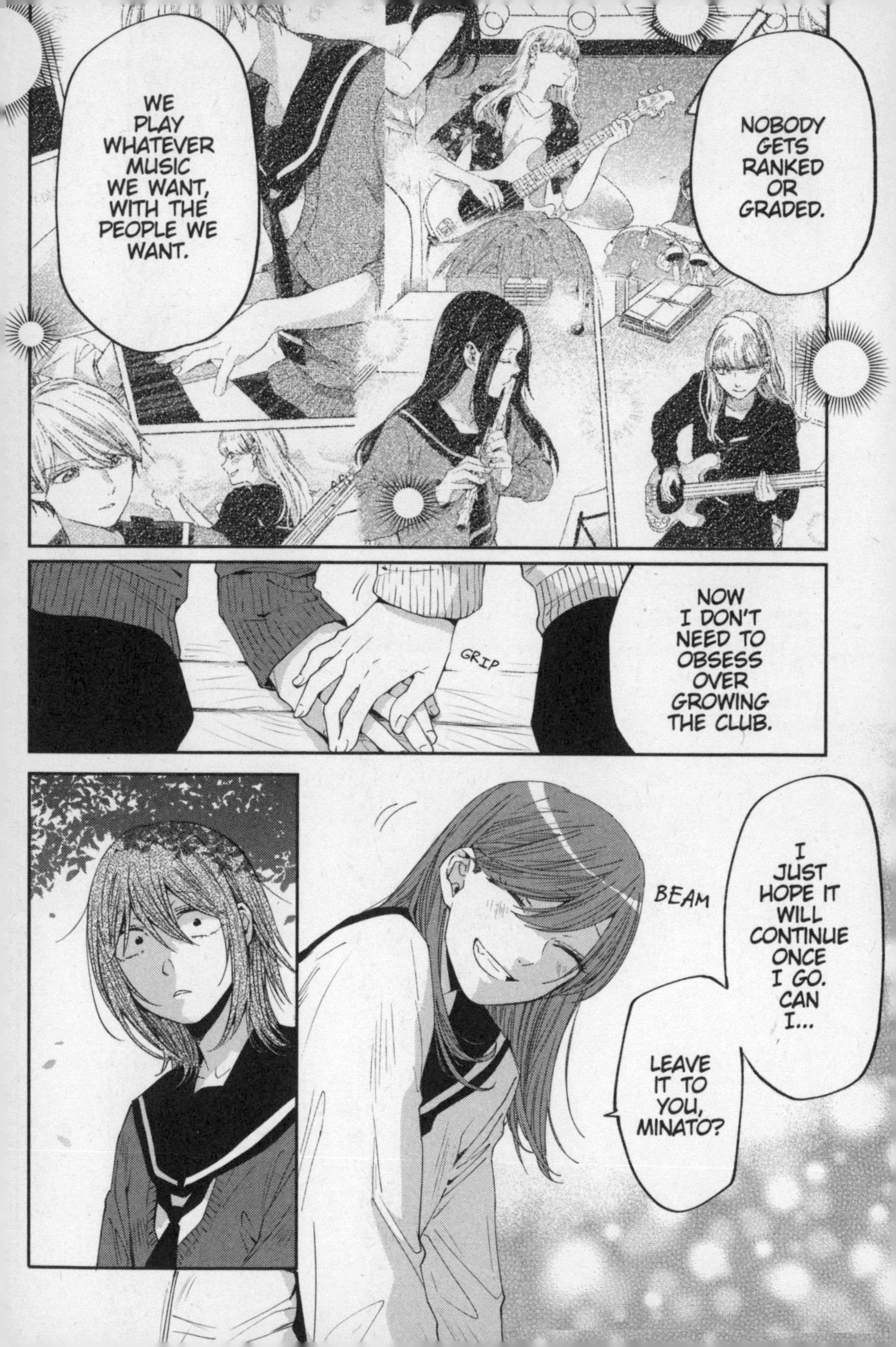
NOBODY GETS RANKED OR GRADED.
WE PLAY WHATEVER MUSIC WE WANT, WITH THE PEOPLE WE WANT.
NOW I DON'T NEED TO OBSESS OVER GROWING THE CLUB.
GRIP
I JUST HOPE IT WILL CONTINUE ONCE I GO. CAN I...
BEAM
LEAVE IT TO YOU, MINATO?

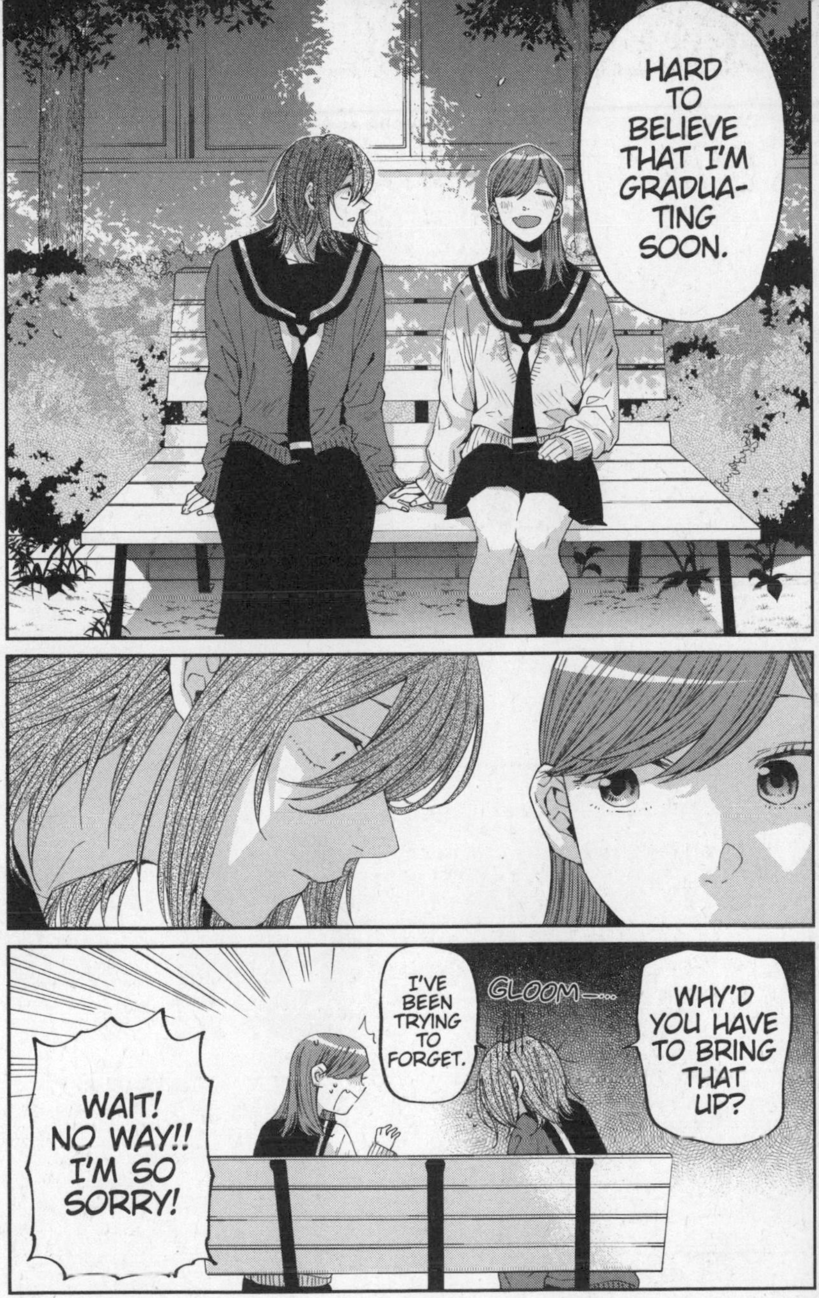
HARD TO BELIEVE THAT I'M GRADUA-TING SOON.
WHY'D YOU HAVE TO BRING THAT UP?
GLOOM....
I'VE BEEN TRYING TO FORGET.
WAIT! NO WAY!! I'M SO SORRY!

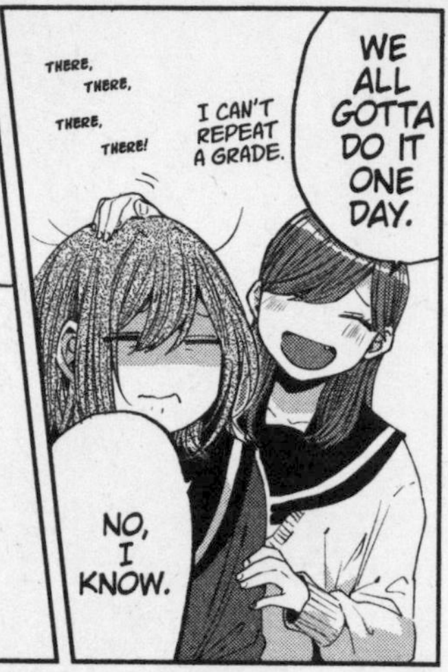
WE ALL GOTTA DO IT ONE DAY.
I CAN'T REPEAT A GRADE.
THERE, THERE, THERE, THERE!
NO, I KNOW.

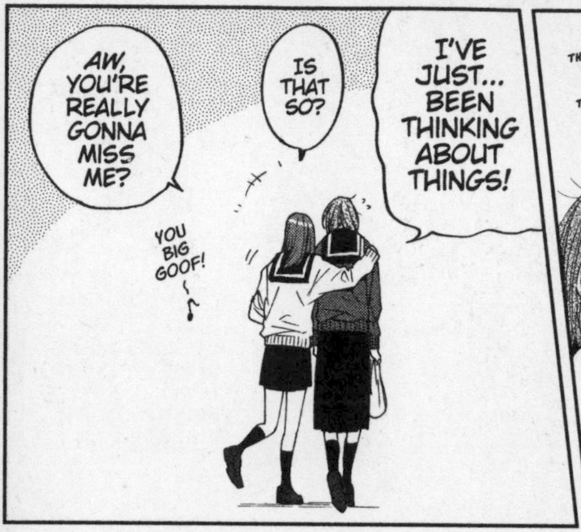
I'VE JUST... BEEN THINKING ABOUT THINGS!
IS THAT SO?
AW, YOU'RE REALLY GONNA MISS ME?
YOU BIG GOOF!

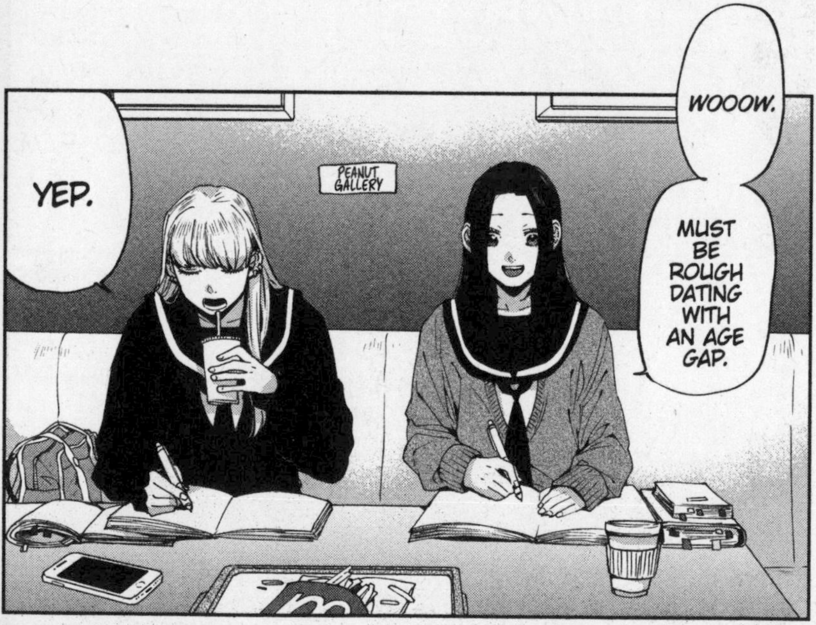
WOOOW.
MUST BE ROUGH DATING WITH AN AGE GAP.
PEANUT GALLERY
YEP.

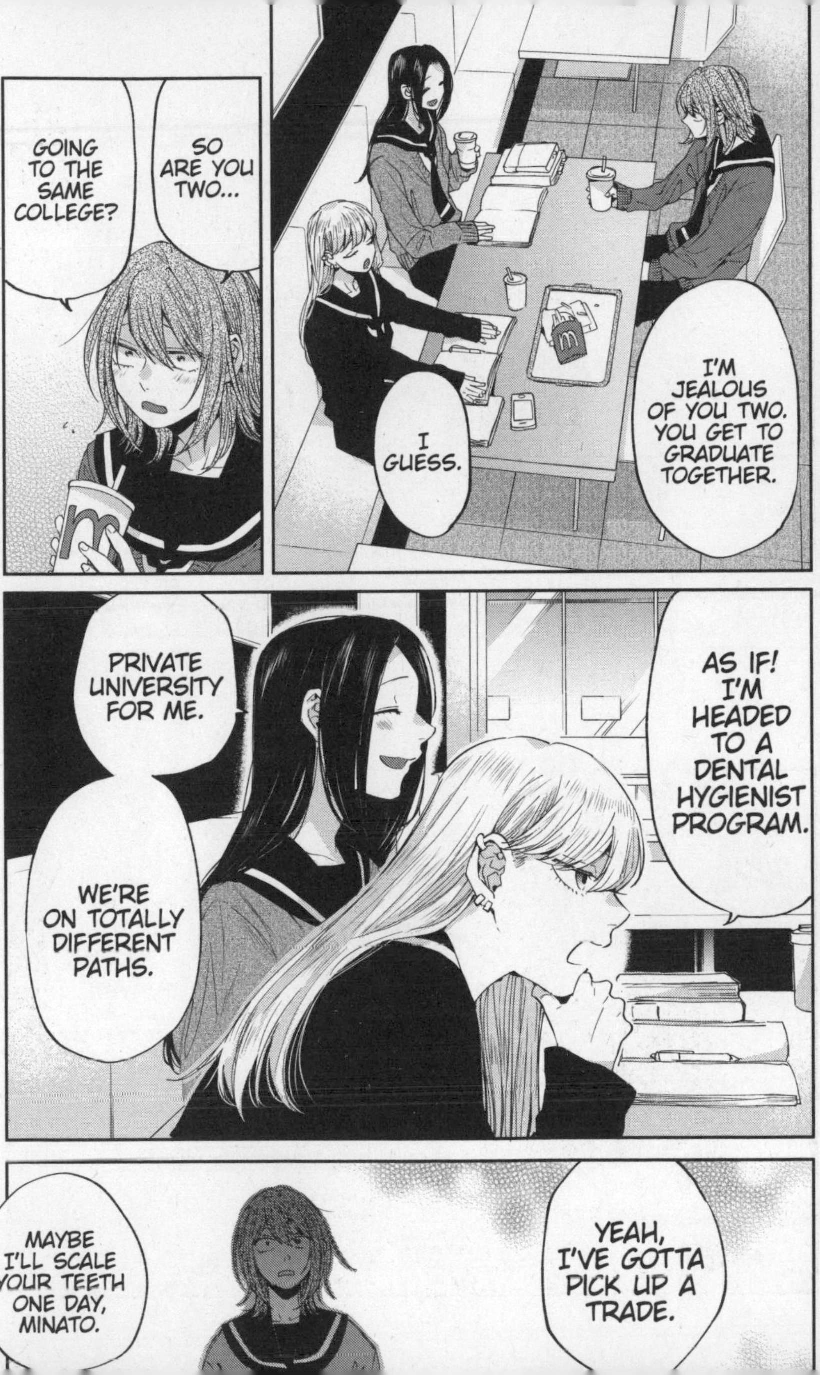
I'M JEALOUS OF YOU TWO. YOU GET TO GRADUATE TOGETHER.
I GUESS.
SO ARE YOU TWO...
GOING TO THE SAME COLLEGE?
AS IF! I'M HEADED TO A DENTAL HYGIENIST PROGRAM.
PRIVATE UNIVERSITY FOR ME.
WE'RE ON TOTALLY DIFFERENT PATHS.
YEAH, I'VE GOTTA PICK UP A TRADE.
MAYBE I'LL SCALE YOUR TEETH ONE DAY, MINATO.

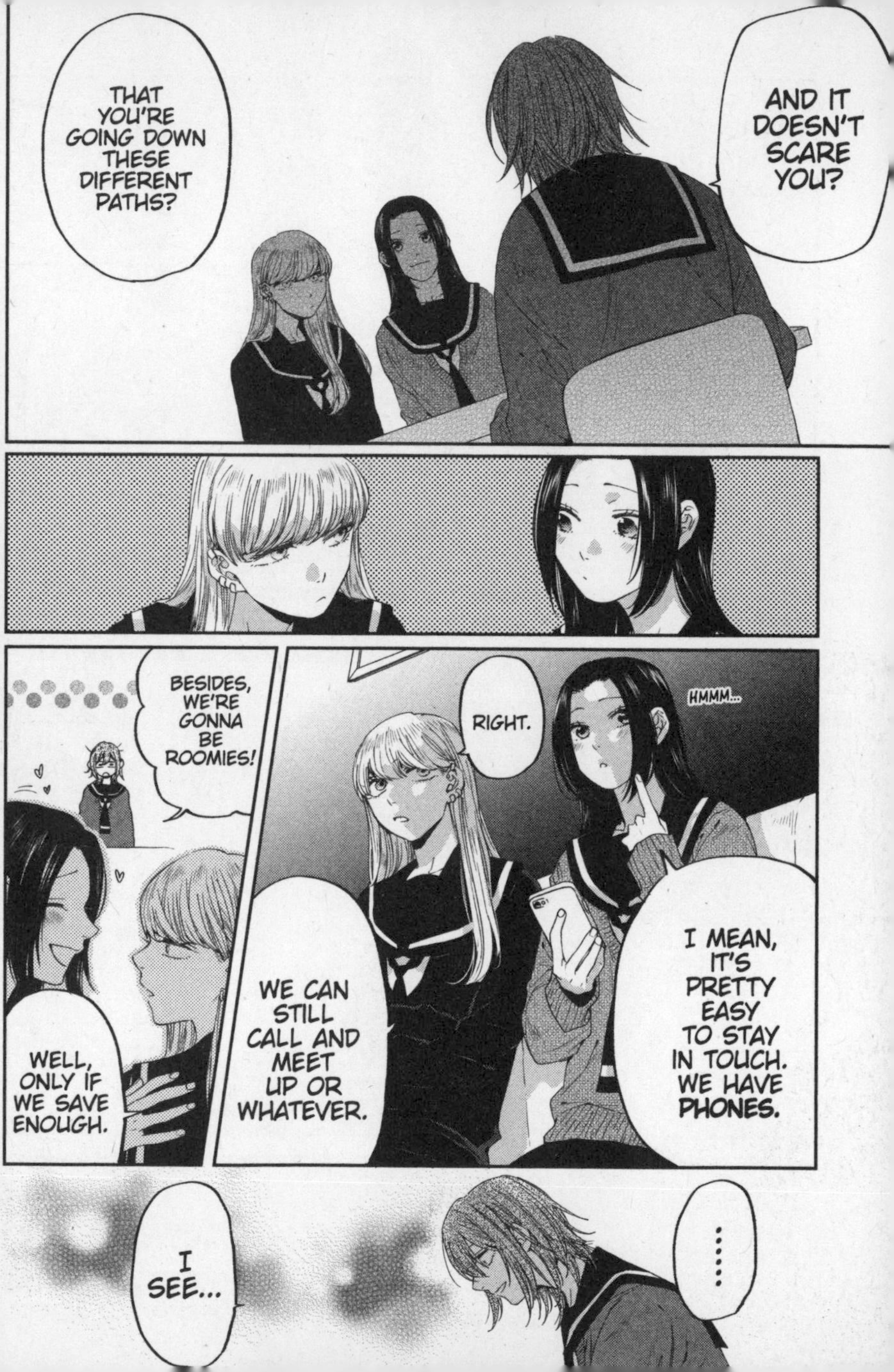
AND IT DOESN'T SCARE YOU?
THAT YOU'RE GOING DOWN THESE DIFFERENT PATHS?
HMMM...
RIGHT.
I MEAN, IT'S PRETTY EASY TO STAY IN TOUCH. WE HAVE PHONES.
WE CAN STILL CALL AND MEET UP OR WHATEVER.
BESIDES, WE'RE GONNA BE ROOMIES!
WELL, ONLY IF WE SAVE ENOUGH.
......
I SEE...

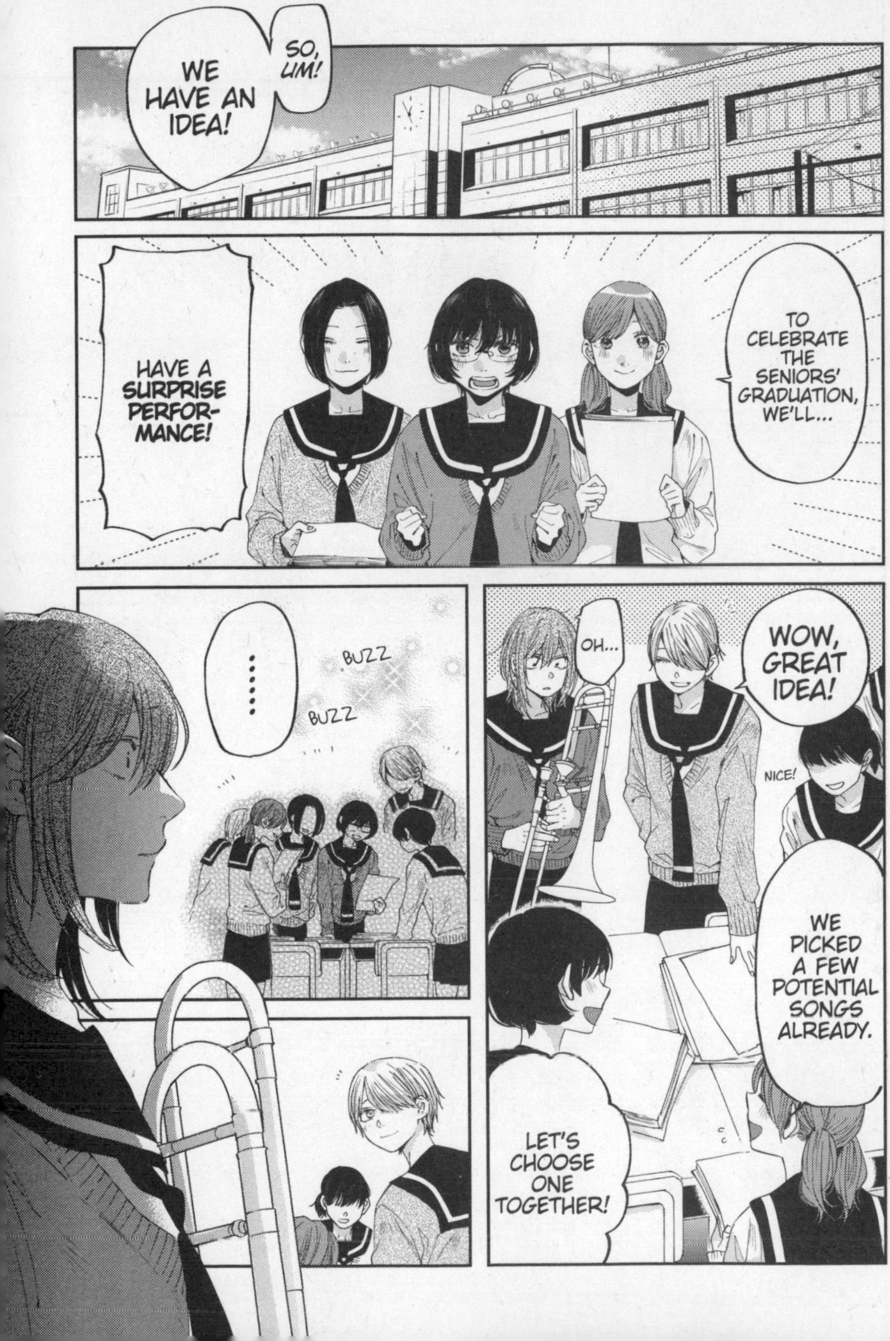
SO, UM!
WE HAVE AN IDEA!
TO CELEBRATE THE SENIORS' GRADUATION, WE'LL...
HAVE A SURPRISE PERFORMANCE!
WOW, GREAT IDEA!
OH...
NICE!
WE PICKED A FEW POTENTIAL SONGS ALREADY.
LET'S CHOOSE ONE TOGETHER!
......
BUZZ
BUZZ

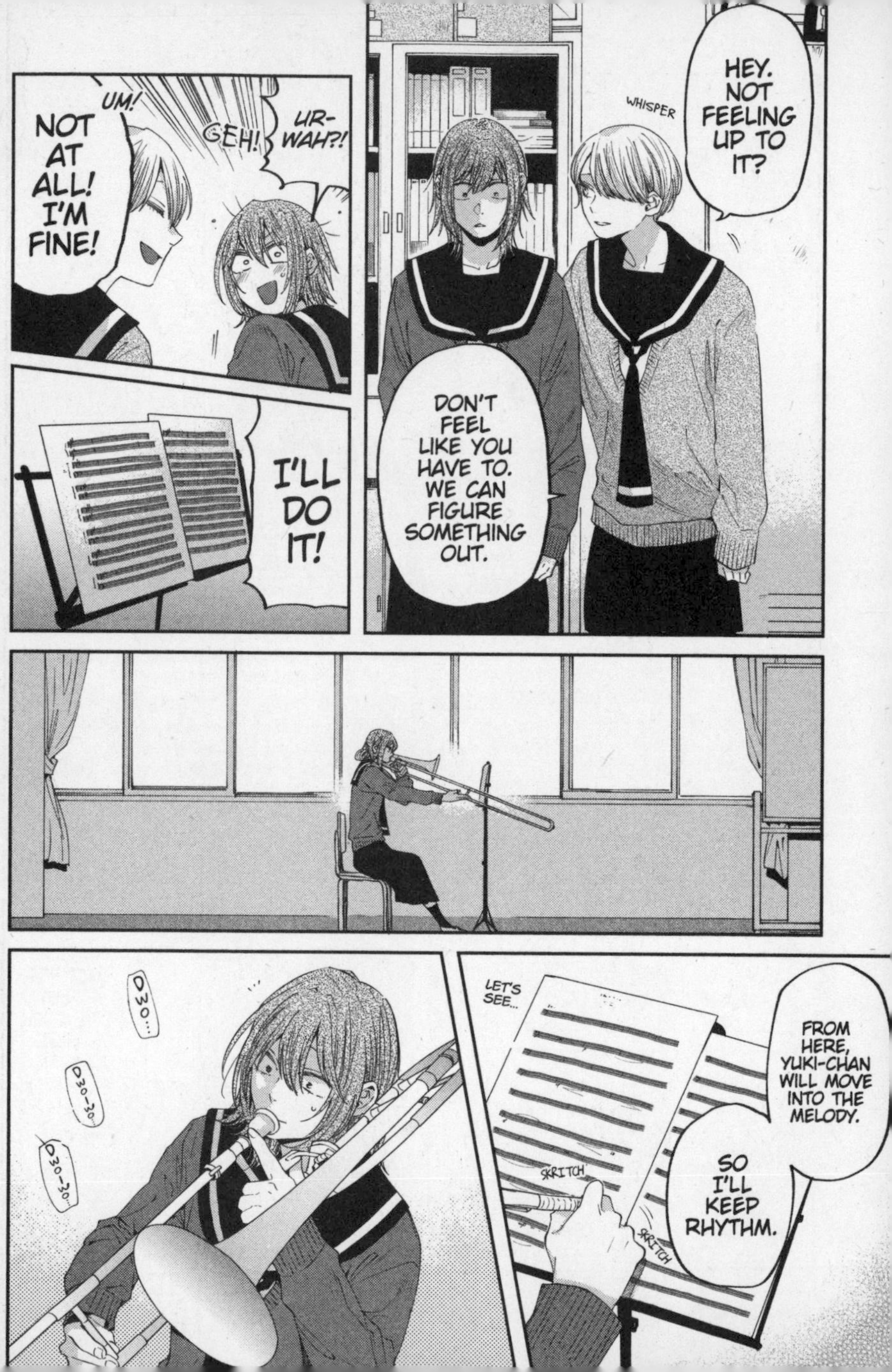
WHISPER
HEY. NOT FEELING UP TO IT?
DON'T FEEL LIKE YOU HAVE TO. WE CAN FIGURE SOMETHING OUT.
UR-WAH?!
GEH!
UM!
NOT AT ALL! I'M FINE!
I'LL DO IT!
LET'S SEE...
FROM HERE, YUKI-CHAN WILL MOVE INTO THE MELODY.
SO I'LL KEEP RHYTHM.
SKRITCH
SKRITCH
DWO...
DWO-WO...
DWO-WO...

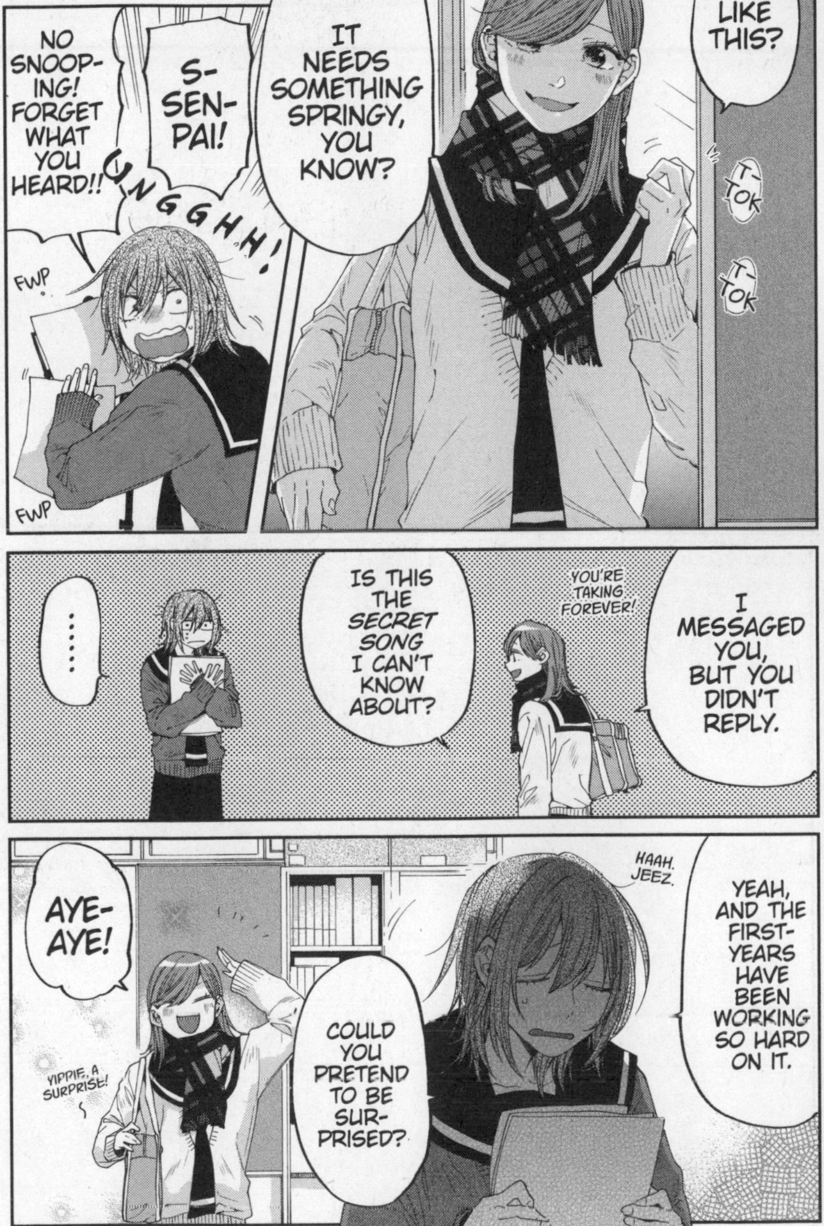
T-TOK
T-TOK
LIKE THIS?
IT NEEDS SOMETHING SPRINGY, YOU KNOW?
S-SENPAI!
UNGGHH!
NO SNOOPING! FORGET WHAT YOU HEARD!!
FWP
FWP
I MESSAGED YOU, BUT YOU DIDN'T REPLY.
YOU'RE TAKING FOREVER!
IS THIS THE SECRET SONG I CAN'T KNOW ABOUT?
......
YEAH, AND THE FIRST-YEARS HAVE BEEN WORKING SO HARD ON IT.
HAAH. JEEZ.
COULD YOU PRETEND TO BE SURPRISED?
AYE-AYE!
YIPPIE, A SURPRISE!

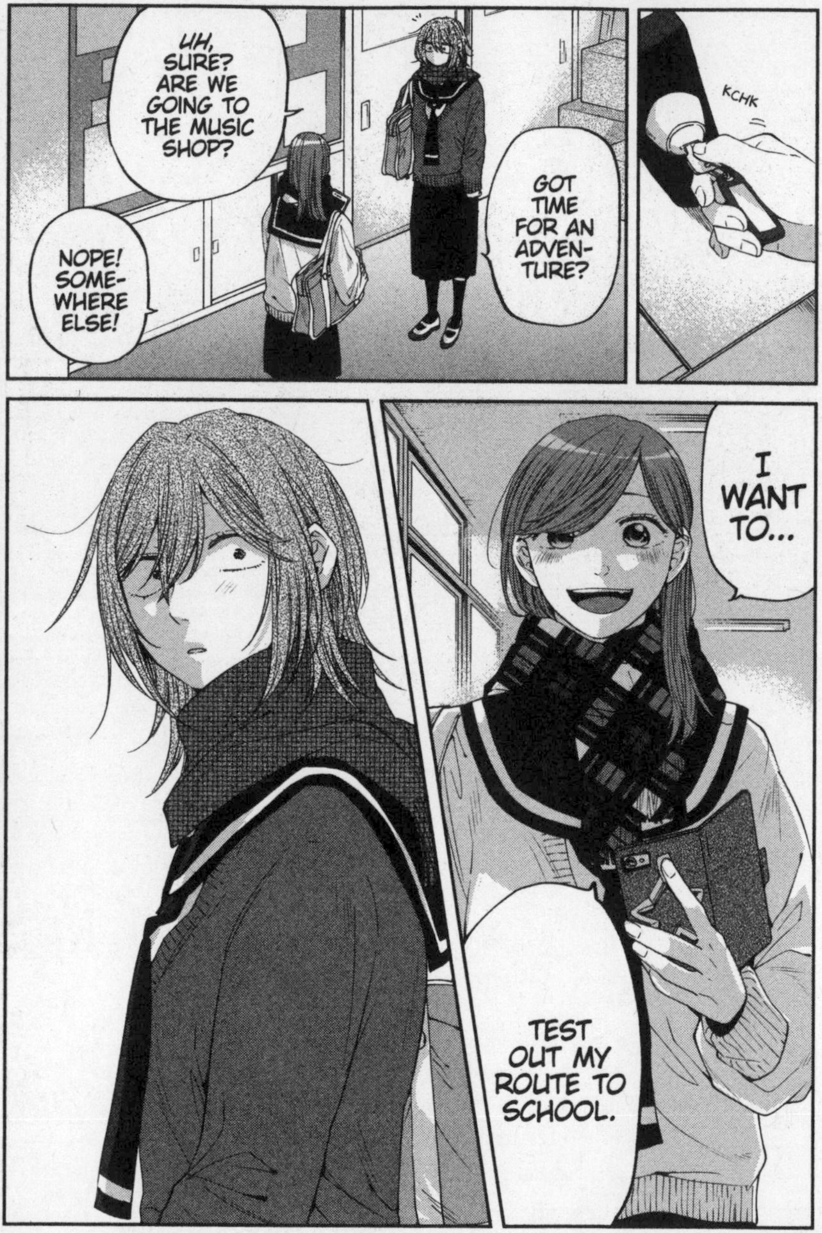
KCHK
GOT TIME FOR AN ADVENTURE?
UH, SURE? ARE WE GOING TO THE MUSIC SHOP?
NOPE! SOMEWHERE ELSE!
I WANT TO...
TEST OUT MY ROUTE TO SCHOOL.

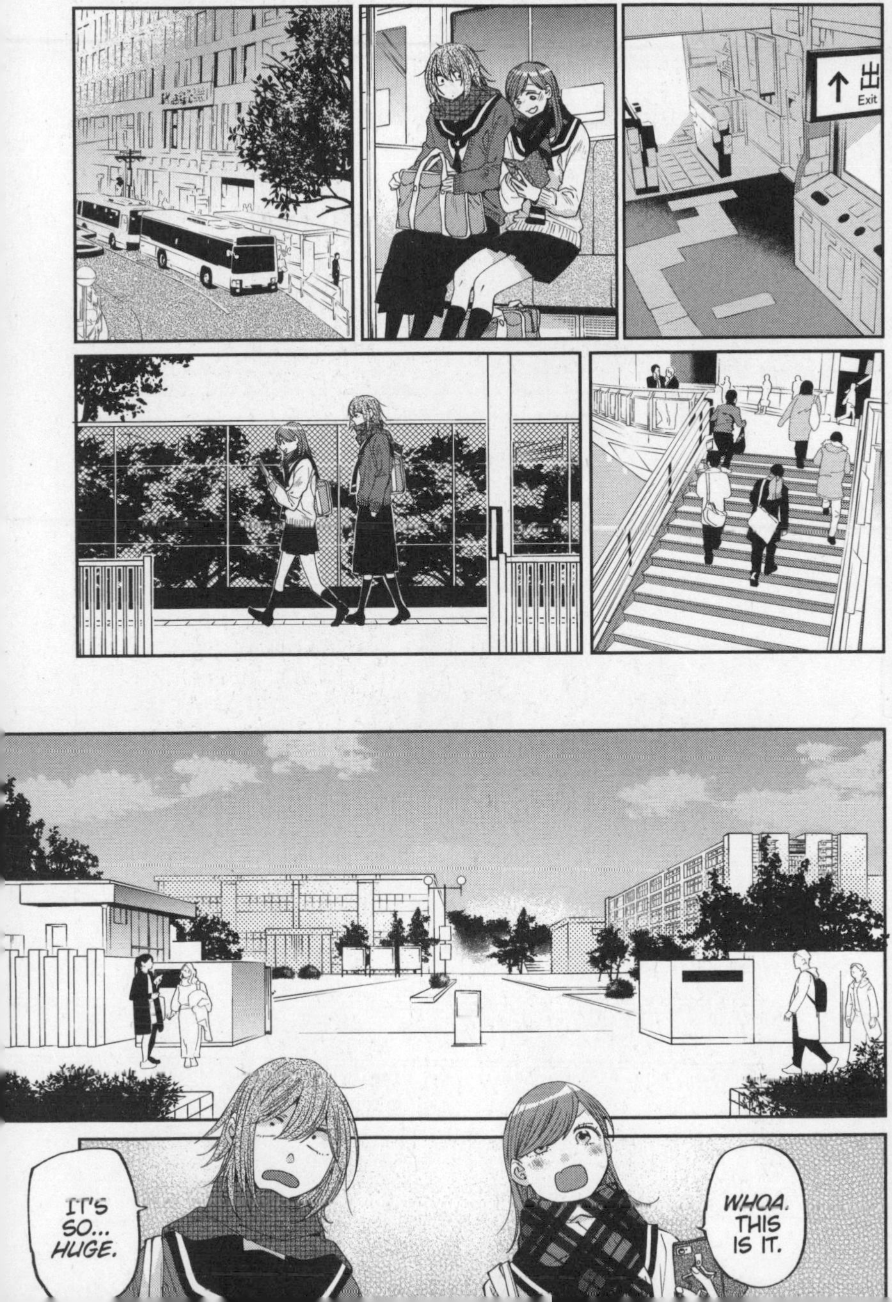
↑ 出 Exit
WHOA. THIS IS IT.
IT'S SO... HUGE.

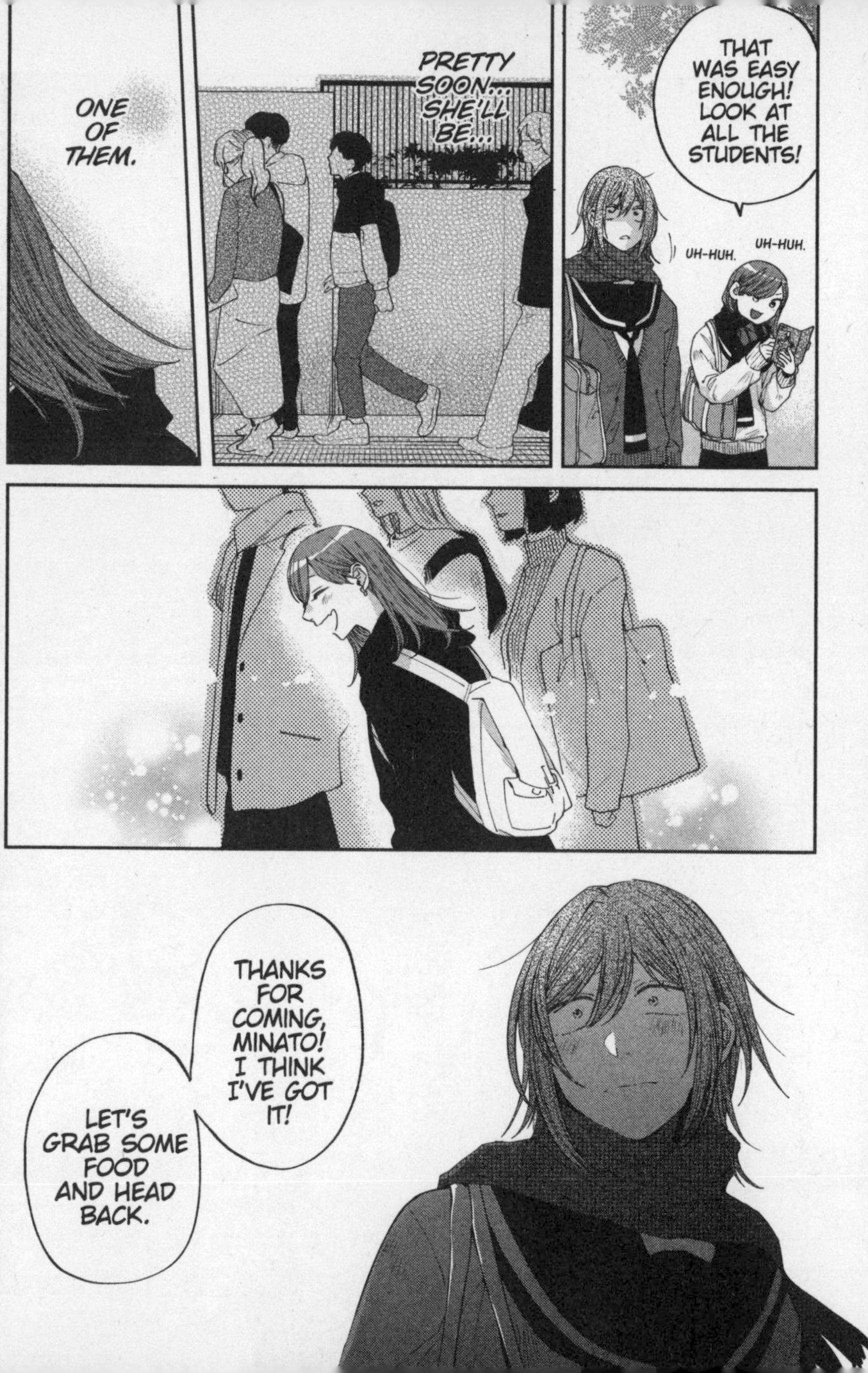
THAT WAS EASY ENOUGH! LOOK AT ALL THE STUDENTS!
UH-HUH.
UH-HUH.
PRETTY SOON... SHE'LL BE...
ONE OF THEM.
THANKS FOR COMING, MINATO! I THINK I'VE GOT IT!
LET'S GRAB SOME FOOD AND HEAD BACK.

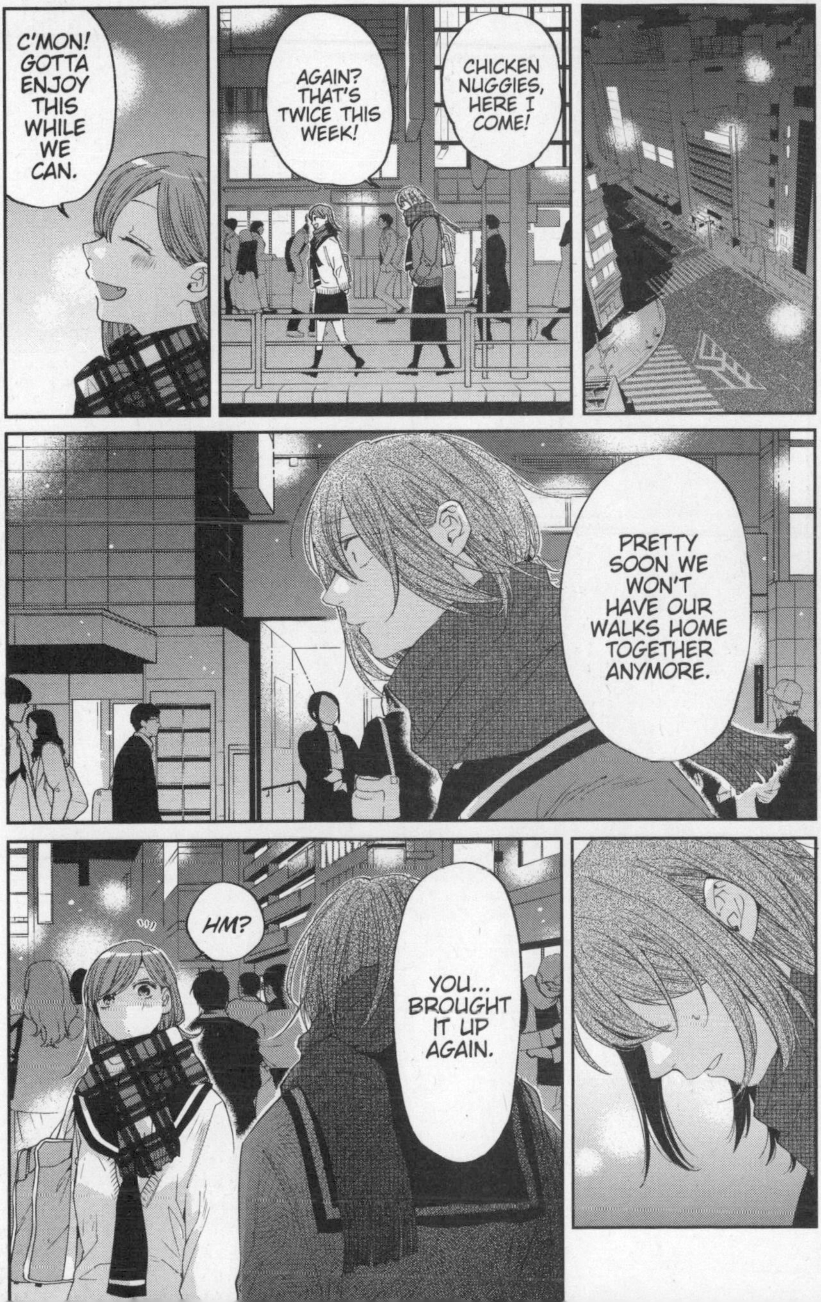
CHICKEN NUGGIES, HERE I COME!
AGAIN? THAT'S TWICE THIS WEEK!
C'MON! GOTTA ENJOY THIS WHILE WE CAN.
PRETTY SOON WE WON'T HAVE OUR WALKS HOME TOGETHER ANYMORE.
YOU... BROUGHT IT UP AGAIN.
HM?

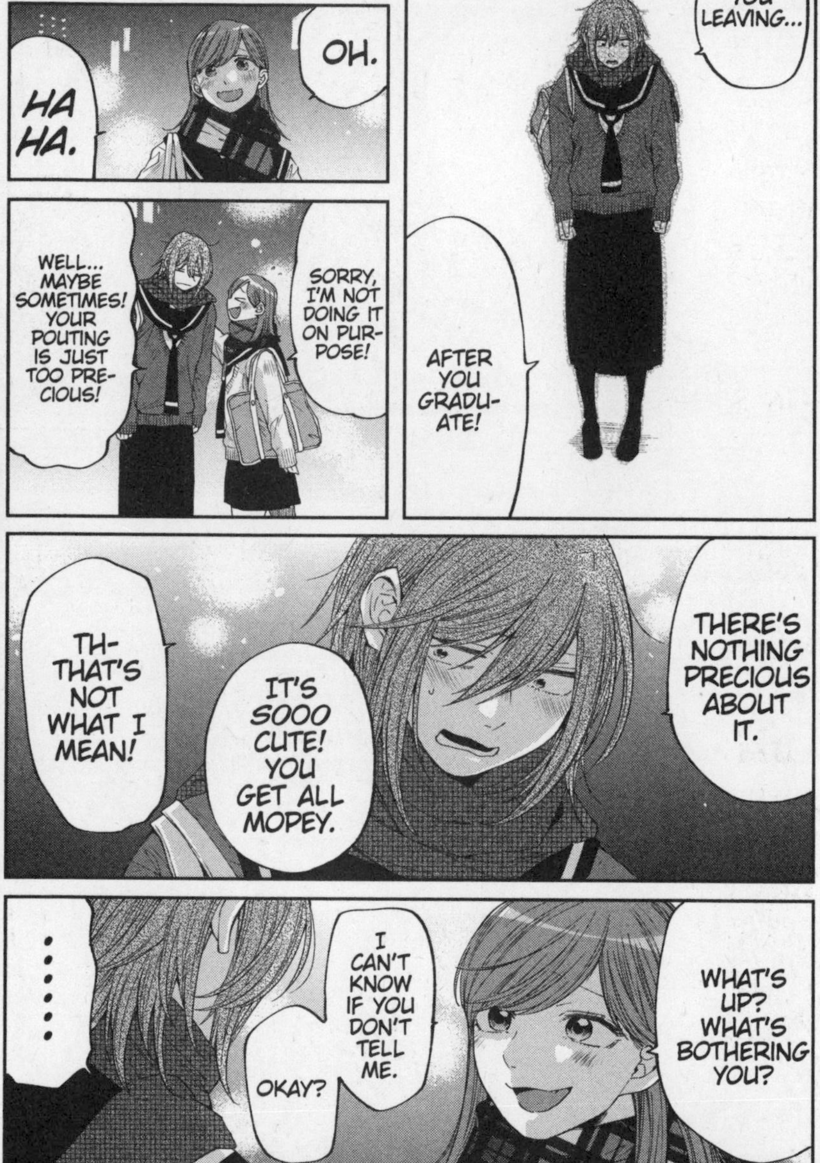

YOU LEAVING...
AFTER YOU GRADUATE!
OH.
HA HA.
SORRY, I'M NOT DOING IT ON PURPOSE!
WELL... MAYBE SOMETIMES! YOUR POUTING IS JUST TOO PRECIOUS!
THERE'S NOTHING PRECIOUS ABOUT IT.
IT'S SOOO CUTE! YOU GET ALL MOPEY.
TH-THAT'S NOT WHAT I MEAN!
WHAT'S UP? WHAT'S BOTHERING YOU?
I CAN'T KNOW IF YOU DON'T TELL ME.
OKAY?
......

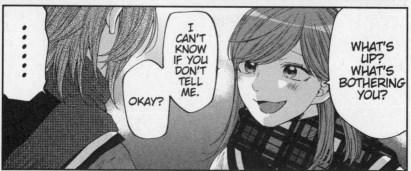

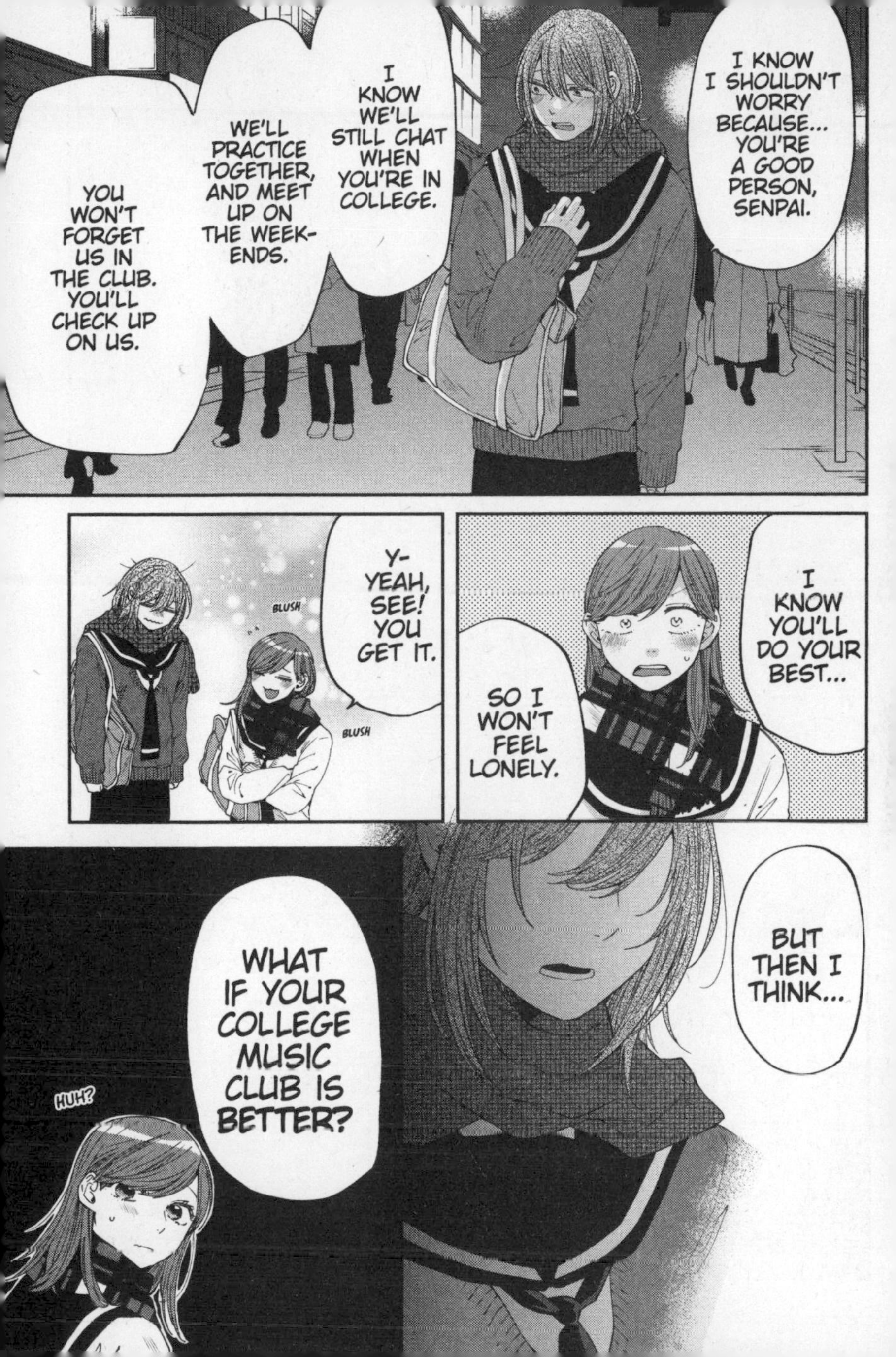
I KNOW I SHOULDN'T WORRY BECAUSE... YOU'RE A GOOD PERSON, SENPAI.
I KNOW WE'LL STILL CHAT WHEN YOU'RE IN COLLEGE.
WE'LL PRACTICE TOGETHER, AND MEET UP ON THE WEEK-ENDS.
YOU WON'T FORGET US IN THE CLUB. YOU'LL CHECK UP ON US.
I KNOW YOU'LL DO YOUR BEST...
SO I WON'T FEEL LONELY.
Y-YEAH, SEE! YOU GET IT.
BLUSH
BLUSH
BUT THEN I THINK...
WHAT IF YOUR COLLEGE MUSIC CLUB IS BETTER?
HUH?

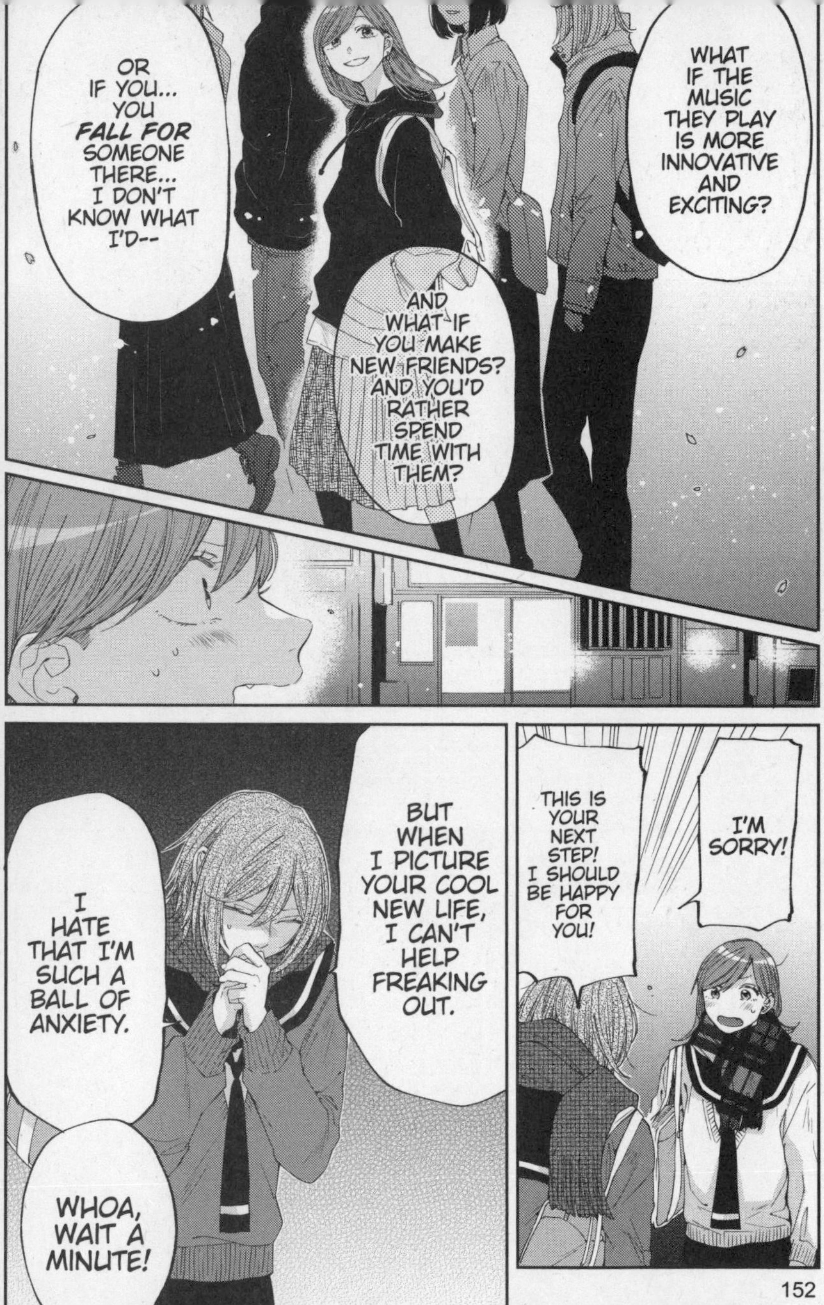
WHAT IF THE MUSIC THEY PLAY IS MORE INNOVATIVE AND EXCITING?
AND WHAT IF YOU MAKE NEW FRIENDS? AND YOU'D RATHER SPEND TIME WITH THEM?
OR IF YOU... YOU ***FALL FOR*** SOMEONE THERE... I DON'T KNOW WHAT I'D--
I'M SORRY!
THIS IS YOUR NEXT STEP! I SHOULD BE HAPPY FOR YOU!
BUT WHEN I PICTURE YOUR COOL NEW LIFE, I CAN'T HELP FREAKING OUT.
I HATE THAT I'M SUCH A BALL OF ANXIETY.
WHOA, WAIT A MINUTE!

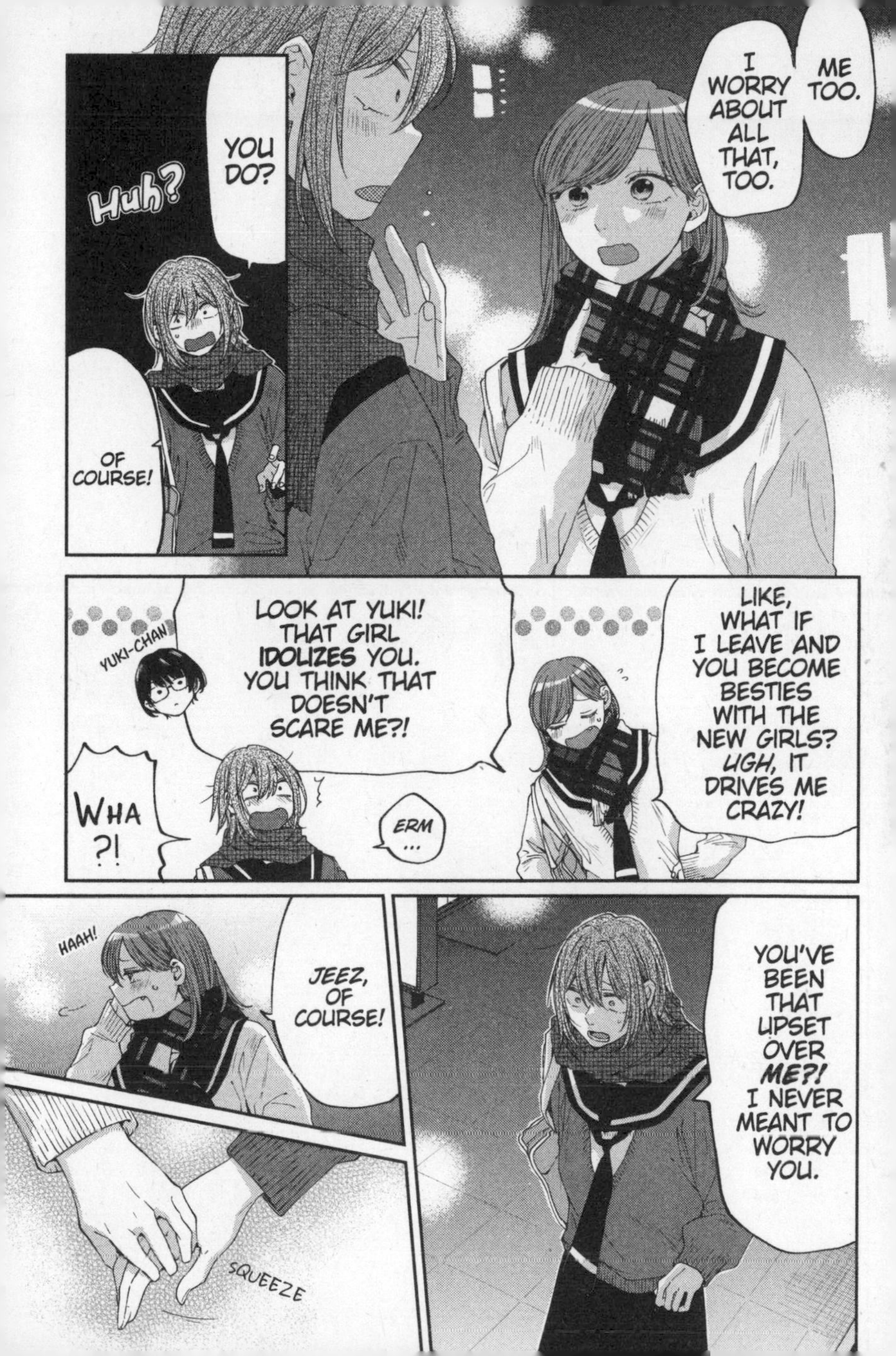

ME TOO.
I WORRY ABOUT ALL THAT, TOO.
YOU DO?
Huh?
OF COURSE!
LIKE, WHAT IF I LEAVE AND YOU BECOME BESTIES WITH THE NEW GIRLS? UGH, IT DRIVES ME CRAZY!
LOOK AT YUKI! THAT GIRL IDOLIZES YOU. YOU THINK THAT DOESN'T SCARE ME?!
YUKI-CHAN
ERM ...
WHA ?!
YOU'VE BEEN THAT UPSET OVER ME?! I NEVER MEANT TO WORRY YOU.
JEEZ, OF COURSE!
HAAH!
SQUEEZE

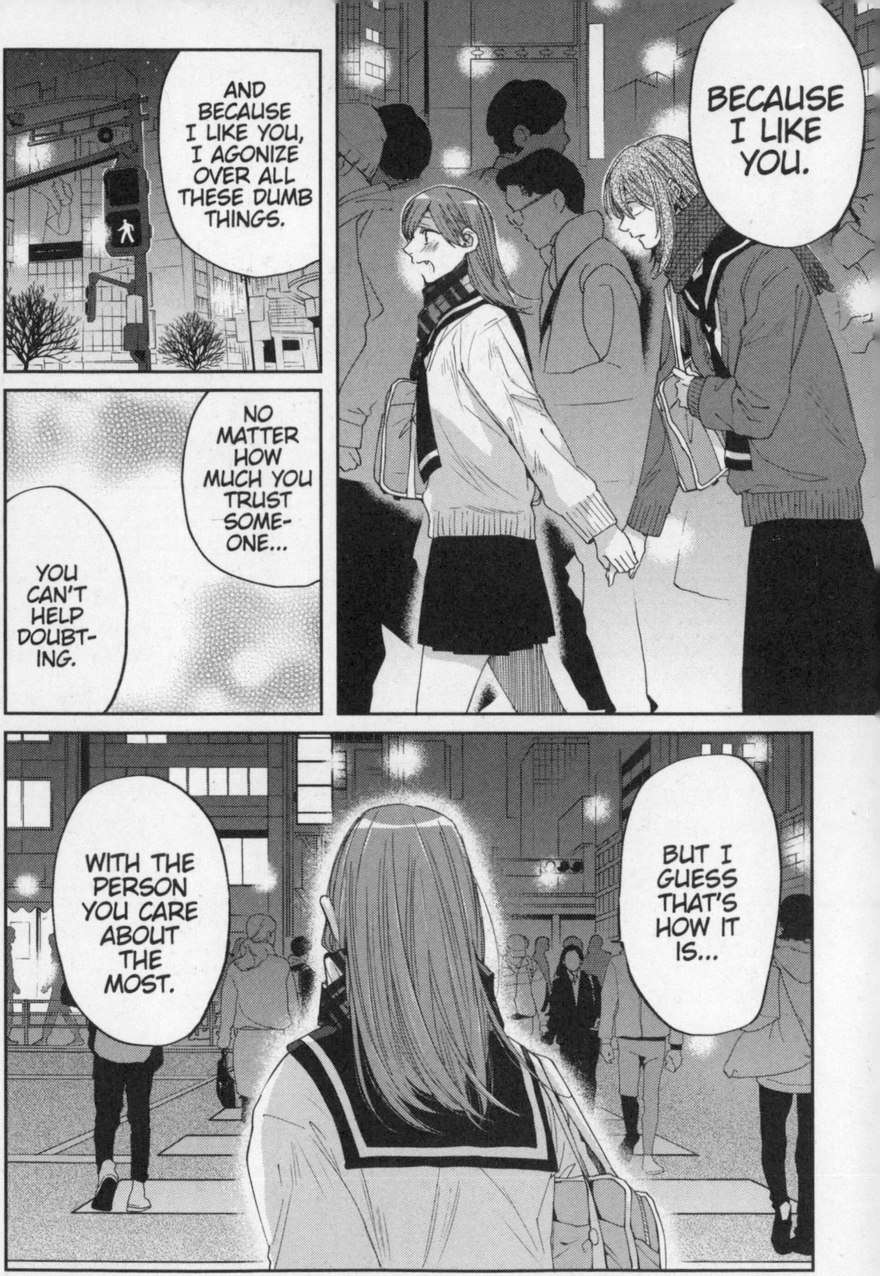
BECAUSE I LIKE YOU.
AND BECAUSE I LIKE YOU, I AGONIZE OVER ALL THESE DUMB THINGS.
NO MATTER HOW MUCH YOU TRUST SOMEONE...
YOU CAN'T HELP DOUBTING.
BUT I GUESS THAT'S HOW IT IS...
WITH THE PERSON YOU CARE ABOUT THE MOST.

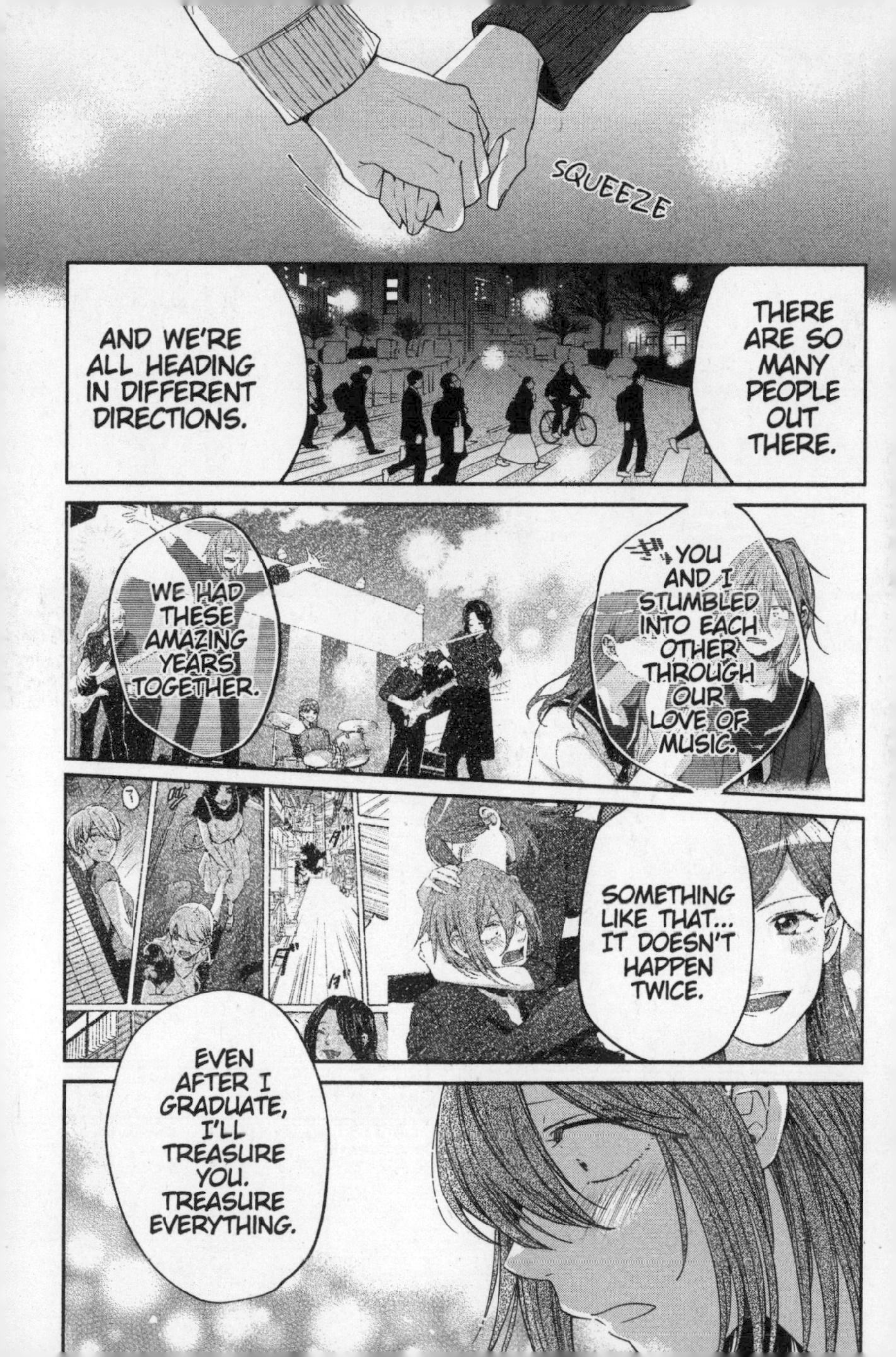
SQUEEZE
THERE ARE SO MANY PEOPLE OUT THERE.
AND WE'RE ALL HEADING IN DIFFERENT DIRECTIONS.
YOU AND I STUMBLED INTO EACH OTHER THROUGH OUR LOVE OF MUSIC.
WE HAD THESE AMAZING YEARS TOGETHER.
SOMETHING LIKE THAT... IT DOESN'T HAPPEN TWICE.
EVEN AFTER I GRADUATE, I'LL TREASURE YOU. TREASURE EVERYTHING.

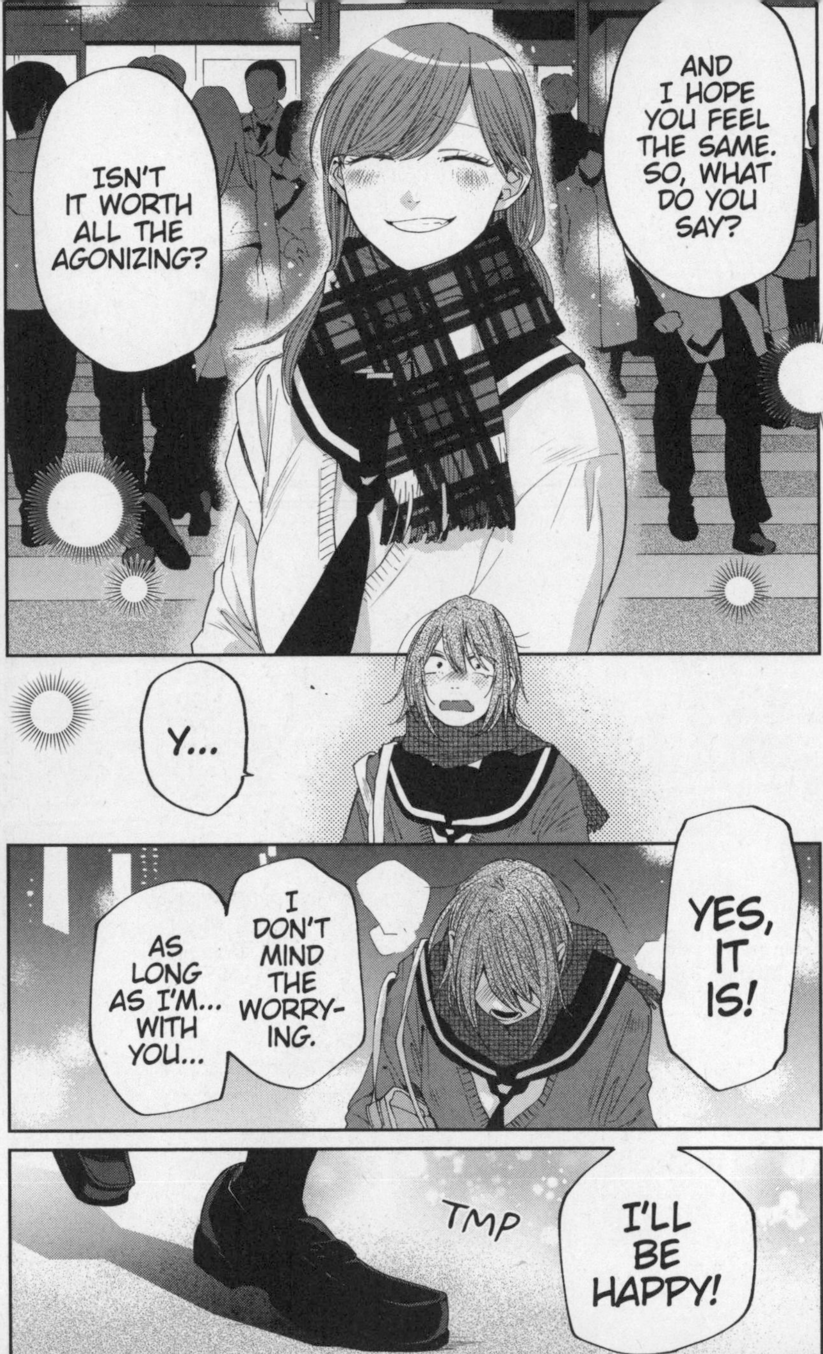
AND I HOPE YOU FEEL THE SAME. SO, WHAT DO YOU SAY?
ISN'T IT WORTH ALL THE AGONIZING?
Y...
YES, IT IS!
I DON'T MIND THE WORRY-ING.
AS LONG AS I'M... WITH YOU...
I'LL BE HAPPY!
TMP

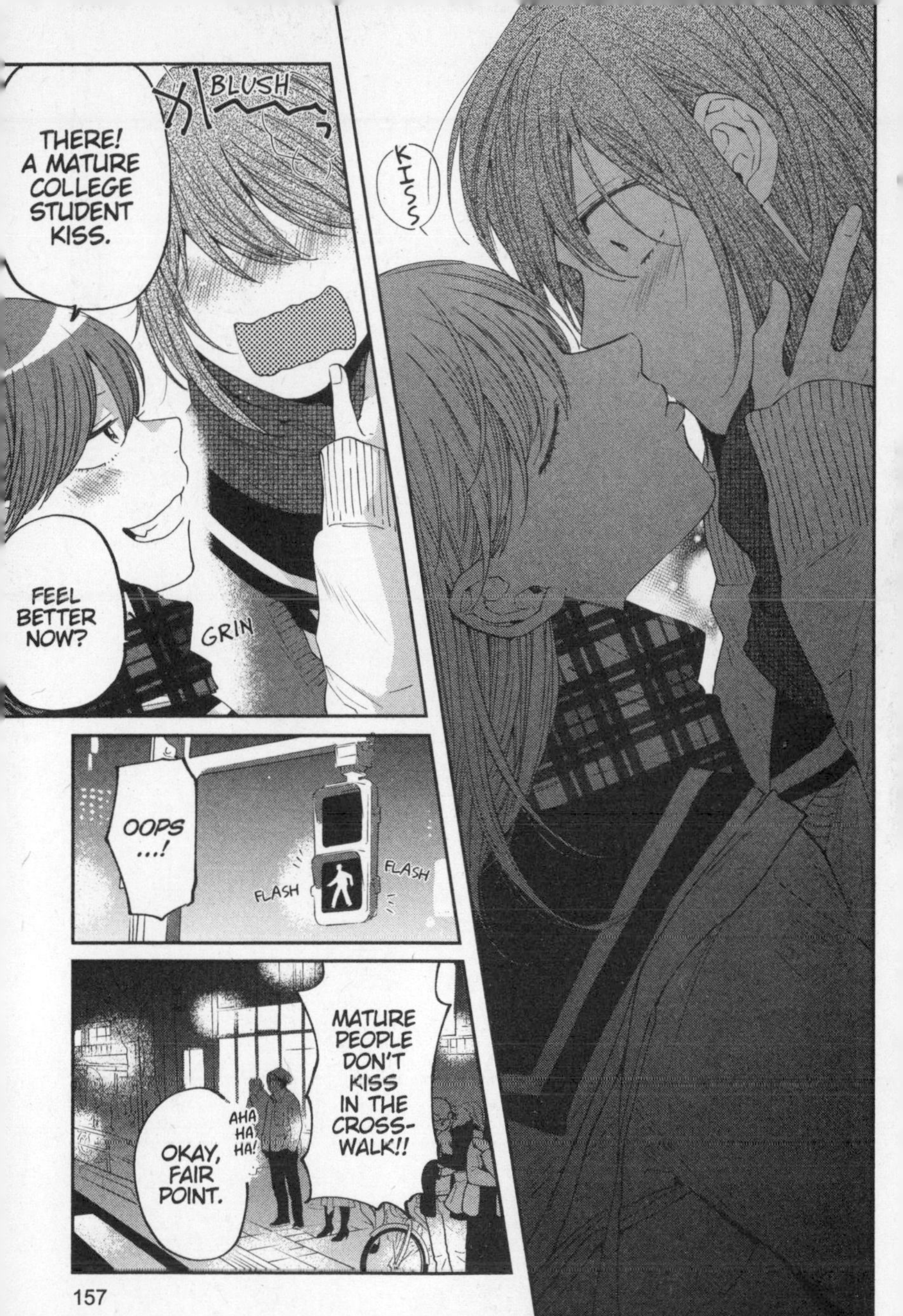
KISS
BLUSH
THERE! A MATURE COLLEGE STUDENT KISS.
GRIN
FEEL BETTER NOW?
OOPS ...!
FLASH
FLASH
MATURE PEOPLE DON'T KISS IN THE CROSS-WALK!!
AHA HA HA!
OKAY, FAIR POINT.

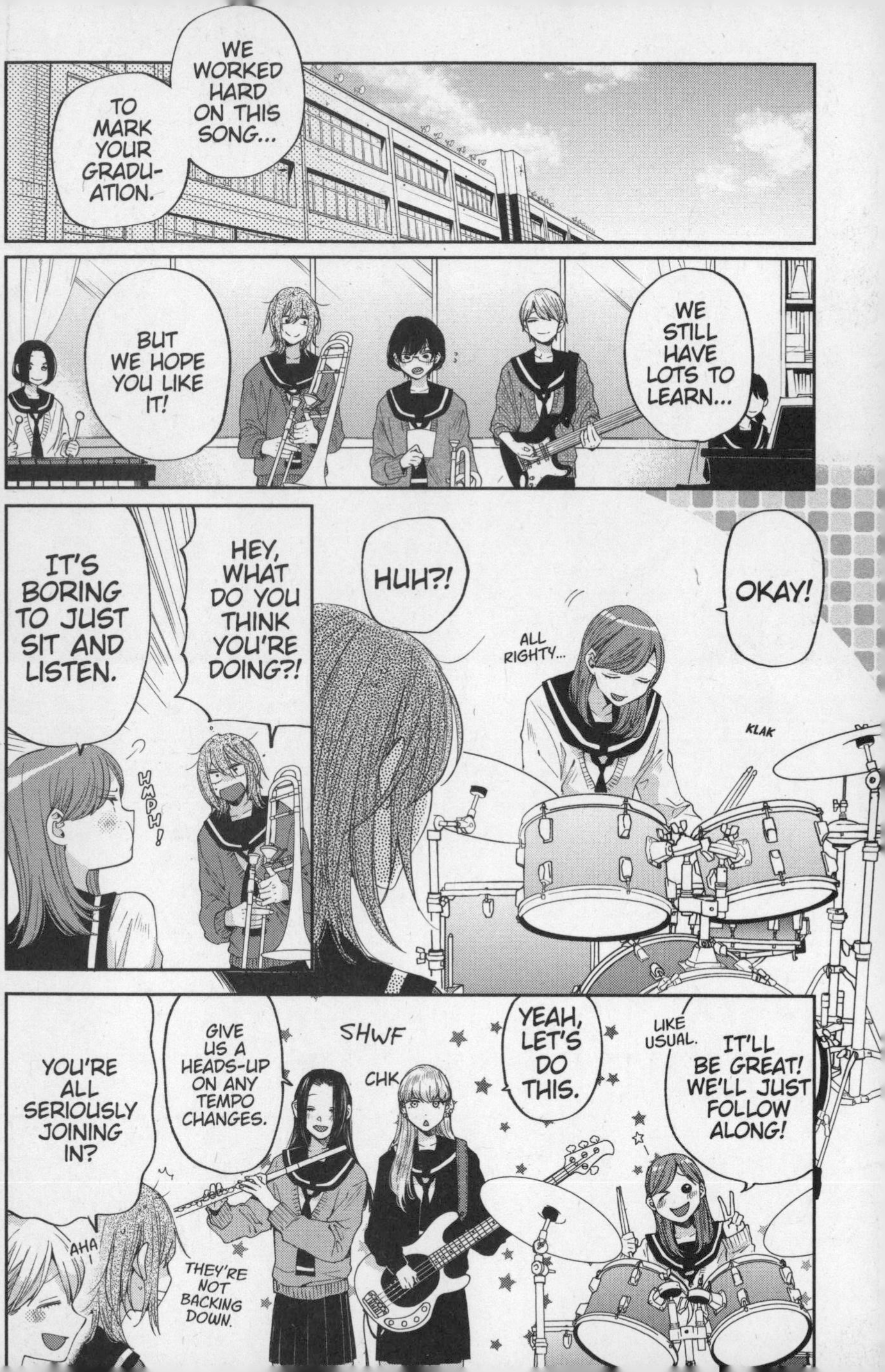
WE WORKED HARD ON THIS SONG...
TO MARK YOUR GRADUATION.
WE STILL HAVE LOTS TO LEARN...
BUT WE HOPE YOU LIKE IT!
OKAY!
ALL RIGHTY...
KLAK
HUH?!
HEY, WHAT DO YOU THINK YOU'RE DOING?!
IT'S BORING TO JUST SIT AND LISTEN.
HMPH!
IT'LL BE GREAT! WE'LL JUST FOLLOW ALONG!
LIKE USUAL.
YEAH, LET'S DO THIS.
SHWF
CHK
GIVE US A HEADS-UP ON ANY TEMPO CHANGES.
YOU'RE ALL SERIOUSLY JOINING IN?
AHA
THEY'RE NOT BACKING DOWN.

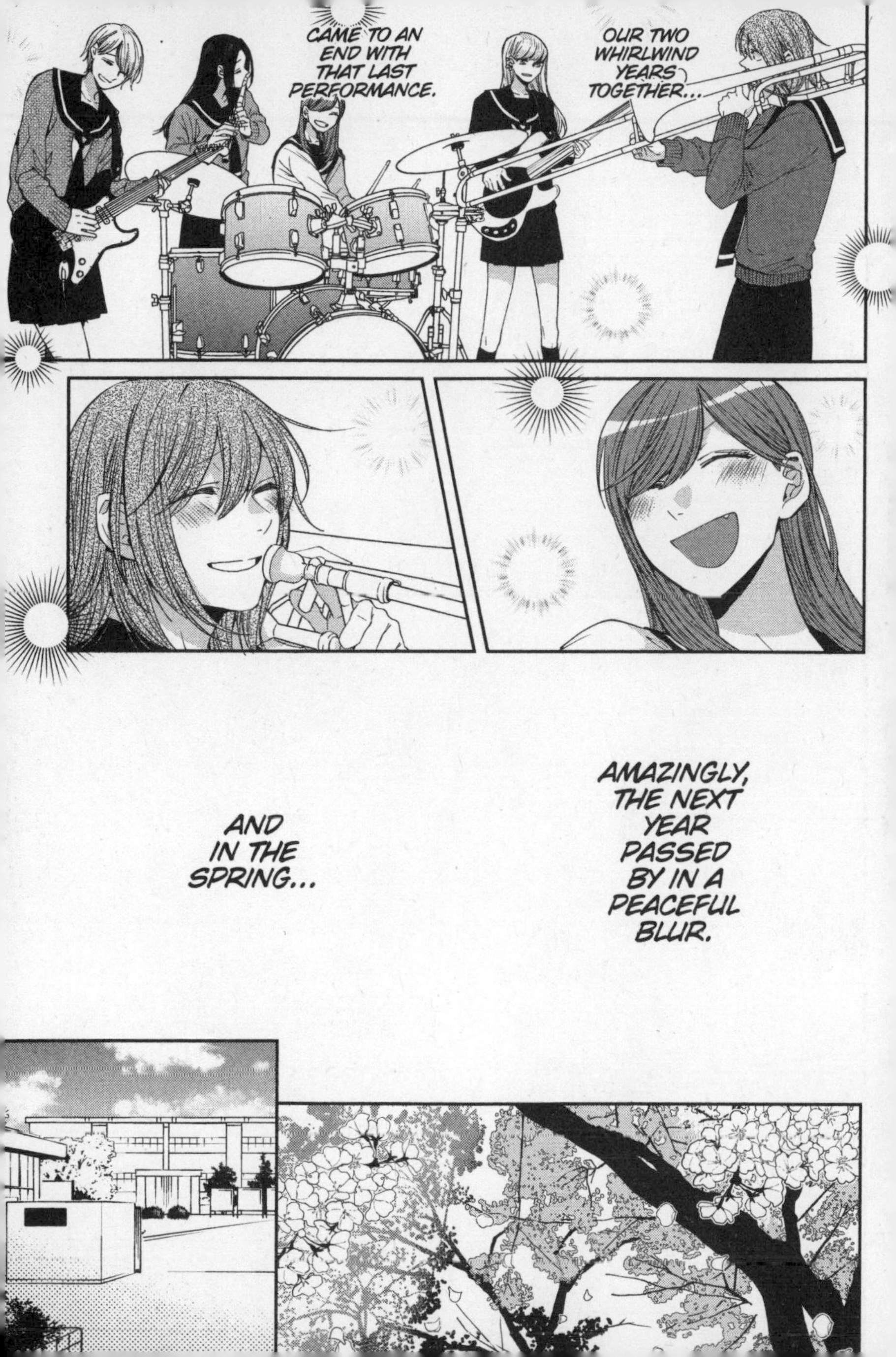
OUR TWO WHIRLWIND YEARS TOGETHER...
CAME TO AN END WITH THAT LAST PERFORMANCE.
AMAZINGLY, THE NEXT YEAR PASSED BY IN A PEACEFUL BLUR.
AND IN THE SPRING...

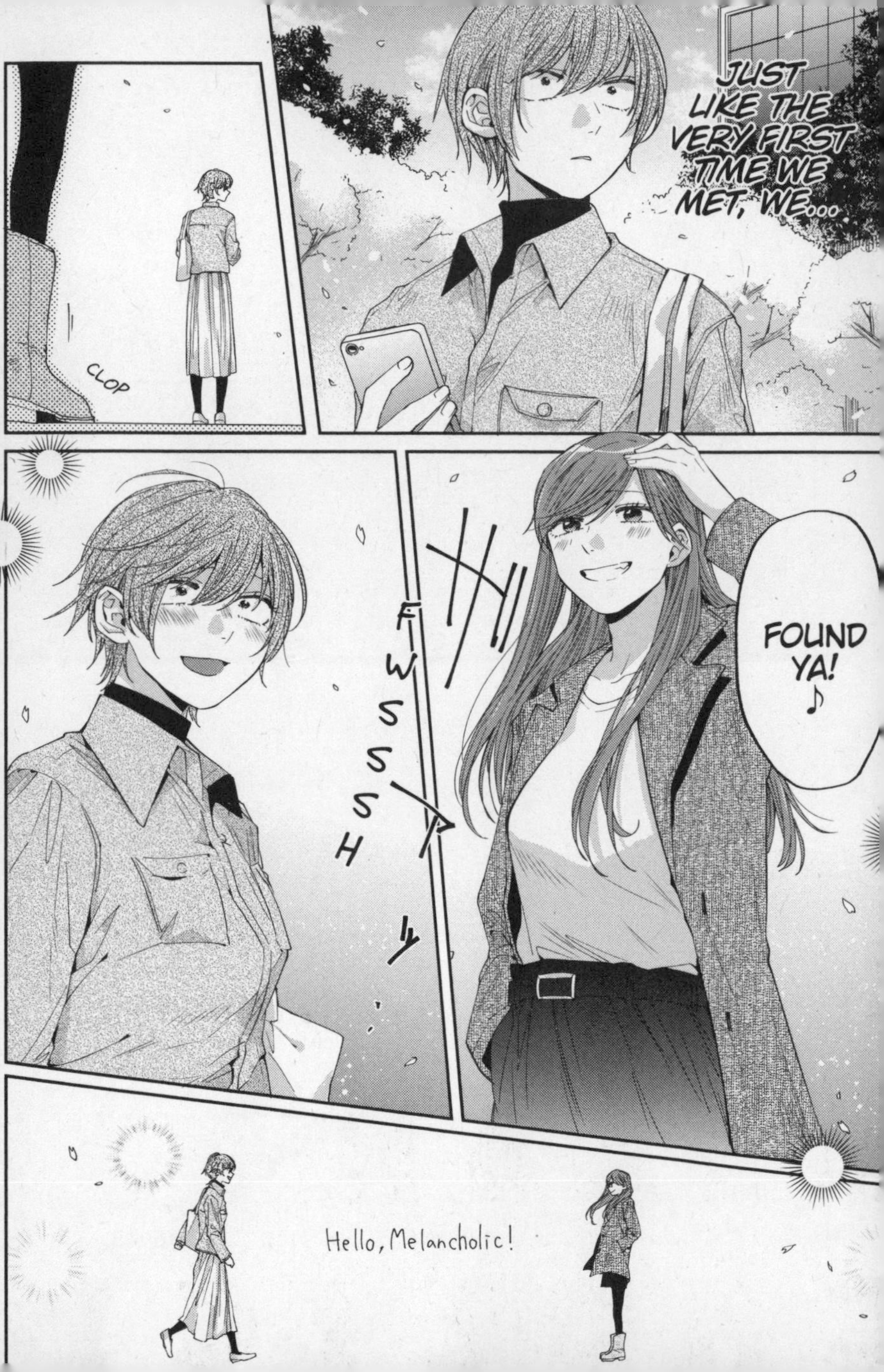
JUST LIKE THE VERY FIRST TIME WE MET, WE...
CLOP
FOUND YA! ♪
FWSSSH
Hello, Melancholic!

HELLO,
MELAN
CHOLIC!

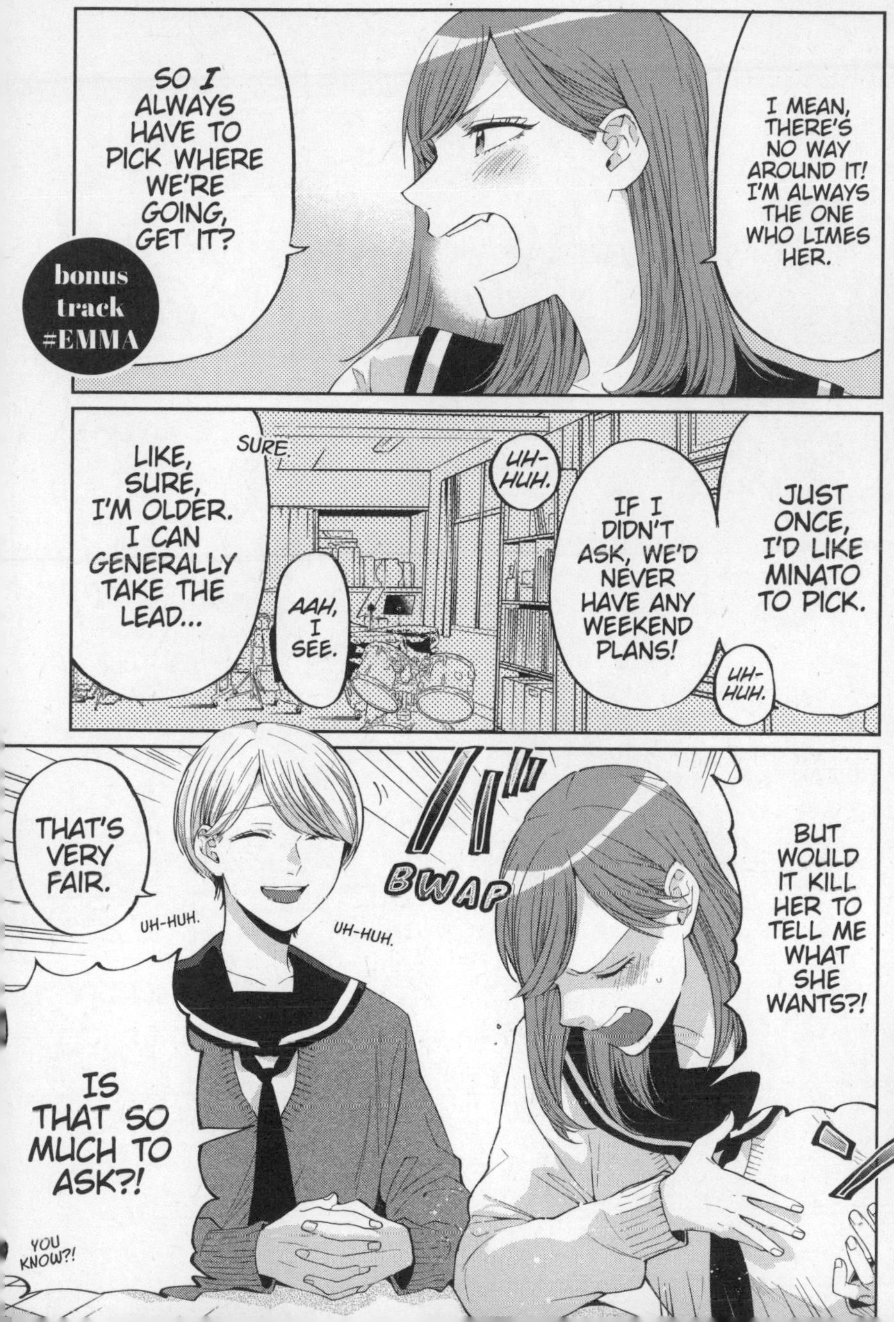
I MEAN, THERE'S NO WAY AROUND IT! I'M ALWAYS THE ONE WHO LIMES HER.
SO I ALWAYS HAVE TO PICK WHERE WE'RE GOING, GET IT?
bonus track #EMMA
JUST ONCE, I'D LIKE MINATO TO PICK.
UH-HUH.
IF I DIDN'T ASK, WE'D NEVER HAVE ANY WEEKEND PLANS!
UH-HUH.
AAH, I SEE.
SURE.
LIKE, SURE, I'M OLDER. I CAN GENERALLY TAKE THE LEAD...
BUT WOULD IT KILL HER TO TELL ME WHAT SHE WANTS?!
BWAP
UH-HUH.
UH-HUH.
THAT'S VERY FAIR.
IS THAT SO MUCH TO ASK?!
YOU KNOW?!

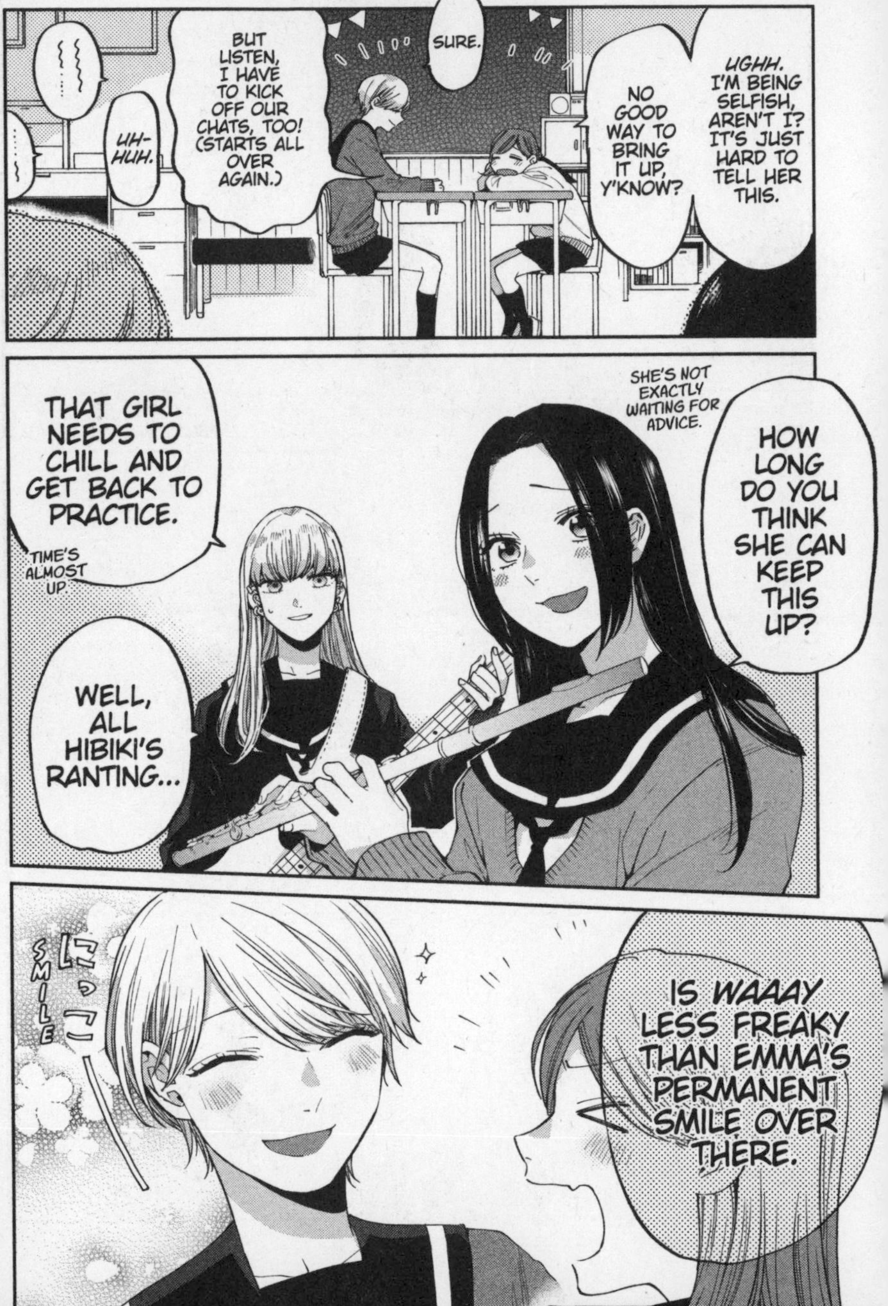
UGHH. I'M BEING SELFISH, AREN'T I? IT'S JUST HARD TO TELL HER THIS.
NO GOOD WAY TO BRING IT UP, Y'KNOW?
SURE.
BUT LISTEN, I HAVE TO KICK OFF OUR CHATS, TOO! (STARTS ALL OVER AGAIN.)
UH-HUH.
SHE'S NOT EXACTLY WAITING FOR ADVICE.
HOW LONG DO YOU THINK SHE CAN KEEP THIS UP?
THAT GIRL NEEDS TO CHILL AND GET BACK TO PRACTICE.
TIME'S ALMOST UP.
WELL, ALL HIBIKI'S RANTING...
IS WAAAY LESS FREAKY THAN EMMA'S PERMANENT SMILE OVER THERE.
SMILE

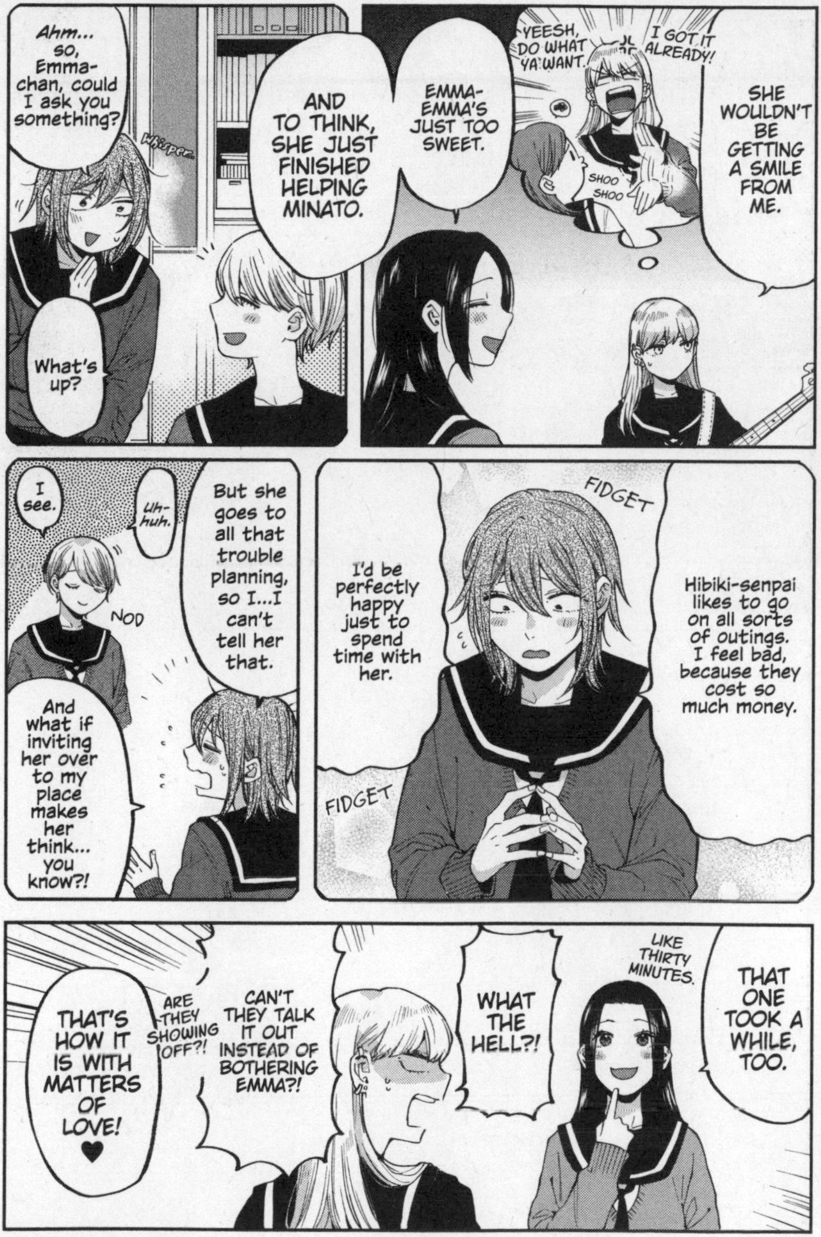

SHE WOULDN'T BE GETTING A SMILE FROM ME.
I GOT IT ALREADY!
YEESH, DO WHAT YA WANT.
SHOO SHOO
EMMA-EMMA'S JUST TOO SWEET.
AND TO THINK, SHE JUST FINISHED HELPING MINATO.
Ahm... so, Emma-chan, could I ask you something?
Whisper
What's up?
FIDGET
Hibiki-senpai likes to go on all sorts of outings. I feel bad, because they cost so much money.
I'd be perfectly happy just to spend time with her.
FIDGET
But she goes to all that trouble planning, so I...I can't tell her that.
Uh-huh.
I see.
NOD
And what if inviting her over to my place makes her think... you know?!
THAT ONE TOOK A WHILE, TOO.
LIKE THIRTY MINUTES.
WHAT THE HELL?!
CAN'T THEY TALK IT OUT INSTEAD OF BOTHERING EMMA?!
ARE THEY SHOWING OFF?!
THAT'S HOW IT IS WITH MATTERS OF LOVE! ♥

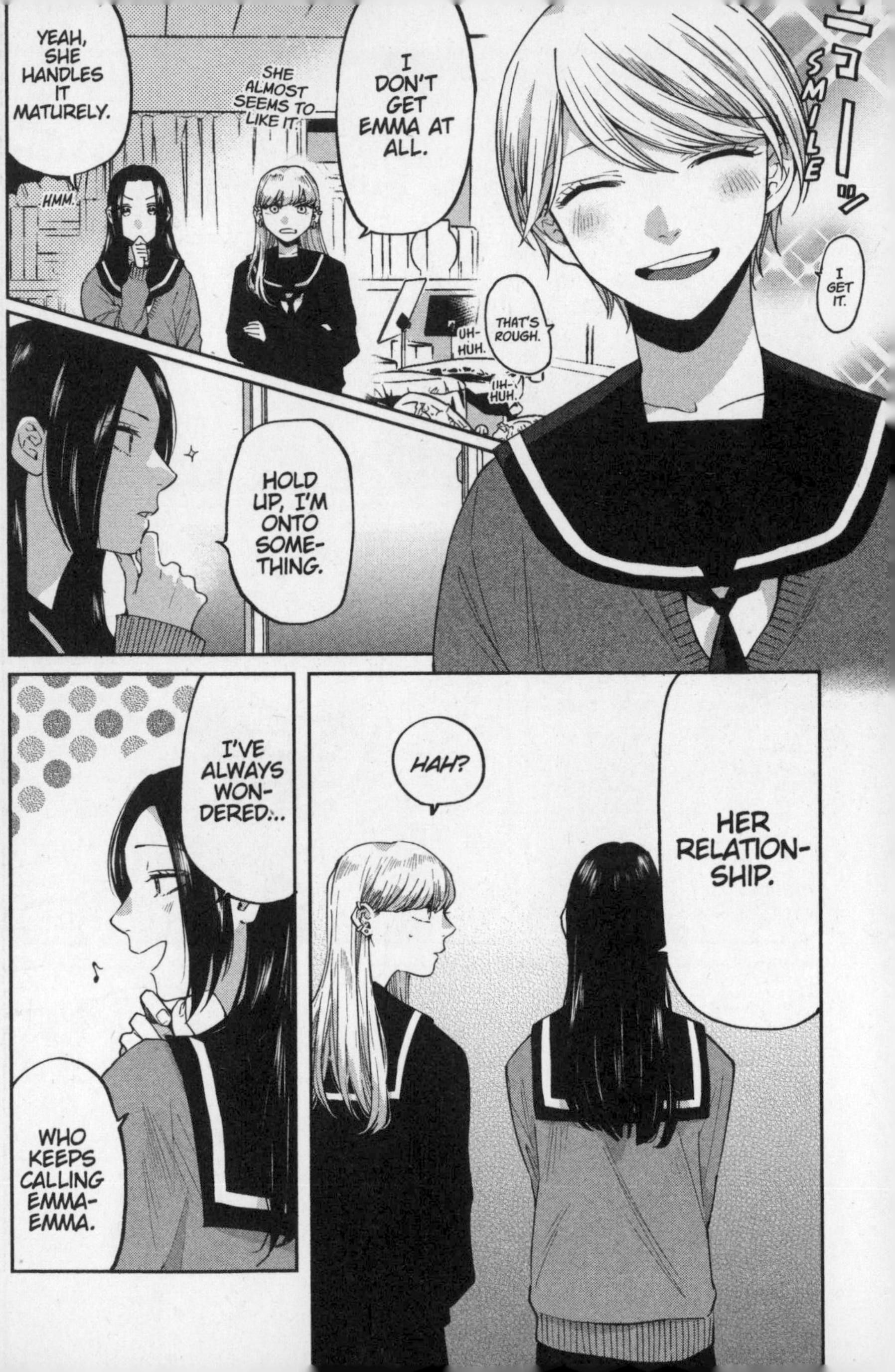
SMILE
I GET IT.
I DON'T GET EMMA AT ALL.
THAT'S ROUGH.
UH-HUH.
UH-HUH.
SHE ALMOST SEEMS TO LIKE IT.
YEAH, SHE HANDLES IT MATURELY.
HMM.
HOLD UP, I'M ONTO SOME-THING.
HER RELATION-SHIP.
HAH?
I'VE ALWAYS WON-DERED...
WHO KEEPS CALLING EMMA-EMMA.

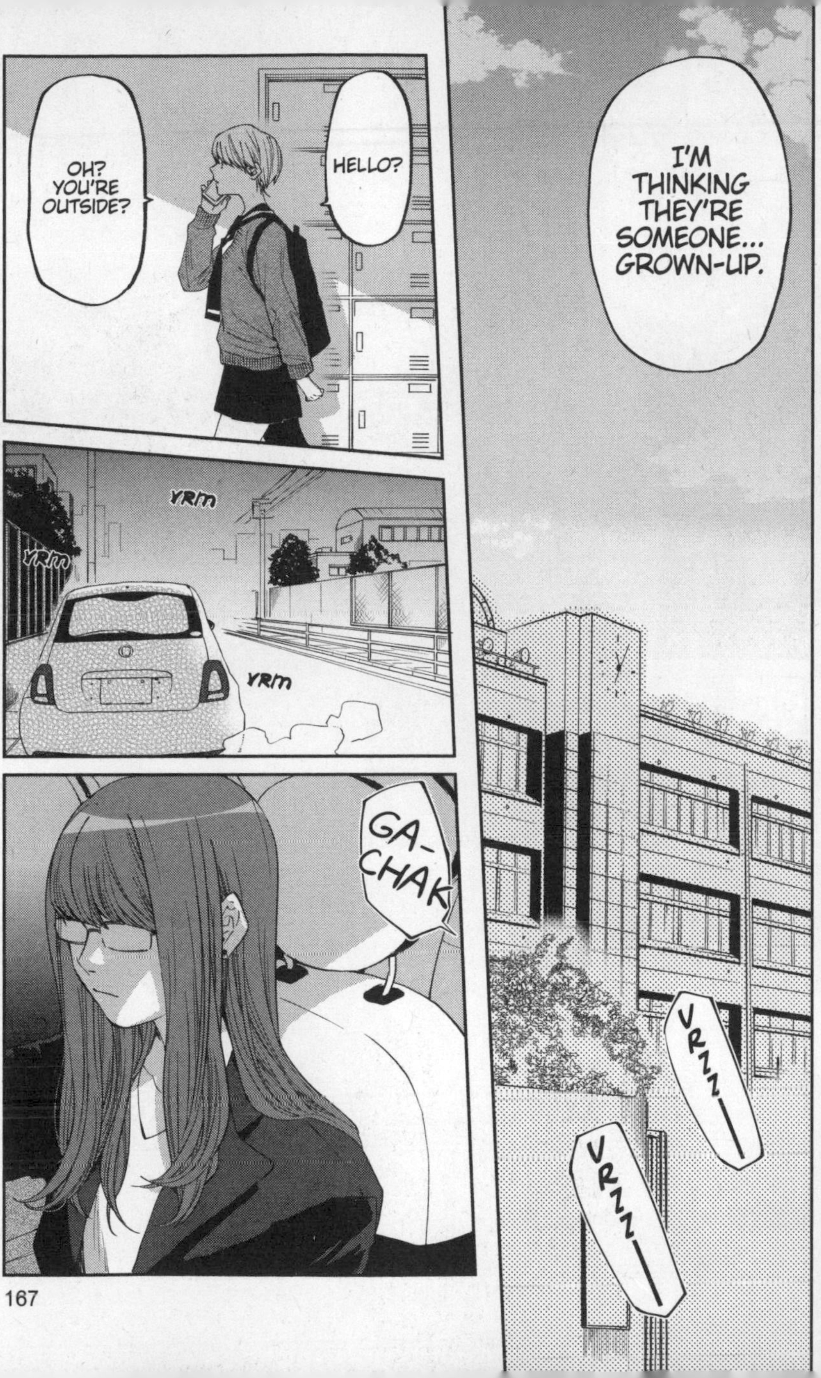
I'M THINKING THEY'RE SOMEONE... GROWN-UP.
VRZZ
VRZZ
HELLO?
OH? YOU'RE OUTSIDE?
YRM
YRM
YRM
GA-CHAK

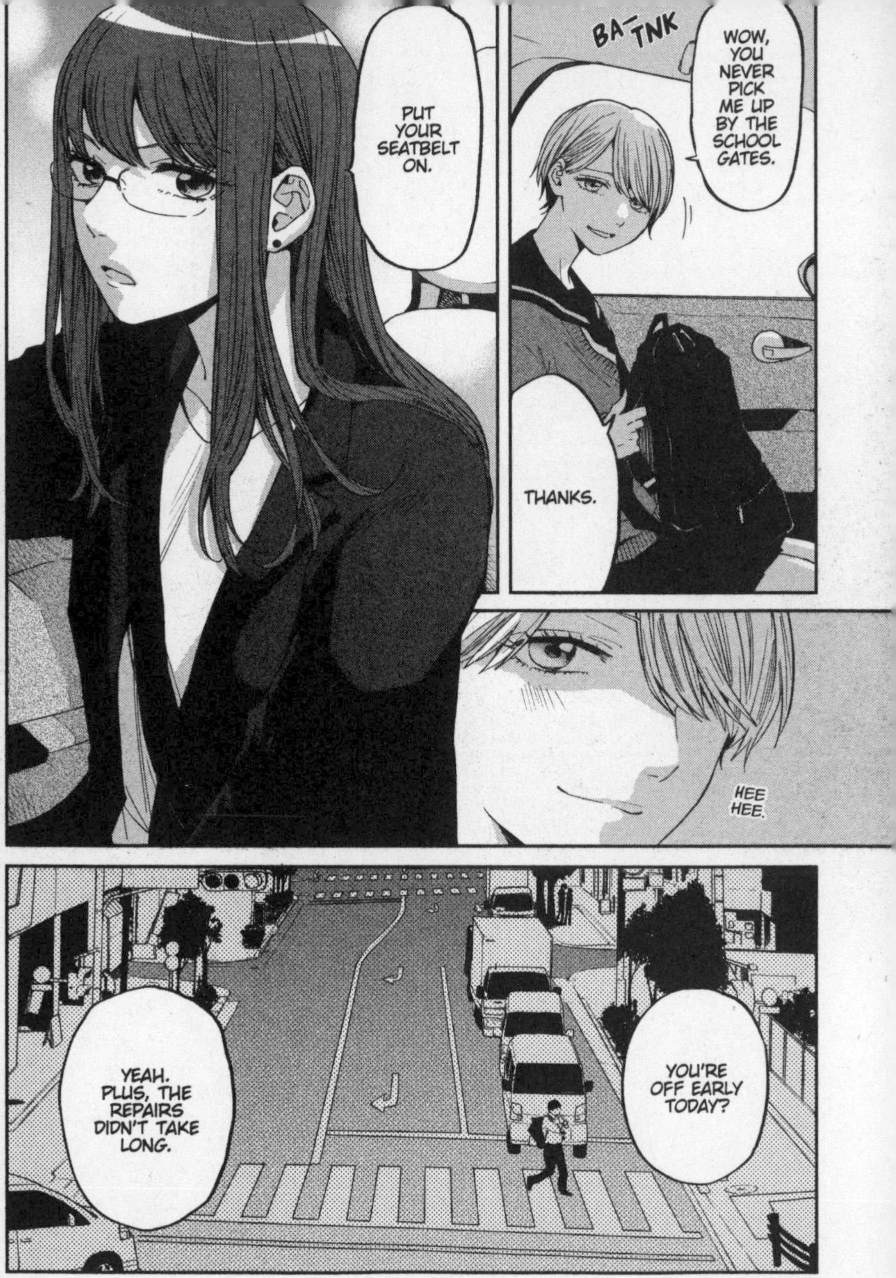
BA-TNK
WOW, YOU NEVER PICK ME UP BY THE SCHOOL GATES.
THANKS.
HEE HEE.
PUT YOUR SEATBELT ON.
YOU'RE OFF EARLY TODAY?
YEAH. PLUS, THE REPAIRS DIDN'T TAKE LONG.

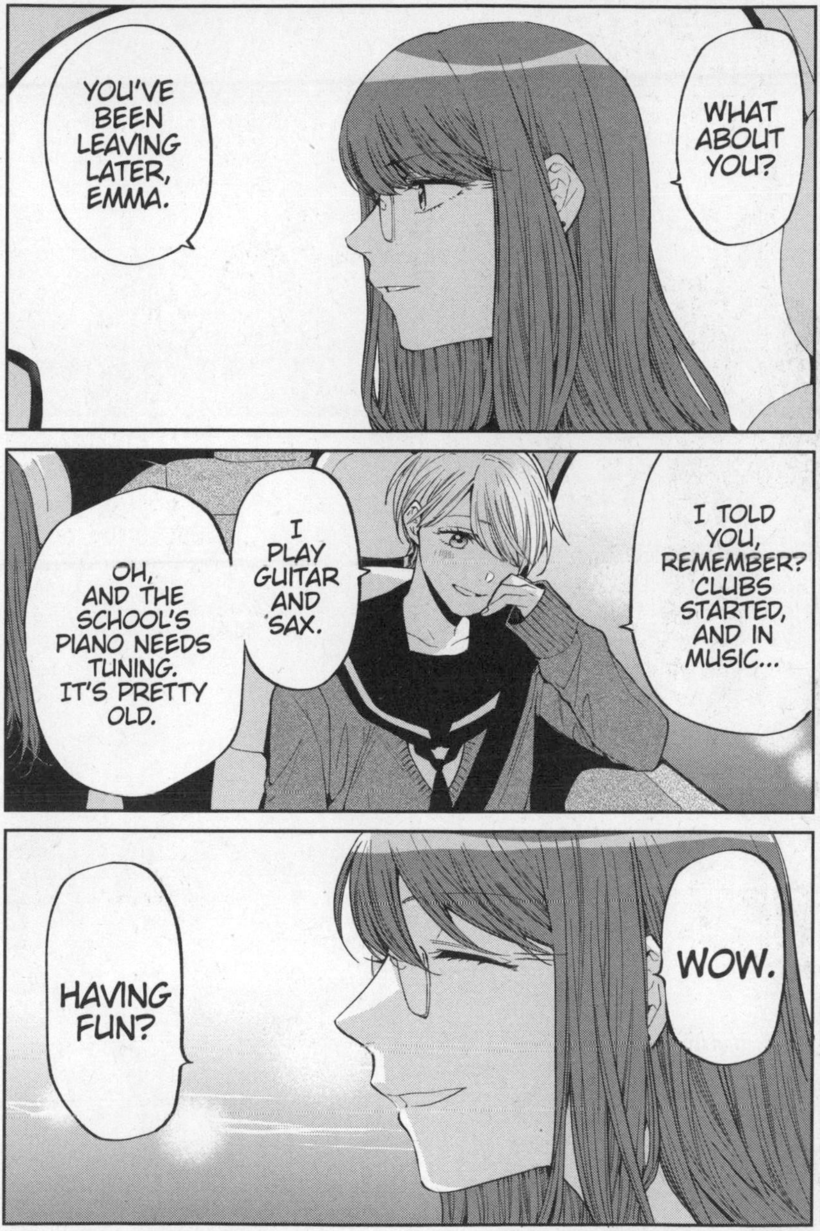
WHAT ABOUT YOU?
YOU'VE BEEN LEAVING LATER, EMMA.
I TOLD YOU, REMEMBER? CLUBS STARTED, AND IN MUSIC...
I PLAY GUITAR AND SAX.
OH, AND THE SCHOOL'S PIANO NEEDS TUNING. IT'S PRETTY OLD.
WOW.
HAVING FUN?

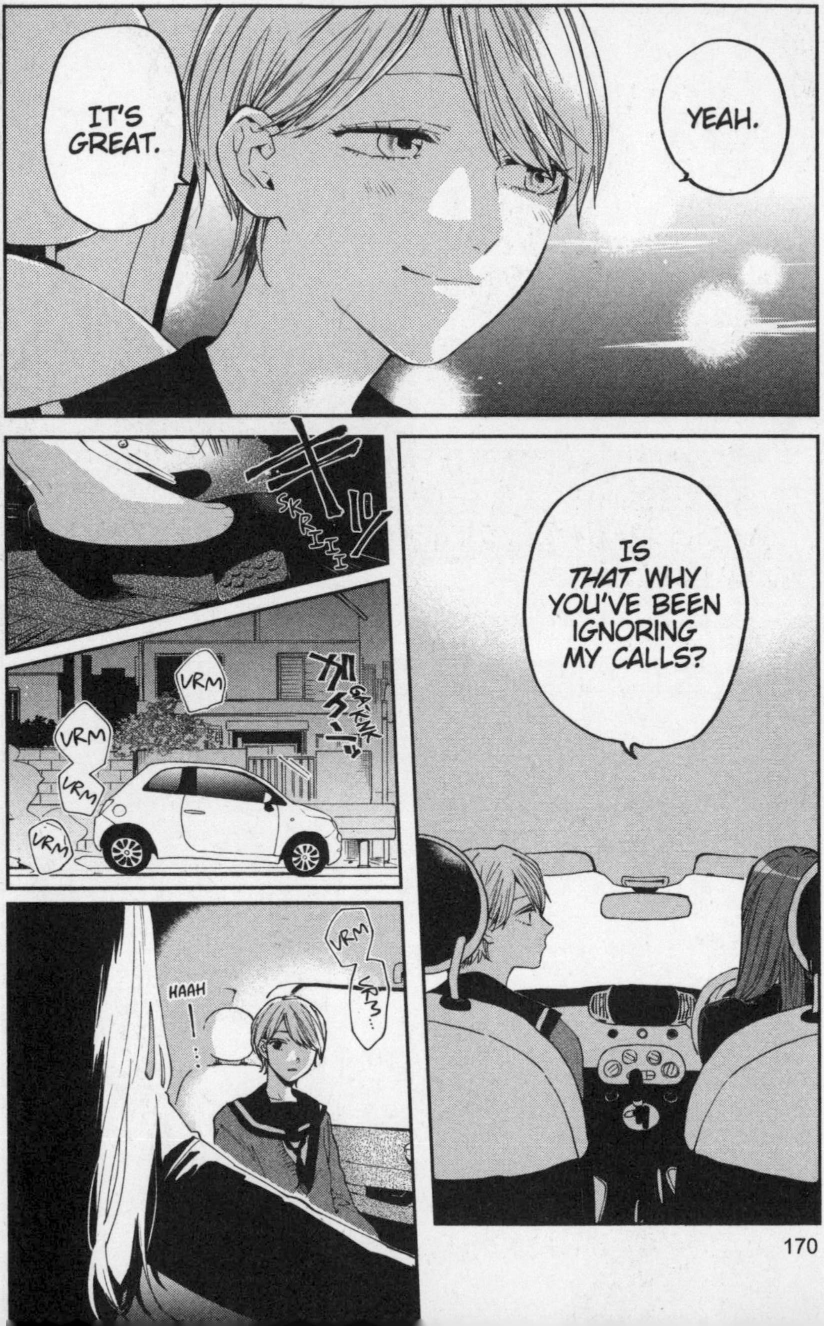
YEAH.
IT'S GREAT.
IS *THAT* WHY YOU'VE BEEN IGNORING MY CALLS?
SKRIIII
VRM
GA-KUNK
VRM
VRM
VRM
VRM
VRM...
HAAH
...

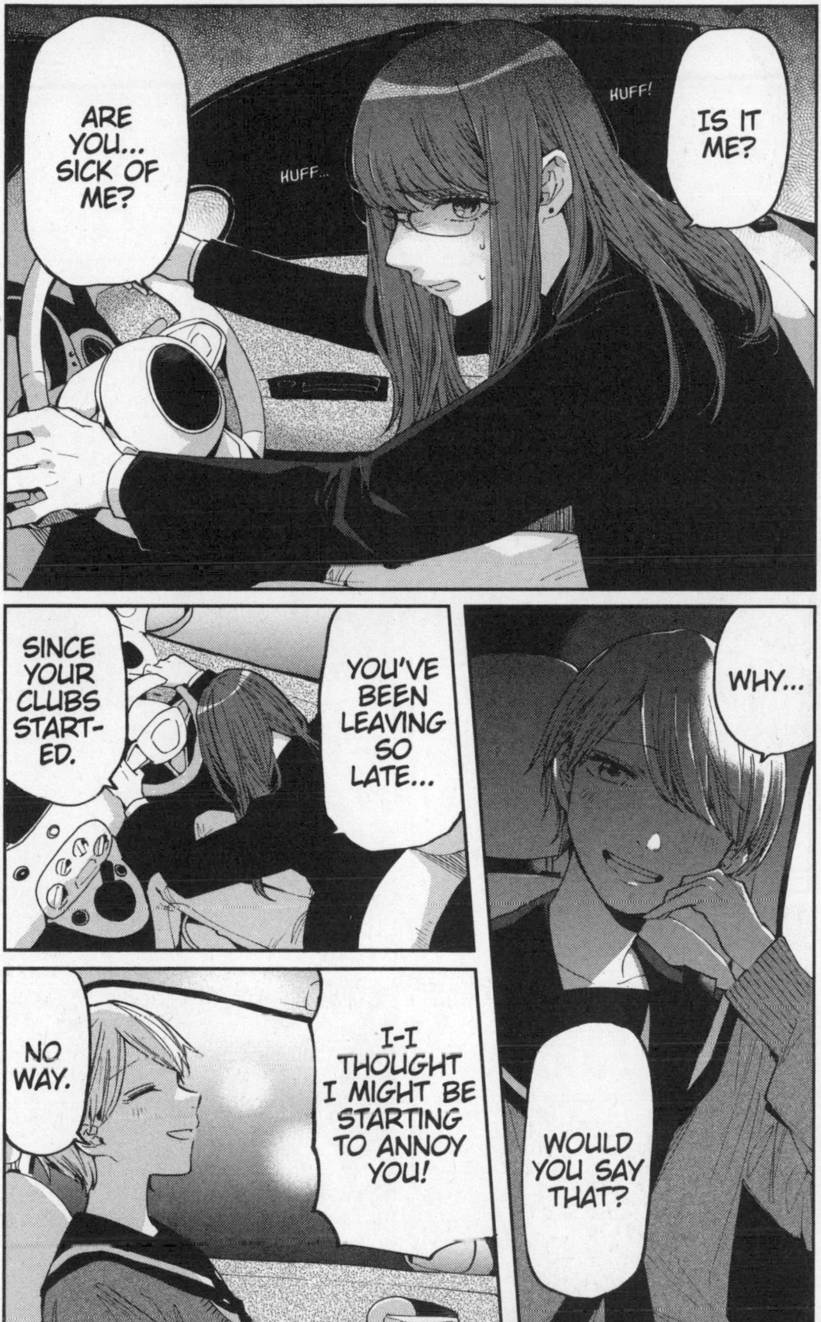
IS IT ME?
HUFF!
HUFF...
ARE YOU... SICK OF ME?
WHY...
WOULD YOU SAY THAT?
YOU'VE BEEN LEAVING SO LATE...
SINCE YOUR CLUBS START-ED.
I-I THOUGHT I MIGHT BE STARTING TO ANNOY YOU!
NO WAY.

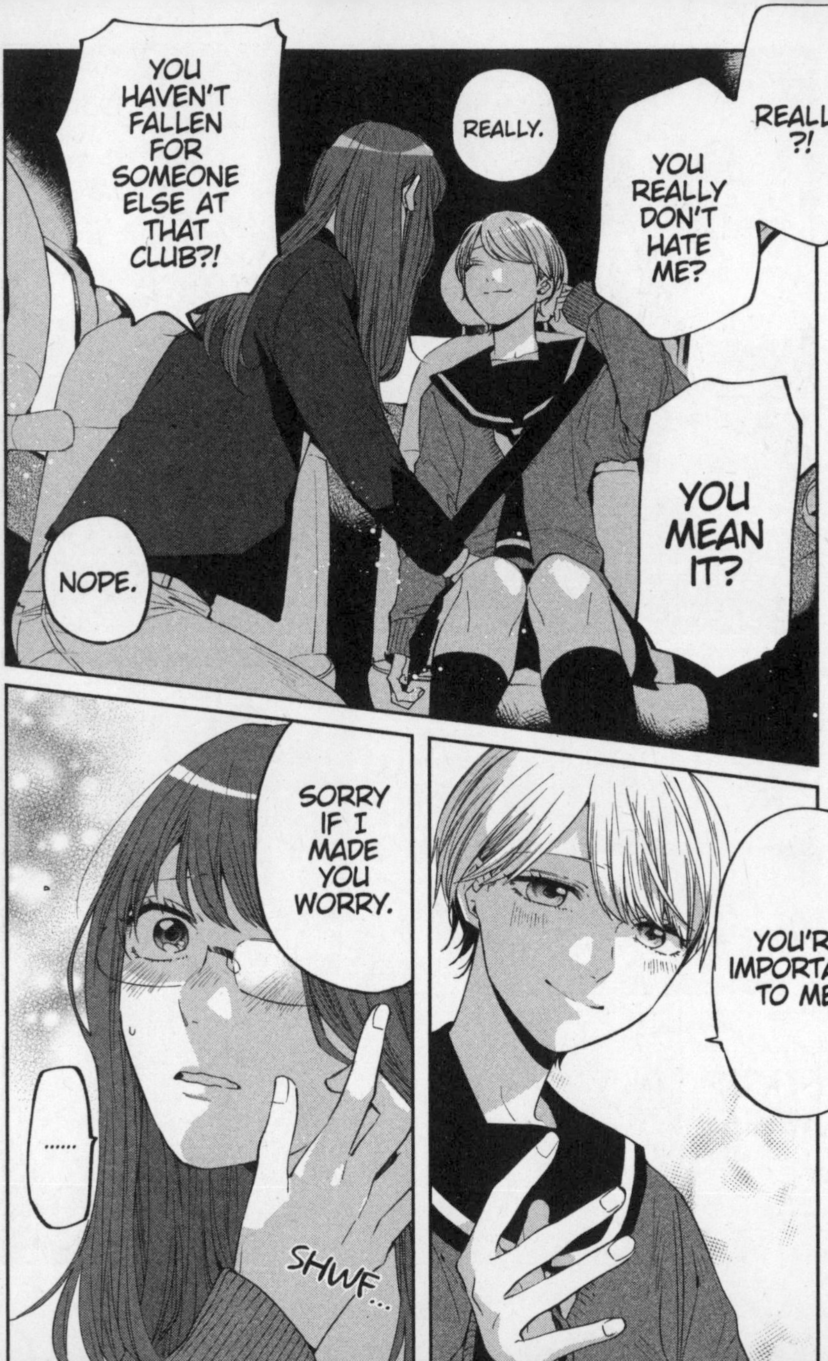
REALLY ?!
YOU REALLY DON'T HATE ME?
REALLY.
YOU MEAN IT?
YOU HAVEN'T FALLEN FOR SOMEONE ELSE AT THAT CLUB?!
NOPE.
YOU'RE IMPORTANT TO ME.
SORRY IF I MADE YOU WORRY.
......
SHWF...

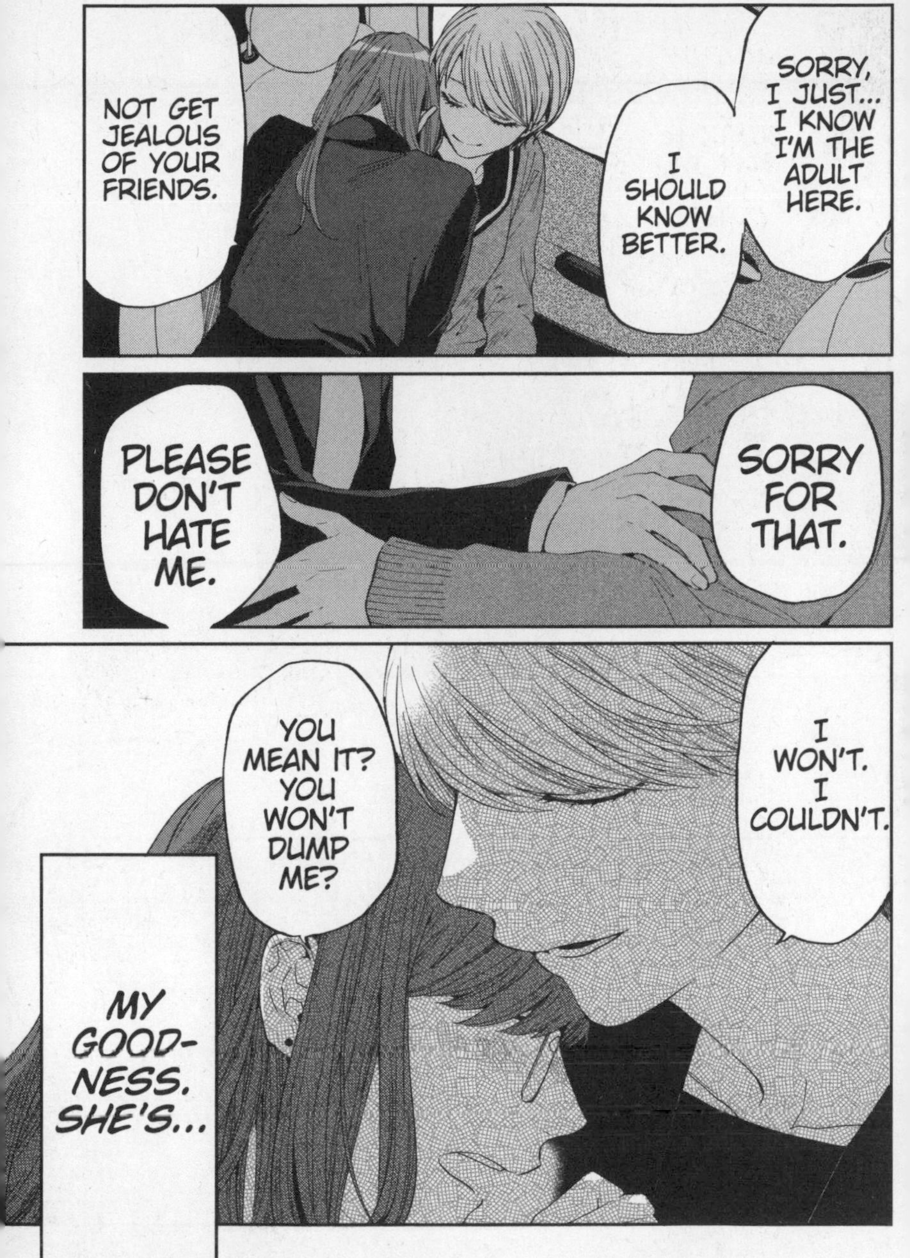
SORRY, I JUST... I KNOW I'M THE ADULT HERE.
I SHOULD KNOW BETTER.
NOT GET JEALOUS OF YOUR FRIENDS.
SORRY FOR THAT.
PLEASE DON'T HATE ME.
I WON'T. I COULDN'T.
YOU MEAN IT? YOU WON'T DUMP ME?
MY GOODNESS. SHE'S...

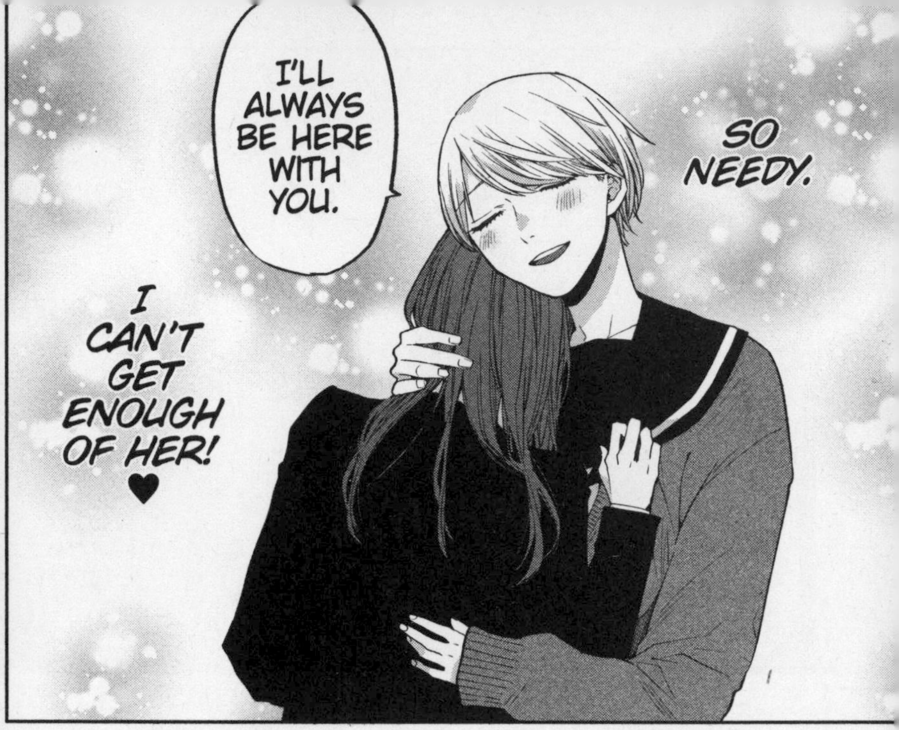
SO NEEDY.
I'LL ALWAYS BE HERE WITH YOU.
I CAN'T GET ENOUGH OF HER! ♥

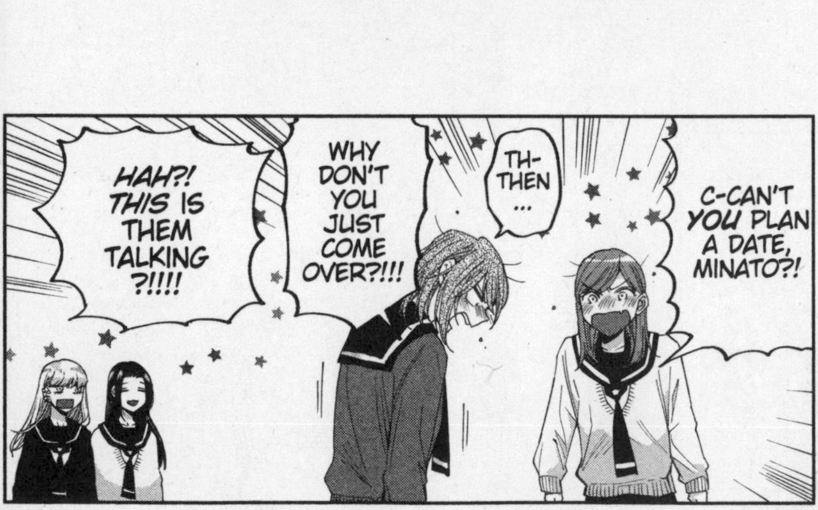
C-CAN'T YOU PLAN A DATE, MINATO?!
TH-THEN...
WHY DON'T YOU JUST COME OVER?!!!
HAH?! THIS IS THEM TALKING?!!!!

End

HELLO, MELAN CHOLIC!

Hello, Melancholic!

Afterword

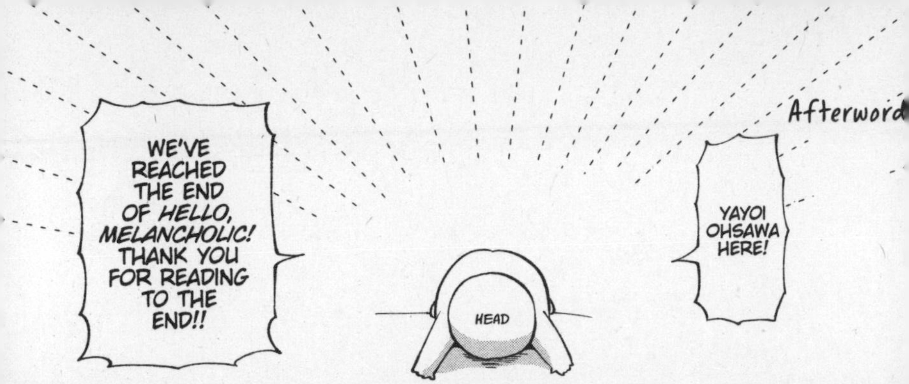
YAYOI OHSAWA HERE!
WE'VE REACHED THE END OF *HELLO, MELANCHOLIC!* THANK YOU FOR READING TO THE END!!
HEAD

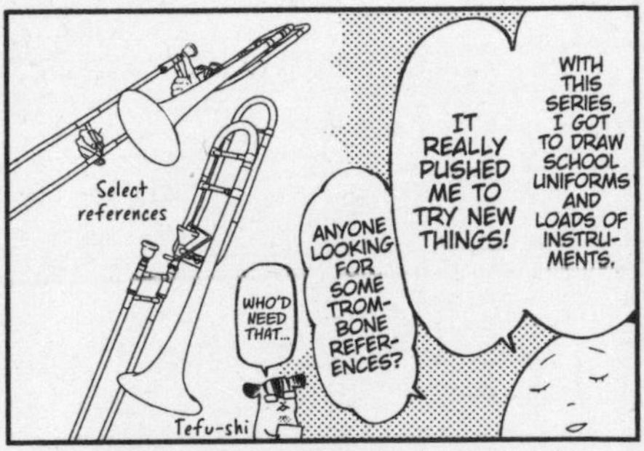
WITH THIS SERIES, I GOT TO DRAW SCHOOL UNIFORMS AND LOADS OF INSTRUMENTS.
IT REALLY PUSHED ME TO TRY NEW THINGS!
ANYONE LOOKING FOR SOME TROMBONE REFERENCES?
WHO'D NEED THAT...
Select references
Tefu-shi

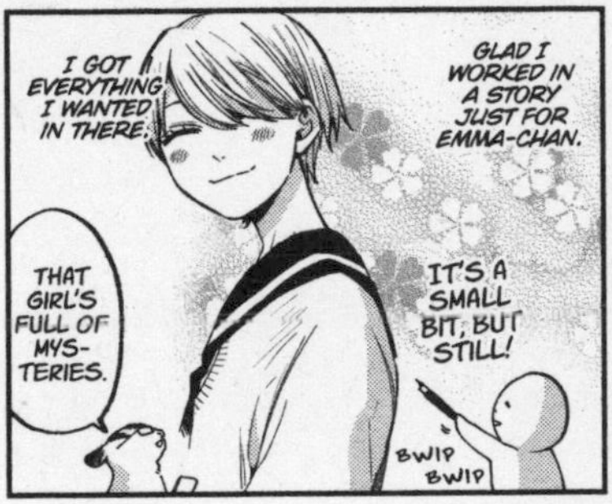
GLAD I WORKED IN A STORY JUST FOR EMMA-CHAN.
I GOT EVERYTHING I WANTED IN THERE.
IT'S A SMALL BIT, BUT STILL!
THAT GIRL'S FULL OF MYSTERIES.
BWIP BWIP

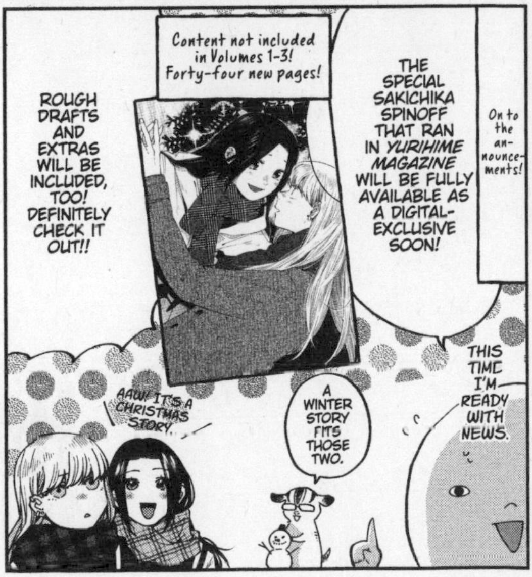
On to the announcements!
THE SPECIAL SAKICHIKA SPINOFF THAT RAN IN *YURIHIME MAGAZINE* WILL BE FULLY AVAILABLE AS A DIGITAL-EXCLUSIVE SOON!
Content not included in Volumes 1-3! Forty-four new pages!
ROUGH DRAFTS AND EXTRAS WILL BE INCLUDED, TOO! DEFINITELY CHECK IT OUT!!
THIS TIME I'M READY WITH NEWS.
A WINTER STORY FITS THOSE TWO.
AAW, IT'S A CHRISTMAS STORY...

Thanks to...

Tefu-san, my manager...

the designer...

everyone over at the Ichijinsha editorial department...

S-shi, my assistant...

T-san, for the trombone materials...

Suzaki Aya-sama, for the shout-out...

and you! Thank you for reading!!

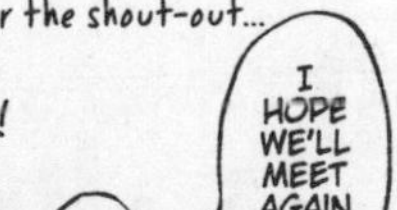
I HOPE WE'LL MEET AGAIN SOON!

March 2021 - Yayoi Ohsawa

Hello, Melancholic!

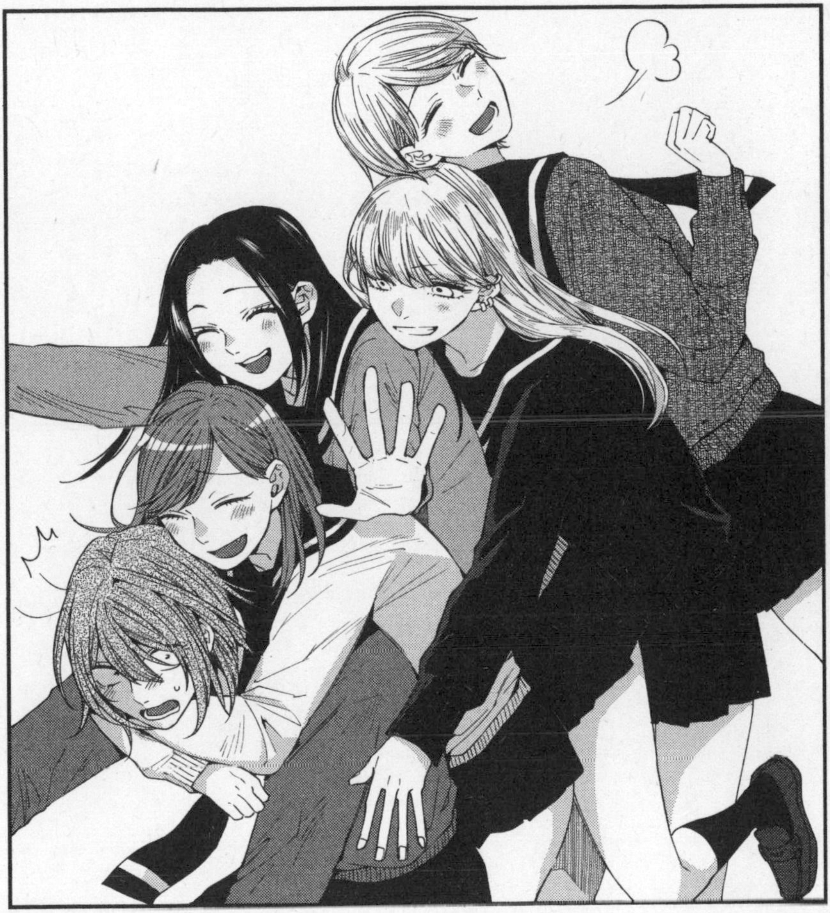

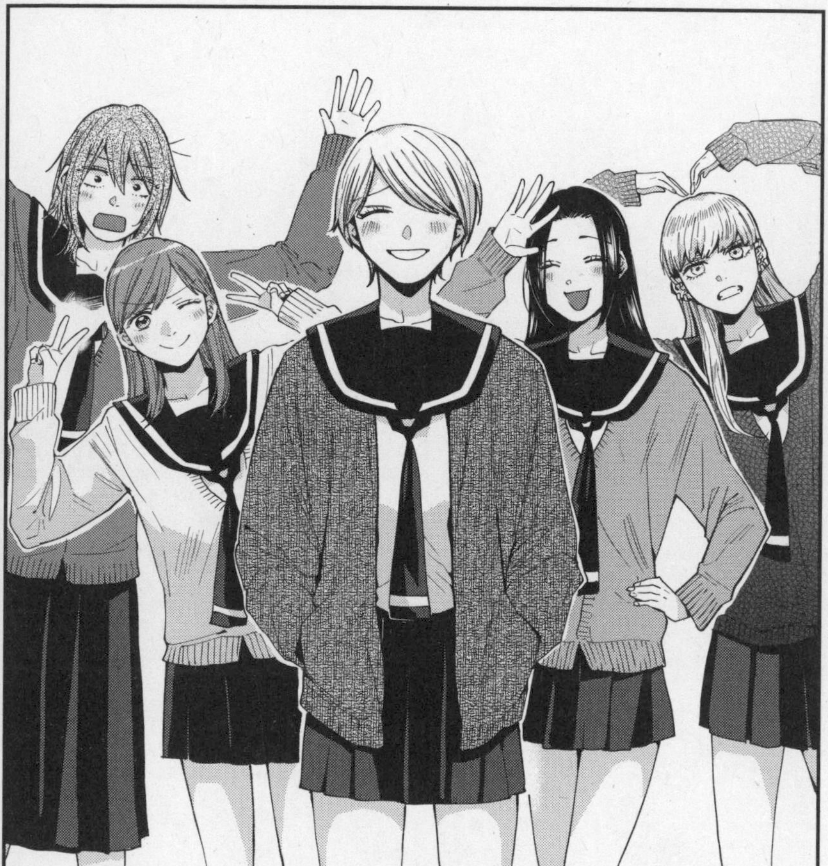

Hello, Melancholic!

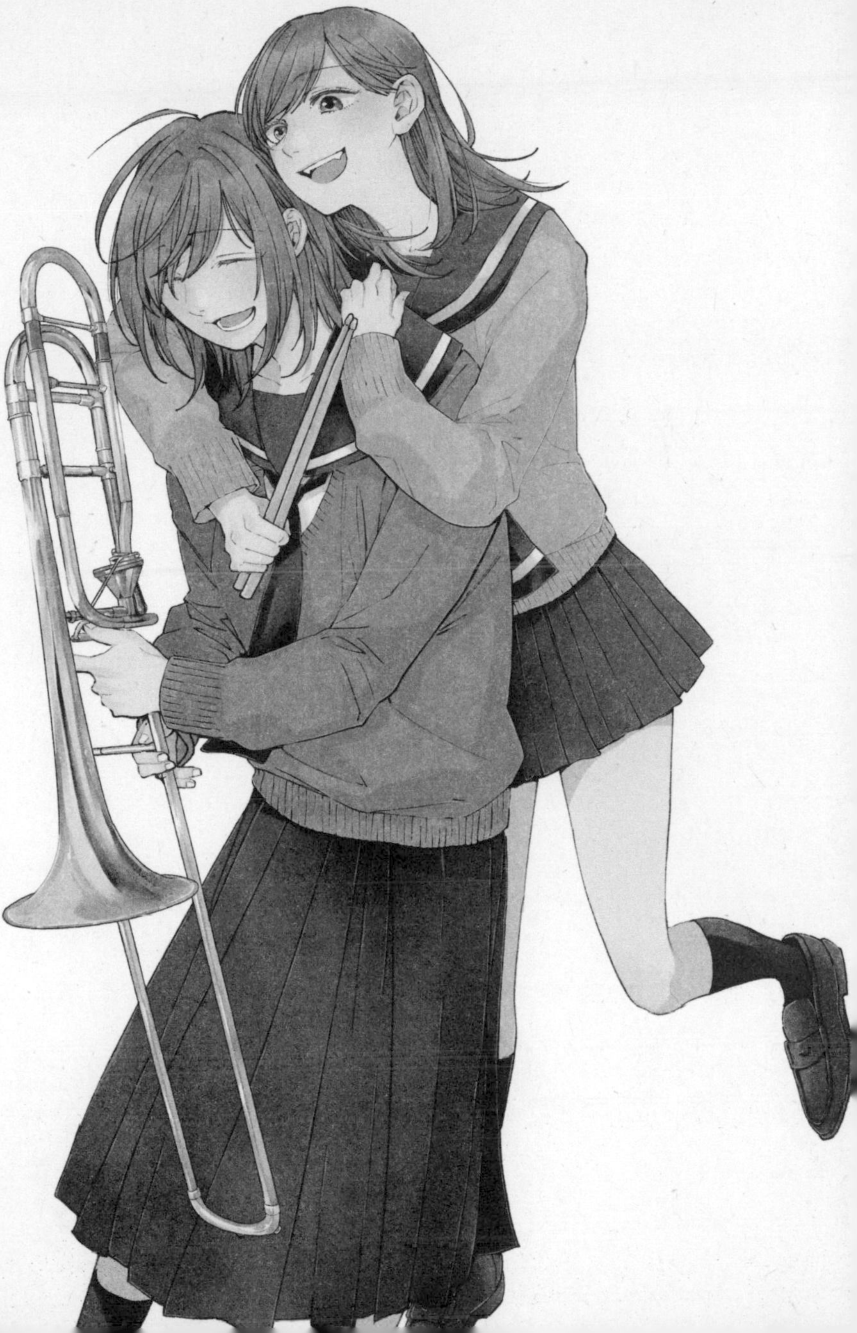

Hello, Melancholic!